RELIGION OR
ETHNICITY?

RELIGION OR ETHNICITY?

Jewish Identities in Evolution

EDITED BY ZVI GITELMAN

RUTGERS UNIVERSITY PRESS
New Brunswick, New Jersey, and London

Library of Congress Cataloging-in-Publication Data

Religion or ethnicity?: Jewish identities in evolution / edited by Zvi Gitelman.

    p. cm.

Includes bibliographical references and index.

ISBN 978–0–8135–4450–2 (hardcover : alk. paper)

ISBN 978–0–8135–4451–9 (pbk.: alk. paper)

1. Jews—Identity. 2. Jews—Civilization. 3. Humanistic Judaism. 4. Judaism and secularism. 5. Jews—Israel—Identity. 6. Secularism—Israel. I. Gitelman, Zvi Y.

DS143.R374 2009

305.892′4—dc22

2008016701

A British Cataloging-in-Publication record for this book is available from the British Library.

Visit our Web site: http://rutgerspress.rutgers.edu

Manufactured in the United States of America

To Felix Posen—visionary activist

Contents

RELIGION OR
ETHNICITY?

Introduction

JEWISH RELIGION, JEWISH ETHNICITY—
THE EVOLUTION OF JEWISH IDENTITIES

ZVI GITELMAN

Is "Jewish" an ethnic or a religious adjective? Can one be Jewish without practicing the religion known as Judaism? This volume analyzes the relationship between Jewish religion and Jewish ethnicity by surveying ways in which Jews over the millennia have defined themselves, with some reference to how they have been defined by others. Jews have long engaged in redefining themselves in a wide variety of countries and cultures. Therefore, the Jewish experience enables us to understand better broader issues of ethnic identity, national formation, the relationship between religion and ethnicity, and the transformation of cultures and identities. Jewish experience is also highly instructive on whether and how a group whose nexus was historically religious can shift the ties that bind to culture and ethnicity in modern societies.

The Jewish collectivity has continually redefined itself, sometimes as a faith community, sometimes as an ethnic group, nation, cultural group, or even a race. The modern distinction between religion and ethnicity was made when the Jews were emancipated in eighteenth-century Western Europe. Today the place of religion in their ethnicity varies widely, from high but declining salience among British and American Jews, to a minor role among most Latin American Jews, and to almost no role among those in and from the former Soviet Union. Jews in the former Soviet Union think of themselves primarily as an ethnic group ("nationality"), not a religious one, because both state and society taught them to do so, while most Jews in Western Europe and America think of themselves as both a religious and an ethnic group. Nevertheless, both groups identify with each other and generally consider themselves part of the same "Jewish" entity.

The aim of this volume is not to classify the Jews "once and for all" but to examine how and why they and others have defined and redefined themselves, and to what effect. We also ask what the history of these transformations reveals about relations among ethnicity, religion, and culture. The chapters examine empirically the proposition that in modern Europe, Israel, and North America there has been a transformation of Jewish identity from a religious basis toward one that can accommodate secular Jewishness, however conceived. But can such a sense of Jewishness take root and be transmitted over generations in societies where Jews are free to adopt the majority culture?

The first section of the book deals with antiquity and the premodern era during which religion (Judaism) and ethnicity (or "Jewishness," which is not quite the same as *Yidishkayt*) were not differentiated. Indeed, in ancient Hebrew/Israelite/Jewish culture, and perhaps in other cultures, the very notion of religion as a belief system that could be described and analyzed may not have existed. While ideas of nationhood are articulated in the Hebrew Bible (*am, le-om, goy*), the modern Hebrew word for religion (*dat*) appears rarely and its meaning is different from today's.

Did the separation between religion and ethnicity begin when Jewish and Greek cultures came into contact? Some have seen a conflict between Judaism and Hellenistic culture as the precursor of the religious/secular divide of modern times. Yaron Eliav argues that this is not the case, and that the boundaries between Jews and non-Jews, and between Jewish and other cultures, were more fluid than many have assumed. Analyzing Judaism around the time of Jesus, Gabriele Boccaccini argues that the important difference between Judaism and Christianity became ethnic, not ideological. Religious ideas preceded notions of Jewish ethnicity. Before the Maccabees, religion defined ethnicity, but afterward religious diversity was confined within the boundaries of an ethnicity, of a shared way of life. Rabbinic Judaism, one of several forms of Judaism in antiquity, emerged as normative and for several centuries defined Judaism in all parts of the Jewish diaspora.

This changed radically in Western Jewish societies in the late eighteenth and nineteenth centuries. As Miriam Bodian shows, the European states weakened Jewish communal authorities—as they were to do later in Eastern Europe—and simultaneously the traditional community was weakened by challenges to rabbinic authority by Sephardi crypto-Jews in Amsterdam and elsewhere. These Jews, who had originated in Spain and Portugal, challenged rabbinic authority and can be considered progenitors of modern religious and secular Jewish movements that challenged traditional rabbinic norms.

Perhaps the most widely known of these Sephardic Jews is Benedict (Baruch) Spinoza. Steven Nadler argues against the popular notion that Spinoza was the first "reforming" or even "secular" Jew. For Spinoza there can be no Jewishness without Jewish law (*halacha*), and since he rejected its validity, he did not claim any Jewishness for himself. Indeed, he might be considered the first Jewish intellectual to articulate an identity in which neither religion nor ethnicity figured.

Jewish identity became complicated in the modern era due to the differentiation of religion and ethnicity and the distinctions drawn in France and elsewhere between religious and civic affiliation. Jews were challenged to find ways whereby their previous identities could be combined with the civic and social affiliations that were opened to them. Could someone be Jewish by religion but French by nationality? Did the acquisition of French or German citizenship mean that French or German ethnicity had been acquired? Scott Spector revisits conventional notions of what it meant to be Jewish and German for certain modern Jewish intellectuals. Todd Endelman shows how uneven and contradictory the process of Jewish emancipation was in Western Europe and concludes that "social acceptance and mixing lagged behind the decline of belief and practice." Many West European Jews abandoned some of their religious beliefs and practices but continued to mix and marry with Jews to a far greater extent than they did with Gentiles.

The second section of the book deals with the twentieth century and beyond.

Using the tools of several disciplines—history, social science, and literature—the authors deal with nonreligious manifestations of Jewishness in several countries. One of the most popular alternatives to Judaism as a basis of Jewish identity was Yiddishism, a movement that regarded the Yiddish language, spoken by perhaps seven million Jews at the beginning of the twentieth century, not just as an instrument of communication but as a multifaceted culture. Other peoples—including Czechs, Ukrainians, and Germans—were pointing to language as the "essence" of their culture; Yiddishists did the same. David Fishman focuses on how Yiddishism played out in the United States. The complexities of synthesizing culture, identity, and religion—always a challenge to secular Jewish movements—were exacerbated in the United States by the realities of immigration to a dominant culture that admitted Jews, but, because the American ethos recognized religion more than ethnicity, accepted them as a religious group. The curricula and ideologies of Yiddish schools in America illustrate the complexities of secular Jewishness.

Charles Liebman and Yaacov Yadgar examine two questions in Israel: has a secular Jewish culture developed in the Jewish state, and do those who define themselves as "traditional," rather than "religious" or "secular," resolve the tension between religion and secularity, particularity and universalism? Another aspect of the relations among religion, culture, and Jewish identity in Israel is examined by Mark Tessler, who uses public opinion data to survey Israeli Jewish attitudes toward the role of religion in the "Jewish state," asking where that leaves the 1.4 million Arabs who are citizens of that state. The relationship between religion and the nature of the state is a burning issue in many Middle Eastern states, and Tessler compares opinion data from Jordan and Egypt to the Israeli data.

The Soviet government, guided by Marxism, aimed to abolish religious belief as incompatible with science and "progress." It classified Jews as an ethnic, not religious, group. Several generations of Soviet Jews were socialized to this conception. Zvi Gitelman and his colleagues examine post-Soviet conceptions of Jewishness in Russia and Ukraine, using extensive surveys of several thousand Jews living there. They find that most have accepted the Soviet conception of Jewishness as ethnicity. Despite efforts to renew Jewish religious practice and belief among them, post-Soviet Jews remain largely secular. Whether they shall be able or even wish to construct a viable nonreligious Jewish culture remains to be seen.

Analysts of American Jewry, the largest diaspora Jewish population in the world, have raised questions about its religious commitment and declining Jewish affiliations. Calvin Goldscheider, a demographer and sociologist, believes that social and especially familial ties, are keeping the American Jewish community connected, perhaps in the same way that Todd Endelman discerns among West European Jews in centuries past. Goldscheider believes that Jewish values undergird these social connections.

There is a small group of American Jews who try to express their Jewishness in an organized, communal, but nonreligious form. While they call their institutions "congregations" or temples, they are not theists but seek to articulate their ethnicity through study and celebration. Adam Chalom, who leads such a congregation, examines the group's ideology and social characteristics in his chapter on secular, humanist Judaism.

Literature often serves as a prism through which to view societies and their values. In recent years, books by Jewish authors on Jewish themes have gained a wide readership, presumably mostly among Jews. Some have suggested that this literature might be the basis for reinvigorating a-religious Jewish identity and culture. Julian Levinson examines three anthologies of Jewish literature published in different periods in order to discern the ways in which American Jews have understood their Jewishness, whether secular or religious. Shachar Pinsker also turns to literature— Hebrew in this case—to analyze how classic modern Hebrew authors tried to adapt rabbinic texts to the a-religious modern Hebrew culture they were constructing. The interplay between Jewish "religious" and Israeli "secular" literatures continues to this day.

In the concluding chapter, Zvi Gitelman shows how Judaism began as a tribal religion and how the attempt to disaggregate religion and ethnicity that began in the eighteenth century has taken different forms in various places and different times. Zionism is perhaps the most successful "secular" movement among Jews, since it achieved its aim of establishing a Jewish state, which, in turn, has produced a heterogeneous Jewish culture, some of it inflected with religion. Outside of Zionism, several forms of secular Jewishness have proved to be evanescent, but new modes of expression of Jewishness arise all the time. This may be read either as a sign of extraordinary adaptability and flexibility or, as others may see it, as a constant futile search for the impossible: Jewishness without Judaism.

Of course, changes in outlook and identification among Jews are closely related to changes in the larger societies in which they live. Their ever greater integration into European and American societies guarantees this will be the case. The very fact that significant numbers of Jews continue to debate issues of Jewish viability, cultural content, and belief indicates that these matter to them and, hence, that Judaism and Jewishness are important components of their individual identities.

To prepare this book, we brought together leading American, European, and Israeli scholars for a series of colloquia and a major conference, where drafts of chapters were thoroughly discussed and revised. This enterprise would not have been possible without the financial support and intellectual stimulation of Felix Posen. He challenged us to think about Jewish culture as evolving, living, and multifaceted, and in continuous dialogue with—but perhaps independent of—Judaism. While expressing his own views vigorously, he did not try to guide or constrain those of others. By the same token, he is unlikely to agree with some of the authors in this collective enterprise. We dedicate this book to Felix Posen with great appreciation and respect.

PART I

JEWISHNESS AND JUDAISM IN THE PREMODERN ERA

It is widely accepted that Jews have been for centuries and remain today both an ethnic and religious group. However, the very concepts of "religion" and "ethnicity" did not exist in antiquity, or at least were not differentiated. Religion was so pervasive that nonreligion was hard to imagine. In the ancient Near East, there seems to have been no concept of religion since it suffused the lives of all peoples to such an extent that it was not a thing apart. There were no atheists or secularists that we know of in the ancient world, and no ancient Indo-European language had a special word for religion.

Nevertheless, some have discerned in the conflict between Hellenizing Jews and the rabbis the antecedents of conflict between modern secular and religious Jews. Yaron Eliav argues that the relationship between Judaism and Greco-Roman culture has nothing to do with the conflicting categories of religion-secularism, which modern Jews have projected on it. Secularism does not provide a meaningful category for the understanding of ancient Judaism. There was a definable Jewish identity, but its texture and content remained fluid for centuries.

Gabriele Boccaccini maintains in his chapter that the important difference between Judaism and Christianity is ethnic, not ideological. Religious ideas preceded notions of Jewish ethnicity, but ethnicity became more salient. Christianity, a movement within Judaism, lost its ethnic Jewishness and became dissociated from it.

By the late Middle Ages, Jewishness was defined as rabbinic Judaism. But in the late eighteenth and nineteenth centuries, there were challenges to rabbinic authority by Sephardi crypto-Jews, whose role in undermining rabbinic rule is addressed by Miriam Bodian. Crypto-Jews from Spain and Portugal sounded the first notes of individuation and the development of a personal religion.

Perhaps the best known of these Jews, certainly outside Jewish circles, was Baruch (Benedict) Spinoza, who preceded the challenges Bodian describes and is often regarded as the first secular Jew. Steven Nadler rejects this idea and maintains that for Spinoza there can be no Jewishness without Jewish law (*halacha*), and since Spinoza rejected the validity of halacha, he did not claim any Jewishness. Thus, he was not the first secular Jew, but perhaps an important early modern model of the secular individual, someone for whom religious affiliation or heritage plays no role whatsoever in his identity.

1

Secularism, Hellenism, and Rabbis in Antiquity

YARON Z. ELIAV

Participants in current discussions, inside and outside academia, about the nature of Judaism often present the conflict between ancient Judaism and Hellenistic culture as the earliest prototype for the antagonism and tension between Jewish religion (particularly in its orthodox, *halachic* manifestation) and the modern secular world. Ironically, this model appeals to both participants in the current cultural debate. For example, in the days preceding Hanukah, it is common to hear teachers in ultra-orthodox educational institutions or community rabbis in synagogue sermons pre-figure the battle of religion against secularism as the struggle of the Hasmoneans against both the Greek kingdoms and Jews inclined toward a Hellenistic way of life. This paradigm places *mityavnim* (Hellenizing Jews) and modern secular (as well as acculturating and assimilating) Jews on the same side of a great divide. Many ortho-dox Jews seem eager to depict themselves as comrades-in-arms of the Hasmonean pietists in Judaism's age-old campaign against its nemeses. Similarly, on the other end of the polemical spectrum, secular Jews, inclined toward and sustained by the ideological characteristics of Western civilization, empathize with the supposed Hellenistic bedrock of that tradition. Adherents of the eighteenth- and nineteenth-century Jewish enlightenment appealed to Hellenistic trends in ancient Judaism, which they identified even among the rabbis of the Talmud. They argued that Judaism should incorporate the positive elements of non-Jewish society, eschew tra-ditional Jewish separatism, and indeed reconstruct the Jewish religion entirely.[1]

The rise of Zionism complicated matters even further, adding a fascinating angle fraught with internal contradiction to the discussion. Advocates of an inde-pendent Jewish state that would empower the Jewish people and end their depend-ence on the protection of other nations harked back to the image of the Maccabees (as well as Bar Kochba); after all, the Zionists considered them to be the last inde-pendent Jewish rulers before the modern state of Israel. The Zionist movement transformed Hanukah into a national festival, overflowing with symbols of free-dom and Jewish might. Such tendencies impacted, for example, the choice of name for the major Zionist youth movement in 1926: the Young Maccabees (Makkabi ha-Tsa'ir), and for the Jewish Olympics: the *makkabiyah*. The same tendency is evident in Israel's choice of the menorah—the seven-branched candelabrum from the Jewish Temple famously kept alight by the Hasmonean rebels—as the national emblem.[2]

However, I suggest that these modern notions about religion and secularism have little, if any, precedent in the ancient world and in the historical encounter of Jews with the Hellenistic, Greco-Roman cultures. To substantiate this assertion, I will first address religious consciousness and experience in the ancient world. A student of early periods must always remain cognizant of the fundamental differences that separate the modern era from previous ages. This is particularly true with regard to the study of religion. The dramatic advances in the natural sciences, the technological-industrial revolution, and the replacement of devout belief with secularism have radically transformed the religious environment. In ancient times, people perceived reality through categories that today we would call "religious." The cosmology of the Greco-Roman Mediterranean basin was replete with divine beings: deities, goddesses, spirits, souls, angels, demons, and mythological monsters.[3] Today we know these entities only from the realm of special effects in Hollywood cinema, but in the classical era they surrounded people everywhere, from the heights of the temples on Mount Olympus, through the abstractions of philosophical writings, down to the latrines in which people relieved themselves. One of these latter facilities, for example, discovered almost intact in Pompeii, contains a fresco of the goddess Fortuna in all her glory. The graffito to her right reads *"cacator cave malum"* (defecator, beware of evil), and beneath it a man crouches over a small altar, probably moving his bowels. To contemporaries of the fresco, this depiction resembled neither a sacrilege nor a derisive caricature. On the contrary, the elementary human function of excretion, with its concomitant odors and physical exertion, demanded expression, just as bathroom graffiti, for all their humorous and scatological intent, demonstrate today. However, in the ancient mind, this basic act was understood in the language of religion, incarnated (in the Roman case) in the guise of Fortuna. Keith Hopkins has captured this quintessential aspect of the ancient world succinctly in the title of his recent book, *A World Full of Gods*.[4]

Pervasive and invasive, religious mentality shaped the lens through which the people of the Roman world viewed their surroundings and performed their everyday routines. Religious vocabulary and imagery seeped into every strata of language, assisting people in mediating, explaining, and interpreting their interactions with their environment. Names and characteristics of gods, myths, legends, and folk beliefs fashioned the cognitive templates that granted validity both to natural phenomena and human situations, just as scientific "truth" shapes the contours of our present world. Although they worshiped one God, ancient Jews shared with their neighbor polytheists the plurality of divine expression—that is, an all-encompassing religious mentality.

Therefore, the historical relationship between Judaism and Greco-Roman culture has nothing to do with the conflict between religion and secularism that modern Jews, troubled by and fixated on the issues of their time, have projected onto it. I will try to place the story of Judaism, Hellenism, and the rabbis in historical context. The subsections of this chapter will examine issues of cultural interaction, identity, and worship during the five hundred years following the destruction of the Jewish Temple in Jerusalem—the era some call (rather misleadingly) the rabbinic period.[5] A twofold claim runs throughout these discussions: First, secularism does not provide a meaningful category for the understanding of ancient Judaism. Second, ancient Jewish religion and way of life are far removed from the rabbinically centered Judaism of the Medieval and Modern eras, even in the eyes of its opponents.

Hellenism and Judaism: General Context

Few events affected the history of the ancient world as profoundly as the conquests of Alexander, son of Philip the Macedonian, also known as Alexander the Great, in the thirties of the fourth century B.C.E. For nearly one thousand years, until the appearance of Islam in the first half of the seventh century C.E., the Mediterranean world in general and its eastern shores in particular—the regions of Phoenicia, Syria, and Palestine-Israel—participated in a great cultural experience that came to be known as Hellenism. A precise elucidation of the multifaceted, convoluted, and complex civilization of this era is beyond the scope of this essay. However, we may take note of its central features: a syncretistic religious landscape in which worship of Greco-Roman gods and belief in Greco-Roman mythologies melded with the worship of local deities; the Greek language gradually becoming the lingua franca of the eastern Mediterranean and functioning alongside the indigenous Semitic dialects as the cohesive element in an otherwise disparate environment; and, most important, a cultural and social milieu structured by a colorful blend of Western and native elements—in architecture and art (and the aesthetic realm in general); in government (in its legal, political, and economic manifestations); throughout the various strata of social hierarchy and affiliations; and in the mundane details of leisure and daily life. In a gradual process that spanned centuries, Hellenism touched and significantly altered almost every aspect of life.[6]

One cannot overemphasize the relevance of these developments to the formation of ancient Judaism. Most, if not all, of the major components of ancient Judaism crystallized during this period; for example, the Bible, as a central sacred composition believed to encompass the direct revelation of God; Jewish law, as a system that directs the lives of its members; and the synagogue, as the communal institution that networks these people. These elements took shape, although in a remarkably fuzzy process, within or in close proximity to the Greco-Roman world. This stands in striking contrast to the underlying tendency in nineteenth- and early twentieth-century Jewish scholarship to describe ancient Judaism according to the famous biblical rubric *"Am levadad yishkon"* (a nation that dwells apart).

Until recently, most textbooks portrayed Judaism throughout its ancient history as a coherent, if not homogeneous, unity. Despite internal conflicts, disputes, and differences over both minor and major issues, according to this view the Jewish people ranged themselves steadfastly against the outside world in its Greek guise.[7] Judaism, in the view that was accepted then and, to a large extent now, was based on monolatry values in stark contrast to Greek polytheism. This contrast prevailed in all other areas of life, such as daily behavior, language, literature, and legal and governing institutions. Consequently, by defining Hellenism and Judaism as two distinct, separate, and largely hostile categories, these modern writers went on to define the connection between them in terms of influence, a category usually carrying negative connotations of assimilation. Some Jews willingly and consciously "Hellenized"—that is, they adopted some aspects of Greek culture, such as language or personal name, or worse, abandoned their original way of life entirely and went to graze in foreign fields. Elsewhere I have characterized this portrayal in modern scholarship as the image of "two fighters in the boxing ring."[8] In other words, despite their mutual influence and cross-fertilization, Judaism and Hellenism were suspicious of and antagonistic toward one another, locked in a perpetual battle that often led to violent conflict and bloodshed.

Current scholars have rejected most of the elements of this view, especially with regard to the Second Temple period—the first four hundred years of the Jewish-Hellenistic encounter. They have shown that the nature of the relationship between the Jews and Greek culture was much more complex, and that Greek-Hellenistic culture percolated into, and in many cases molded, the most basic components of Jewish life. Even the first Hasmoneans, portrayed in I and II Maccabees as the saviors of Judaism from the grips of Hellenism, were immersed in the fundamentals of the Greek worldview.[9] Legal and governing institutions, such as the Sanhedrin (a Greek word), and even the most inward levels of human experience, such as perceptions of the world and nature, not to mention the Jewish God, were imprinted with the general cultural textures of the Mediterranean basin, namely Hellenism.[10]

But did this cross-fertilization and mutually influential relationship persist in the period after the Second Temple, from 70 C.E. to the Muslim conquest at the beginning of the seventh century? The rest of this chapter endeavors to illuminate this period. By conservative estimates, scholars assess the population of the Roman Empire at the beginning of the first millennium C.E. to have been between fifty to sixty million, inhabiting the lands around the Mediterranean basin. An educated guess numbers about five (conservative estimates say two) million Jews among them.[11] Between 10 and 20 percent of the empire's Jewish population lived in present-day Israel or Palestine, then a Roman province, first called Judea and later Syria-Palestina. The rest lived in cities and villages throughout the Mediterranean world, in Egypt and North Africa, Syria, Asia Minor, Greece, Rome, and beyond, in Gaul (today France) and the Iberian peninsula—noncontiguous islands of Jewish habitation usually referred to as the Diaspora. These numbers, albeit imprecise, and their geographical distribution establish the Jews as the largest and most widely dispersed ethnic minority under Roman rule. Such noticeable presence immediately raises questions about the nature of this community, the substance of its life, and its relation to the world in which it existed. Thus we turn from geography and statistics to politics, society, culture, and religion.

Identity and Lifestyle

The question "Who is a Jew?" has been answered in myriad ways, and defining Jewish identity in the ancient world involves no less complexity or difficulty. The rubric "Jewish" (*yehudi*), which began as a geographical-tribal marker (one who lived in the territory called Judea or who belonged to the tribe of Judah), had developed into a signifier of cultural, religious, and national identity by the second century B.C.E. (2 Macc. 2:21 offers the earliest testimony). Roman law—and before that, Hellenistic imperial correspondence—as well as many non-Jewish authors acknowledged a Jewish reference group with unique characteristics and a discernable historical heritage anchored in ancient times.[12] These sources confirm the existence of a definable Jewish identity while simultaneously assailing the signifiers of Judaism. But, most important, the texture and content of that identity remained fluid for centuries. Jewish identifying marks, such as dress and language, which later demarcated the boundaries between members of this group and others, had not yet matured into sharp identifiers in antiquity. In a cultural environment in which identity is not hermetic, a person could be "a good Jew," at least by self-definition, while being an Idumean and a Roman at the same time.[13] Alternatively, a Jew could also be a Christian and vice versa.[14]

Theologically, and in hindsight, it may be possible to locate clusters of ideas that could represent the nucleus of ancient Judaism, or at the very least denote a certain strand within it. Yet clearly no consensus beyond the superficial level has ever been reached on such notions; various groups and sects differed among and within themselves about any number of principles. Even if all acknowledged the importance of a given tenet in the world of Judaism, such as belief in the God of Israel and the traditions conveyed about him by the scriptures (that is, he created the world, brought Israel out of Egypt, gave the Torah, and so on), people perceived the nature and essence of this God in contradictory ways. Philo of Alexandria's philosophical divinity, for example, modeled on the high god of Greek *paideia* and his subordinate agent (the *logos*), was nothing like the concrete, almost flesh-and-blood God who nearly rubbed shoulders with Bar Kochba's armies, according to some rabbinic tales.[15] And both of these images fall far from the heavenly, sometimes dualistic God who emerges in many mystical and apocalyptic works. Yet it seems that if we brought Philo and Bar Kochba together (even though historically impossible) and overcame the language gap between them (Philo spoke and thought in Greek, whereas Bar Kochba's mother tongue was Aramaic), both would have agreed that they believed in the same deity—the God of Abraham, Isaac, and Jacob who granted the Torah to Israel.

But even this kind of (modernly constructed) consensus does not resolve the problem of identity. Diversity and flexibility characterized the ancient marketplace of faiths and views, and people mixed and matched their spiritual groceries eclectically and without product loyalty (at least not in modern terms). Instances of unabashed gentiles who believed in the God of Israel and took part in worship of him in synagogues are well documented.[16] Likewise, many of those who professed Jesus' messianic status retained their adherence to the God of Israel and continued to observe his laws in later generations, even when criticized by other Christians who felt that the very meaning of their faith involved separation from Judaism.[17]

Finally, many (or even all) Jews took part at some level or other in the Roman experience (*romanitas*) that pervaded the Mediterranean and did not necessarily see their participation as contradictory to Judaism. For example, some Jews who held official positions in municipal administrations must have participated actively and centrally in the city cult, which was the norm in those days, even if certain Roman legislation pronounced their exemption from such obligation.[18] Jewish communities that chose to depict the image of the sun god Helios, mounted on his chariot and bearing identifying attributes, on the mosaic floors of their synagogues offer another example.[19] These instances point to the messiness of the cultural environment of the ancient world. In this context, the very act of searching for a coherent ancient Jewish theology is fundamentally mistaken, and is perhaps an outgrowth of the theological intensity of Christianity. For reasons beyond the scope of this essay, Christian thinkers tended to arrange the set of ideas that defined their way of life into an organized system by Late Antiquity and even more so in the Middle Ages. In this sense, premedieval Judaism was, with a handful of exceptions, a nontheological religion. If a certain framework did exist, it encompassed amorphous and noncompulsory traits.

More than theology, ancient Judaism featured a shared historical heritage based freely and without concrete obligation on the biblical ethos. Jews identified themselves and were perceived by their Gentile neighbors as the descendants of Abraham, Isaac, and Jacob, members of a nation who had been enslaved in Egypt, taken out of bondage with signs and wonders, received the Torah at Sinai, and whose twelve tribes had inherited the land of Canaan.

In this pre-theological environment, Jewish experience centered on a way of life, a long list of smaller and larger details that shaped the time and space of the individual and the family, weaving the practitioners, even if only loosely, into what was called "the Jewish people." In addition to the Temple, which already lay in ruins by this period, and the Jewish God, who naturally attracted much attention, this way of life included the following components:

1. the Sabbath, the seventh day of the week on which labor was prohibited, a day devoted to prayer, family feasts, and rest;
2. dietary laws, which proscribed certain foods, in particular specific types of meat and especially pork, a common ingredient in the Roman diet;
3. circumcision.

These core practices are supplemented frequently in our sources with references to burial practices, the sabbatical year, and annual festivals. Jewish writers of different strands articulate this almost obsessive tendency to encapsulate Judaism in practical paradigms, and itemize its essence in (what we now call according to the Rabbis) "halachic" details. The roots of this legal propensity are found in the sacred writings that Second Temple Jews revered as their foundation texts: first among them, the Five Books of Moses, also known as the Torah. At their core, these scriptures convey the God of Israel's requirement that his subjects observe strictly his precepts (the *mitsvot*). The Torah communicates these guidelines as legal strictures, dictating permitted and forbidden actions for God's people. Through the mitsvot, the Torah endeavors to shape the Jew's entire way of living—from his diet to his farming, his family, the marketplace and economy, not to mention his army and its wars. Of course, the Torah also devotes much attention to the laws that lay out the proper procedures for the sacrificial process of the Temple, the highest institution in the life of ancient Jews (see below). It also specifies a series of annual feasts, which created a link between agriculture and the changing seasons of the year, on the one hand, and the nation's mythological-historical heritage on the other, producing a Jewish dimension of time, a calendar. These holidays included festivals in memory of the exodus from Egypt (Passover), receiving the Torah (Shavu'ot), and later the victories of the Hasmoneans (Hanukah), as well as fasts and days of mourning commemorating the destruction of the Temple and the exile of the nation.

Many Jewish writers from the Second Temple period recognize the importance of the divine way of life. Philo endowed the laws with allegorical-philosophical meaning; Josephus explained them in language comprehensible to his Greek-Roman readership; while other books, such as *Jubilees*, addressed a solely Jewish audience.[20] The brevity and ambiguity with which the Torah formulates its decrees stimulated Jewish groups in the Second Temple era to interpret and shape them in varied ways, each group disputing the interpretations of the other. The Judean Desert (or "Dead Sea") scrolls provide a lively example of such a legal-polemical debate.[21] Many of the messages the authors of the canonical Gospels attribute to Jesus also express his disagreement with legal interpretations that the Pharisees, one of the central groups at the end of the Second Temple period, bestowed upon the Torah. Yet, at the same time, they confirm the centrality of the mitsvot in his world (contrary to later Christian claims that Jesus rejected the Torah's practical commandments and advocated their replacement with a spiritual doctrine).[22] The Sages built upon this legal tendency and enhanced it in the years after the destruction.

However, one caveat is necessary in this regard: many modern scholars are not sufficiently sensitive to the necessary distinctions between the function of Jewish law in ancient Judaism and the supremacy of rabbinic halacha in the medieval and early modern world. Clear-cut and considerable differences set these two historical moments and their legal systems apart. Ancient Jewish law existed in a relatively rudimentary, and therefore amorphous, state; at the time, no one had yet produced a legal code that would regulate Jewish life beyond the important but rather vague statements of the Torah. By contrast, through the Middle Ages, the great rabbinic legal scholars including Rabbi Isaac of Fez (1013–1103), Maimonides (1135–1204), and Rabbi Jacob *ba'al haturim* (died c. 1340) produced any number of codices, each expanding, elaborating, and clarifying their predecessors. Furthermore, Jews in antiquity lived in a relatively flexible and unenforceable legal environment. They were able to navigate more freely than their medieval descendants, who lived according to a much more organized written system of halacha that predominated and determined Jewish religious experience (even if, as some scholars convincingly claim, the system was not as rigid as we tended to think in the past). Jewish life in antiquity should be seen as a diversified and porous continuum on which individual Jews and groups (families, communities, geographical settings) located themselves differently, appropriating some aspects of Jewish law and rejecting others, intentionally or otherwise.

Yet another characteristic of Jewish life in the Roman world distinguished it from both earlier and later periods. Like other minorities at the time, and unlike the Jews of the medieval world, when firm boundaries encompassed many facets of daily routines and alienated Jews from Christians, Jews in the Roman era lived in a relatively open and commonly shared cultural environment that extended to even the furthest reaches of the empire and embraced its members regardless of their ethnic or religious orientation. Two examples from Asia Minor illustrate this point: In the city of Aphrodisias, some high-ranking non-Jewish city officials (called *theosebeis* or God-fearers in the Jewish inscription of the story) cooperated with their Jewish neighbors in the establishment of a public kitchen for the needy.[23] Toward the center of Asia Minor, in the city of Acmonia, one Julia Severa, a high priestess of the house of the divine emperors and president of the city's competitive games, donated the "house" of the local synagogue.[24]

The same social and cultural dynamics emerge from an examination of the Roman bathhouse. Scholars who have reconstructed Jewish life in the Roman world by applying norms developed later could not conceive of Jews participating in the cultural milieu that transpired in the bathhouse. After all, this institution encapsulated the essence of the romanitas, with its nudity, sports, and hedonistic fixation on the human body. In fact, the opposite is true. Not only did Jews attend the bathhouse regularly, they also lauded its benefits and partook in its cultural proceedings.[25] This flexibility applied even to features of Roman life that, at first glance, seem to be highly problematic for Jews, such as the numerous statues that permeated the Greco-Roman urban landscape. Rabbinic literature expresses surprisingly lenient and diverse attitudes to these statues. The rabbis' views about three-dimensional sculpture are articulated in accordance with common modes of viewing sculpture throughout the Mediterranean.[26] Magic is yet another feature that Jews happily shared with other constituents of the ancient world, as could be seen vividly in the many magical texts (a full Jewish recipe book of magic formulae survived in the Cairo Genizah, *Sefer ha-Razim*), amulets, and curse tablets that exhibit Jewish traits, as well as numerous references to magic (not all unfavorable) in rabbinic literature.[27] Such shared cultural textures undermine the modern scholarly view which reconstructs the encounter between Jews and Hellenistic, Greco-Roman culture as two distinct and predominantly hostile entities that at the most negotiated with and influenced each other. At least with regard to Late Antiquity, this model must be revised.

Ritual

This period also witnessed a total revision of the ritual system of the Jewish world, one of the most significant revolutions ever undergone by any religion. The worship of gods was one of the basic and indispensable elements of human experience in the ancient world. At their core, Israelite and subsequent Second Temple Judaism were cultic religions, which means they exhibited two basic components:

1. the existence of Temple or Temples;
2. the worship of God through offerings—mainly animal sacrifices, but also vegetarian offerings (called "meal offerings," especially all kinds of grain breads) and liquids (like oil and wine, or "libations").

In this respect, Judaism resembled all other religious systems in the ancient Near East and the Greco-Roman world, which formed the cultural environments of the Israelite tradition and Judaism, respectively. While sacrifices and offerings may seem fetishistic, if not primitive, to the modern observer, to ignore them is to overlook a fundamental aspect of the ancient Jewish experience. On the grounds of the Temple, up to one hundred animals a week (thousands during the major holidays) were butchered, skinned, and burned on a huge altar. The odor of flowing blood, massive quantities of spoiling meat, and thousands of pounds of scorched livestock was overpowering. This is what ancient religious procedures consisted of, and for contemporaries of these rituals, the odor was sweeter than the finest perfume. In fact, a Jewish tradition configured the spatial layout of the Temple as "Mount Moriah," from the Hebrew *mor*—myrrh, a kind of perfume. Ancient texts tell us that the appearance of smoke coiling up from the altar prompted the highest joy from the populace (e.g., Sir. 50:16–9). After all, it signified that God had received their sacrifice. This seemingly simple act embodied no small achievement in a world that had not yet witnessed the modern technological-industrial revolution, which radically transformed the religious landscape. In the ancient Mediterr-anean, gods supplied the necessary safety nets in an environment replete with agony and insecurity. They helped people interpret, understand, and control their fate, and thus everyone strove to be in their favor.

Ancient people, in general, and Israelites and then Jews, in particular, conceived of the temple as the house of a god, any god. Within this domestic conception of sacred space, sacrifices functioned as the "communication lines" through which the public, standing outside the house (a gap representing the cosmological breach between the human and the divine), could connect with the godly entity who resided within.[28] Simultaneously their doctor, lawyer, financial advisor, and psychi-atrist, God existed beyond immediate reach but remained accessible nevertheless. Accordingly, the common belief held that God must dwell among his people. Judaism differed from other religions throughout the Roman Mediterranean in that the latter viewed their gods as a human or semi-human figure, and therefore placed their images in the temples. The Torah insisted on the non-anthropomorphic nature of God, and thus prohibited his depiction. So the Temple in Jerusalem stood naked, devoid of statues. Instead, ancient Israelite thinkers formulated the elusive concept of *Shechina* (presence), meaning that only the intangible essence of God inhabited the sanctuary. Beyond this difference, however, all ancient religions shared common practices with regard to the spatial organization of worship. The Jewish Temple resembled a huge house, consisting of two main chambers: the

Holy of Holies, where the Ark of the Covenant stood and God's presence resided; and the outer chamber, called *kodesh* or *heichal*, containing the sacred vessels (furniture). The vessels included the menorah, a golden table holding a dozen loaves of bread, and a small bronze altar for incense (analogous in the domestic conceptuality to electricity, a pantry with food, and a ventilation system to dissipate the potent smell). The huge altar for sacrifice stood just outside the entrance to the building (functioning as the "intercom" that established communication).[29]

Another important aspect of the cultic religion involved the location of the masses during worship. They were neither permitted to enter the Temple, which was considered "sacred" (i.e., off-limits), nor were they allowed to participate in the sacrifice of their own offerings. These privileges were granted exclusively to the priests (*kohanim* in Hebrew), who were seen as God's servants and in charge of maintaining the house (Temple) and implementing the entire sacrificial process. The populace would gather in the courts and the huge compound surrounding the Temple, and bring their offerings to a certain point to hand over to the priests. They then watched the procedures from a distance. Thus the individual was separated from the core of religious activity, and the encounter with God remained indirect through a sacrifice handled by someone else.

In the ancient world nearly everyone (as far as we know) seemed happy with this arrangement. Jews everywhere revered the Temple of God, even if some—like Jesus, who according to the Gospel writers overturned the tables in the Temple's court (*Mk.* 11:15–9 and parallels)—criticized the priests who controlled it or disapproved of the corruption that developed around it.[30] Notwithstanding these occasionally dissonant voices, by the last centuries of the First Temple period (seventh and sixth centuries B.C.E.), the Temple had become the most beloved institution of the people of Israel. In the days of the Second Temple, this popularity reached an unprecedented peak. Hundreds of thousands flocked to its compound during the Jewish holidays to be in the vicinity of God. From all over the world, Jews voluntarily raised a special annual levy, called the half-shekel, for the maintenance of the Temple. On the conceptual level, the Temple served as a fundamental and, in their minds, irreplaceable element of the encounter with God, i.e., the hub of the religious experience. Prayers were directed towards the Temple; sins were absolved through the offering of sacrifice; and in general, the practice of Judaism was dependent upon its existence. It is no surprise, therefore, that the Temple exceeded its practical religious status and became the best-known emblem of the nation of Israel.[31]

Although not instantly, all of this changed after the destruction of the Temple. Beyond the horrendous physical blow—tens, if not hundreds, of thousands dead (a number doubled and tripled by later rebellions) and the loss of property and land—the Jews remained without the institution that had enabled their lives. It is no surprise that many Jews (although certainly not all) concluded that Judaism had reached its end. With the eradication of the mechanism that had linked them with God, Israel's connection with its protector had been cut off, and the way of life nourished by that union terminated.[32] The paucity of sources from this period prevents us from measuring fully the circulation of such beliefs. I surmise it is no coincidence that it is in this period when Jewish groups that believed in Jesus formulated their first comprehensive narratives about his teaching. These accounts should be seen, at least in part, as responses to the vacuum created by the Temple destruction. The gospel accounts offer a formula of redemption in place of the security the Temple provided. The halachic framework of the Sages also sought in a fundamental way to supplant the loss of the Temple by providing an answer to the question of what constituted a Jewish way of life in its absence.

In time, the synagogue filled the spatial void left by the Temple's destruction.[33] The origins of this institution reach back to centuries prior to the Temple's destruction, which explains the stories about Jesus set in synagogues. At that time, the synagogue was a gathering place for a local community, mainly for the sake of reading the Torah publicly on the Sabbath. But after 70 C.E., the synagogue's appearance and role changed dramatically. Although we cannot firmly date the stages of its development, the synagogue gradually became (as it remains) the prime locus for the worship of the God of Israel, and unquestionably the most important institution in Jewish life.

The ancient synagogue emerges as a multifunctional cultic and communal establishment, diversified in appearance and substance. In addition to the worship of God through prayer and the housing of the torah scroll in a special ark, some communities, for example in the Bosphoros kingdom, practiced and documented the manumission of slaves in this institution.[34] Other synagogues held the public archives of the people associated with it (non-Jews included?) and housed other functions of community life such as schools for the youth. Most of all, the building embodied the spatial layout so central to ancient identity—its iconography (most but not all of which is later to the period discussed here), brought to life and perpetuated the memories of a shared past as communicated by the scriptures; and a space for various Jewish celebrations, such as the Sabbath, annual holidays, marriages, and other local festivities, as well as for the pronouncement of local hierarchy and power (evidenced by who sat where, honors inscribed on stone or mosaic, etc.).

To summarize, the synagogue, a religious institution par excellence in the modern world, functioned on many levels of communal life that would be labeled secular today. More importantly, ritual and worship in their ancient context were not confined to the realm of religion, but rather were an essential component of human experience, an existential mode that transcended the boundaries of a particular faith or conviction. This point of view blurs the dividing lines between Jewish and Hellenistic, Greco-Roman institutions of worship. Apart from the essential (though trivial) fact that people invoked different divinities in these institutions, they all partook in the same human experience of the ancient world and its most basic sensibilities, in which gods were everywhere, and everyone worshipped something.

The Rabbis in Antiquity

The Rabbinic Movement (generally called in Hebrew *HAZAL*, an acronym for "our sages, may their memory be blessed") is the anachronistic title given to the men who created rabbinic literature.[35] The term intends to exalt and set them apart as a homogeneous group with a distinct ideology and systematic philosophy of life, which shaped the character of Judaism, its institutions, and its way of life to the present. According to this view, rabbinic literature contains the essence of Judaism after the destruction of the Temple: a way of life developed, honed, and led by those who wrote these works—the rabbis. Thus the common label in collective Jewish memory for the centuries after 70 C.E. was the rabbinic period (or, in some cases, the period of the Mishnah and the Talmuds, after the two major rabbinic texts). The foundation of this view lies in the Middle Ages (although doubted by some modern scholars), when most streams in the Jewish public accepted rabbinic literature as a cornerstone of Jewish life and as the soul of Judaism. The leaders of Jewish communities in the Medieval Jewish Diaspora viewed themselves as the successors and followers of the rabbinic sages who created this literature. Accordingly, they adopted for themselves the collective title of "rabbi," which they had bestowed upon their predecessors.

The veneration of rabbinic texts ensured their preservation from one generation to the next—first as handwritten scrolls and then codices—and also assured their printing in thousands of copies. Yet this process of perpetuation undermined the ability of modern scholars, many of whom came from circles that revered the rabbis, to reconstruct the context in which the texts were composed. In fact, many times the process entirely distorted that context. The result is that most current scholars reject the view that emerged in the nineteenth and early twentieth century: that most Jews in the ancient world defined themselves and lived their lives according to the ideas and instructions found in rabbinic literature.[36]

The sages' status in antiquity was much more modest, and their authority—if they had any at all—was more meager than the traditional view would allow. The creators of rabbinic literature were learned Jews—scholars—who were active in Palestine in the generations after the destruction of the Second Temple, and from the third century, in the Persian Empire (or "Babylonia," now part of Iraq; a few of those scholars arrived there even earlier). Like other intellectuals throughout history, both Jewish and non-Jewish, the rabbis seem to be animated by their natural proclivity toward learning. They devoted their lives to scholarship and erudition. The focus of their studies, the foundation texts of their curriculum, consisted of the Jewish scriptures, which later became the Bible. Their preferred field of study centered on legal discourse, which did not preclude other branches of learning, such as philosophy and mysticism, although these latter do not seem to stand out in the rabbinic material. Accordingly, rabbinic sages endeavored to channel what they believed to be the eternal truth of God as articulated in the Torah (the first five, most important books of the Bible) into meticulous and well-structured legal formulae. In a long and gradual process, rabbinic legal scholarship grew into an all-embracing legal system. They named it *Halacha*—God's way of life.[37]

The small group of intellectuals who crafted the rabbinic tradition had limited impact on the Jewish public in Palestine, and even less on the Jewish communities elsewhere in the Mediterranean region. There were never more than a few dozen active at any given time, and sometimes even fewer.[38] At first, and for several generations, the sages functioned as individual scholars, teachers who gathered small numbers of students on a personal basis. Whatever links existed among them were loose and limited, and generally restricted to intellectual interests and scholarly debates.

The situation began to change slowly only at the beginning of the third century C.E. with the project of redacting and publishing the Mishnah, the first comprehensive compilation of rabbinic legal material. Dating from approximately 200 C.E., the Mishnah is a legal text, a type of compendium (or legal anthology) to which there are but few parallels from this early period. The quality and precision of its phraseology and scrupulous editing, combined with its intellectual vigor, rank the Mishnah at the top of the ancient world's legal documents. The view, embraced by some modern scholars (as well as orthodox Jews), that the Mishnah is a type of legal codex, a charter or rule of behavior addressed to the public at large and meant to lay out and dictate the Jewish way of living, should be roundly rejected.[39] Texts of such pragmatic nature are well known in the Middle Ages; for example, Maimonides's *Mishneh Torah* and Joseph Karo's *Shulkhan Aruch*. The earliest such works date back to the end of the Byzantine period and were discovered in the Cairo Genizah, a repository of ancient Jewish texts discovered in the nineteenth century. The genre continued to evolve in Persia after the rise of Islam under the guidance of a group known as the Geonim, hundreds of years after the Mishnah.

However, the editors of the Mishnah executed an entirely different agenda, evident in the fact that the work does not provide clear and unambiguous legal ruling on nearly any subject. On the contrary, its editors gathered and then offered several opposing positions on every issue. Those who wished to conduct their life according to the Mishnah would find themselves quickly at a dead end. Whose views should they follow? Rabbi Eliezer's, Rabbi Yehoshua's, Rabbi Meir's, or Rabbi Shimon Bar Yohkai's? Lacking the sophisticated hermeneutic tools that developed in much later generations and which enabled choice between opposing positions, there was no way to decide between the dissenting voices of the Mishnah. The editors were apparently uninterested in reaching such a verdict. Furthermore, as shown in the work's first line, the text ignores the larger public. It requires prior knowledge of nuances and complex legal concepts the sages had developed. The Mishnah itself does not convey this preliminary knowledge, and without it the text is accessible only to those conversant with the sages' legal thinking—a doctrine so difficult to grasp that the untrained person could hardly understand it.[40] The Mishnah contains no hint that its editors presumed, expected, or hoped that their text would turn out to be what it eventually became: a Jewish foundation document of the same, and in some cases even higher, standing than the Torah itself. The original target audience of the Mishnah were the sages themselves.

Thus the Mishnah was the *creator* (or at least the instigator) rather than the *creation* of the rabbinical movement. It wove the fabric that brought together individual intellectuals who had previously been linked, if at all, only loosely and informally and turned them into a group founded on recognition of the importance of the text it had created.

The third century opened a new stage in the history of the sages. First, they diverted their intellectual focus from the scriptures to the Mishnah itself. Some of the rabbis, apparently displeased with the final product, launched a supplementary work, the Tosefta. But this new composition assumed the Mishnah's internal organization—six orders, each covering a large category of subjects, and further divided into subsections called tractates—thus acknowledging its appreciation of the older work.[41] In the third century, centers of learning (*yeshiva*) were organized, some with dozens of students who arrived from distant communities such as Persia to hear the teachings of the sages and study the Mishnah.[42] Some students even transported the Mishnah outside the borders of the Roman Empire and founded centers of study in Sasanid Persia. Other works amassing the sages' commentaries on the Bible—*the Midrash*—began to appear at this time as well. The third century is the first period where one can discern a movement led by the sages, even if they still had a long way to go until accepted by most, if not all, strata of the Jewish public, and until the legal products of their scholarship—the halacha—became the obligatory infrastructure of Jewish life. That happened only after the rise of Islam, outside the traditional borders of the Roman world, in Persia, and from there back to Palestine, and thence to North Africa and Europe.

Conclusion

History plays a tricky game with modern analogies, blurring what from a distance of time might seem like clear-cut dichotomies, and churning the various constituents of current discussions into unfamiliar blends. This is particularly true when present debates are modeled on ancient precedent, such as the one that stirred around the role of secularism in Jewish society. Here I have striven to nuance and complicate (and to a large degree dismiss) the too-neat picture of continuity that locates the roots of the strife between Jewish religion, in particular in its orthodox, rabbinic form, and secularism in the ancient world. First, as I have shown, there was no secular experience in the ancient world, at least not in the way this category is grasped today. The various facets of Jewish life in antiquity reviewed here, including the practical aspects of daily routines, ritual procedures, and more abstract notions of consciousness and identity, were overwhelmingly anchored in the religiosity of the time. Secularism does not find a place along the gamut of Jewish manifestations in ancient times. Nevertheless, the decisively religious world of antiquity was nothing like the orthodox, predominantly rabbinic version that governed the Jewish sphere from the Middle Ages and on. No firm lines separated the Jews from their fellow Mediterraneans, and even the most intimate aspects of the worship of God shared large conceptual ground with other forms of worship. Moreover, the rabbis of that time were quite different from orthodox figures of today; it would be unimaginable, for example, for a present-day haredi rabbi to attend a Roman bathhouse. The so-called rabbinic version of Judaism and the ascent of rabbinic figures to social and political power were practically nonexistent in those early days, and were perhaps only in a rudimentary stage of development that by no means could have been the core of Jewish life. Thus from every angle, the modern paradigm that ties disputes around secularism to the ancient world should be abandoned.

NOTES

1. For an exhaustive discussion of the image of Hellenism in modern Jewish discourse, see Yaacov Shavit, *Athens in Jerusalem: Classical Antiquity and Hellenism in the Making of the Modern Secular Jew*, trans. Chaya Naor and Niki Werner (London: Littman Library of Jewish Civilization, 1997).

2. Another source for the menorah's significance in modern Zionist symbolism comes from its appearance on the arch of Titus, which ties it to the same paradigm of freedom/power; see Rachel Hachlili, "The Menorah, the Ancient Seven-Armed Candelabrum: Origin, Form and Significance," *Journal for the Study of Judaism Supplement Series* 68 (2001).

3. An illuminating articulation of this all-embracing religious spirit that prevailed in the ancient world, with emphasis on the period under discussion, can be found in Peter Brown's extensive work on the subject. See, for example, the chapter on religion in Peter R. L. Brown, *The World of Late Antiquity: From Marcus Aurelius to Muhammad* (London: Thames and Hudson, 1971), 49–112; and his recent article "Christianization and Religious Conflict," in *The Cambridge Ancient History XIII: The Late Empire, A.D. 337–425*, ed. Averil Cameron and Peter Garnsey (Cambridge: Cambridge University Press, 1998), 632–664. There he has characterized the "religious common sense" of the period as "a spiritual landscape rustling with invisible presences—with countless divine beings and their ethereal ministers" (632).

4. Keith Hopkins, *A World Full of Gods: The Strange Triumph of Christianity* (New York: Free Press, 1999). The wall painting from Pompeii is reproduced in plate 1.

5. On the misconceptions in naming periods and what informs them, see Yaron Z. Eliav, "Jews and Judaism, 70–429 C.E.," in *A Companion to the Roman World*, ed. David Potter (Oxford: Blackwell, forthcoming).

6. The best summary for English speakers is still Frank W. Walbank et al., eds., *The Cambridge Ancient History*, vol. 7, *The Hellenistic World* (Cambridge: Cambridge University Press, 1984), part 1.

7. Among the numerous examples, see the classic Haim H. Ben-Sasson et al., *A History of the Jewish People* (London: Weidenfeld and Nicolson, 1976). For more recent scholars who have continued to apply this model, see my study in the following note.

8. Yaron Z. Eliav, "The Roman Bath as a Jewish Institution: Another Look at the Encounter between Judaism and the Greco-Roman Culture," *Journal for the Study of Judaism* 31, no. 4 (2000): 416–454 (quote on 417).

9. Martha Himmelfarb, "'He Was Renowned to the Ends of the Earth' (1 Macc. 3:9): Judaism and Hellenism in 1 Maccabees" (forthcoming).

10. An example of a recent study that makes these arguments rather convincingly for the Second Temple period is Erich S. Gruen, *Heritage and Hellenism: The Reinvention of Jewish Tradition* (Berkeley: University of California Press, 1998).

11. Keith Hopkins, "Christian Number and Its Implications," *Journal of Early Christian Studies* 6, no. 2 (1998), 185–229; Seth Schwartz, *Imperialism and Jewish Society, 200 B.C.E. to 640 C.E.* (Princeton: Princeton University Press, 2001), 10–11; cf. Brian McGing, "Population and Proselytism: How Many Jews Were There in the Ancient World?" in *Jews in the Hellenistic and Roman Cities*, ed. John R. Bartlett (London: Routledge, 2002), 88–106.

12. The various sources are collected in Miriam Pucci ben Zeev, *Jewish Rights in the Roman World: The Greek and Roman Documents quoted by Josephus Flavius* (Tübingen: Mohr Siebeck, 1998); Amnon Linder, *The Jews in Roman Imperial Legislation* (Detroit: Wayne State University Press, 1987); Menaham Stern, *Greek and Latin Authors on Jews and Judaism*, 3 vols. (Jerusalem: Academy of Sciences and Humanities, 1974–84).

13. Shaye J. D. Cohen, *The Beginnings of Jewishness: Boundaries, Varieties, Uncertainties* (Berkeley: University of California Press, 1999), 13–24. Herod, the Jewish king of the last part of the first century B.C.E., represents a classic example.

14. Daniel Boyarin, *Border Lines: The Partition of Judaeo-Christianity* (Philadelphia: University of Pennsylvania Press, 2004).

15. Philo *Quod Deus est immutabilis*, PT Ta'an. 68d.

16. Paul R. Trebilco, *Jewish Communities in Asia Minor* (Cambridge: Cambridge University Press, 1991), 127–166.

17. Paula Fredriksen, "What 'Parting of the Ways'? Jews, Gentiles, and the Ancient Mediterranean City," in *The Ways That Never Parted: Jews and Christians in Late Antiquity and the Early Middle Ages, Texts and Studies in Ancient Judaism* 95, eds. Adam H. Becker and Annete Yoshiko Reed (2003): 35–63.

18. Linder, *The Jews*, 103–107, 120–124.

19. Martin Goodman, "The Jewish Image of God in Late Antiquity," *Jewish Culture and Society under the Christian Roman Empire, Interdisciplinary Studies in Ancient Culture and Religion* 3, eds. Richard Kalmin and Seth Schwartz (Leuven: Peeters, 2003), 133–145.

20. Philo, *De specialibus legibus*, Jos. *AJ* 4:196.

21. The best example is the text known as the Halachic Letter (*MMT*; 4Q 394–399); see Elisha Qimron and John Strugnell, eds., *Qumran Cave* 4, *Discoveries in the Judaean Desert X* (Oxford: Clarendon Press, 1994).

22. Paula Fredriksen, *From Jesus to Christ: The Origins of the New Testament Image of Jesus* (New Haven: Yale University Press, 1988), 98–106.

23. Joyce Reynolds and Robert Tannenbaum, *Jews and God-fearers at Aphrodisias: Greek Inscriptions with Commentary* (Cambridge: Cambridge Philological Society, 1987), 5 line 1, 26–27.

24. Tessa Rajak, *The Jewish Dialogue with Greece and Rome: Studies in Cultural and Social Interaction* (Leiden: Brill, 2002), 463–478.

25. Eliav, "The Roman Bath," 416–454.

26. Yaron Z. Eliav, "Viewing the Sculptural Environment; Shaping the Second Commandment," *The Talmud Yerushalmi and Graeco-Roman Culture*, vol. 3, *Texts and Studies in Ancient Judaism* 93, ed. Peter Schäfer (2002): 411–433.

27. Peter Schäfer, "Magic and Religion in Ancient Judaism," in *Envisioning Magic: A Princeton Seminar and Symposium*, ed. Peter Schäfer and Hans G. Kippenberg (Leiden: Brill, 1997), 19–43.

28. *GenR*. 68:12 (Theodor and Albeck 784–786) is one rabbinic articulation of this idea.

29. The notion of *shechinah* finds an intriguing parallel in Greco-Roman conceptualities of the divine presence in statues; see Yaron Z. Eliav, "On Idolatry in the Roman Bath House—Two Comments," *Cathedra: For the History of Eretz Israel and Its Yishuv* (in Hebrew) 110 (2003): 173–180. The best comprehensive presentation of the Jewish Temple and its various features remains Théodore A. Busink, *Der Tempel von Jerusalem von Salomo bis Herodes; eine archäologisch-historische Studie unter Berücksichtigung des westsemitischen Tempelbaus*, 2 vols. (Leiden: Brill, 1970–80).

30. Craig A. Evans, "Opposition to the Temple: Jesus and the Dead Sea Scrolls," *Jesus and the Dead Sea Scrolls*, ed. James H. Charlesworth (New York: Doubleday, 1992), 235–353; Edvin Larsson, "Temple-Criticism and the Jewish Heritage: Some Reflections on Acts 6–7," *New Testament Studies* 39 (1993): 379–395.

31. This idea is nicely reflected, for example, in the wide range of articles in William Horbury, ed., "Templum Amicitiae: Essays on the Second Temple Presented to Ernst Bammel," *Journal for the Study of the New Testament Supplement Series* 48 (1991).

32. E.g. *2 Bar.* 10 (Charles 39–41), 44 (Charles 60–61); *Sotah* 15:10–15 (Lieberman 4.242–4).

33. The ancient synagogue, with its numerous references in ancient texts and abundant archaeological material, attracted much attention in modern scholarship. Much of the following is loosely based on the sometimes divergent views of Lee I. Levine, *The Ancient Synagogue: The First Thousand Years* (New Haven: Yale University Press, 2000); Shaye J. D. Cohen, "The Temple and the Synagogue," *The Temple in Antiquity: Ancient Records and Modern Perspectives*, Religious Studies Monograph Series 9, ed. Truman G. Madsen (Provo: Brigham Young University, 1984), 151–174; Steven Fine, *This Holy Place: On the Sanctity of the Synagogue during the Greco-Roman Period* (Notre Dame: University of Notre Dame Press, 1997); Rajak, *The Jewish Dialogue*, 301–499.

34. Elizabeth Leigh Gibson, "The Jewish Manumission Inscriptions of the Bosporus Kingdom," *Texts and Studies in Ancient Judaism* 75 (1999).

35. For good summaries of the relevant details in this section, consult Shmuel Safrai, ed., "The Literature of the Sages," *Compendia Rerum Iudaicarum ad Novum Testamentum* 2, no. 3 (1987); Hermann L. Strack and Günter Stemberger, *Introduction to the Talmud and Midrash*, 2nd ed., trans. Markus Bockmuel (Edinburgh: Clark, 1996).

36. The secondary literature on this topic is too vast to list here. For a concise summary, see Catherine Hezser, "The Social Structure of the Rabbinic Movement in Roman Palestine," *Texts and Studies in Ancient Judaism* 66 (1997): 1–42, 353–404.

37. Cf. Safrai, *The Literature*, 121–209.

38. Lee I. Levine, *The Rabbinic Class of Roman Palestine in Late Antiquity* (Jerusalem: Yad Izhak Ben-Zvi, 1989), 66–69; Shaye J. D. Cohen, "The Place of the Rabbi in Jewish Society of the Second Century," in *The Galilee in Late Antiquity*, ed. Lee I. Levine (New York: Jewish Theological Seminary of America, 1992), 157–173.

39. Abraham Goldberg, "The Mishna—A Study Book of Halacha," in *The Literature of the Sages*, ed. Safrai, *The Literature*, 213–214.

40. A fascinating development occurred in tandem with the invention of print, which allowed the wide dissemination of rabbinic texts among many strands of society, to the extent that even young children gained access to this overly difficult material. Many of the new consumers of rabbinic literature, by and large intellectually unequipped to wrestle with these texts, endorsed alternative methods to engage with them. In other words, they conceived a learning system for rehearsing the texts without fully understanding them, in which melodies, *pilpul,* and other means replaced comprehension.

41. For recent reconsideration of this text and its relationship with the Mishnah, see Judith Hauptman, "The Tosefta as a Commentary on an Early Mishnah," *Jewish Studies, an Internet Journal* 3 (2004): 1–24.

42. Levine, *The Rabbinic Class*, 25–29; Hezser, *The Social Structure*, 195–214.

2 What Is a Judaism?

PERSPECTIVES FROM SECOND TEMPLE
JEWISH STUDIES

GABRIELE BOCCACCINI

In the last few decades, scholars of ancient Judaism and Christian origins have been engaged in a debate about the nature and essence of Judaism. Such a debate concerns not only what Judaism was in antiquity, itself and in relation to Christianity, but also has profound implications for our understanding of what Judaism is today.

Everything started when the normativity of Rabbinic Judaism and the myth of its antiquity and unchangeability, at least in premodern times, began to be openly questioned. Until the early 1970s, the model of Judaism as a monolithic system of thought, troubled only by the presence of marginal sects and by the confrontation with rival Christianity, was still largely accepted.[1] In the words of Jacob Neusner, "People were used to thinking in terms of a single, encompassing and normative Judaism, which defined the context in which all religious writings deriving from Jews—except for that of Jewish followers of Jesus—found a place. The other writings attested to yet another unitary and normative religion, Christianity."[2] In between, in the no-man's-land at the border between Judaism and Christianity, there were writings rejected by both. They fell into yet another category, that of sectarianism. They were Jewish apocrypha and pseudepigrapha—bizarre fantasies of radical sectarian (if not dysfunctional) minds, doomed to theological oblivion and historical insignificance.

The irony was that in spite of their differences, Jews and Christians had effectively worked as a team for centuries to create and sustain the idea of Judaism as an unchanging, unchanged (and perhaps unchangeable) system: the idea that since Moses' time there had been only one Judaism—that is, Rabbinic Judaism. Such an idea had proven to be functional to both Jewish and Christian self-understanding. It also provided a setting convenient to both for their conflict. For oppressed Jews, the model served to emphasize their enduring fidelity to an ancient and unaltered tradition as well as polemically to sanction the complete otherness of Christianity (as well as any other "heresy") compared to the one Judaism. On the other hand, triumphant Christians used the same model to stress the absolute newness and uniqueness of their religion and to support their contention of having replaced an outmoded, sclerotic religion.

Although the continuous fortune of Josephus (and of his Christian and Jewish doubles, Hegesippon and Josippon) throughout the Middle Ages demonstrated the diversity of ancient Judaism, the Jewish sects aroused no interest, their memory being only occasionally resurrected by the curiosity of the erudite (Philastrius and Epiphanius among the Christians; Ibn Daud and Maimonides among the Jews).[3] The decisive dramatic conflict between the Synagogue and the Church, both so well defined in their respective roles, certainly had no need of other, minor characters—in fact, they were quickly forgotten. In either triumph or distress, both the rabbis and the Christians had good reasons to consider themselves the only authentic heirs of the one Judaism, which the former claimed to have faithfully maintained and the latter to have faithfully fulfilled.

The legacy of the single-Judaism model extends well into modern times and shaped the origins of modern scholarship. It took the Second World War and the Holocaust to change things. In the post-Holocaust climate of reconciliation between Christians and Jews and in the wake of the breathtaking discovery of the Dead Sea Scrolls, the entire framework of certainties that for centuries had regulated Jewish-Christian relations suddenly collapsed. If Jesus was a Jew (not the blue-eyed, Scandinavian hero of the movies) and "sectarian" movements like the Essenes looked perfectly at home in the diverse environment of the first century, something had to be wrong with the perception of what Judaism and Rabbinic Judaism were in antiquity. In the late 1970s, the works of Ellis Rivkin and Jacob Neusner conclusively showed that Rabbinic Judaism was not normative Judaism, but a reform movement that became normative only at a later stage in Jewish history.[4] The synchrony between biblical and rabbinic origins was broken, and so was the very foundation of the continuity and stability of the entire history of Judaism, based on the equation "Judaism = Rabbinic Judaism = Orthodox Judaism." A seemingly limited historical problem such as redefining the relationship between Second Temple Judaism and Rabbinic Judaism had led scholars to nothing less than the monumental task of redefining Judaism.

From Judaisms Back to Judaism

The task of defining what Judaism was would prove to be much harder than defining what Judaism was not. In the early 1990s, the idea of multiple Judaisms gained momentum and recognition, so much so that in 1994 Neusner could boldly announce: "The issue, how to define Judaism, is now settled: we do not. We define Judaisms."[5] We were, on the contrary, only at the beginning of a long process of theoretical clarification. Philip R. Davies raised the timely question: "The replacement of the concept of Judaism by the concept of Judaisms solves one problem only to create another, perhaps even more fundamental one—namely what it was that made any Judaism a Judaism. . . . The plural Judaisms require some definition of Judaism in the singular, in order itself to have any meaning."[6] The Neusner model offered a refreshing emphasis on Jewish diversity, but its potential to develop into a comprehensive model was somehow restrained by its inability to engage in a constructive dialogue with other approaches and by its disturbing tendency to freeze and isolate each variety of Judaism from the others in almost impermeable systems without a coherent theory of what "Judaism" (singular) was. "In the history of Judaism, we can identify numbers of different Judaisms. . . . All together, of course, we observe continuities but these prove hardly definite of the distinctive traits of any one system. So, in all, Judaisms flourished side by side. Or they took place in succession to one another. Or they came into being out of all relationship with one another."[7]

Three post-Neusner models have emerged that challenge or correct his multiple Judaisms model. The most conservative and minimalistic approach is that advocated by E. P. Sanders since the late 1970s and recently revived by Seth Schwartz.[8] According to this view, any discourse about Jewish diversity and historical changes must be taken as regarding only the accidents, not the essence, of Judaism.

E. P. Sanders strongly rejects "the assumption that Judaism was divided into parties"[9]—that is, that there may have been not one Judaism but many. Underneath the diversity of Second Temple Judaism, he recovers the profound unity of "common Judaism" as "that of the ordinary priests and the ordinary people. . . . [W]hat was common in two senses: agreed on among the parties, agreed on by the populace as a whole."[10] The result of Sanders' "common-denominator theology" is the conceptualization of the essence of Judaism as "covenantal nomism."[11]

What in Sanders's view is the result of a sophisticated sociological analysis of Jewish literature and Jewish "practice and belief" in the Second Temple period becomes, in the work of Seth Schwartz, little more than a polemical assumption. "I reject the characterization of Judaism as multiple."[12] "The three pillars of ancient Judaism—the one God, the one Torah, and the one Temple—cohere in a single neat, ideological system."[13] Whereas Sanders saw sectarianism as a marginal yet actual phenomenon of dissent, Schwartz has stressed unity and cohesion. "The main sects were in fact an integral part of the Torah-centered Judaean mainstream elite."[14] Even the apocalyptic material was "the product of the same scribal and priestly elites and subelites who produced Jewish literature in general, and presumably it reflects their attempt to neutralize, judaize (i.e., interpret in Jewish terms), and assert control over problematic, perhaps in part magical, elements of Judaean religion."[15] The very concept of conflict, dissent, and competition, which specialists in Second Temple Judaism and apocalypticism have been emphasizing as the most characteristic element of the period,[16] is entirely dismissed as a mere optical illusion, "a trick of perspective."[17]

Such an approach is essentially apologetic. In spite of any diversity, Judaism regains its familiar and reassuring unity. Of course, Judaism is ever-changing and diverse, and the Second Temple period does not equal the rabbinic period. However, Jewish society in late antiquity was "complex, loosely centralized but still basically unitary"; "fragmentation" occurred as a result of "accommodation to direct Roman rule,"[18] not as a consequence of internal conflict and competition. The emergence of Rabbinic Judaism as well as of any other new stage in the history of Judaism does not signal any breakthrough but the continuous adjustment of "common Judaism" to different historical forms and circumstances. Accidents may change it (and in fact they continuously change it over time), but in its essence

Judaism has no history: over the centuries, beyond the plurality of its diverse historical manifestations, Judaism was, is, and always will be "covenantal nomism."

Lawrence Schiffman has parted from Sanders and Schwartz as he unreservedly accepts the dynamism and pluralism of Judaism and the existence of competing groups: "Can we speak of a normative tradition at any time in pre-Rabbinic times? I think not."[19] Schiffman also, however, has supported the idea of an intellectual unity of Judaism over the centuries, but this unity is demonstrated not by the permanence of an unchanged essence but by a gradual and consistent process of evolution of an ever-incremental tradition. In his words, "continuity can only be achieved in a tradition which adapts and develops."[20] Evolution means diversity, discontinuity, conflict, and dead possibilities before mainstream Judaism finds its natural course. Sectarianism provides the necessary antitheses on which new, more advanced syntheses are built. "What Judaism and the Jewish people needed was to experiment by playing out the results of the old conflicts to see how the various approaches would work in this new era. Thus, the sects were a proving ground from which emerged an answer to which way Judaism would move in the post-70 C.E. period."[21] Out of the Judaisms of the Second Temple period, "the rise of the rabbinic form of Judaism . . . was no accident. The Judaism that emerged at the end of the Talmud era had been chosen by a kind of natural selection process in the spheres of history and religion."[22] In other words, while Sanders and Schwartz stress that the essence of Judaism remains unchanged in spite of its history, Schiffman claims that the essence of Judaism is given by the history of its intellectual evolution. Judaism is what it has become.

Schiffman is definitively correct in his criticism of the Neusner model when he points out that we cannot "isolate each Judaism from the others, not only from those that existed at the same time, but also from those that came before."[23] In history there is no such thing as a group or movement that suddenly appears from nowhere. A group or movement always emerges from somewhere, as a modification or outgrowth of a previous group or movement, upon the foundations that others have laid before them. However, forcing the diversity of Judaism into a single line of evolution, as Schiffman has done, is a Hegelian enterprise, aimed to present one's own tradition, philosophy, or religion as the providential synthesis of historical processes. The problem of Jewish diversity is not merely a diachronic problem to be solved from a teleological perspective. With the same criterion, one could consider Christianity as the climax of Judaism, following the history of the "Jewish Church" from its biblical and prophetical foundations until the time of Christ, dismissing Pharisaism and Rabbinic Judaism as late and erroneous "antitheses," and then following the Christian synthesis through the progress of the Christian Church up to the present. This is what the *historiae sacrae* (so popular in the eighteenth and nineteenth centuries) used to do, before the genres of the "History of Israel" and of "Church History" established themselves as autonomous units.[24]

Shaye J. D. Cohen and Martin S. Jaffee have offered quite an interesting variant to the evolutionary model.[25] They doom as theologically motivated and absolutely hopeless any attempt to find an ideological unity of Judaism, be it described as an unchangeable essence or a single incremental tradition. Where Sanders and Schwartz find "a single body of doctrine and practice"[26] and Schiffman "a straight evolutionary line culminating inevitably in a victorious rabbinic Judaism,"[27] Jaffee sees "patterns of disharmony and points of intellectual and social stress, a picture of flux and experiment, rather than one of continuity and broadly recognized authority."[28]

Cohen has compared Judaism to a "bumblebee which continues to fly, unaware that the laws of aerodynamics declare its flight to be impossible."[29] The absence of any internal logic or law of ideological continuity does not mean, however, that there is no "unity within diversity."[30] It only means that this unity must be sought elsewhere, in the ethnic bond that links the Jewish people to its religious expressions. Neither for preserving the Jewish "essence" uncontaminated, nor for reaching the most perfect ideological synthesis, but for keeping the ethnic bond, "the rabbis were the winners of ancient Jewish history."[31] Judaism is the history of its people.

The ethnic model has the great advantage of discarding concepts of "race" or "genetics" in defining the Jewish identity. Quoting authors such as Anthony D. Smith and Ernest Gellner,[32] Cohen has identified an *ethnos* as "a named group, attached to a specific territory, whose members shared a sense of common origins, claimed a common and distinctive history and destiny, possessed one or more distinctive characteristics"—among which "the most distinctive . . . was the manner in which they worshiped their God, what we today would call their religion . . . and felt a sense of collective uniqueness and solidarity."[33]

The ethnic model also has the great advantage of almost completely getting rid of disturbing theological assumptions. Christianity, for example, is neither a "heresy" of covenantal Judaism nor an "antithesis" that before being discarded helped lay the foundations for the rabbinic synthesis. Christianity is simply a variety of Judaism that ceased to be such when it broke its bond with the Jewish people and "became a religious movement overwhelmingly gentile in composition and character."[34]

The problem is that by stressing the ethnic bond we miss entirely the ideological continuity that still ties Christianity to Rabbinic Judaism even after the ethnic bond was broken. This is what scholars of the "partings of the ways" have discovered—an unbroken "fraternal link" as that between "twins" born from the same womb. In the words of Alan F. Segal:

> The time of Jesus marks the beginning of not one but two great religions of the West, Rabbinic Judaism and Christianity. . . . As brothers often do, they picked up different, even opposing ways to preserve their family heritage. . . . Rabbinic Judaism maintains that it has preserved the traditions of Israel. . . . Christianity maintains that it is the new Israel, preserving the intentions of Israel's prophets. Because of the two religions' overwhelming similarities and in spite of their great areas of difference, both statements are true.[35]

As the title of a recent book edited by Adam Becker and Annette Reed points out, "the ways never parted"—Rabbinic Judaism and Christianity are simply different outgrowths of ancient Judaism.[36]

Judaism, Jewishness, and Judaicness

In order to define the unity of Judaism, some scholars have chosen to privilege the intellectual approach, which identifies Judaism primarily as a coherent system of thought, be it described as a temporal essence (Sanders, Schwartz) or an incremental historical tradition (Schiffman). Other historians have taken the ethnic approach instead, which identifies Judaism primarily as the expression of the religious identity of the Jewish people over the course of centuries (Jaffee, Cohen).

In my work on middle Judaism, I have focused on the intellectual dimension of Judaism while rejecting apologetic and theological assumptions.[37] The results have confirmed the conclusions of Segal; no clear boundary can be set between Christianity and Rabbinic Judaism in their relation with the previous tradition of Israel. From the intellectual point of view, Second Temple Judaism is neither the end point of an already established monolithic Judaism before Jesus (late Judaism) nor the starting point of a linear process of evolution naturally leading to the rabbinic stage (early Judaism). Those centuries are the transitional and diverse age (middle Judaism) of many competing Judaisms, in which both Christianity and Rabbinic Judaism had their intellectual roots and experienced their social origins.

The Christian and the rabbinic systems of thought are certainly distinct and very different from one another. However, each movement is in an analogous line of continuity and discontinuity with ancient forms of Second Temple Judaism.

The Christians built their system of thought on the theological foundations that the Enochic tradition had laid for centuries before Jesus around the principle of the demonic origin of evil.[38] The result was a parallel development of the ancient religion of Israel according to a trajectory different from that of Rabbinic Judaism, a trajectory in which ultimately the Torah was subordinated to the Messiah and ethnicity was no longer considered a prerequisite for membership. In so doing, the Christians undoubtedly sacrificed part of the rich intellectual heritage of ancient Judaism while enhancing the aspects they found more congenial; but this is also what the rabbis did.

Rabbinic Judaism built its system of thought on the theological foundations of the covenantal theology that the Pharisees (and before them the Zadokites) had created in the post-exilic period.[39] The rabbis stressed the centrality of the Torah by claiming its preexistence and expanding its boundaries to include the oral Torah,[40] thereby strengthening the bond between ethnicity and religion into an unprecedented identification. In so doing, the rabbis enhanced part of the rich intellectual heritage of ancient Judaism while sacrificing other aspects, exactly as the Christians did. While each party has for centuries claimed just the opposite and even agreed on the rival's claim, Christianity is no less conservative than Rabbinic Judaism, and Rabbinic Judaism is no less innovative than Christianity.

In sum, the clear discontinuity between Christianity and Judaism, emphasized by Jaffee and Cohen on the ethnic level, is not as apparent on the intellectual level, where continuity prevails over discontinuity. Should we then conclude that Christianity is still a Judaism, as it is an intellectual outgrowth of previous Judaic systems just as Rabbinic Judaism is? And if this is true for Christianity, what should we say about Samaritanism and Islam? They are also religious systems that developed from the ancient religion of Israel. Should we also define Samaritanism and Islam as varieties of Judaism?

It seems that scholars have arrived at a standstill. The ethnic approach alone does not account for the special and permanent bond that still links Judaism to Christianity (and also to Samaritanism and Islam). On the other hand, the intellectual approach alone is unable to set clear boundaries between these religions without having recourse to the historically unacceptable categories of "heresy" or "antithesis." Where the ethnic approach is too exclusive, the intellectual approach seems to be too inclusive.

If we keep taking either the ethnic or the intellectual element as the only marker of the unity and identity of Judaism, we will never find a coherent solution. We need to build a more sophisticated model that would reconcile both elements in a harmonious framework. I have maintained the importance of a conceptual and terminological distinction between the ethnic and the intellectual aspects of Judaism, or between "Jewishness" and "Jewish," on the one hand, and "Judaicness" and "Judaic," on the other. These terms in modern English (when used) are actually synonyms, but ours are no longer the happy times when scholars still used to speak the language of ordinary people. In a technical vocabulary, "Jewishness" and "Jewish" should refer to the people, history, and culture of ethnic Jews, while "Judaicness" and "Judaic" should be used with reference to the monotheistic religion of YHWH.

Studies of Jewishness and Judaicness are very important and complementary, and may be pursued autonomously according to each scholar's own legitimate research interest. It is one thing to trace the history of the cultural and religious expressions of Jewish ethnic identity (the history of "Jewishness," or of what is "Jewish"), and another thing to trace the history and intellectual evolution of Israelite monotheism (the history of "Judaicness," or of what is "Judaic"). Both histories overlap, yet they do not coincide. A history of Jewishness would give room to the secular (not only religious) manifestations of Jewish thought, but would only marginally include Samaritanism and Christianity (limited to their Jewish stage) while totally excluding Islam (which never knew a Jewish stage). A history of Judaicness, on the other hand, cannot ignore the enduring intellectual relations of Judaism with Samaritanism, Christianity, and Islam.

Even more important, neither the history of Jewishness nor the history of Judaicness equals the history of Judaism. A Judaism is not simply a Judaic system believed or practiced by just anyone (this would be the necessary conclusion if the emphasis is placed exclusively on the intellectual element—that is, on Judaicness without Jewishness). Nor is Judaism only whatever a Jewish group believes or does (this would be the necessary conclusion if the emphasis is placed exclusively on the ethnic element, or Jewishness without Judaicness).

In order to have "Judaism," we must have both Jewishness *and* Judaicness (not necessarily in precisely the same proportion). Only the presence of, and tension between, these two elements defines the boundaries of Judaism. Some examples from ancient history will help illustrate my contention.

At the Beginning It Was Judaicness

Most specialists of ancient Israel would characterize the ancient Israelite religion as a Canaanite religion and the Israelites as a Canaanite people. During the monarchic age, polytheism was normative. Henotheistic trends became more apparent only with the reform of King Josiah, and monotheism finally developed among the exiled Judahite elites in Babylon.[41] At the time of the "return," the monotheistic religious system elaborated by the priestly House of Zadok won its battle for leadership against the House of David and its prophets and defined in Judah a new entity in people of Israelite descent. Although later sources would romantically speak of an "emptied land" that welcomed the exiles, in reality a bitter confrontation occurred between the returnees and the remainees. At the beginning, therefore, it was religion (Judaicness), not ethnicity (Jewishness), that set the boundaries of Judaism as the new "community of the exile." In order to strengthen their ideological diversity, the returnees, through the creation of genealogical lists of exiled families and the prohibition of intermarriage outside the community, transformed what originally was only a regional branch of the Israelite people (the Judaeans) into an ideological category (the Jews). This category increasingly took the features of an ethnic entity distinct not only from the Canaanite peoples of the land but also from the pre-exilic Israelite identity. By the time of Sirach (beginning of the second century B.C.E.), the Samaritans, who shared common Israelite descent and even assimilated the Mosaic Torah and yet did not recognize the Zadokite leadership or conform to their practice and belief, were not considered "Jews," members of the same community or *ethnos:* they became the "others": "the foolish people that live in Shechem" (Sir 50:26), "not even a people" (Sir 50:25).[42]

Before the Maccabean period, however, the emphasis remained on Judaicness, not on Jewishness. The Tobiads are a case in point. This influential family of Israelite descent lived long on the fringes of Jewish society and resisted several attempts to exclude them from the community of the exile, only to be accepted at the end of the third century B.C.E. by virtue of political alliance and ideological compromise with the ruling Zadokite priesthood. Once tested, the ideological boundary proved to be still stronger than any ethnic boundary.

Then Came Jewishness

The Maccabean crisis started as a theological conflict that divided the more Hellenized urban upper class from the less Hellenized (and largely oppressed) rural class. The end of the Zadokite rule, which neither faction had the interest to restore, created a split among rival priestly families, the Hellenized party's attempt at replacing the Zadokite Torah being led by no one less than the high priest, Menelaus.

The genius of the Maccabees was to turn the Zadokite Torah from a priestly law into the national law of Israel. What originally was a theological conflict about Judaicness became a matter of Jewishness, a national war of liberation against Greeks and "false" Jews. It is in the aftermath of the Maccabean revolt that the term "Ioudaismos" first emerged to define the national identity of the Jews based on the observance of the Mosaic Torah.[43]

This did not guarantee uniformity; on the contrary Judaism remained even more divided.[44] The Maccabean war, however, changed the nature of Judaism. While before the Maccabees religion defined ethnicity, religious diversity was then confined within the boundaries of an ethnicity, of a shared way of life. Leaving or entering Judaism was increasingly understood as implying a crossing of an ethnic boundary. Even those varieties of Judaism (for example, Hellenistic Judaism), which went further in their allegorical interpretation of the Torah and were more eager to attract Gentiles, preserved the ethnic distinction between Jews and Gentile God-fearers. If Judaism was the religion of the cosmos, the Jews remained separated by birth from the Gentiles as the chosen priests of humankind. In the words of Philo, "a priest has the same relation to a city that the nation of the Jews has to the entire inhabited world" (*Spec. Leg.* II.63).

From the Persian period to the Hellenistic-Roman period, the situation curiously reversed. In the Persian period there were people (Tobiads and Samaritans) who could claim to share the same ethnicity and yet were excluded because they did not share the same religion. In the Hellenistic-Roman period, there were people (Gentiles) who could claim to share the same religion, yet were excluded because they did not share the same ethnicity. God-fearers could enjoy many of the privileges of Jewish monotheism and even being associated with Jewish communities, yet it was taken for granted that for the proselyte full membership was open only through a process of ethnic adoption (see Philo, *Spec. Leg.* I.51). Jewishness had then become the most conspicuous and least flexible boundary of Judaism.[45]

A Judaism (Christianity) Lost Its Jewishness

Christianity was born as a Jewish messianic movement. The Jesus movement, even in its more radical expressions, was one of the Judaisms of the Second Temple period. Jesus and his first followers sparked much controversy. Their Judaism attracted large crowds but also generated a lot of opposition by other competing groups. The temple elite (the Sadducees) tried to suppress the movement, and Christians repaid them with equal contempt. As for the Pharisees, the early Christian tradition preserves a sort of ambivalent memory of them as both friends and foes. Apparently, the Pharisees were no less harsh in their theological opposition, yet they defended the right of the Christians to exist and dissent—an attitude apparent in the Acts of the Apostles, where the Pharisees are praised for siding with the Christians against the Sadducees (Acts 5:17–40; 23:6–10), and confirmed by Josephus's account of the death of James, which outraged the Pharisees against the

Sadducean High Priest (Ant. 20:197–203). We know little about the reaction of the Essenes or para-Essene groups. Theologically, they seem to have been the closest to the Christian positions, but this does not mean that they welcomed the Christian message unreservedly. At least in the case of the followers of John the Baptist and the Enochic group who authored the Parables of Enoch, we have evidence of groups who preserved their distinct identity from the new Christian movement.

This variety of reactions is exactly what one would expect in the diverse and competitive environment of the Second Temple period. From its inception, the Jesus movement was controversial, yet no one questioned its being both Judaic and Jewish.

Then it happened that a minority branch of Christianity, namely Pauline Christianity, openly trespassed the boundaries of Jewishness, not simply by accepting Gentile members (Christian Jews and Hellenistic Jews also used to do this) but by abolishing the distinction between Jews and Christians within the new table fellowship. The Judaism of Paul was still fully Judaic, but its Jewishness was now largely compromised. Not surprisingly, the position of Paul created a conflict not only with the other forms of Judaism, but also within the Jesus movement—a conflict that ceased only when after the year 70, the balance of power in the early Church shifted decisively toward the Pauline communities. The "new" Israel, in which the first Christians intended to welcome the Gentile converts, gradually lost its cultural and ethnic continuity with the "old" Israel. Jewishness was neglected, forgotten, and even despised as a bizarre heresy of minority fringes. Christianity turned from a variety of Judaism that welcomed Gentile members into a Gentile movement.

Yet, Christianity has never ceased to be Judaic, as Judaic as its Jewish sibling. The most radical positions (like Marcion's), which aimed to sever the Judaic nature of the new religion, were contained and eventually rejected. The loss of Jewishness, in spite of the preservation of Judaicness, prevents us, however, from calling any of the modern Christianities a Judaism.[46]

And a Non-Jewish Community (Islam) Gained Judaicness

While Christianity provides the example of a Judaism that lost its Jewishness, Islam is a non-Jewish community that gained its Judaicness. Unlike Christianity, Islam was not born from within the Jewish people, nor was it ever a Judaism. Islam is a religious community that took from Judaism (and Christianity) the element of Judaicness and grafted itself into the tradition of the God of Israel. This ideological continuity, which automatically would assimilate Islam to Judaism if only the intellectual dimension were considered, does not make Islam a Judaism, as the element of Jewishness is completely missing. Even in its mythological expression, the Islamic tradition clearly marks such a distinction by claiming descent from the "other" son of Abraham, Ishmael.

In relation to Christianity and Judaism, Islam applied the same supercessionist attitude that the Christians had applied to Judaism, and Judaism and Christianity reacted with the same claim of heresy that the Jews also applied to Christianity. But once again this is a theological disputation. The fact that Islam is not and never was a Judaism, does not signify in any way a lower degree of legitimacy. If only the element of Jewishness were considered, we would miss an essential element of continuity that links Islam to Judaism. From the intellectual point of view, Islam is no less Judaic than its Jewish, Samaritan, and Christian siblings.

Conclusion: Judaism as a Genus

The distinction between Judaicness and Jewishness offers the possibility of a taxonomy that fully respects the diversity of Judaisms (plural) and at the same time clearly defines what "Judaism" is (singular). It also has the advantage of setting objective, nontheological, and nonjudgmental boundaries between Judaism and its siblings (Samaritanism, Christianity, and Islam), while unreservedly acknowledging what all these religions still have in common.

We have to think of Judaism as a genus. A genus is by definition a major category in the classification, ranking above a species and below a family. The family is that of "Abrahamic religions," which includes the whole set of monotheistic systems that sprang forth from the same Middle Eastern roots as a multibranched tree, or as Martin Jaffee would say, "all religions claiming to possess revelations from the God who first made himself known to Israel." The family of Abrahamic religions includes several genera: Judaism, Samaritanism, Christianity, and Islam, each of them being very rich and diverse in species.

Thanks to the distinction between Judaicness and Jewishness, both the link between Judaism and its siblings (the other religions belonging to the same family), as well as the particular identity of Judaism, are immediately apparent. While Judaicness is the common element of all Abrahamic religions, the term "Judaism" applies exclusively to the genus encompassing those many species (Judaisms), which show both the features of Jewishness and Judaicness.

Since its inception, Judaism was made of several parallel systems. Some of them had a short history; some flourished and developed side by side for centuries. No Judaism ever existed in isolation. Intellectual diversity challenged the inner development of each species, suggesting experiences of merging and synthesis and offering a continuous opportunity for borrowing and dialogue.

Sometimes the competition among species happened to increase so much that not only was any sense of mutual recognition destroyed, but also the ties of a previously shared ethnicity were severed (as in the case of Samaritanism) or the original Jewishness of a movement was repressed and forgotten (as in the case of Christianity). Sometimes the seed of Judaicness happened to produce fruit in a non-Jewish land (the fertile land of Islam). Thus, new genera and new species within each genus were born, fueling a more and more complex mechanism of borrowing, dialogue, and competition that has characterized and still characterizes the history of the Abrahamic family in the extraordinary diversity of its historical manifestations.

After more than twenty-five hundred years, the life blood of the family tree does not show any signs of exhaustion. Contemporary times have seen the rise of new conflicts and bitter crises with the revival of fundamentalism, but also an exciting season of Christian-Jewish dialogue in the post-Holocaust era that has reshaped the identity of two long-estranged genera.

The discussion about Judaicness—that is, about which Abrahamic religion is "more Judaic"—is a theological problem about their Truth, a crucial question for the religious conscience, yet a meaningless question from the historical point of view. What defines and distinguishes Judaism vis-à-vis its siblings is the combination of Judaicness and Jewishness, not the claim of a higher or purest degree of Judaicness. Judaism, Samaritanism, Christianity, and Islam belong to the same family; they are all Judaic religions. On the other hand, what defines a Judaism vis-à-vis the other varieties of Judaism is the different balance between these two constitutive elements. This problem—as we have seen—marks the entire history of Judaism since its very beginning. We see it still in action in the post-Enlightenment question about whether Judaism is primarily a religion or an ethnos, and in the contemporary confrontation between secular and religious Jews.

In fact, the entire history of Judaism offers many different examples of how these two elements are combined. We proceed from the identification of Jewishness and Judaicness in Rabbinic Judaism to opposite varieties of contemporary Judaism, where Judaicness is emphasized over against Jewishness (as in Reform Judaism) or, vice-versa, Jewishness is emphasized over against Judaicness (as in Secular Humanistic Judaism). The question to what extent one element can be emphasized over against the other without breaking the boundaries of Judaism has created and continues to create endless controversy in modern Judaism and in some cases even prevents mutual recognition among different species of Judaism. But once again, what the balance between Judaicness and Jewishness is or should be is an ideological (or theological) problem, not a historical problem. Scholarly models do not solve problems and conflicts; the most we can expect is that they help us better understand the nature of conflicts. Not a small accomplishment.

NOTES

1. See Alexander Guttman, *Rabbinic Judaism in the Making: A Chapter in the History of Halakhah from Ezra to Judah I* (Detroit: Wayne State University Press, 1970); Louis Finkelstein, *Pharisaism in the Making: Selected Essays* (New York: Ktav, 1972); J. Weingreen, *From Bible to Mishna: The Continuity of Tradition* (Manchester: Manchester University Press, 1976).

2. Jacob Neusner, "What Is a Judaism? Seeing the Dead Sea Library as the Statement of a Coherent Judaic Religious System," in *Judaism in Late Antiquity*, ed. A. J. Avery-Peck and B. D. Chilton, vol. 3 (Leiden, NY: E. J. Brill, 2001), 3–21 (quotation on p. 3).

3. See Gabriele Boccaccini, *Portraits of Middle Judaism in Scholarship and Arts* (Turin: Zamorani, 1992).

4. Ellis Rivkin, *A Hidden Revolution: The Pharisees' Search for the Kingdom Within* (Nashville: Abingdon, 1978); and Jacob Neusner, *From Politics to Piety: The Emergence of Pharisaic Judaism* (New York: Ktav, 1978).

5. Jacob Neusner, *The Judaism the Rabbis Take for Granted* (Atlanta: Scholars Press, 1994), 12.

6. Philip R. Davies, "Scenes from the Early History of Judaism," in *The Triumph of Elohim: From Yahwisms to Judaisms*, ed. Diana Vikander Edelman (Grand Rapids: Eerdmans, 1995), 145–182 (quotation on pp. 147, 151).

7. Jacob Neusner, preface to *Judaisms and Their Messiahs at the Turn of the Christian Era*, ed. Jacob Neusner, William Scott Green, and Ernest S. Frerichs (Cambridge: Cambridge University Press, 1987), xi–xii.

8. See E. P. Sanders, *Paul and Palestinian Judaism* (Philadelphia: Fortress Press, 1977); E. P. Sanders, *Judaism: Practice and Belief, 63* B.C.E.–66 C.E. (Philadelphia: Trinity Press International, 1992); and Seth Schwartz, *Imperialism and Jewish Society, 200* B.C.E. to 640 C.E. (Princeton: Princeton University Press, 2001).

9. Sanders, *Paul and Palestinian Judaism*, 11.

10. Ibid., 11–12.

11. Sanders, *Paul and Palestinian Judaism*.

12. Schwartz, *Imperialism*, 9.

13. Ibid., 49.

14. Ibid., 49.

15. Ibid., 15.

16. See Paolo Sacchi, *History of the Second Temple Period* (Sheffield: Sheffield Academic Press, 2000); Lester L. Grabbe, *Judaic Religion in the Second Temple Period* (London: Routledge, 2000); and John Joseph Collins, *The Apocalyptic Imagination: An Introduction to Jewish Apocalyptic Literature* (Grand Rapids: Eerdmans, 1998).

17. Schwartz, *Imperialism*, 2.

18. Ibid., 291.

19. Lawrence H. Schiffman, "Jewish Sectarianism in Second Temple Judaism," in *Great Schisms in Jewish History*, ed. Raphael Jospe and Stanley M. Wagner (New York: Ktav, 1981), 1–46 (quotation on p. 35).

20. Lawrence H. Schiffman, *From Text to Tradition: A History of Second Temple and Rabbinic Judaism* (Hoboken, NJ: Ktav, 1991), 26.

21. Schiffman, "Jewish Sectarianism," 35.

22. Schiffman, *From Text to Tradition*, 15.

23. Ibid., 4.

24. Boccaccini, *Portraits of Middle Judaism*, xv.

25. Shaye J. D. Cohen, *From the Maccabees to the Mishnah* (Philadelphia: Westminster, 1987); Shaye J. D. Cohen,, *The Beginnings of Jewishness: Boundaries, Varieties, Uncertainties* (Berkeley: University of California Press, 1999); and Martin S. Jaffee, *Early Judaism* (Upper Saddle River, NJ: Prentice Hall, 1997).

26. Jaffee, *Early Judaism*, 245.

27. Ibid., 246.

28. Ibid..

29. Cohen, *From the Maccabees to the Mishnah*, 26.

30. Ibid., 26.

31. Ibid., 18.

32. Anthony D. Smith, *The Ethnic Revival* (Cambridge: Cambridge University Press, 1981); and Ernest Gellner, *Nations and Nationalism* (Ithaca: Cornell University, 1983).

33. Cohen, *The Beginnings of Jewishness*, 7.

34. Cohen, *From the Maccabees to the Mishnah*, 37.

35. Alan F. Segal, *Rebecca's Children: Judaism and Christianity in the Roman World* (Cambridge, MA: Harvard University Press, 1986), 1, 179; see also James D. G. Dunn, *The Partings of the Ways between Christianity and Judaism and Their Significance for the Character of Christianity* (London: SCM Press, 1991); and Hershel Shanks, ed., *Christianity and Rabbinic Judaism: A Parallel History of Their Origins and Early Development* (Washington, DC: Biblical Archaeology Society, 1992).

36. Adam Becker and Annette Yoshiko Reed, eds., *The Ways That Never Parted* (Tübingen: Mohr Siebeck, 2003).

37. Gabriele Boccaccini, *Middle Judaism: Jewish Thought, 300* B.C.E. to 200 C.E. (Minneapolis: Fortress Press, 1991).

38. Gabriele Boccaccini, *Beyond the Essene Hypothesis* (Grand Rapids: Eerdmans, 1998).

39. Gabriele Boccaccini, *Roots of Rabbinic Judaism: An Intellectual History, from Ezekiel to Daniel* (Grand Rapids: Eerdmans, 2002).

40. Gabriele Boccaccini, "The Preexistence of the Torah: A Commonplace in Second Temple Judaism, or a Later Rabbinic Development?" *Henoch* 17 (1995): 329–350; and Martin S. Jaffee, *Torah in the Mouth: Writing and Oral Tradition in Palestinian Judaism, 200* B.C.E.–400 C.E. (Oxford: Oxford University Press, 2001).

41. Edelman, *The Triumph of Elohim.*

42. James D. Purvis, "Ben Sira and the Foolish People of Shechem," *Journal of Near Eastern Studies* 24, (January–April 1965), 88–94.

43. Cohen, *The Beginning of Jewishness*, passim; Doron Mendels, *The Rise and Fall of Jewish Nationalism* (Grand Rapids: Eerdmans, 1997).

44. Albert I. Baumgarten, *The Flourishing of Jewish Sects in the Maccabean Era: An Interpretation* (Leiden: Brill, 1997).

45. John M. G. Barclay, *Jews in the Mediterranean Diaspora: From Alexander to Trajan, 323* B.C.E.–117 C.E. (Edinburgh: T & T Clark, 1996).

46. The only possible (and indeed, controversial) exception is "Messianic Judaism," which claims (ideological not historical) continuity with the experience of the Christian Jews of the first centuries and strenuously vindicates its Jewishness: "When we call our movement a type of Judaism, we are affirming our relationship to the Jewish people as a whole, as well as our connection to the religious faith and way of life which that people have lived throughout its historical journey." See Mark Kinzer, *The Nature of Messianic Judaism: Judaism as Genus, Messianic as Species* (West Hartford: Hashivenu Archives, 2000), 5.

3

Crypto-Jewish Criticism of Tradition and Its Echoes in Jewish Communities

MIRIAM BODIAN

In the late medieval period, rabbinic law provided the legal and theological foundation of Jewish communal life throughout the Diaspora. It shaped the educational system, the structures of communal self-government, and Jewish-Gentile relations, as well as the activities of worship and ceremony usually associated with religion. "Religious life," that is, was not separable from "Jewish life." A Jew paid taxes to the Jewish community, ate ritually slaughtered meat, was married under a *khuppah*, and was buried by a Jewish burial society. The only alternative was to convert and join another religious community.

All of this changed radically in western Jewish societies in the late eighteenth and nineteenth centuries. The governing and policing powers of the traditional Jewish communal authorities were dismantled, first and foremost by the centralizing state. But the traditional community was weakened by other factors as well. The opportunities that beckoned as a result of their emancipation lured Jews "out of the ghetto." Assimilation to one degree or another followed. Leaving the synagogue behind was made easier by the fact that doing so no longer necessarily entailed conversion. For some, philosophical skepticism provided the impetus for rejecting all traditional religious belief.

Because Jewish secularization was so strongly (and suddenly) impelled by external developments in European society, it showed few manifestations of a phase that was of the utmost importance in European secularization, namely the individuation of belief *within the traditional context of revealed religion.* To be sure, such individuation can be discerned in the unique career of Moses Mendelssohn, who became deeply immersed in Enlightenment thought in late-eighteenth-century Berlin without abandoning the fundamentals of traditional Jewish theology. Among other issues, Mendelssohn pondered the problem of individual conscience when it conflicted with prescribed religion. (This problem was not recognized in traditional Judaism and had become widely recognized in Christian Europe only in the sixteenth century.) Mendelssohn's thinking on this problem led him to oppose coercive religious authority of any kind. However, by this time the coercive powers of the traditional community were already being seriously eroded from without. (Most of Mendelssohn's followers abandoned traditional Judaism after his death and adopted some form of deism, for which they suffered no penalty.)

However, well before Mendelssohn, some noteworthy figures with strong Jewish religious convictions were unwittingly developing a conception of Judaism that would, when transplanted to normative Jewish communities, pose a challenge to rabbinic authority. These figures have been ignored in the study of Jewish secularization for several reasons. First, they were not Ashkenazim, but Sephardi crypto-Jews. Moreover, they are largely unknown to scholars, as a result of which their connection to anticlerical and individualist religious currents in Portuguese-Jewish communities has not been charted. But even if their careers had been known to scholars, they would not necessarily have been regarded as material for an essay on Jewish secularization, for the simple reason that they believed ardently in "the Law of Moses."

They did not, in short, fit the stereotypical models of secularizing Jews. By this I mean such types as the traditional immigrant lured by the American dream, the yeshiva *bocher* turned socialist Zionist, or the German-Jewish poet who sought to be simply a German poet. It is obvious how these types became agents of secularization. It is more difficult to understand how fervent believers in a private conception of the Law of Moses became such agents. If anything, such a "type" might bring to mind twentieth-century American experimentation among Havurah youth or in New Age circles. But we would tend to associate these phenomena with religious revival in a secular society rather than with secularization.

It might be helpful in addressing the phenomenon of early modern "personal" Judaism (or Judaisms) if we first consider the parallel phenomenon in Christian societies and its link to secularization. This is an area that has long drawn the attention of Reformation scholars, who have acknowledged the importance of marginal, sectarian Christian groups and thinkers in bringing about the elimination of state-supported clerical authority and laying the foundations for a rejection of all religious belief.[1] They have recognized that only with the elimination of such clerical authority could a "secular" society emerge. That is, only in a society undergirded by the principles of freedom of conscience and the separation of church and state could a wide array of religious groups function on a voluntary basis, along with secular ideologues of every stripe.

In the sixteenth and seventeenth centuries, with the Protestant Reformation, there were increasing manifestations of anticlericalism among pious Christians that were directed not only at the Catholic Church, but at *any* church that dictated belief and disciplined behavior. In the early Dutch Republic, a rather broad sector of the public adhered to what Benjamin Kaplan has described as "a vehemently anticonfessional form of piety whose most important strands were composed of spiritualism and a distinctly Protestant brand of anticlericalism."[2] There are many parallels between the phenomenon described by Kaplan and the phenomenon I will describe in this essay. The "Libertines" he has described were conditioned to anticlerical attitudes during the Dutch Revolt against Spain and Catholic clerical authority. "But where the revolt succeeded," he has written, "Libertines were not about to comply with renewed demands for discipline, this time from the Calvinists."[3] The "Libertines" were for the most part not, as this pejorative contemporary term suggests, without religion. Many of them were deeply pious. They believed that salvation was a matter between the individual and God, with divine authority residing in Scripture. Their position, however, opened the way for unbelief as well. As Kaplan has observed, "Once Libertines had positioned themselves beyond the reach of the churches, free from the threat of discipline, they could believe anything they wished. They could be spiritualizers, but they could also be humanists, neostoics, skeptics, nicodemites, eclectics, or 'rustic pelagians.' They could be truly indifferent to religion."[4]

In his classic work, *The Secularization of the European Mind*, Owen Chadwick has succinctly articulated the relationship between the fight for freedom of conscience and the processes of secularization. According to Chadwick,

> Christian conscience was the force which began to make Europe "secular"; that is, to allow many religions or no religion in a state, and repudiate any kind of pressure upon the man who rejected the accepted and inherited axioms of society. My conscience is my own. It is private. Though it is formed and guided by inherited wisdom and by public attitudes and even by circumstances which surround me, no man may intrude upon it. . . . How I may be true to it, whether I may be true to it, whether allegiance to it is compatible with comfort or with happiness, these decisions are for me and no one else. It shows me that I cannot trample upon other people's consciences, provided they are true to them, provided they do not seek to trample upon mine, and provided they will work with me to ensure that our differing consciences do not undermine by their differences the social order and at last the state.[5]

It is important to note that in their fight against clericalism, heterodox Christians employed tools of criticism against ecclesiastical traditions that would eventually be used to reject all religious belief. In particular, they carried the use of the historical criticism of tradition, as well as biblical criticism, far beyond the limits established by "mainstream" Protestants (that is, Lutherans, Zwinglians, and Calvinists). Moreover, at least among the rationalists, they relied on arguments that reflected a strong sense of the "naturally impossible,"[6] from a point of view that assumed unalterable laws of nature.

Such a sensibility was mostly alien to European Jewish culture before the Enlightenment. But it was not entirely absent. What I will argue in this chapter is that while, in general, the fundamental fight that brought into being "secular" societies—the fight for freedom of conscience—took place mostly in the Christian arena, it was introduced directly into the Jewish arena in the seventeenth century by crypto-Jews from Spain and Portugal. [7]

Historical Encounters with Portuguese Jewish "Heretics" in Western Europe

The western Sephardim of converso background—the "Portuguese Jews"—were notorious in the eyes of their Jewish contemporaries, Sephardi and Ashkenazi alike, for indifference to the strict observance of rabbinic law and for certain "heretical" opinions. Rabbi Hayyim Yosef David Azulai, an emissary from Eretz Israel, recorded his shock at what he witnessed during his visits to the Bordeaux community in 1755 and again in 1777–78.[8] Many of the Sephardim he encountered exhibited a rather unconscious but open laxity of a kind that could be found in Ashkenazi communities only in the eighteenth century.[9] But he also encountered Jews who, as respectable members of their Jewish communities, openly articulated their rejection of the very foundation of rabbinic Judaism, namely the Oral Law. Such thinking was not new in Portuguese-Jewish circles at the time of Azulai's visit. From as early as the second decade of the seventeenth century, certain Portuguese Jews were expressing opposition *in principle* to rabbinic Judaism, a kind of opposition that did not appear among Ashkenazim until the end of the eighteenth century.

In *Out of the Ghetto*, Jacob Katz argued the importance of distinguishing between religious laxity, which can be found in any traditional society, and ideological opposition to tradition.[10] The emergence of "secular Jews" occurred along different paths, often including a process of gradual, unconscious alienation from traditional religious life. But a conscious ideological reorientation was necessary before secular Jewish life could be institutionalized. Such a reorientation has appeared, over time, within all modern Jewish populations. But the earliest manifestations emerged in the ex-converso population of Western Europe in the early seventeenth century.

There is now a considerable scholarly literature on rationalistic "heresy" among the Portuguese Jews of seventeenth-century Amsterdam. Among these Jews, heterodox thought tended to combine philosophical rationalism with a literalist, bibliocentric theology. For such Jews, there was little more reason to accept rabbinic Judaism as it was expounded in their day than there was to accept Catholicism or Calvinism. All of these traditions struck them as contrary to reason.

The names of the most notorious Portuguese-Jewish "heretics" who rejected rabbinic Judaism are familiar—Uriel da Costa, Juan de Prado, and Benedict (Baruch) Spinoza. In fact, all of these men were forced to leave the Jewish community. But criticism of rabbinic tradition was a fairly widespread phenomenon *within* Portuguese-Jewish communities, and an internal anti-rabbinic current persisted up to the Enlightenment.[11]

The classic text describing the process of disillusionment with rabbinic tradition among the Portuguese Jews is Uriel da Costa's "Autobiography," which he wrote shortly before his suicide in 1640. This is how da Costa briefly but vividly described his initial encounter with rabbinic Judaism in Amsterdam, after he left the Iberian Peninsula: "I had not been there [in Amsterdam] many days before I observed that the customs and ordinances of the modern Jews were very different from those commanded by Moses. Now if the Law was to be strictly observed, according to the letter, as it expressly declares, it must be very unjustifiable in the Jewish doctors to add to it inventions of a quite contrary nature. This provoked me to oppose them openly: nay, I looked upon it as doing God service to defend the Law with freedom against such innovations."[12]

In this passage da Costa strongly suggests that his idea of Jewish law had been formed in the Peninsula on the basis of an independent reading of the

Old Testament. When he arrived in Amsterdam and Hamburg in 1616, he discovered to his dismay that the Jews there were not observing the Law as literally expounded in the Books of Moses, but rather a vast and intricate "law" that bore little relationship, in his view, to the precepts given at Mount Sinai.

The important Spinoza scholar Carl Gebhardt accepted da Costa's account more or less at face value. As Gebhardt described it, da Costa, while still in the Peninsula, "had gained a certain bare picture of the Law and Prophets; the postbiblical religious sources were not accessible to him due to his lack of knowledge of Hebrew. But the Judaism he encountered in Amsterdam was a Judaism formed by a two-thousand-year-old tradition, which Moses Uri Halevi first taught the [ex-converso] émigrés in Ashkenazi form, and which around 1616 was being taught in Amsterdam by the rabbis Joseph Pardo of Salonica, Isaac Uziel of Fez, and Saul Levi Morteira of Venice."[13]

However, subsequent authors have questioned da Costa's account from several angles. There is, first of all, the problem of the integrity of the text of the "Autobiography."[14] Second, there is the fact that da Costa's mother and her family practiced a crypto-Judaism that I. S. Révah has described as *"marranisme normale"*— a practice that included elements of postbiblical Judaism.[15] If this was the case, da Costa could not have been entirely surprised by the fact that contemporary Judaism did not mirror a literal understanding of the biblical Law.

Yirmiyahu Yovel has speculated that da Costa unconsciously suppressed his prior, though admittedly meager, knowledge of postbiblical Judaism. According to the scenario Yovel proposed, da Costa began his career (as a student of canon law at the University of Coimbra) as a reform-minded Catholic, with a notion of moving toward a "pure" religious belief. After he turned to Judaism, he "expected Judaism to be more amenable to a purifying reform than the Catholicism of inquisitorial Iberia." But he brought to this expectation little knowledge of Judaism: "Above all, he did not realize the prodigal extent to which rabbinical laws and precepts had taken over in Jewish life, or the rigid and powerful resistance they would therefore show to any attempt at reform."[16]

Da Costa, however, nowhere mentions a time when he sought a reformed Catholicism, and it is difficult to understand why Yovel's hypothesis is helpful or necessary in order to understand da Costa's career. Nor does his hypothesis address the important question: Why in his account did da Costa fail to mention the crypto-Judaism of his mother's family, of which (thanks to Révah) we can be sure? That is, *why* did he misrepresent his background?

This was, I believe, a matter of self-image. The idealized self-image Uriel da Costa cultivated and sought to project in his writings was that of a fiercely independent person who relied entirely on his own powers of reason to interpret Scripture. This self-image had already been formed at the time he wrote his angry work of 1623, *Exame das tradições phariseas*—a work that was incontestably of his authorship.[17] In the *Exame*, he presented himself as a person driven solely by an interest in the truth— unlike the conforming Jews of the community, who in his view were motivated by self-interest, or cowardice, or accident of birth, or conditioning. Da Costa regarded himself as having achieved a higher level of insight than these Jews—not only the rank and file but also the Jewish rabbinic and communal leaders who persecuted him.

Such a basic self-image was common to the leading "heretics" in the Portuguese-Jewish diaspora. It was also common to certain university-educated crypto-Jews in the Peninsula, some of whom became famous martyrs for Judaism. These men—crypto-Jews and Jewish heretics alike—*did* see things differently from most of their contemporaries. Leaving aside the question of superior wisdom, they *had* achieved a high degree of detachment from traditional religious life. They were liable to suffer considerable disenchantment when they encountered rabbinic Judaism, in large part because while in the Peninsula they had constructed a conception of Judaism that relied on individual reason and the conviction that the Bible had a self-evident, literal meaning. This conception of Judaism was unconsciously formed in a way that made it impregnable to the critical arsenal they used to attack Catholicism.

Let us consider for a moment Isaac Orobio de Castro's opinion about the origins of Portuguese-Jewish heresy. This prominent defender of Rabbinic Judaism, an educated Portuguese Jewish physician, pointed the finger at men who had received a university education before coming to Judaism. These men "had learned sundry secular sciences, such as logic, philosophy, metaphysics, and medicine. Their ignorance of God's Law was no less than that of the others [i.e., other ex-conversos who joined Jewish communities], but they reeked of pride, superciliousness and arrogance, being convinced that they were expert in every subject under the sun, and knew all that there was to be known."[18] This opinion, stated in Orobio's *Epístola Invectiva*, has puzzled scholars. Orobio himself had such university training, as did Isaac Cardoso, the staunch defender of rabbinic orthodoxy in Verona. Indeed, for both of these men, a university education was crucial in their path to rabbinic Judaism.

It seems probable that Orobio intuitively grasped a connection—one that seems from the evidence to have had a basis in reality—between converso upbringing, education in Iberian universities, and subsequent anti-rabbinic "heresy." He himself had been able to distance himself from the philosophical criticism of religion by associating such criticism with the "idolatrous" Christian world.[19] By doing this, he was able to assimilate a rather sophisticated rabbinism as a new framework for belief. For others, however, a conception of "true Judaism" remained entangled with a structure of thought formed in intellectual circles in the Peninsula—a structure that had once helped provide a basis for a crypto-Jewish critique of Catholicism.

The case of Juan de Prado is also instructive. While still in the Peninsula, during his studies at the Colegio Menor de la Madre de Dios of Alcalá de Henares, he was already toying with deistic ideas. He was reported to have asserted that all religions were equally good, and that Jews, Christians, and Muslims could achieve salvation by observing the laws of their religions, since all three religions derived from natural law, differing from one another only as a consequence of political necessity.[20] Such a view might seem difficult to reconcile with Prado's ardent crypto-judaizing. It is reasonable to assume, however, that a notion of rational natural religion underlay his particular version of crypto-Judaism, and allowed it to coexist with an otherwise fundamentally skeptical position. This may have served him very well in the Peninsula. However, when he actually encountered rabbinic Judaism in the Diaspora, his fragile (and illusory) idea of historical Judaism was shattered.

In what follows, I will try to show the close connection between (a) the emergence of an aggressive, critical attack on Catholicism among converso intellectuals; (b) the formation of an "unassailable" but illusory conception of Judaism in the Peninsula; and (c) attacks on rabbinic authority in the Portuguese Jewish diaspora. First I will elucidate the major rationalist lines of anti-Catholicism among crypto-Jews in the Peninsula. Then I will compare these with the major rationalist lines of attack on rabbinic Judaism in the Diaspora—lines of attack that often began as part of a defense of individualist notions of "authentic" Judaism.

Crypto-Jewish Criticism of Catholicism

A fundamental and widely articulated crypto-Jewish criticism of the Catholic tradition was that it was a human fabrication, one with no divine origins.[21] Of course this idea had always been *implicit* in classical Jewish anti-Christian polemics, but it had not been the *focus* of those polemics. In the late sixteenth and seventeenth centuries, certain learned crypto-Jews believed they could *show for a certainty* that Christianity was a human fabrication. Their numbers were small, but their impact considerable.

In these elitist circles, it was common to disparage belief in Christianity for the reason that the Gospels were the work of low-born, ignorant men. This attack was no doubt partly a mobilization of Iberian social prejudices to disparage the earliest "Christians." But it was more than that. It was an attack by crypto-Jews for whom the truth could be discerned only by the learned. Low birth was associated with superstition and foolish beliefs. Such a view is evident in the remarks of Gonçalo Vaez, a Portuguese student who appears to have studied in Salamanca, and who told inquisitors in 1571 that "there was no reason to believe the law of the Gospels, because they had been written by fishermen."[22] Moses, in contrast to Jesus, was a learned man, worthy of receiving revelation. Francisco Maldonado de Silva, an inquisitorial prisoner in Lima, wrote in a statement of 1638 that if—as Christians claim—the Trinity was a divine doctrine, God would not have hidden it from Moses, "seeing that he was a scholar [*doctor*] and teacher of the people of God."[23]

In keeping with the social deprecation of Jesus and his circle, Jesus was portrayed as a magician who was able to fool his small, gullible following.[24] In 1615, a Mexican crypto-Jew belittled Jesus' miracles, saying that "in those days there were lots of spell casters who brought back the dead."[25] Francisco Maldonado de Silva told inquisitors that his father had taught him "that Jesus Christ . . . had learned magic arts with which he deceived a few ignorant people."[26] Diogo d'Assumpção asserted "that the law of Christ was made by men who had to flee and hide among rocks"—that is, outlaws or outcasts from society.[27] The apostles, he said, were all relatives of Jesus[28]—the implication being that no one else would have supported his absurd aspirations. Social contempt for Jesus and his disciples could be extended to the symbols of Jesus that played a role in Catholic practice. Luis Carvajal, for example, told inquisitors that he found comical the idea that the consecrated host was the body of Christ, since this object of worship and elaborate ceremony would in fact be the body of a man who was born among shepherds, and whose disciples were lowly and vulgar men.[29]

In general, literalist, bibliocentric crypto-Jews found the Church's allegorical exegesis ludicrous. As we have noted, Maldonado de Silva found no evidence for the doctrine of the Trinity in the Books of Moses. He further found "that there was no place *in all of Scripture* that said there were three Divine Persons [my emphasis]."[30] Similarly, a manuscript work found by the Portuguese Inquisition in the converso João de Fonseca's possession argued that "neither the Old Law nor the New recognized the mystery of the Trinity."[31] The author of this work also noted that nowhere was it written that the Messiah promised by "the Law" (the Hebrew Bible) would be divine.[32]

Fixity and stability were considered, in an age untouched by Foucault, key characteristics of the truth. Adherents of all orthodoxies sought to show the greater rootedness and continuity of their own beliefs in comparison to others. It was thus supremely important to crypto-Jews that God repeatedly emphasized in the Pentateuch that the Law he had given Moses was eternal and *was not to be changed*. Some crypto-Jews even argued, no doubt savoring the irony, that Jesus had shared this view. As Baltasar Carvajal reportedly said to his brother Gaspar, a Dominican friar, "Even in the Gospel it is written that your Crucified One said, 'Do not think that I came here to annul the laws of the prophets or their holy and truthful prophecies!' "[33]

It was more usual, however, for crypto-Jews to identify Jesus with the "false prophet" defined in Deuteronomy, someone who was able to perform signs and wonders, but who was to be judged an imposter because he sought to turn God's people away from the commandments. Given the frequency with which the passage concerning the false prophet was cited by crypto-Jews, it is not surprising that Luis Carvajal, when asked by the inquisitors on what basis he had rejected the Law of Christ for the Law of Moses, cited the relevant passage in Deuteronomy 13 as the second of nine reasons.[34] The same passage was part of an important conversation between the Old Christian Hebraist Lope de Vera and a Portuguese judaizer at the University of Salamanca. Don Lope was apparently impressed by the difficulty of reconciling with Christianity the criterion God gave the people in this passage to distinguish between a true or false prophet, saying that "if [a person who claims to be a prophet] says 'Abandon the Law,' you mustn't believe him."[35]

For the most part, the crypto-Jewish attack on the Gospels was consistent with centuries of Jewish anti-Christian polemic (except for its dogged insistence on the exclusive authority of *literal* interpretation). Ultimately more threatening from the point of view of rabbinic Judaism was the crypto-Jewish attack on the postbiblical traditions of the Catholic Church. To some extent, this attack paralleled humanist criticisms and Protestant propaganda. It is difficult to know how familiar such ideas were to crypto-Jews, but there was clearly some direct appropriation. In 1545, for example, an Old Christian *fidalgo* charged as being a *luterano* stated that "the Old Law called only for mental confession," and that the Pope had ordered verbal confession to a priest only "so that lay people would be more subject to the Church."[36] At about the same time, inquisitors confiscated a manuscript work in the home of a converso in Pombal that asserted that confession was ordered by the bishops, not by God.[37] Likewise, the judaizing martyr Diogo d'Assumpção made a distinction between an "Ur-Christianity" with a basis in a revealed text, and a falsified later tradition, arguing "that originally the mass was only a 'pater noster' and that all the rest was an invention and addition of the popes."[38] It is almost unimaginable that such formulations of crypto-Jewish belief would have appeared in the fifteenth century.

Diogo d'Assumpção's view of Christianity merits a closer look. At a time when he had probably not definitively abandoned Christianity for "the Law of Moses," he regarded as "authentic" only practices which had their source in the New Testament, and viewed all other Christian practices as human accretions. As he put it, "The popes and councils, not understanding Scripture, made and followed human laws."[39] (It is clear that by "Scripture" he meant at this time both the Old and New Testaments.) Using the same basic analytic technique, he argued that, "in the primitive Church [*na igreja primitiva*] they recited [only] the words of consecration [which appear in Mt 26:26–28, and are supported by 1 Cor 10:14–17]," and that St. Peter and the Apostles "added all the other things as a [false] tradition of Christ."[40] Particularly in the case of Diogo d'Assumpção—a judaizing martyr who had little or no Jewish ancestry—"Protestantish" trends in Portugal seem to have played an important role in his theological development. This underscores the important fact that nonconformist Catholics in the Reformation period were in contact with crypto-Jews; that "Protestantish" trends resonated with crypto-Jewish trends and vice versa; and that there was a sharing of critical tools between both parties that may have had important implications for ex-converso attacks on rabbinic Judaism.

Educated conversos were well aware of the events that had an impact on theological perception throughout Europe. Something of the enormity of these events for crypto-Jews is conveyed in the testimony of a conversa of Baeza in 1572. "When the Council of Trent was coming to an end," the record of her testimony reads, "her mother had fasted forty days without eating until nightfall, and had kept silent, and prayed repeatedly that it [the Council] should rule that all Christians should keep the Law of Moses and praise God instead of Jesus Christ, because they [the Christians] were living in deception."[41] There is more than a hint of apocalyptic thinking in this passage. But apocalyptic thinking draws power from the awareness of real historical upheaval. The passage may reflect a growing theological self-confidence among crypto-Jews who observed the havoc in the Christian world wreaked by the Reformation.[42]

For intellectual crypto-Jews of the type I am describing, one of the "proofs" that Christianity was a human fabrication was that there was such wide disagreement among Christians about doctrine. Interestingly, Diogo d'Assumpção pointed not only to the split between Luther and the Church, but also to splits within the Church of Rome itself. The Franciscan friars, he argued, followed Duns Scotus or Domingo de Soto, whereas the Dominicans followed Thomas Aquinas. "They had great controversies among themselves, and what good was a Law with no stability [*firmeza*]?"[43] But he saw the divisiveness among the Protestants as a sign that these "sects," too, were human fabrications, which their leaders had produced to satisfy their own ambitions.[44]

This fascinating former Capuchin monk also raised an issue that disturbed other contemporary Christians in the wake of the overseas discoveries and conquests. "If the Law of Christ was valid," he said, "it would have to be communicated to the entire world." Yet it had reached "neither the *negros* nor [the people of] another hundred thousand lands."[45] Indeed, Frei Diogo maintained that one of the reasons he converted to Judaism was his realization that he "could not be obligated to live in the Law of Christ since most of the world did not have access to it."[46]

The crypto-Jews could not have known that in pursuing their polemic with the Church they were participating in a dramatic shift in the way Europeans perceived religious authority and the locus of that authority. This shift has been voluminously documented for the Protestant world, with sweeping speculations about the consequences for the structures of politics, social organization, and philosophical thought. However, it has been addressed in relation to converso populations (to the degree that it has been addressed at all) only impressionistically.

Especially among crypto-Jewish intellectuals, religious authority was a key issue, and further study of Inquisition documents will no doubt furnish better evidence of their views about it. It was natural for these men to arrogate to themselves the authority to decide for themselves in religious matters. This was partly a result of circumstances: As crypto-Jews, they lived in the absence of a religious hierarchy and had no choice but to rely on their own judgment.

Yet they did not, it should be stressed, conceive of freedom of conscience as freedom to concoct a new religion. (That is, after all, what they accused the Church of doing.) "Conscience," as they conceived of it, was a human faculty that permitted all men (and perhaps even women) to gain access to the truth directly, without clerical intervention. It was associated with: the God-given ability to interpret Scripture according to its self-evident meaning; the God-given ability to differentiate between truth and falsehood through the exercise of reason; and/or a special relationship with God, in which God illumined them concerning the truth. The conviction that God had implanted in them the faculty they called "conscience" justified their uninhibited exercise of religious autonomy, and fortified them in their struggle against clerical authority.

The language of the inquisitors and their notaries, on whose written record we depend for most of what we know about the crypto-Jews, often reveals the continental divide that separated these officials from crypto-Jewish intellectuals in terms of their assumptions about authority. Inquisitors regarded it as provocative and insolent when crypto-Jews (or other types of heretics) used Scripture to defend their views. The Portuguese university student Gonçalo Vaez, for example, was accused of teaching many persons the Law of Moses, "inciting them with verses from the Old Testament" (*provocandoselo por autoridades de la escriptura del testamento viejo*). When Vaez taught that there was no purgatory or hell, he deviated from permissible behavior not only by teaching erroneous doctrines, but also by using verses of Scripture for this aim.[47]

Crypto-Jewish resort to "reason" (or "natural reason") has been insufficiently studied to allow for far-reaching conclusions. Crypto-Jews mentioned these terms often enough, but not necessarily in a uniform sense. Sometimes reliance on reason was implied indirectly, when a crypto-Jew stated that a certain Catholic dogma was "impossible." For example, Gonçalo Vaez argued that the Virgin Birth could not have happened simply "because it is impossible for a woman to give birth as a virgin."[48] At other times the term was mentioned explicitly, the teachings of the Church being condemned as "contrary to reason."

The most fully articulated defense I have seen for crypto-Jewish reliance on reason was made by a Portuguese student with whom Lope de Vera had discussions. (The student's name is not given in the surviving documentation.) Lope de Vera described one of his encounters with this student, and the inquisitorial notary recorded it as follows:[49]

> [Lope de Vera] said that . . . he knew this student was a Jew [i.e., a converso judaizer] and had the intention of leaving Spain in order to judaize . . . and on this occasion as on others they discussed certain ceremonies and articles of faith of the Roman Church, condemning some of them. In particular [they agreed] that it seemed impossible that God could be three and one, and that He could be incarnate, and that He could be present in the consecrated host. And to support this [criticism], his companion cited a passage in Psalms [31:9] that states *no lise fijeri sicut equs et mulus In quibus non est Intelectu [sic]*,[50] which he recited, meaning that God said we do not have to subjugate our understanding [*entendimiento*] "like a horse or a mule" to things that seemed impossible to the understanding.

One wonders whether this was a semi-humorous scriptural "source" for a conviction Lope de Vera already took for granted: that the "best" religion was the one that most conformed to natural reason, and that one's God-given reason entitled one to make a choice about belief. Such a conviction is also implicit in a conversation reported by another witness, who testified

> that when Don Lope was with other students in a group, he said that our Holy Catholic Faith contained many things that were difficult to believe, and that he found there were other religions that were more in conformity with natural reason (*raçon natural*), possessing doctrines that were less difficult and that seemed closer to reason.[51]

Those "other religions" were Judaism and Islam. Indeed, Lope de Vera had considered fleeing to Muslim lands to adopt one or the other, after he had had a chance to study both of them.

Even before his arrest, Diogo d'Assumpção had apparently weighed the question of whether he had a right to distinguish what was true or false for himself. His outlook appears to have drawn from illuminist currents in the Peninsula. He saw himself as an exceptional person, and seems to have believed that the very fact that he was tormented by his *consciencia inquieta* was evidence of his superior spiritual qualities. "Seeing that God had given him discernment (*juizo*) and understanding (*entendimento*) to recognize these things," he had told a witness, "he would deserve the highest penalty if he did *not* seek his salvation; and anyone who knew the Law of the Jews and didn't observe it was damned."[52]

But when confronted directly by the inquisitors on the question of authority, he gave a somewhat different answer. The exchange came when Frei Diogo asked rhetorically, with characteristic audacity, "Who were St. Augustine and St. Jerome to interpret the knowledge (*sabiduria*) of God?" The notary's record continues blandly:

> And when it was said to him, Who was *he* to say this about St. Augustine and St Jerome . . . ? He answered [in Latin], "I am thy servant, the son of thy handmaid" [Ps 115:16], and [he said] that St. Augustine was subject to the devil when he said the messiah had come, whereas he himself was subject to God because he was a Jew and observed the Law of the Jews, and that God did not reveal [the meaning of] His Scripture to St. Augustine because he was a gentile, and revealed it only to Jacob and Israel because [again in Latin] "He declares His word to Jacob, his statutes and ordinances to Israel; He has not dealt thus with any other nation" [Ps 147:19–20].[53]

Diogo d'Assumpção was far from being a consistent thinker or even a balanced person. He did not embrace the idea that all persons were entitled to pursue the truth for themselves, or that they possessed a natural God-given gift of reason that would allow them to do so. Rather he claimed the special entitlement of the illuminist, chosen by God because of his spiritual qualities (and, it would seem, his blood). He did, however, share with the more generic rationalist "judaizers" a rejection of the Church's monopoly on exegesis and doctrine, a conviction of the transparent artificiality of Catholic tradition, and a highly abstract and personal notion of "Judaism."

Ex-Converso Perspectives on Postbiblical Rabbinic Judaism

It was not the mere discovery of postbiblical Judaism that came as an unpleasant surprise to some of the intellectuals who made their way to Jewish communities in northern Europe. It was the discovery that rabbinic Judaism did not conform to the contours of a "pure religion" as they had constructed them. The intriguing question remains, of course, why some educated, rationalist crypto-Jews responded differently and embraced rabbinic Judaism. It may be that persons who harbored strong feelings of solidarity, identification, and responsibility toward their coreligionists, like Orobio de Castro and Isaac Cardoso, were more likely to find rabbinic Judaism compelling. The Jewish "heretics," in contrast, tended to regard the rank-and-file of the émigrés with contempt, as mediocrities who readily mocked the absurdities of Catholicism while accepting the absurdities of the Talmud as "Torah from Mount Sinai." It may be said that these "heretics" were just as intolerant of foolish ideas among Jews as they were of foolish ideas among Catholics—perhaps more so. The "heretic" Juan de Prado, not surprisingly, "mocked the statement of the Sages that the dead must go [rolling] underground [to Eretz Israel for resurrection]. He said that it was impossible and irreconcilable with what reason (o entendimento) dictates."[54]

Such criticism of the irrationality of rabbinic Judaism suggests structural parallels between the crypto-Jewish attack on postbiblical Catholic tradition and the ex-converso attack on postbiblical rabbinic tradition. A key proof-text for both critiques was Deuteronomy 4:2—"You shall not add to the word which I command you, nor take from it." While the Church was mainly culpable for "taking from it," the rabbis had been prodigal, in the view of the Portuguese Jewish "heretics," in adding to it. When Uriel da Costa accused a defender of Jewish tradition of deviating from the true Law of God, he could just as well have been rebuking a family member who had become a Jesuit: "With a *false cult*," he wrote [emphasis added], "strange and foreign to what He asks of you, you are breaking and undoing His laws, in a deluded effort to serve Him."[55]

One of the traditional arguments in defense of the Oral Law was that the Written Law, by itself, raised innumerable questions and contained apparent contradictions that required explanation. A "chain of tradition" going back to Moses had been established whereby each generation of rabbinic scholars passed the torch to those they had ordained with the authority to address new issues as they arose. In traditional Jewish societies, the vesting of authority in a small number of men who had undergone intensive scholarly training was accepted as entirely natural. Although the Written Law and the Oral Law technically retained their separate status, Jews were conditioned from a very young age to see each as embedded in the other. Thus when during the sabbath Torah reading, for example, the verses were read prescribing "an eye for an eye," a traditionally conditioned Jew would not even *register* the literal meaning.

Educated ex-crypto Jews, in contrast, had learned as an important strategy of crypto-Jewish existence to distill out the "true meaning" of the text from the Church's "perversion" of it. They believed in the sufficiency of the revealed text and in the capacity of the human mind to capture its correct meaning. The Church's tradition of exegesis was not only a distortion but also unnecessary. Quite naturally, they brought this model with them to the Jewish community, where they expected to find the "true" meaning of Scripture honored. For some, it may have been humbling to discover that their knowledge of Torah was so unsophisticated from a rabbinic point of view. Others, however, viewed themselves as superior in sophistication to the rabbis, just as they had regarded themselves as superior to the theologians of Rome. They regarded their untarnished logic as unassailable. "If the Law [of Moses] were not comprehensible without an oral explanation," da Costa insisted, "it would follow that the Law was imperfect and not open to understanding."[56]

Considerable efforts were made by rabbinic figures entrusted with the guidance of ex-converso congregations to inculcate a less absolutist perspective and an appreciation of rabbinic reasoning. The Venetian rabbi Immanuel Aboab wrote a work entitled *Nomologia*—a classic text in the Portuguese Jewish library—to refute those who rejected the interpretations of the Sages on the naive grounds, as he saw it, "that one may understand Scripture . . . from within itself, and that all of them [the neophytes] will understand it fully with a little bit of study, and that one need merely read it and observe it as it is written."[57]

Aboab had had direct experience of such claims, as he related in the book:

> In the year 1615, when I was in Italy, I was approached by two of our opponents. (I can't think of a more appropriate term for them, since they oppose the truth all Jews accept.) I tried to understand the foundations underlying their words, since only by understanding a disease can one offer the appropriate cure. One of them said to me angrily that he didn't believe the words of our Sages to the effect that Jacob was seventy-seven years old when he entered the house of his father-in-law Laban, and eighty-four years old when he married Laban's daughters. How did they [the Sages] know such a thing? . . . The second ["opponent"] . . . presented several challenges: First, how did the Sages derive all the details and fine points of ritual slaughter, to such an extent that they prohibited eating [animals] that had been slaughtered with a flawed knife, since in the Torah there is no hint of this? . . . And he presented another argument, namely that the Torah explicitly commands observing Passover for seven days, Shavuot for one day, Rosh ha-shanah for one day, and Sukkoth for eight days; this being so, why did the Sages alter the Torah, adding a day to each holiday, contrary to God's command, "You shall not add to the word which I command you, nor take from it" [Dt 4:2], and to the verse, "Everything that I command you you shall be careful to do; you shall not add to it or take from it" [Dt 13:1]?[58]

Some ex-conversos responded to rabbinic efforts as hoped and developed an understanding of rabbinic controversy and irony, while others simply acquiesced to the new reality and accepted rabbinic discipline. However, there were also those who resisted what they experienced as a Jewish version of clerical propaganda. They sometimes viewed the rabbis and sages as gullible and superstitious, while they impugned others' motives. Da Costa, for example, regarded the *halacha* that prohibited eating cheese after a meal at which meat was served (as well as a multitude of other *halachot*) as "ridiculous and superstitious."[59] But these laws were not just foolish. The sages, he argued, "invented" the great edifice of Talmudic law because they "saw the advantage [their innovations] would give them in dominating and subjugating the people to their dictates and rule."[60]

Probably no other text reflects the Iberian rationalist crypto-Jewish perspective applied to rabbinic Judaism as succinctly as the seventh of the eleven propositions that Uriel da Costa sent to the leaders of the Spanish and Portuguese synagogue in Venice in 1616. Da Costa's original text of the propositions is not extant, but fortunately we have a Hebrew version prepared by Leon de Modena for the purpose of refutation.[61] I will quote the seventh proposition of da Costa's text, in Modena's version:

> It is tantamount to destroying the foundations of the Torah to say that we must rule, in questions of the Law, according to the Tradition, and that we must believe in it [the Tradition] just as we do in the Law of Moses itself. This is nothing less than tampering with the Torah and creating a new Torah in contradiction to the true one, when in fact there exists no Oral Law, only the Written one.
>
> First, nowhere in the Torah itself is there mention of another Torah, whereas [if such existed] it would have been proper to explain [the existence of another Law] in the Torah itself. For anything aside from what is actually stated in the Torah has no proof. Moreover, even if people who performed miracles would testify to the existence of an Oral Law, we would have to disregard their words, because since the Torah was given by God to the master of all prophets [Moses], there is nothing by which we can distinguish a true prophet from a false except [the prophet's] endorsement of the Torah.
>
> Second, the Torah itself makes clear that no other Law exists and that we must follow its words alone, and none other. . . . Similarly we find in chapter 27: "Cursed be he who does not confirm the words of this Torah" etc., that is to say, there is no Torah besides this one and I shall give you no other.
>
> Third, even the new rulings in the time of Moses were included not in the Tradition but in the Torah, as it says: "Difficult cases they brought to Moses" [Ex 18:26], and the Torah commanded that this [procedure] should be followed in the future, i.e., that difficult questions should be taken to the priest or the judge, not that they should be ruled upon according to another Torah, but that God should bestow His spirit upon them [the priest or judge] to rule according to the Written Law.
>
> Fourth, King Solomon . . . asked God for the spirit to understand and judge according to the Torah. He did not judge difficult cases according to the Oral Law but according to reason, and the people, seeing this, were amazed by his wisdom. Judges must have the characteristics that Jethro told Moses they should have, "able men . . . such as fear God, men who are trustworthy and who hate a bribe" [Ex 18:21]. That [way of doing things] is the "Tradition" that belongs to the Torah, no other.
>
> Having shown that there is no other Torah or interpretation than the Written one from God, it is evident that what has been called "Tradition" is merely human, and it can be disputed, quite aside from the fact that it is in itself a great breach to give a person reason to turn from the Law of Moses and to interpret and distort and disseminate human interpretations in place of divine ones. It is great heresy to regard these human [interpretations] as equal to divine ones, to say that we are obligated to observe all the laws of the Talmud just like those of the Law of Moses. However, it is possible that if we find in it [the Talmud] a solution to a practical need, we should examine it, and if it conforms to the Torah we can follow it, but if not, it should be disregarded.

In his later *Exame das tradições phariseas*, da Costa raised another "proof" for the inauthenticity of the Oral Law. This "proof" is particularly interesting in view of the fact that Portuguese Jewish apologetes frequently pointed to the unity of the Jewish people, in contrast to the fragmentation of the Christian world, as evidence of the truth of Judaism. But da Costa took a view of rabbinic tradition that recalls crypto-Jewish criticisms of the divided Christian world. If rabbinic tradition was, as it was claimed, an integral part of the Torah conveyed at Mount Sinai, how, he asked, can one account for the discord between the Sages themselves?[62]

Da Costa was the earliest figure, as far as I know, to point to the historical Karaites (he conflated them with the "Sadducees") as having perpetuated authentic Judaism.[63] Other Portuguese Jews would follow in his footsteps.[64] There would also be Protestant observers who would adopt this idea. In a variation on the early modern European search for a universal, pure, natural religion, some Protestants took an interest in contemporary Karaites as possible adherents of a pure, unadulterated Judaism, a counterpart to their own pure, unadulterated Christianity.[65]

Deism was but a step away, and Uriel da Costa eventually took that step, if we can rely on the "Autobiography." At a certain point, the cerebral contortions necessary to reconcile Scripture with his notion of reason became too great, and da Costa dispensed altogether with belief in a revealed religion. In this regard he anticipated the great "heretics" of the 1650s—Spinoza, Juan de Prado, and Daniel de Ribera.

The little evidence we possess about the later radical "heretics" during the time they were members of the Amsterdam community indicates that, in their rejection of the Written Law, they used the kind of rhetoric crypto-Jews used in the Peninsula to discredit Jesus and his followers. Daniel de Ribera was reported to have said that Moses "was a great magician"; that as a leader he acted "in his own interest and that of his brother [Aaron]"; and that Abraham "was merely a miserable shepherd, so that it was impossible that God had spoken with him."[66] Such characterizations not only harked back to Diogo d'Assumpção, but also anticipated Voltaire.

One of the most important legacies of the Iberian experience was the sense of entitlement it gave such Jewish "heretics" to rely on their own judgment (or on "natural reason," as they were more likely to put it). The religious autonomy that was necessary to sustain crypto-Jewish life in the Peninsula became not only a habit but also a right that could be defended. The very fact that Uriel da Costa, as a young émigré from Portugal who had only recently arrived in a Jewish community, sent his propositions against the Oral Law to the leaders of the Spanish and Portuguese Jewish community in Venice reflects his very powerful sense of entitlement.

A generation later, Juan de Prado articulated the issue clearly when he asked a student the following question: "In matters of conscience, should a man act according to what others tell him, or according to his own understanding?"[67] He posed the question again somewhat differently to another student, asking, "Why should we believe in the Law of Moses more than in the teachings of other sects?" He then provided his own answer: "If we believe in Moses rather than in Mohammed, there should be some cause for it; but in fact it is all in the imagination."[68] The very posing of such questions was regarded as evidence against him in the proceedings that led to his excommunication.

A few years after their excommunication, Prado and Spinoza attended some social gatherings in Amsterdam where they met a certain Spanish captain. As fate would have it, the captain later reported to the Inquisition, leaving a little piece of evidence for scholars to unearth about how these men understood their separation from the Jewish community. The captain reported as follows: "He heard Dr. Prado and Spinoza say many times that they had previously been Jews and had observed the Jews' law, but they had distanced themselves from it because it was not good, it was a falsehood, and for that reason they had been excommunicated. *They had investigated which was the best religion, in order to profess it*, but to him [the witness] it seemed that they did not profess any religion at all" [emphasis added].[69] Whether or not this is what Prado and Spinoza actually said, it is consistent with their belief that they were qualified to judge for themselves what constituted the "best religion," and that being "born into" or conditioned to a certain religion was not a reason for observing it or accepting it as true.

By now, this conviction was held by a number of educated Europeans. The fact that the first *Jews* to articulate such a conviction publicly were members of the Portuguese Jewish population in seventeenth-century Amsterdam was not an accident. It should not, however, be explained simply as the result of a psychological condition some scholars have identified as "marranism"—that is, a psychic condition of conflict and doubt induced by the experience of living in a netherworld between Christianity and Judaism.[70] The confusions of the converso milieu no doubt contributed to the psychic detachment that was required before an early modern thinker could view religions relatively. But other factors were equally important. First, there was the experience of living in a clandestine subculture in which there was no hierarchy of authority, no means of monitoring or disciplining practice or belief, and no possible reason to exclude idiosyncratic thinkers, as long as they opposed Catholicism. Second, and no less important, there was the exposure to heterodox intellectual currents in Spain and Portugal (often but not always through university studies)—currents that scholars have too often assumed to have been suppressed in the Peninsula.[71]

Conclusion

The complex history of secularization in modern Europe has been told in numerous ways, with varying emphases and according to different theoretical models. The particular trajectory of Jewish secularization has usually been plotted starting with the Ashkenazi Jews of eighteenth-century Germany. Yet the earliest Jewish ideological justifications for the rejection of rabbinic authority predate those of the German Jews by a century and a half and correspond to a different point of development in European society.

Nevertheless, a systematic comparative study might yield some surprising results. It might appear at first glance, for example, that the Sephardi "enlighteners" of the seventeenth century were not troubled by the ethnic, nationalist aspects of Judaism in the way that German *maskilim* would have been. Their explicit criticism of rabbinic Judaism did not include an attack on Jewish ethnic exclusivity. This can be explained, in part, because there was as yet no pressure on European Jews to assimilate into the majority society. Yet the Amsterdam "heretics" hinted at a discomfort with the idea of an obligation to Judaism that proceeded from a collective covenant with God. They insisted that their commitment to the Law of Moses stemmed from individual rationalistic inquiry or illumination by God. Da Costa and Prado, in particular, demonstrated a need to distinguish themselves from their coreligionists by minimizing or even concealing the role of particularistic Jewish ethnicity in their careers. The path of religious individuation they had taken—one that dovetailed with emerging trends in European thought—implied a conviction that individual conscience alone should determine a person's choices in matters of faith. In this respect, their thinking foreshadowed demands that would come from Christian sectarians to remove religion from the public sphere. But the religious individualists of the western Sephardi diaspora were not men with a social program; nor could they have begun to anticipate the consequences of secularization in modern western societies for the practice of the "Law of Moses."

NOTES

I would like to express my thanks to the Center for Advanced Jewish Studies at the University of Pennsylvania for providing ideal conditions in the summer months of 2003 for writing a first draft of this essay.

1. See, in particular, the discussion of this scholarship in Silvia Berti, "At the Roots of Unbelief," *Journal of the History of Ideas* 56 (October 1995): 555–575. The religious roots of skepticism and secularism have been explored (or at least adumbrated) in several areas of research: the so-called radical Reformation; the emergence of ideas about toleration; and the tangled knot of skepticism, rationalism, and mysticism in early modern thinking. Among the major contributors to this literature are George Huntston Williams, Jonathan Israel, and Richard Popkin.

2. Benjamin Kaplan, "'Remnants of the Papal Yoke': Apathy and Opposition in the Dutch Reformation," *Sixteenth-Century Journal* 25 (Autumn 1994): 658.

3. Ibid., 660.

4. Ibid., 668.

5. Owen Chadwick, *The Secularization of the European Mind in the Nineteenth Century* (Cambridge and New York: Cambridge University Press, 1975), 23–24.

6. On the importance of the development of a "sense of the naturally impossible" for the emergence of unbelief, see David Wootton, "Lucien Febvre and the Problem of Unbelief in the Early Modern Period," *Journal of Modern History* 60 (December 1988): 695–730, esp. 714–723.

7. A word on terminology: I will use the term "converso" to refer to all persons descended from forcibly converted Jews who lived as Catholics in Iberian lands. The term "ex-converso" will refer to such Jews who had permanently left Iberian lands. The terms "crypto-Jew" and "judaizer" will refer only to those conversos who adhered to Jewish beliefs or practiced Jewish rituals, and not to the many conversos who had fully assimilated into Iberian Catholic society. I should add that a few Old Christians, who possessed no Jewish blood, also became "judaizers."

8. See Hayyim Yosef David Azulai, *Ma'agal tov ha-shalem*, ed. Aaron Freimann (Jerusalem, 1934), 113–124.

9. Azriel Shohet has documented this development in Ashkenazi Jewry. See Azriel Shohet, *Im hilufe tekufot: Reshit ha-haskalah be-yahadut germania* (Jerusalem: Mosad Bialik, 1960).

10. Jacob Katz, *Out of the Ghetto: The Social Background of Jewish Emancipation, 1770–1870* (Syracuse: Syracuse University Press), 34–38.

11. On R. Immanuel Aboab's report of his debate in 1615 with two Portuguese Jews in Italy who challenged aggadic exegesis and the Oral Law, see his *Nomologia o discursos legales* (Amsterdam, 1629), 2:29, 272–273. On the David Farar/Abraham Farar episode(s), which entailed a challenge to aggadic exegesis and the Kabbalah, see Miriam Bodian, "Amsterdam, Venice, and the Marrano Diaspora in the Seventeenth Century," *Dutch Jewish History* (Jerusalem: Tel-Aviv University, 1984–89), 2:51–57. Discussions of the wider phenomenon of rejection of the Oral Law among the Portuguese Jews can be found in Shalom Rosenberg, "Emunat Hakhamim," in *Jewish Thought in the Seventeenth Century, ed.* I. Twersky and B. Septimus (Cambridge, MA: Harvard University Center for Jewish Studies, 1987), 285–341; Yosef Kaplan, "'Karaites' in Early Eighteenth-Century Amsterdam," in *Sceptics, Millenarians and Jews*, ed. D. Katz and J. Israel (Leiden: E. J. Brill, 1990), 202–208; Yosef Kaplan, *From Christianity to Judaism: The Story of Isaac Orobio de Castro*, trans. Raphael Loewe (Oxford: The Littman Library, 1989), 122–178; Jakob Petuchowski, *The Theology of Haham David Nieto: An Eighteenth-Century Defense of the Jewish Tradition* (New York: Ktav Publishing House, 1970), 32–105.

12. *Uriel da Costa's Own Account of His Life (Exemplar humanae vitae)*, trans. John Whiston (London, 1740), republished in Solomon and Sassoon, trans., Uriel da Costa, *Examination of Pharisaic Traditions*, trans., notes, and intro., H. P. Salomon and I.S.D. Sasson (Leiden: E. J. Brill, 1993), 557.

13. Carl Gebhardt, *Die Schriften Uriel da Costa* (Amsterdam: M. Hertzberger, 1922), xxvii.

14. The Hamburg Lutheran pastor Johann Müller possessed a copy of the text, which he said was written shortly before da Costa's death and was found near his corpse. (See A. M. Vaz Dias, *Uriel da Costa* [Leiden: E. J. Brill, 1936], 28–29.) A copy of the manuscript text in Latin is preserved in the library of the University of Amsterdam, but it is not written in da Costa's hand. In 1687, Philip van Limborch published the text as *Exemplar humae vitae*, as an appendix to his work *De veritate religionis Christianae amica collatio cum erudito Judaeo*. There has been considerable speculation that Limborch may have tampered with the text. However, many details treated in the text have been corroborated by other sources.

15. I. S. Révah, "La religion d'Uriel da Costa, Marrane de Porto," *Revue de l'histoire des religions* 161 (1962): 72–76.

16. Yirmiyahu Yovel, *Spinoza and Other Heretics: The Marrano of Reason* (Princeton: Princeton University Press, 1989), 46–47.

17. A copy of this work was discovered only in 1990; it was published in facsimile with an introduction and translation by H. P. Salomon and I. S. D. Sassoon in 1993.

18. Kaplan, *From Christianity*, 149.

19. See ibid., 149–150.

20. O I. S. Révah, "Aux origines de la rupture spinozienne: Nouvel examen," *Annuaire du Collège de France* 72 (1972): 651.

21. In 1595, a Portuguese conversa in Granada told inquisitors that during the time she judaized, "creyo . . . que el hir a misa y confesar y comulgar y todo lo demas que hacian los christianos eran cosa compuesta e yinbentada por los hombres" (Garcia Fuentes, Inquisición en Granada, 474). More than a century later, Francisco Maldonado da Silva's father, an educated surgeon in seventeenth-century Peru, taught his son "que todo lo que enseñaba la Iglesia de Jesucristo . . . era fingido y compuesto." (Günter Böhm, *Historia de los Judíos en Chile: El Bachiller Francisco Maldonado de Silva, 1592–1639* [Santiago de Chile: Editorial Andrés Bello, 1984], 222).

22. José Maria Garcia Fuentes, *La Inquisición en Granada en el siglo XVI: Fuentes para su estudio* (Granada: Autor, 1981), 98.

23. *"Por ser doctor y preceptor del pueblo de Dios"* (Böhm, *Historia de los Judíos en Chile*, 299).

24. This was actually a rather widespread and common idea among crypto-Jews in general. (It was also a theme in the medieval Jewish tract *Toledot Yeshu*.) See David Gitlitz, *Secrecy and Deceit: The Religion of the Crypto-Jews* (Philadelphia: Jewish Publication Society, 1996), 140.

25. Gitlitz, *Secrecy and Deceit*, 140, 170n29. Criticism of this kind undoubtedly had pre-Inquisition roots. In a very early trial in 1483 in Ciudad Real, a converso was reported to have said that Jesus had not brought Lazarus back from the dead but rather the Church "had invented this and it was ridiculous." (Haim Beinart, *Records of the Trials of the Spanish Inquisition in Ciudad Real*, 4 vols. (Jerusalem: Israel National Academy of Sciences and Humanities, 1977–85), 2:217. Similarly, a conversa of Soria said about the commemoration of the Passion, "God be cursed if I can believe that it happened this way; rather someone must have invented it to cause trouble for the Jews." Carlos Carrete Parrondo, *El Tribunal de la Inquisición en el Obispado de Soria (1486–1502). Fontes iudaeorum regni castellae*, vol. 2 (Salamanca: Universidad Pontificia de Salamanca, 1985), 143.

26. "Que Jesucristo . . . habia aprendido el arte magica con que habia engañado algunos ignorantes" (Böhm, *Historia de los Judíos en Chile*, 1984], 288).

27. Arquivo Nacional de Torre do Tombo (hereafter ANTT), Inquisição de Lisboa, processo no. 104, 12r.

28. Ibid., 14r. Diogo d'Assumpção was by no means typical even for an educated crypto-Jew. He was not known to be a converso at all, although more than one witness testified to rumors that he had a Jewish ancestor, and at times he himself claimed Jewish ancestry. One witness testified to overhearing him in conversation on religious matters with a known New Christian [189r]. On this crypto-Jew, see Miriam Bodian, "In the Cross-Currents of the Reformation: Crypto-Jewish Martyrs of the Inquisition, 1570–1670," *Past and Present* 176 (August 2002): 85–90.

29. *Procesos de Luis de Carvajal (el Mozo)*, ed. L. Gonzalez Obregón (Mexico City: Talleres gráficos de la nación, 1935), 266–267.

30. Böhm, *Historia de los Judíos en Chile*, 283.

31. António Borges Coelho, *Inquisição de Évora*, 2 vols. (Lisbon: Caminho, 1987), 2:79.

32. Ibid.

33. *Procesos de Luis de Carvajal*, 473.

34. ibid., 235.

35. AHN Inq. Leg. 2135, no. 17, 25r.

36. António Baião, *A Inquisição em Portugal e no Brazil: Subsidos para a sua historia* (Lisbon, 1921), 145; José Sebastião de Silva Dias, *Correntes de sentimento religioso em Portugal (seculos XVI a XVIII)*, 2 vols. (Coimbra: Universidade de Coimbra, 1960), 2:514.

37. Coelho, *Inquisição de Évora*, 79.

38. ANTT, Inquisição de Lisboa, processo no. 104, 44r.

39. Ibid., 42r, 208v. This was, of course, a common Protestant criticism of Catholic tradition.

40. Ibid., 44b.

41. Rafael Gracia Boix, *Autos de fe y causas de la Inquisición de Córdoba* (Cordova: Excma. Diputación Provincial, 1983), 133.

42. On this phenomenon, see Miriam Bodian, "In the Cross-Currents of the Reformation: Crypto-Jewish Martyrs of the Inquisition, 1570–1670," *Past and Present* 176 (August 2002).

43. ANTT, Inquisição de Lisboa, processo no. 104, 12r-v, 184v.

44. Ibid., 5r, 14r-v.

45. Ibid., 14v.

46. Ibid., 102v.

47. The denial of an afterlife is a crypto-Jewish theme that has been associated with a lingering medieval Averroist current. In particular, Francisco Márquez Villanueva, in his "'Nacer e morir como bestias': Criptojudaísmo y criptoaverroímo" (in *Inquisição: Ensaios sobre mentalidade, heresias e arte* [Rio de Janeiro: Expressão e Cultura, São Paulo: Edusp, 1992], 11–34), argues that this line of thought was a clandestine continuation of medieval Spanish Jewish Averroism—he calls it "criptoaverroísmo" (14)—that was repressed by the Inquisition in Iberian lands, but resurfaced in full force among ex-conversos in the Diaspora (24–25). This may be so,

but among crypto-Jewish and Portuguese-Jewish intellectuals, this line of thought lacked the nihilist thrust it had gained in popular thought and was integrated into a broader critique of tradition (Catholic or rabbinic) based on a literalist reading of the Bible.

48. "Porque era ynposible una muger parir virgen." Garcia Fuentes, *Inquisición en Granada*, 99.

49. AHN *Inq. Leg.* 2135, no. 17, 25r-v.

50. "Be not like a horse or a mule, without understanding" (RSV). The Vulgate, which was being cited, reads "nolite fieri sicut equus et mulus quibus non est intellectus."

51. AHN *Inq. Leg.* 2135, no. 17, 24v.

52. ANTT, Inquisição de Lisboa, processo no. 104, 13v and see 5r.

53. Ibid., 120v and see 185r.

54. I. S. Révah, "Aux origines de la rupture spinozienne: Nouveaux documents sur l'incroyance dans la communauté judéo-portugaise à l'époque de l'excommunication de Spinoza," *Revue des Etudes Juives* 123 (1964): 395.

55. Da Costa, *Examination of Pharisaic Traditions*, 52. Da Costa was addressing Samuel da Silva, who had written a tract attacking da Costa's ideas.

56. Ibid., 55.

57. Immanuel Aboab, *Nomologia, o discursos legales* (Amsterdam, 1629), preface to part 1.

58. Ibid., part 2, chap. 29.

59. Da Costa, *Examination of Pharisaic Traditions*, 90.

60. *Ibid.*, 59.

61. It is published in his *Magen ve-Tsina*, along with a rebuttal, and was republished in Gebhardt, *Schriften*, 3-10. The translation is mine.

62. *Examination of Pharisaic Traditions*, 58-59.

63. See *Examination of Pharasaic Traditions*, 141-142, 153-154, 234, 240. Da Costa draws a characteristically dichotomous distinction between the authentic "Sadducees" and the so-called Pharisees in the first of these passages: "The Book of Daniel was not accepted by the Jews called Sadducees, and this fact alone should discredit it. (As we have said, very little faith can be placed in the testimony of the Pharisees, seeing how these men made it their business—or their madness—to change words, modify, twist, and misinterpret Scripture in order to confirm their confused delusions.)"

64. See Yosef Kaplan, "'Karaites' in Early Eighteenth-Century Amsterdam," in *Sceptics, Millenarians and Jews*, 196-236.

65. See Richard Popkin, "The Lost Tribes, the Caraites and the English Millenarians," *Journal of Jewish Studies* 37, no. 2 (1986): 213-227; Popkin, "Les Caraïtes et l'Emancipation des Juifs," *Dix-Huitième Siècle*, 13, *Juifs et judaïsme* (1981), 137-147. The Puritan millenarian John Dury portrayed the rabbanite Jews, or "Pharisees," as "full of superstitious imaginary foolish conceits, and thalmudicall questions and nicities in their Sermons and Bookes," while Karaites were "rational men that take up no doctrines but what the Scriptures teach, by comparing one text with another" (Popkin, "Lost Tribes," 218).

66. Révah, "Aux origines," 402, 406.

67. Ibid., 392.

68. Ibid., 395.

69. I. S. Révah, *Spinoza et le Dr Juan Prado* (Paris, 1959), 67.

70. For a classic description of the "marrano psyche," see J. A. van Praag, "Almas en litigio," *Clavileño* 1 (1950): 14-26.

71. See Bodian, "In the Cross-Currents of the Reformation," 66-67, 100-101.

4   *Spinoza and the Origins of Jewish Secularism*

There is a common conception that the seventeenth-century Dutch Jewish philosopher Baruch de Spinoza played an important role in the secularization of Judaism. This claim has been expressed in an interesting variety of ways: that Spinoza made secular Judaism possible, that Spinoza laid the groundwork for an assimilated or Reform Judaism, and even that Spinoza was himself the first secular Jew. In fact, nothing could be further from the truth. Although it is not difficult to imagine why one would give credence to the claim—given Spinoza's critique of sectarian religion and other features of his philosophy—I will show that to believe that Spinoza envisioned a Judaism unencumbered by the prescriptions of *halacha*, Jewish law, and the strict observance of Jewish ritual is to misunderstand much of what Spinoza said about both Judaism in particular and religion in general.

Let me begin by stipulating what I mean by the secularization of Judaism, although other contributors to this volume offer different, perhaps more thoughtful, understandings of the phenomenon. I do not intend this to be a rigorous definition, but rather a working definition that is good enough for my limited purposes. By "secularized Judaism," I understand what is sometimes called a cultural or nonreligious Judaism. This would be exemplified by an individual who is (according to halacha) Jewish and who expressly identifies himself or herself as Jewish, but who does not follow Jewish law or order his or her life by Jewish ritual. I might be willing to add to this definition the qualification of "who does not *strictly* follow Jewish law" or "who does not *strictly* order his or her life by Jewish ritual," but because this raises too many contentious and (I believe) absurd questions about whether or not Conservative or Reform Jews are "secular" Jews, I would rather draw the line at a cleaner breaking point and stick with the simpler idea that a secular Jew is a Jew for whom Jewish law and ritual play practically no part in his or her life. It is a person for whom his or her Jewishness lies outside regular normative observance or even membership in a community. Such a person must still maintain a strong sense of Jewish identity, a sense of belonging to a certain culturally or ethnically circumscribed group and to a certain history, and this must make some practical difference in his or her life. This person may also have a self-conscious commitment to what might be called secularized "Jewish beliefs and values"—that is, certain moral and social principles that, while divorced from religious and theological foundations, nonetheless derive in some way from Torah and Jewish history.

To say that Spinoza played a role in the origin of secular Judaism could mean one of two things. First, it could mean that he explicitly envisioned the possibility of living and thinking as a secular Jew, as a Jew outside any organized Jewish community and observance, and perhaps even that he himself led such a life. It could also mean that Spinoza, while not explicitly envisioning such a thorough secularization of one's Jewish identity or complete break from Jewish belief and observance, nonetheless argued for what Miriam Bodian has called "the individuation of belief within the traditional context of revealed religion."[1] According to this somewhat weaker reading of his contribution to the secularization of Judaism, Spinoza's role was to defend a kind of freedom of conscience *within* a sectarian religion—in this case, Judaism—such that one could pursue individualistic or assimilated or even heterodox forms of observance and nonobservance while remaining within traditional Jewish communal life; that is, unlike the first case, without leaving observance and communal membership completely behind. On either reading of Spinoza's contribution to the secularization of Judaism, what he is supposed to have seen is that one could be an unorthodox Jew but, nonetheless, still a Jew.

I would like to approach this question of Spinoza and the secularization of Judaism from two vantage points: first, from the perspective of his life and, second, from the perspective of his thought.

Any discussion of Spinoza's life, and especially one focused on his relationship to Judaism, must begin with the following document, read from in front of the ark of the Torah in the synagogue of the Portuguese Jews of Amsterdam on July 27, 1656:

> The *Senhores* of the *ma'amad* [the congregation's lay governing board] having long known of the evil opinions and acts of Baruch de Spinoza, they have endeavored by various means and promises, to turn him from his evil ways. But having failed to make him mend his wicked ways, and, on the contrary, daily receiving more and more serious information about the abominable heresies which he practiced and taught and about his monstrous deeds, and having for this numerous trustworthy witnesses who have deposed and born witness to this effect in the presence of the said Espinoza, they became convinced of the truth of this matter; and after all of this has been investigated in the presence of the honorable *hakhamim* ["wise men," or rabbis] they have decided, with their consent, that the said Espinoza should be excommunicated and expelled from the people of Israel. By decree of the angels and by the command of the holy men, we excommunicate, expel, curse and damn Baruch de Espinoza, with the consent of God, Blessed be He, and with the consent of the entire holy congregation, and in front of these holy scrolls with the 613 precepts which are written therein; cursing him with the excommunication with which Joshua banned Jericho and with the curse which Elisha cursed the boys and with all the castigations which are written in the Book of the Law. Cursed be he by day and cursed be he by night; cursed be he when he lies down and cursed be he when

he rises up. Cursed be he when he goes out and cursed be he when he comes in. The Lord will not spare him, but then the anger of the Lord and his jealousy shall smoke against that man, and all the curses that are written in this book shall lie upon him, and the Lord shall blot out his name from under heaven. And the Lord shall separate him unto evil out of all the tribes of Israel, according to all the curses of the covenant that are written in this book of the law. But you that cleave unto the Lord your God are alive every one of you this day.

The document concludes with the warning that "no one should communicate with him, not even in writing, nor accord him any favor nor stay with him under the same roof nor [come] within four cubits in his vicinity; nor shall he read any treatise composed or written by him."[2]

It was the harshest writ of *herem*, or ban, ever issued by Amsterdam's Sephardim, and unlike other bans in the period—and there were quite a few, of varying degrees of severity—it was never rescinded. That is, Spinoza was not just punished by his Jewish community, he was expelled. What was his response to this vitriolic act of ostracism? According to one early biographer, someone who knew Spinoza personally, Spinoza said, "All the better; they do not force me to do anything that I would not have done of my own accord if I did not dread scandal. But, since they want it that way, I enter gladly on the path that is opened to me, with the consolation that my departure will be more innocent than was the exodus of the early Hebrews from Egypt."[3] Clearly, by this point, Spinoza's faith was gone and his commitment to communal Jewish life practically nonexistent. Most likely, he did not even regret having to give up running his late father's importing business, which he could not do without membership in good standing in the Portuguese Jewish community.[4]

Was he not, then, after the *herem*, a Jew living a secular life, a cultural if not a religious Jew? Does he not provide the perfect model for nonobservant Judaism? The problem with looking at Spinoza in this way is that not only did he, after his *herem*, cease to have any formal relations with the Sephardic congregation within which he had been raised and educated, and not only did he, as I am absolutely certain, cease to practice any of the rituals and observances of a halachic Jewish life, but the mature Spinoza seems to have had practically no sense of Jewish identity. Being Jewish apparently played no role whatsoever in his self-image (although it did continue to play a role in the image that others had of him, as we can see by Christiaan Huygens's reference to him as "the Jew of Voorburg").[5] For the rest of his life Spinoza clearly did not regard himself as a Jew, other than the nominal way in which someone born to Jewish parents but raised in a perfectly secular household might feel compelled to admit that he is, in a sense, "technically Jewish." One is struck, for example, by the way the Jewish people are regarded in the *Theological-Political Treatise* from the third-person perspective. "They" are the ones who lack any kind of theological or moral "chosen-ness"; "they" are the ones who have emasculated themselves through their laws. More generally, Spinoza seemed in his writings, including his extant correspondence, to lack all identification or sympathy with Jewish religion and history, and even to go out of his way to distance himself from them. But to be even a secular Jew—as opposed to being a secular individual whose background happens to be Jewish—would seem to demand some sense of Jewish identity, even if the source of that identity lies not in any specific religious beliefs or practices, or even in any religious beliefs whatsoever, but rather in at least partially distinguishing oneself from others by one's belonging to a certain histori- cal, ethnic, or social community. I do not think we can say that this was true of Spinoza.

Thus, from the perspective of his life, I would insist that Spinoza was not the first secular Jew, for he was not a secular Jew at all. If anything, he was an important and perhaps the most prominent early modern model of the secular individual, someone for whom religious affiliation or heritage—Jewish or otherwise—plays no role whatsoever in his self-identity

But even if Spinoza did not see himself as a Jew in any sense and thus cannot be said to have lived the life of a secular Jew, did not his philosophy in its entirety, with its powerful argument for a secular, liberal, democratic, tolerant state, in which there is freedom of religion and thought and a general assimilation of all citizens to its core values; with its dismissal of Jewish law and ceremony as irrelevant to contemporary life; and with his reduction of the "true religion" to ethics, that is, to a basic set of rational moral and social principles without any theological-metaphysical dogma— indeed, without any real theology at all—lay the groundwork for what might be called secular Judaism? Did Spinoza at least make it possible to be a modern Jew, one who, while remaining a Jew, nonetheless makes certain essential accommoda- tions to modern secular society and even leads a completely secular life—a Jew for whom the demands of civil citizenship and social assimilation take precedence over the requirements of a strictly Jewish life?

It is important to distinguish this strong kind of assimilation from the strictly political assimilation with which Spinoza was sometimes concerned, the kind of assimilation that would accompany emancipation. Spinoza certainly saw political assimilation as in principle compatible with the continued existence of Jewish reli- gious life. There is no reason why Jews could not maintain their particular beliefs and rigorously practice their religion as well as participate as full, emancipated cit- izens in a secular state. Indeed, the principles of toleration demand this possibility. To be sure, it is also important to remember that Spinoza feared that such societies within society ultimately threatened the peace and unity of the state. In Spinoza's ideal polity, at least, there would be no sectarian differences either to dilute the alle- giances of citizens to the state (or to the state religion) or to cause divisions among citizens. But that does not mean that such a scenario of sectarian emancipation within a larger secular society, while undesirable, is not a possible one.

But this is political assimilation—a space within the state for the Jews to prac- tice Judaism while nonetheless enjoying all the benefits and responsibilities as full citizens. The stronger and more general assimilation that threatens the halachic observance of Judaism is another issue entirely. This kind of assimilation raises the question of whether Jews can even survive as a group in the absence of the rigor- ous observance of their laws and the strict practice of their rituals.

Now there are a number of reasons why one might think that for Spinoza the answer to the question is that they can, that Judaism in the absence of the Law is certainly possible. First of all, Spinoza believed that the hatred directed at the Jews has, over the generations, and even in the absence of halachic observance, helped to preserve them as a separate people. Indeed, Spinoza insisted that even after Jews have left Judaism behind and converted to some other religion, as happened in Portugal in the fifteenth and sixteenth centuries, anti-Semitism, based not only religion but also on blood, served to maintain Jewish identity. "As to their continued existence for so many years when scattered and stateless, this is in no way surprising, since they have separated themselves from other nations to such a degree as to incur the hatred of all. . . . That they are preserved largely through the hatred of other nations is demonstrated from historical fact [*experientia*]."[6] And then there is Spinoza's remark, one that I am hesitant to take seriously, that "I consider the mark of circumcision to be such an important factor in this matter that I am convinced that this by itself will preserve their nation forever"[7]—just as, he insisted, the Chinese have been able to maintain their identity solely through the pigtail. This is not Spinoza at his finest, and I suggest we ignore this particular piece of evidence.

More important, there is Spinoza's claim, so central to the *Theological-Political Treatise*, that the Jewish ceremonial law is no longer valid. The laws were instituted by Moses and enforced by later Israelite political leaders solely for the purpose of establishing a secure and stable state and for political and social well-being. With the destruction of that state, and especially the Temple to which so much of the ceremonial law was directed, the Law has lost its legitimizing context. It is now a body of laws without a state, thus without a purpose. Of course, Jews continued to observe those free-floating laws. But what would happen if the laws themselves, in the absence of their legitimation, withered away? Would the Jewish people disappear as well? Or, on the other hand, would the Jewish people continue in the absence of their laws, only now as a more secular group? When Spinoza said, in chapter 5 of the *Treatise*, that the Mosaic Law is no longer binding on latter-day Jews, was he not recommending that they should pursue their Jewishness without the Law? And isn't this just to foresee a kind of secular Judaism?

The answer to this question, at least insofar as we are talking about what Spinoza envisioned, is a clear "no." Spinoza believed, I would insist, that without the Law, the Jewish people have no sustaining source of difference and identity, and thus for him the notion of a secular Jew—even in the face of hatred and even with his circumcision—would be incoherent.

In chapter 3 of the *Theological-Political Treatise*, Spinoza argued that there is no theological or metaphysical or moral sense in which the Jews are "chosen" by God and selected out from all other peoples. Their "chosen-ness" or "vocation" consists only in the fact that for a long time the Israelites enjoyed political and social good fortune and a secure and powerful commonwealth. This is not something that they possessed uniquely, and, since by the seventeenth century the commonwealth was gone, it is not something that continues to distinguish the Jew from the Gentile. In Spinoza's eyes, of course, there can be no innate or internal factors that distinguish the Jew from any other person. No special moral quality, no divine advantage, and especially no peculiar gifts of nature make a Jew. As we know from Spinoza's philosophical masterpiece, the *Ethics*, all human beings are a part of Nature to the same degree and in exactly the same way, and there are no intrinsic differences among them and no natural kinds to distinguish them one from another. The only thing that separates the Jew from the Gentile is the Law. He emphasized that "the individual Jew, considered alone apart from his social organization and his government, possesses no gift of God above other men, and there is no difference between him and a gentile."[8]

Spinoza took a long view on this question. Why, he asked, have the Jews survived over so many centuries as a people, despite no longer having a commonwealth and being scattered over all the nations of the world? What makes a Jew? The answer, he said, is not because of God's having chosen and favored them, but simply because, as we have seen above, "they have separated themselves from other nations . . . through external rites." Indeed, he noted that were the Jews to give up those rites, the observance of Jewish law, then political assimilation would lead to total assimilation, and Jewish identity would disappear. In the *Theological-Political Treatise*, he cited the case of the Babylonian exiles. "They turned their back on the entire Mosaic Law, consigned to oblivion the laws of their native land as being obviously pointless, and began to be assimilated to other nations."[9] In other words, the result of secularity and assimilation is not secular and assimilated Jews; it is secular and assimilated individuals who have left their Judaism behind. He also mentioned (perhaps a little too optimistically) the case of the Jews of Spain, whose full political assimilation was conditional upon their giving up their religion—understood as the observance of the Law—and the result of which was the disappearance of this group of Jews; "no trace of them was left," he wrote.[10] The fact that Spinoza here overlooked the laws of blood purity by which the Spanish themselves continued to distinguish true Christians from Jewish Conversos indicates that for him there was nothing to being a Jew other than the observance of the Law.

For Spinoza, then, the Law, halacha, was essential to Judaism. Judaism without a robust divine "chosen-ness" is relatively unproblematic. But there can be no Judaism unbounded by the observance of Jewish law. Take away the Law, and you take away the Jew. To put it another way, for Spinoza, to be a Jew was to be a halachically observant Jew. For what defined Jewish life for Spinoza were the tenets of its religion and the set of ceremonial and other practices and laws that, with the destruction of the Temple, have lost their raison d'être. And what defined Jewish self-identity for him was to belong to a Jewish community that is constituted by the self-conscious observance of those commandments.

In fact, we can generalize this point and say that for Spinoza any sectarian religious group was defined solely by its observance of a particular set of laws and rituals. The contrast is with those partisans of what he called the "true religion," which is defined not by ceremonial observance but by the inner commitment to what he called the "divine law"—that is, a simple set of basic moral principles that can be summed up by the proposition "Love God and your fellow human being." There are Christians, and then there are Christians. The former are sectarian, committed to an elaborate body of rites, historical and theological doctrines, and a determinate hierarchy of authority; the latter are those who see the true, nonsectarian, universal moral message of Jesus' preaching. They recognize that external modes of observance are totally accidental to religious virtue and, as Spinoza said, "contribute nothing to blessedness."[11]

For Spinoza, then, to be a secular or assimilated or accommodationist Jew is nonsense. It is to be a nonsectarian sectarian. For him, Judaism without an observance of its textually and historically defined tenets, laws, and ceremonies would be an empty shell, a masquerade. These laws and rituals—along with Gentile anti-Semitism—are what have preserved Judaism since the destruction of the Temple, and what its essence now boiled down to. Of course, Spinoza had great contempt for traditional sectarian religions, and Judaism in particular. And he certainly did argue that Jewish law was no longer binding on contemporary Jews; perhaps in this sense he unwittingly opened the door for a nonhalachic, even secular Judaism. But it seems to me that he also had a very strict understanding of what was to count as Judaism. Spinoza may have been a religious reformer. But what he envisioned was not reform *within* Judaism. Rather, what he had in mind was a universal rational religion that eschewed meaningless, superstitious rituals and focused instead on a few simple moral principles—above all, to love one's neighbor as oneself.

After his ban from the Amsterdam congregation, Spinoza belonged to and participated in no organized religion. I could just as easily have addressed in this essay the oft-repeated claim that the post-*herem* Spinoza was a Christian, but that is not even worth discussing. Sectarian religions represented, for him, one of the greatest threats to social harmony and political well-being. They weaken the fabric of society by introducing allegiances that may, in fact, be inconsistent with one's allegiance to the state and thus run counter to the general public good. If Spinoza represented anything, it was as the first truly secular citizen, someone for whom religious affiliation played no role whatsoever in his self-identity and who argued that traditional religious beliefs generated only superstition and the harmful passions of hope and fear. Far from being the means to salvation and blessedness, he held that such beliefs represented the most serious obstacle to our highest good. This, I believe, is Spinoza's greatest contribution to the origins of secular modernity.

NOTES

1. See the chapter by Miriam Bodian in this volume.

2. The Hebrew text is no longer extant, but the Portuguese version is found in the Book of Ordinances (*Livro dos Acordos de Naçao e Ascamot*), in the Municipal Archives of the City of Amsterdam, Archives for the Portuguese Jewish Community in Amsterdam, 334, no. 19, fol. 408.

3. Jean-Maximlien Lucas, in *Die Lebensgeschichte Spinoza's in Quellenschriften, Urkunden und Nichtamtlichen*, ed. J. Freudenthal (Leipzig: Verlag Von Veit, 1899), 8.

4. For a more detailed study of this event in Spinoza's life, see Steven Nadler, *Spinoza: A Life* (Cambridge: Cambridge University Press, 1999), esp. chap. 6; and Steven Nadler, *Spinoza's Heresy* (Oxford: Oxford University Press, 2002).

5. Christiaan Huygens, *Oeuvres complètes*, 22 vols. (The Hague: Martinus Nijhoff, 1893), 6:81.

6. *Theological-Political Treatise* (TTP), chapter 3, "Spinoza Opera," ed. Carl Gebhardt, 5 vols. (Heidelberg: Carl Winters Verlag, 1925 [1972]; henceforth cited as "G"), 3:56. Translation from *Theological-Political Treatise*, trans. Samuel Shirley, 2nd ed. (Indianapolis: Hackett Publishing, 2001; henceforth cited as "S"), 45.

7. TTP, chap. 3, G, 3:57; S, 45.

8. TTP, chap. 3, G, 3:50; S, 40.

9. TTP, chap. 5, G, 3:72; S, 62.

10. TTP, chap. 3, G, 3:56–7; S, 46.

11. TTP, chap. 5, G, 3:76; S, 65.

PART II

CHALLENGES OF SECULAR
JEWISHNESS IN MODERN TIMES

Influenced by socialism and nationalism in the late nineteenth and early twentieth centuries, some East European Jews proposed that the key attributes of Jewishness were homeland, language, history, and/or culture. Religious faith and observance were no longer essential but only one dimension of the Jews' national cultural heritage. Yiddishists, for example, championed the vernacular of East European Jews as the vehicle for Jewish national revival and set up school networks to promote this ideology and its culture. But, as David Fishman points out, when these schools were transplanted to the United States, where Jews were regarded largely as a religious group, the intrinsic problems of creating a secular Jewish culture and identity were exacerbated, as can be seen in the curricula and ideologies of Yiddish secular schools in America.

The separation of Jewish ethnicity from the Jewish faith is often seen as having begun with the Reform movement in early-nineteenth-century Germany. "Classic" Reform Judaism rejected the idea that Jews are a people or nation, declared them a faith community only, and held that this allowed Jews to become Germans, Frenchmen, Englishmen, and others, while restricting their Jewishness to Judaism. Scott Spector explores Jewish identity as dealt with by Central European Jewish intellectuals. He reexamines critically the usual conception of a spectrum of identities, ranging from complete assimilation to total Jewish identification. By the turn of the twentieth century, the classical liberal-assimilationist position, with its optimism about a potentially unproblematic fusion of Jewish (private) identities and German public ones, was no longer available.

Until the eighteenth and nineteenth centuries, lines between Jews and others were clearly drawn. But with emancipation, acculturation, secularization, and integration, Jews and non-Jews in Europe debated how Jews should transform themselves and the extent to which they should do so. According to Todd Endelman, "ordinary" emancipated Jews did not imagine a future in which they would renounce or transcend their Jewish attachments, though they were willing and even eager to redefine them. Christian emancipationists clearly envisioned a more radical break with the Jewish past. In reality, integration and secularization were uneven processes, so that social acceptance and mixing lagged behind the decline of belief and practice. By the late nineteenth century the bonds among West European Jews had become more social and ethnic than religious.

5

Yiddish Schools in America and the Problem of Secular Jewish Identity

DAVID E. FISHMAN

A self-consciously secular Jewish identity emerged in Eastern Europe in the late nineteenth and early twentieth centuries under the influence of two great systems of ideas: nationalism and socialism. Jewish nationalism created a paradigm shift in the construction of Jewishness, in which the key attributes of the Jews were now considered to be their markers as a nation: their homeland, language, history, and/or culture. Jewish nationalists did not consider religious faith or observance to be essential to the perpetuation of the Jews and instead ascribed primacy to one's fidelity to the Jewish homeland, language, history, and/or culture. They looked upon the Jewish religion as one aspect of the Jews' national cultural heritage.

Meanwhile, the spread of socialism among East European Jews, usually in combination with some form of Jewish nationalism, brought an overtly atheistic and antireligious worldview into the Jewish sphere of discourse. Jewish socialists not only deemphasized the position of the Jewish religion but also rejected religious Judaism as a false system of ideas, harmful to the cause of social progress—and to the Jews' own political and social liberation.[1] Those Jews who were influenced more strongly by the combination of nationalist and socialist ideas were usually the ones who embraced an avowedly secular Jewish identity more clearly and sharply.

In Eastern Europe, a secular national identity was compelling to many Jews, because it corresponded to political and social realities. The political realities are well known: Eastern Europe was rife with nationalist movements, national conflicts, and virulent anti-Semitism, all of which together made it natural, and—given the social exclusion and rejection of Jews—almost necessary, for the Jews to define themselves as a distinct national group struggling for its liberation.

But the underlying social conditions that spurred the adoption of a secular, national identity by many Jews were equally important. In late-nineteenth-century and early-twentieth-century Eastern Europe, the Jews were a rapidly modernizing group. They became urbanized, industrialized, politicized, and, concomitant to all of those processes, secularized. The secularization of the Jews' everyday lives in the rising urban centers (Warsaw, Lodz, Odessa, Vilna, etc.) was ubiquitous, with the role of religion shrinking in authority, scope, and intensity. But the Jews' acculturation to either Russian or Polish language lagged considerably behind their secularization (and other aspects of their modernization). In 1897, the vast majority of the Jews in the Russian Empire spoke Yiddish, and only 27 percent could read and write in Russian. The Jews' social integration with their Polish, Russian, and Ukrainian neighbors in the Pale of Settlement was also modest. All of which is to say that in turn-of-the-twentieth-century Eastern Europe, "the secular Jewish nation" was not just an ideological construct, but a term that seemed to correspond to a growing social reality.

One version of Jewish nationalism that grew in popularity at the time was Yiddishism—the movement that championed the Yiddish language, the vernacular of East European Jews, as the vehicle for Jewish national revival. Yiddishists considered strengthening Yiddish language, literature, and cultural institutions to be a central aspect of Jewish nation-building in the modern era.[2] While Yiddishism was in many ways similar to other ethno-linguistic nationalist movements in Eastern Europe, it faced a particular problem that other movements did not: Most of the Jewish cultural heritage over the preceding three millennia had been religious in character and Hebrew in language. Just what did a secular Jewish national identity based on the Yiddish language mean? What was the relationship of secular Yiddish culture to Jewish religious texts, concepts, rituals, and doctrines? Many Yiddishist writers, artists, and intellectuals addressed and alluded to this issue, but more often than not it was either skirted or ignored. The one arena where the question of secular Jewish national identity was confronted directly was education. The creation of modern Yiddish schools required that the abstract idea of secular Jewish nationality be concretized into a curriculum for Jewish children. What, if anything, of the Jewish religious legacy would be taught, and how would it be presented?

This chapter examines the American Yiddish schools' conundrum of synthesizing secularism and Judaism. These schools were created by immigrant educators and intellectuals who operated with East European ideological conceptions of Jewish nationalism, socialism, and secularism. While the schools themselves were in America, the educators' minds were distinctly East European. I focus on the period from 1910 until 1947—the time of the schools' establishment, upswing, and strength, and prior to the hemorrhaging of Yiddish culture in America, the proliferation of the synagogue congregational school, and the establishment of the State of Israel, all of which had a profound weakening impact on the Yiddish schools.

The Creation of Yiddish Schools in America

At the time of the Czernowitz conference for the Yiddish language in 1908, modern Yiddish schools were more of an idea than reality. The conference, famous for declaring Yiddish a national language of the Jewish people, resolved to create a World Bureau for the Yiddish Language, one of whose tasks would be "to establish and support Yiddish model schools, and assist in the publication of model textbooks."[3] While the planned World Bureau never materialized, Yiddish schools opened independently in the years immediately after the conference, both in Tsarist Russia and in North America, as part of the general upswing of modern Yiddish culture of that time.

In North America, the opening of the schools was preceded by appeals for their establishment by Yiddish intellectuals and journalists. Joel Entin (1875–1959) noted

in April 1909 on the pages of the daily *Di varhayt* that the question of providing a
Jewish education to the children of immigrants as a supplement to their public
school education was growing in urgency. While religious parents could send their
children to *heders*, talmud torahs, and yeshivas, and Zionists had established a few
private schools of their own, there were no schools for the children of "parents
who are not religious and not Zionists, but are interested in Judaism (*yidishkayt*)
because of Jewish history or Jewish culture." Entin called for such parents to form
new Jewish schools "which would not teach religion or inculcate national ideas
which were repugnant to the parents. They would instead provide good instruction
in Jewish history, the Hebrew language, its ancient and modern classics, and in our
Yiddish language and literature."[4]

In a follow-up article, Entin sharpened his definition of the schools' constituency.
They were needed for the children of the tens of thousands of Jewish radicals in
America, the vast majority of whom was "opposed to the Jewish religion . . . but do
not want their children to become totally estranged from Judaism (*yidishkayt*)." The
schools were to provide a "Jewish cultural education." Entin proposed that the socialist Zionists were the most appropriate movement to establish such schools; he himself went on to establish and head the Farband schools, associated with Poale Zion of
America.[5]

At about the same time, the Bundist émigré journalist Tsivyon (pseudonym for
Ben-Tziyon Hoffman, 1874–1954), fresh off the boat from Europe, expressed similar
thoughts and sentiments. In an article on the cultural tasks of the Workmen's
Circle, Tsivyon dismissed the organization's existing Sunday schools, which gave
children a socialist education in English, as an educational and moral abomination.
Instead, Tsivyon advanced what he called a "heretical" idea: the Workmen's Circle's
Sunday schools should teach Jewish history and Yiddish.

> Jewish children need to know Jewish history and Yiddish literature, just as
> Russian children need to know Russian history and Russian literature, German
> children need to know German history and German literature etc. . . .
>
> I would like for the Jewish worker's children to grow up to be not just social-
> ists, but Jewish socialists. . . .
>
> Should we radicals hold fast to the opinion that we have nothing to do with
> Judaism, and leave the monopoly over Jewish education in the hands of the
> bourgeoisie? Or should we make, call it if you want, a compromise, and take
> Judaism into our own hands? Instead of prayers and religion, we will teach our
> children modern Judaism: Jewish history and Yiddish literature. From a socialist
> perspective Jewish history and Yiddish literature are certainly "kosher," or at
> least not "*treyf.*"[6]

Shortly thereafter Tzivyon became a member of the Educational Committee of
the Workmen's Circle and one of the main supporters of its Yiddish schools.

The tension between a commitment to Judaism and an insistence on secularism
found in Entin's and Tsivyon's articles became a hallmark of the Yiddish schools
in America. While both authors self-consciously used the word *yidishkayt*, the

traditional term for Judaism, and embraced it as a value, they were, by virtue of their being socialists, openly "opposed to religion" and rejected "teaching prayers." Therefore Yiddish schools in America became a laboratory for exploring the meaning of secular Jewish identity.

Yiddish Schools in America: Four Systems

Now mostly forgotten, the Yiddish school movement was a dynamic and growing educational trend in America during the years between the two World Wars. In their heyday in 1934, some twenty thousand Jewish children were enrolled in Yiddish schools in America and constituted 10 percent of American Jewish children receiving a Jewish education.[7] These were supplementary schools whose classes met three to six days per week for one or two hours per day. Yiddish schools were neighborhood institutions, averaging sixty children per school; the Yiddish school system consisted overwhelmingly of elementary schools for children between the ages of eight and twelve (only one thousand children, or 5 percent of the total were enrolled in 1934 in Yiddish *mitlshuln*).[8]

The Yiddish schools in America were divided into four separate systems, with different sponsorships and orientations. The Jewish National Workers' Alliance (*Yidish-natsionaler arbeter farband*, or simply Farband), the fraternal order associated with Poale Zion of America, founded the first Yiddish schools in America in 1910, and the first Yiddish teachers' seminary in 1918. The Farband schools were distinguished from the others in that they taught Yiddish and Hebrew equally and developed the students' interest in the *yishuv* in Palestine. Enrollment in 1934 stood at 5,598 students.

The Sholem Aleichem Folk Institute was established in 1918, based on a number of nonpartisan Yiddish schools, the first of which was founded in 1913. The Sholem Aleichem Institute was committed to nonpartisan Yiddish education and did not teach Hebrew in its elementary schools until 1940. Enrollment in 1934 reached 1,976 students.

The Workmen's Circle resolved to create Yiddish socialist schools in 1916; the first such schools appeared in 1918. They paid equal attention to teaching Yiddish and instilling socialism, and did not teach Hebrew in their elementary schools. In 1934 enrollment stood at 6,013 students.

When the Workmen's Circle split in 1926 between the Communists and anti-Communists, the Communist faction took with it a significant number of schools. In 1930 these came under the organizational sponsorship of the International Workers' Order (IWO). These schools were primarily committed to instilling the values of communism and support for the Soviet Union. They did not teach Hebrew. These schools had 6,800 students enrolled in 1934.

Ideological and Programmatic Statements

The ideological positions taken by Yiddish school systems were expressed in programmatic statements issued by their umbrella organizations during their formative years, the 1910s and 1920s. These statements revolved around three issues or tensions: socialism versus Jewish nationalism, Yiddish versus Hebrew, and secularism versus religion. The schools positioned themselves in various ways in relation to these three topics.

With regard to the first dichotomy, Yiddish schools defined themselves alternately as exclusively socialist and not Jewish national schools (e.g., the IWO), as primarily socialist and secondarily Jewish national schools (e.g., the Workmen's Circle), as primarily Jewish national schools and secondarily socialist or progressive (e.g., the Farband schools), or as exclusively Jewish national schools and not socialist (e.g., the Sholem Aleichem schools). With regard to the second dichotomy, the Yiddish schools could attribute educational importance only to Yiddish and not to Hebrew (e.g., the IWO and Workmen's Circle schools), primarily to Yiddish and only secondarily Hebrew (e.g., the Sholem Aleichem schools), or equally to Yiddish and Hebrew (e.g., the Farband schools).

But when it came to the third dichotomy, secularism versus religion, there was basic agreement on the surface level of pronouncements. All of the Yiddish school systems defined themselves as secular and not religious. None defined themselves as primarily secular and secondarily religious, or as both secular and religious. The two terms were considered mutually exclusive.

The underlying ideological unity of the Yiddish schools lay in the fact that they all defined themselves as secular schools for Jewish children that taught in Yiddish. The other variables were open to disagreement. In fact, while the Yiddish schools were referred to early on by various names, such as *natsyonal-radikale shuln* (national-radical schools), *yidishe folk-shuln* (Jewish people's schools), *moderne yidishe shuln* (Modern Jewish/Yiddish schools), the name that became most popular and endured was *yidish veltlekhe shuln* (Yiddish/Jewish secular schools). The name embodied their primary commitments—to Yiddish and to secularity.

While the programmatic statements of the Yiddish schools systems all agreed on using the term *secular*, they did not necessarily agree on its meaning, its relative importance, or its curricular implications. For example, secularity occupied a modest place in the Farband schools' declaration of principles, adopted at their first convention in April 1914:

> As Jewish nationalists we believe in the unity of the Jewish nation, and seek to preserve it with all our energy and means. We wish to give our children an education that will preserve that unity, and bind Jewish children with their brethren across all times and lands.
>
> As radicals and democrats, we seek to give Jewish children an education that will be in harmony with the progress of science and free thought, and with progressive views on social justice and love for fellow men. Our education will therefore include the following elements: Yiddish, Hebrew, Yiddish literature, Hebrew literature (both old and new), Jewish history and Jewish folklore (folksongs, folk-tales etc.).
>
> Our education seeks to develop in the child a healthy approach toward the Jewish religion, viewing it from a cultural-historical perspective. Teachers

should attempt to highlight to the children the national, ethical, and poetic aspects of the Jewish religion. . . . As part of our education, the Jewish national holidays should be celebrated in the schools.

Yiddish and Hebrew are equal in the National-Radical schools. Instruction in both languages should begin simultaneously.[9]

The key phrases in this text are those of providing an education in harmony with "science and free thought," while nonetheless offering "a healthy approach to the Jewish religion" and highlighting its "national, ethical and poetic aspects." The declaration thus assumed that there were aspects of the Jewish religion that were of enduring value for secular nationalist Jews.

Secularism occupied a much more central position in the Declaration of Principles of the Sholem Aleichem Schools, adopted at the 1927 conference of the Sholem Aleichem Folk Institute. It opened with the sentence that "the new Yiddish school became possible and necessary thanks to the *Jewish secular* environment, which arose during the last several decades, and which has become a creative force, destined to play a great role in Jewish history." It went on to state:

The language of the Jewish secular environment is Yiddish. Its culture is modern Yiddish culture. Its world view is in accordance with the results of scientific research. It does not consider religion to be the foundation of our spiritual life. Jewish religious customs are only a part of our people's creativity throughout the generations. Hebrew, and those parts of Jewish creativity connected with Hebrew (Aramaic), belong to our national cultural heritage. They are considered from an objective historic point of view. . . .

Yiddish secular schools must . . . give priority to subjects and activities which relate to Jewish secular life and creativity, such as Yiddish, Yiddish literature, Jewish folk creativity, and Jewish history. Jewish religious beliefs and customs should be considered from a cultural-historical perspective. Hebrew and Hebrew literature should be studied in upper grades (that is, in high school) as a part of the accumulated Jewish cultural heritage.[10]

In this text, the relegation of religion to a minor position in Jewish culture and to the past is made quite bluntly: "not . . . the foundation of our people's spiritual life" and "only a part of our people's heritage." Hebrew is mentioned in the context of reference to religion and as a subject to be studied in advanced grades.

The first statement on the goals of the Workmen's Circle schools, adopted in 1919 by its Education Department and a council of educators, did ot address the issue of secularism directly. Instead it focused almost entirely on the polarity between socialism and Jewishness, giving more weight to the former than to the latter. The stated goals were the following:

1. To teach children to read, write and speak Yiddish well.
2. To familiarize them with the best works of Yiddish literature.
3. To familiarize them with the life of the workers and of the Jewish masses in America and in other lands.

4. To familiarize them with the history of the Jewish people, and with events in the struggle for freedom in general history.
5. To develop in them a sense of justice, love for the oppressed, love of freedom, and honor for those who struggle for freedom.
6. To develop the feeling for beauty.
7. To develop in them idealism and the aspiration for great deeds, which are necessary for every child from an oppressed class, on the path to a better social order.[11]

An official brochure, issued by the Education Committee of the Workmen's Circle in 1920, explained that the schools had been formed to counteract the harmful influence of the American public school—which alienated Jewish workers' children from their parents, the Jewish people, and the struggles of the working class—and to offer an alternative to Talmud Torahs. On the latter, it noted, "The Talmud Torahs do not teach children the living language of the Jewish masses. Instead they teach the language of the old decrepit Jewish past, which is absolutely superfluous for the children, at least during their first several years of study. And besides, the Talmud Torahs give children a religious education, which the great majority of worker-parents would like to avoid."[12]

The curriculum of the schools was set as Yiddish language, Jewish history, Yiddish literature, biographies of strugglers for freedom, and music/dance/recitation. The exclusion of religion from the curriculum as something "decrepit" (*opgelebt*) required no explanation or statement. It was taken for granted.

Finally, the 1929 declaration of principles of the Non-Partisan Jewish Workers' Schools (which became the International Workers' Order Schools in 1930), defined the schools exclusively as socialist. Its goal was "to develop a multi-faceted, bold, joyful and struggling, proletarian personality, which will be able to participate in the revolutionary struggle for power, and in the revolutionary work of building a new socialist order. . . . The language of our school is Yiddish, but the language serves to develop the internationalist spirit among the children." It did not address at all the question of Jewish nationality or secular Jewish identity.[13]

As is evident from the list of subjects given in these programmatic statements, the American Yiddish schools did not teach Bible, *siddur*, Mishna, Talmud, or *halacha*, at least not as distinct subjects. The curriculum was modeled after that of a secular public school in America or Europe and provided for instruction of the Jewish national language (or languages), literature, and history. Jewish religious texts, concepts, and practices were either excluded from the curriculum or subsumed under one of the above-mentioned subjects.[14] The curriculum of language, literature, and history allowed for considerable flexibility and difference of opinion as to what was to be included or excluded. As will be discussed below, beyond the formal curriculum, the question of holiday celebrations loomed large.

Yiddish Language and Literature

The schools devoted their greatest energy and effort to teaching Yiddish reading and writing, spelling, and grammar. Already in the 1920s pedagogues noted that

Yiddish was not the children's native tongue, but rather a second language whose proper acquisition required great effort. Yiddish educators were preoccupied with the methodology of Yiddish language instruction, and many primers, readers, grammar textbooks, and workbooks were published that addressed this objective.

Yet language and content were inextricably connected. What kind of Yiddish texts would children read as they studied Yiddish over the course of five or more years? What kind of Jewish knowledge would the primers and readers impart? The answers varied according to the Yiddish school system. A comparison of two representative and popular readers illustrates this point.

Joel Entin and Leon Elbe published a reader for the Farband schools in 1916, called *Fun idishn kval: A yiddish lehr-bukh un khrestomatye* (*From the Jewish Well-springs: A Yiddish Textbook and Chrestomathy*), which took a Jewishly maximalist approach to the subject of Yiddish. It consisted of 153 short texts, mainly by modern Yiddish writers, including poets Yehoash, Avrom Reisin, and Morris Rosenfeld, and prose writers I. L. Peretz and Mendele Mokher Seforim, who authored the most pieces in the collection.

Generally speaking, while *Fun yidishn kval* was a reader of Yiddish literary texts, thematically it was devoted predominantly to the Jewish holidays, religious traditions, and ancient Jewish heroes. Thus, the poems by Yehoash included "Passover," "David's Harp," "The Hidden Saint" (*Der lamed vovnik*), "Rachel's Tomb," "Shabbat Nahamu," "A Song to the Sabbath," "The Night before the Giving of the Torah," and "Elijah the Prophet's Vision." The Mendele selections were not satirical or critical depictions of the *shtetl*, but rather romantic depictions of traditional Jewish life found in Mendele's later works, entitled "A Day in Elul," "Midnight," "Selichos Time in the Forest," and so forth. What is interesting about this selection of Yiddish literary texts is the use of Yiddish literature as a vehicle for teaching about Jewish religious traditions. Children learned about "Shabbes Nahamu" and "Selikhos" not from going to synagogue and reciting the special prayers for these occasions, but from a Yiddish poem or story that told about them. Entin and Elbe sifted and mined Yiddish literature for a specific Jewish educational function—teaching about Jewish traditions—which had been far from the original writers' minds and intentions. (Yiddish schools did not even exist until the last few years of Mendele's and Peretz's lives.)

Moreover, a good part of Entin and Elbe's Yiddish reader consisted of material which was not originally in Yiddish but in Hebrew. It included eighteen rabbinic *agadot* taken from the Yiddish edition of Bialik and Ravnitsky's *Sefer ha-agadah*, among which were tales about Moses, the giving of the Torah, King David, King Solomon, Rabbi Akiva, the Temple, and the Prophet Jeremiah. And it included Yiddish translations and adaptations of chapters from the Pentateuch, the prophets Isaiah, Jeremiah, and Amos, and a poem by Yehuda Ha-Levi. *Fun yidishn kval* opened with an agadah in which God praised Moses for being a faithful shepherd and concluded with a complete translation of Isaiah 2, "And it shall come to pass in the end of days."

It is noteworthy that the Farband schools did not restrict the teaching of biblical and rabbinic material to the Hebrew language and literature part of their curriculum, but included them in the Yiddish curriculum as well. (In part, this was a pragmatic decision. Children came to the schools knowing some Yiddish from home and thus acquired it more quickly than Hebrew. Teaching biblical and rabbinic material in Hebrew meant delaying its instruction for several years.) Of equal interest is the occurrence of God, revelation, angels, and prophets in a textbook used by schools which were committed to providing "an education that will be in harmony with the progress of science and free thought." We shall see just how this was rationalized below.

An approach diametrically opposed to the teaching of Yiddish is provided by *Der onfanger (The Beginner)* by Jacob (Yankev) Levin (1884–1958), the most popular Yiddish primer in the Workmen's Circle schools during the 1920s and 1930s. Published in six books for six successive years of study, book one of *Der onfanger* went through thirteen printings between 1922 and 1935.

Books one (116 pages) and two (136 pages) taught the alphabet, basic words and sentences, and then offered graded texts on topics from everyday life: family, school, animals, nature, the seasons. Parables and fables about animals were the most frequently represented genre. No specifically Jewish content appeared in books one and two at all. There were no references to Jewish holidays, biblical stories, or even edited texts from modern Yiddish literature.

Book three (136 pages) was devoted to introducing children to the Hebrew component of the Yiddish language. Levin noted in his introduction that the spelling and use of the Hebrew component in Yiddish were controversial topics in the Workmen's Circle schools, with many on the left favoring a phonetic Yiddish spelling of words of Hebrew origin and some supporting the minimization or elimination of the Hebrew component. Levin supported moderate use of the Hebrew component and its traditional spelling, but he saw his task exclusively in terms of language arts. The book's Jewish content was minimal. In fact, it contained as many tales translated from Russian and world literature (eight) as it did translations from Hebrew aggadic sources.

Only in the final, sixth book of *Der onfanger*, which was presumably intended for use in the last of the five-year Yiddish school or the first year of a Yiddish *mitlshul*, was material related to Jewish religion included. Book six was an anthology of literary texts, arranged in sections named "The Bizarre" (*oysterlishs*), "Of Life," and "Labor." Some of the tales and poems in the first section revolved around rabbis and Hasidic masters—Peretz's "If Not Higher," Joseph Opatoshu's "Reb Itche," and a poem by Avrom Liesin on Rabbi Akiva. There were also some stories by Peretz that included supernatural themes (for example, angels and Elijah the prophet), such as "The Seven Good Years" and "At a Corpse's Deathbed." The section with these tales was apparently entitled "The Bizarre" to mark them as unrealistic and thereby justify their inclusion along with other tales of the fantastic. Jewish holidays and biblical heroes were absent from the sixth book of *Der onfanger*, and the section called "Labor" dominated the book, occupying 110 of its 250 pages.[15]

Der onfanger leaves one to wonder how, if at all, students in Workmen's Circle schools learned about Judaism.

Jewish History

Part of the answer is provided by the second main subject in the curriculum of the Yiddish schools: Jewish history. Biblical narratives were taught in the framework of Jewish history, despite the fact that treating the Bible as history raised many problems for avowed secularists.

Chaim Lieberman (1890–1963), one of the founders of the Farband schools, argued for the inclusion of biblical myths and miracles in teaching Jewish history. "The history of facts and events appeals only to reason, whereas mythology and its fascinating legends stimulate the imagination. The legendary part of history is just as necessary for the child's development as the dry, colorless facts."[16] Specifically, Lieberman advocated beginning instruction of Jewish history with the Genesis story of creation, then continuing to the Flood, Tower of Babel, and so on. This would powerfully convey to the children that the Jewish people were an integral part of nature and an organic outgrowth of universal history.

Chaim Bez (Bezprozvany) (1904–1983), the pedagogue who developed the teaching of Jewish history in the Workmen's Circle schools, took the opposing position. Teaching the myths of Genesis would go against the schools' secular worldview. It would also clash with the theory of evolution and with progressive ideas on evil and the means by which evil should be combated. The teaching of Jewish history, he argued, should not begin with the story of creation, but with Abraham.

Bez did agree with the idea, which was raised by Lieberman and others, that the teaching of biblical tales, though formally conducted under the rubric of Jewish history, had mainly literary and aesthetic objectives: "to let the children enjoy the pretty fables, stories, and poems that are contained in the Bible." In selecting Bible stories to be taught to children, their artistic value was the paramount criteria. "One should tell only those legends which, because of their artistic value, would be told even if they had nothing to do with the Jews."

Bez advocated altering the Biblical tales so that they would not convey theological and religious ideas, which were inimical to atheists. He went to some length to refute the view that the legends contained in the Bible were specimens of primordial Jewish folk-creativity and should be maintained in their original form, much like the tales of Greek mythology. He marshaled scholarly opinion to argue that the original *oral* tales had been rational narratives, which only centuries later were embellished with religious elements and messages. Therefore, by removing the theological elements from biblical tales, one restored them to their original form. The act of altering the stories was, consequently, justified from a scholarly perspective, ideologically and educationally necessary, and even artistically beneficial to the stories themselves.

In balancing the principles of the aesthetic enjoyment of Bible tales and maintaining the schools' secular worldview, Bez struck the following compromise: "We should liberate the legends from their theological coating, but not empty them of the charm of extraordinariness. A donkey can speak, a rock can give forth water, the sun and moon may stand still. But God does not reveal himself to people.

Angels do not go up or down from heaven, and they do not visit Abraham. Three *men* visited the old patriarch."[17]

A textbook which presented the tales of the Pentateuch according to Bez's approach was composed by Jacob (Yankev) Levin. Entitled *Mayses un legendes fun der Yidisher geshichte (Stories and Legends from Jewish History)* (with no intended irony), it was published in 1928 and achieved four printings by 1938. *Mayses un legendes* began with the birth of Abraham and ended with the death of Moses, weaving together biblical tales and some rabbinic Midrash, but completely eliminating God from the narrative. Thus, Abraham destroyed the idols in his father's shop, telling his father that the idols had quarreled with each other, but he did not conclude, as in the Midrash, that there was one supreme and incorporeal God.[18]

Certain stories where God figured as an actor were deleted, such as the binding of Isaac, and others were modified, such as the burning bush, where Moses "heard something, as if a voice were speaking to him." Elsewhere, miraculous events were retained, but not attributed to God: Sodom was destroyed by a storm of fire and sulfur, Egypt was struck by ten plagues, but no attribution was given as to who or what caused these events. The Dead Sea parted when Moses lifted his staff.[19]

Levin even rewrote the giving of the Ten Commandments, which in his version were declared by Moses when he went up on Mount Sinai. Gone was the first commandment ("I am the Lord your God who took you out of the Land of Egypt"), the second commandment was truncated to read "you shall not make idols or images, you shall not bow down to them or worship them," and the third was rendered "you shall not swear falsely." The tenth commandment was split into two to retain the number of ten commandments.[20] Levin justified his editorial method as follows:

> While we have freed ourselves from the entire religious world-view, and lost our awe for the Bible as a religious book, we have retained our respect for it as an artistic-literary monument. . . . These are no longer religious tales, which are the foundation of the Jewish religion. They are simply pretty stories which children can enjoy, and which give them some cultural-historical information. . . .
>
> All the stories in the Pentateuch are, after all, only stories, which have behind them almost no historical background. . . . The removal of their religious and supernatural elements helps to enlarge and elevate their heroes. Beforehand, the heroes acted as heroes only thanks to the aid and inspiration of God. Now they act on their own responsibility, at their own initiative, thanks to their own greatness or smallness.[21]

The inclusion of Bible stories under the rubric of Jewish history was an ingenious device, laden with irony. (Where else did the teaching of history consist largely of material which the teachers considered nonhistorical?) It also involved excising the laws and commandments from the Pentateuch. The law—whether ritual, social, and ethical, whether it be the laws of Passover, *kashrut*, charity, or honesty in weights and measures—was not part of the Bible as taught in Workmen's Circle schools. Only stories remained.

A rationalist and secular approach to postbiblical Jewish history was much easier to sustain. Chaim Bez's *Yidn amol* (*Jews in the Past*), a text and workbook on Jewish history from the Babylonian exile to the Bar Kochba uprising, offered a quasi-Bundist reading of Jewish history. It began with an excursus on the Jews as a worldwide nation, for whom dispersion was a historical norm rather than an anomaly. The opening section also stressed that Jewish life had undergone many changes throughout the centuries: economically (from agriculture to commerce and later crafts), socially (from rural life to cities), and culturally (from one language to another and one worldview to another) as Jews interacted with different peoples. Thus, from the very outset, *Yidn amol* disassociated itself from Zionist and religious views on the centrality of the land of Israel, Judaism, and Hebrew in the Jewish historical experience.[22]

The textbook favored social and political history over cultural and religious history in its narrative. It did not discuss the development of the oral law, rabbinic literature, or the ancient synagogue. Religious divisions in ancient Jewry were presented in secular, cultural terms. The Hellenists abandoned the Jewish language, did not celebrate Jewish holidays, admired all that was Greek, and were not perturbed by Greek persecution of the Jews. They were, in short, portrayed as the ancient prototypes of "assimilationists." *Yidn amol* depicted the Maccabean revolt as a struggle for freedom against foreign imperial rule and brutal political oppression, without reference to the religious edicts of Antiochus.

The clash between the Pharisees and Sadducees was presented in Marxist, class-based terms. The Pharisees were "a people's party which expressed the moods of the masses. . . . The Sadducees were the party of the rulers, the money-men and the landowners." Whereas the Pharisees opposed war, aggression, and imposing Judaism on vanquished peoples, the Sadducees sought to conquer the port cities on the coast in order to advance their economic interests. There was no mention of religious differences between the two groups in *Yidn amol*, other than with regard to the doctrine of the afterlife. The latter was explained as an article of faith developed by the poor masses, which gave them comfort in their suffering, and which was adopted by the Pharisees. The Sadducees, who were wealthy, had no need for such a doctrine. While the Pharisees were always ready to ameliorate old, harsh laws, the Sadducees were very strict. "The strictness of the Saducean judges was simply a means to punish harshly the dissatisfied members of the people." In short, the political and social divides of late Imperial Russia were transposed onto ancient Judea.[23]

Yidn amol did not include a section on the sages of the Mishnah or legends about individual sages (with the exception of Hillel). The teaching of legends under the rubric of history was apparently restricted to the Bible, which was taught to younger children. Interestingly enough, the book did have an extensive, and sympathetic, chapter on Jesus of Nazareth.

Jewish Holidays

As noted earlier, beyond the formal curriculum, Jewish holiday celebrations remained an issue for the secular Yiddish schools. The first conference of

Workmen's Circle schools, held in 1920, resolved that the following holidays be observed:

> Passover—as the liberation holiday of the Jews, Lag Ba'omer—in commemoration of the struggle of Bar Kokhba and Rabbi Akiva, May 1st—as the holiday of workers' brotherhood and world peace, Chanukah—as the holiday of liberation from Greek oppression, March 8th—the holiday of the workers' struggle for liberation, Purim—as a children's holiday (costumes, *shalakh-manos* and other forms of entertainment), 4th of July—the liberation of America, February 12th (Lincoln's birthday)—the liberation of the Negroes, Russian revolution—the conference leaves the choice of day to the individual school [February or October], Sukkos—one day.
>
> The celebration of Shavuos as a nature-holiday was rejected by the conference, twelve votes vs. eleven.[24]

This list was noteworthy not only for its mixture of Jewish, socialist, and American holidays, but also for its selections and deletions. As for the Jewish holidays, the notable absences were first, the high holidays, Rosh Hashanah, and Yom Kippur. The latter were presumably considered to be overtly religious, with their themes of divine judgment and repentance. Second, Simhas Torah and Shavuos, with their focus on the Torah, were excluded. The traditional day of mourning for the destruction of the Temple, Tishah B'av, was also absent.[25]

Perhaps a more basic, and probably unconscious, omission was the celebration or observance of the Sabbath. Indeed, most Workmen's Circle and Sholem Aleichem schools in the 1920s and 1930s held classes on Saturdays and did not mark the Sabbath in any way.[26]

While Jewish holidays were not a formal subject in the curriculum, time was set aside both to teach about them and to celebrate them. In the classroom, the holidays were largely taught "from a cultural historical perspective." This meant that the teacher told the children how the holiday had been celebrated *in the past*. He or she described the stories and legends, preparations, rituals, liturgical texts, and customs traditionally associated with the holiday. Then the teacher could, if he or she desired, mention the critical scientific view of the holiday, which cast some doubt on the historicity of the events it commemorated, or which placed the holiday itself in the context of Ancient Near Eastern cultures. In either case, the teacher drew the conclusion, either explicitly or obliquely, that while the holiday's religious rituals were no longer applicable, there was great Jewish-national and/or social significance to the idea of the holiday.[27]

In the Farband schools, the critical, scholarly view on the holidays was not presented as a counterweight to the traditional one. Instead, the Jewish national aspects of the holidays were accentuated. The Farband schools were, after all, socialist-Zionist in orientation, and stressed the holiday's relationship to the land of Israel and Jewish national sovereignty, something the Workmen's Circle and

Sholem Aleichem schools did not and could not do. Nevertheless, in describing rituals, the approach was "cultural historical." As Entin explained:

> One might say that while we do not caution our children to "keep the Sabbath day," we do teach them quite well to "remember the Sabbath day." We do not study the laws of Sabbath with young children, but we do instill in them a sense of the beauty and holiness of the Sabbath.
>
> We are Jewish nationalists, and we therefore explain to the children the national significance of the Jewish holidays, and we celebrate them accordingly. But we do not conceal from the children how Jews in the past, and the religious Jews today, conceive of and observe the Jewish holidays.[28]

Talking *about* the rituals of the holidays in the past tense rather than performing the rituals themselves was the central feature of holiday instruction in all three Yiddish school systems. Yiddish educator Yudl Mark later scoffingly dubbed this approach "museum Judaism."[29] The Workmen's Circle took the most restrictive approach—one could talk about rituals, but not display or demonstrate them. A teacher who brought a *lulav* and *esrog* into class was reprimanded by his colleagues. The Farband schools, on the other hand, were the most expansive in offering a "cultural historical" exposition of religious rituals, and introduced a separate subject into the school curriculum of the middle grades called "Jewish ethnology." Jewish ethnology was the curricular framework for teaching about Jewish religious rituals, texts, and concepts. The academic-sounding title intended to make clear that the attitude was one of dispassionate distance and not religious belief.[30]

Holiday celebrations in the Yiddish schools usually took the form of school assemblies, often with parents in attendance, at which the children presented a literary, dramatic, and musical program.[31] Yiddish poems with holiday themes were recited, and poets such as Avrom Reisin, Y. Goichberg, and others wrote holiday pieces especially for the schools. Holiday material was gleaned from the pages of the two main Yiddish children's magazines, *Kinder tsaytung* and *Kinder zhurnal*, published respectively by the Workmen's Circle and Sholem Aleichem schools. Dramatic presentations were common. In practice, the main holiday celebrations were Chanukah, Purim, and Passover, and in many Yiddish schools, they were the only Jewish holidays celebrated.[32]

There were, however, clear boundaries to the school celebrations. Blessings, prayers, and liturgical texts were not recited. Indeed, Chanukah candles were not lit in Workmen's Circle and Sholem Aleichem schools in the 1920s and 1930s, because this was considered a religious ritual (with a blessing) which commemorated an ostensible divine miracle.[33]

The Shift toward Tradition: 1938–1947

The attitude of Yiddish educators toward Jewish religious tradition began to shift in the late 1930s. The growing sympathy toward tradition was, to a large extent, part of a broader trend among Yiddish intellectuals who became disillusioned with European civilization as the brutality of German Nazism and Soviet Communism became evident, and as they observed the indifference of the West toward the plight of European Jewry. In 1938, Jacob Glatstein published his well-known poem *"A gute nacht velt,"* with its putative call for a return to the ghetto, and a group of Yiddishist intellectuals headed by Elias Tcherikower published the journal *Oyfn sheydveg*, which renounced socialism, emancipation, and secularism as false gods. The turn to tradition among Yiddish educators was, consciously and unconsciously, an expression of their rapprochement with the rest of Jewry—with the nonsocialist and non-Yiddishist Jews—in a time of common peril. As such, it gained even greater momentum during the years of World War II and the European Jewish catastrophe.

Other, more internal forces underlay the shift toward tradition in the Yiddish schools. Foremost was the changed complexion of the schools' student population in the quarter century since their establishment. In the 1910s, Jewish religious traditions were strong in the students' homes and immigrant neighborhoods. The children came to the Yiddish school with a certain pool of traditional Jewish religious ideas and knowledge, which the schools sought to either combat, transform, or supplement. But by the late 1930s, educators noticed that the children in the Yiddish schools were clean slates when it came to knowledge about traditional Judaism. Whatever knowledge the schools did not provide, the children would simply not have. The sight of graduates who could speak Yiddish, but knew virtually nothing about Judaism and felt no connection to it, led some educators to revise their thinking.[34]

The intellectual leader of the movement for traditionalism was Leybush Lehrer (1887–1964), the director of the Sholem Aleichem Institute, as well as the head of YIVO's psychological-pedagogical section. In a series of books and articles, lectures, and meetings, Lehrer argued that Judaism was not a religion at all, but a national cultural system of symbols, collective memories, and rituals. Lehrer contended that the meaning and value of Jewish customs was social-psychological rather than rational, and that many of them could be practiced, even without any belief in God.[35] While not supporting all of Lehrer's theories, Yudl Mark (1897–1975), the Consultant for Yiddish schools at the Jewish Education Committee of New York and editor of the Yiddish school's pedagogical bulletin, also advocated greater tradition in the schools. The Sholem Aleichem schools led the trend toward tradition, and the larger network of Workmen's Circle schools followed, albeit more slowly and cautiously.

In 1938, the conference of the Sholem Aleichem school teachers resolved to introduce Chumash as a separate subject, to celebrate *all* Jewish holidays, and instill a positive attitude toward Jewish customs and practices.[36]

In 1940 *Khumesh far kinder* (*Chumash for Children*), compiled by Shloyme Simon (1895–1970) and based on the Yehoash Yiddish translation of the Bible, was published. This 260-page book was intended for somewhat older children than the targeted audience of Levin's *Mayses un legendes fun der yidisher geshichte*. Although abbreviated and linguistically edited, it was in many ways a traditional Chumash. It did not attempt to read God out of the text: It opened with "In the beginning God created the heaven and the earth," the Ten Commandments were presented in their original form, as was the text of *shema yisrael*. Narrative still overwhelmingly outweighed law, with Genesis occupying half of *Khumesh far kinder*, but a crucial twenty-three-page section gave a digest of biblical laws by subject: fair justice, damages, supporting the weak, loans, slaves, death penalty, cities of refuge, war, the king, *shemita*, *yovel*, agriculture, Sabbath, holidays, idolatry, and everyday behavior.[37]

A Sabbath ritual began to appear in the Sholem Aleichem schools at about this time—a Friday afternoon school assembly, or a Friday night program for parents (with occasional student participation) called an *oyneg shabbes* (joy of the Sabbath). First introduced by Lehrer at the Sholem Aleichem Institute's summer camp, Camp Boiberik, the following ceremony was adopted in the Sholem Aleichem schools: candles were lit (without a blessing) and the traditional hymn "Sholem Aleichem" and Yiddish Sabbath songs were sung in unison. Selections from the weekly Torah portion were read (in Yiddish). An intermission for refreshments and conversation followed. After the break, selections from Yiddish literature were recited. The Yiddishist *oyneg shabbes* was thus a mix of traditional religious ritual (candles, the hymn "Sholem Aleichem"), communal singing, and a literary program. While some schools charged an admission fee to the parent *oyneg shabbes*, teacher Shloyme Simon noted in his memoirs that "we can say with complete confidence that there was often more religious feeling in our *oyneg shabbes*, than in many synagogues during their *davening*."[38]

Similarly, holiday celebrations also developed away from the concert or literary-dramatic program in the direction of public ceremonial ritual. In 1940, the Sholem Aleichem Institute published *Undzer hagode* (*Our Hagadah*), a Yiddish language hagadah compiled by a committee of educators, which became the basis for the Workmen's Circle's *A naye hagode shel peysekh* (*A New Hagadah for Passover*), published in 1946. Here, as in the *oyneg shabbes*, the syncretism of religious ritual and secular culture was on display.

In the Workmen's Circle's *A naye hagode shel peysekh*, much of the structure of the traditional hagadah was maintained. It opened with the raising of a cup of wine (and reciting a poem instead of a blessing), and ended with the singing of "Had gadya." Many sections were identified by Hebrew names (*ke-ha lahma anya, avadim hayinu*), although the text itself was entirely in Yiddish. The hagadah featured the traditional four questions, a rhymed dramatic reading based on the four sons, and the traditional passages on *matzah* and *maror*.

But otherwise, this hagadah was different from all others. It consisted largely of Yiddish poems on the Egyptian slavery and Moses, and of select biblical passages (not from the hagadah) on the Exodus. God was not mentioned even once in its account of the story of the Exodus. (He did make a brief appearance toward the end, in the text of Isaiah's vision on the end of days.) The tension between tradition and secularism reached its culmination in the section entitled *"ve-hi she-amdah."* In the traditional *hagadah*, it read:

> And it [the promise from God to Abraham] stood by our ancestors and us. For more than one has risen up against us to destroy us. For in every generation they rise up against us to destroy us. But the Holy One, blessed by He, saves us from their hand.

In *A naye hagode shel peysekh*, the passage was rendered quite differently:

> LEADER: And what stood by us in all generations, our ancestors and us? For more than one has risen up against us to annihilate us. For in every generation, enemies arise to destroy us! What stood by us in all generations?

> ALL ASSEMBLED: Our faith in truth and justice, and our courage to dedicate ourselves to all that is holy and dear—rescue us from the hands of our enemies.[39]

The Workmen's Circle hagadah also negotiated carefully between the themes of Jewish national liberation and universal liberation. While it included the traditional passage of anger against the Gentiles, "pour out thy wrath," and a short song on Elijah the prophet coming "with Messiah the son of David," it did not offer the traditional concluding exclamation "next year in Jerusalem" or any other reference to a return to the Land of Israel. Instead, *A naye hagode shel peysekh* inserted poems by S. An-sky and A. Liessin that celebrated the Jews' moral passion, derived from centuries of wandering and suffering, to build a better world. The final poem in the booklet, before *"had gadya,"* was Avrom Reisin's paean to world peace, *"Dos naye lid"* (The New Song):

> Un zol vi vayt, nokh zayn di tsayt
> fun libe un fun sholem;
> dokh kumen vet, tsi fri tsi shpet
> di tsayt—es iz keyn kholem.[40]

As part of this turn toward tradition, the Sholem Aleichem schools, which had initially been adamantly Yiddishist and anti-Hebrew (see their 1927 declaration of principles above), resolved in 1940 to introduce the teaching of Hebrew into their elementary schools. Despite pedagogical objections that teaching two languages simultaneously would be too difficult and despite ideological objections to creeping Zionism, the argument which won the day was that without Hebrew the children would be deprived of the possibility of ever using a siddur.[41]

The reevaluation of tradition in the 1940s also made an impact on the central subject in the Yiddish schools—Yiddish language and literature. The canon of literary texts taught in the higher grades of the Yiddish elementary schools and in Yiddish *mitlshuls* shifted quite sharply. One need only compare two anthologies prepared by the same authors—Chaim Bez and Zalmen Efroikin's *Undzer vort* (Our Word) of 1935 with their *Dos yidishe vort* (The Jewish Word) of 1947.

The thrust of *Undzer vort* was to integrate the teaching of socialism and Yiddish literature, rather than having them taught as separate subjects. (See the seven goals of the Workmen's Circle schools above.) Parts 1 and 2 of the anthology, entitled "Worker Children" and "Poverty and Struggle," featured Yiddish literary selections on Jewish poverty in the old country and America, strikes, demonstrations, the socialist movement (including the texts of the "International" and the Bundist anthem *"Di shvue"*), and racism in America. Part 3, "War," depicted the horrors of the First World War from the antiwar perspective of American socialism. These three sections occupied 70 percent of the anthology. Judaism was relegated to the back of the book, to the sections called "The Jewish Child in the Old Country" and "Stories and Legends." Stories on the Jewish holidays were presented in the section on the foreign and far-off old country past, whereas the immediate past and present were occupied with social struggle.[42]

Twelve years later, Bez and Efroikin's was an entirely different kind of literary anthology. Social struggle shrank to a theme inside the section entitled "America." The major rubrics were those on the Jewish holidays and collections of aggadic tales in sections called "From the Old Well." There were separate sections for three major writers—Sholem Aleichem, Avrom Reisin, and I. L. Peretz—and a section on the Holocaust. Instead of the biographies of socialist leaders (Eugene V. Debs, Ferdinand Lassalle, Karl Marx) found in *Undzer vort, Dos yidishe vort* offered biographies of medieval rabbis (Rashi, Yehudah Ha-Levy, Judah the Pious, and Meir of Rothenburg).

The enhanced position of Sholem Aleichem and Peretz was the main revision in the Yiddish literary canon for young readers. Sholem Aleichem's stories were used to portray the shtetl, the heder, and Sabbath and Jewish holidays; Peretz's *folkstimleche geshichtn* and *khsidish* were used to present religious and Hasidic themes in artistic form. Whereas these two classic authors occupied 12 percent of *Undzer vort* (fifty-five pages), their selections constituted 25 percent of *Dos yidishe vort* (eighty pages). The reevaluation of the religious tradition and longing for the destroyed world of East European Jewry went hand in hand and together led educators to place greater emphasis on Sholem Aleichem and Peretz. Youth editions of two of Sholem Aleichem's major works, *Funem yarid* and *Motl peysi dem khazns*, appeared for the first time in New York in 1940 and 1946, during the period of increased traditionalism. And the first anthology of Peretz's works for Yiddish mitlshuls appeared somewhat later, in 1952.[43]

Secular Jewish Identity in the Yiddish Schools

While the American Yiddish schools embraced the idea of secular Jewish identity, there was considerable disagreement, internal tension, and ambivalence when it came to concretizing this idea in a school curriculum. The Workmen's Circle and Sholem Aleichem schools, while opposed to religion, hedged when it came to conducting the radical surgery of excising the religious out of Jewish identity altogether. Secular rationales—sometimes quite artificially contrived—were found to justify the telling of Bible tales, the celebration of Jewish holidays, and the teaching of (or rather *about*) Jewish religious customs. Only in the Soviet Union and among

American Jewish Communists was the idea of a new, fully secular Jewish identity based on Yiddish taken to its logical conclusion.

The one firm antireligious taboo in the American Yiddish schools of the 1920s and 1930s was God—speaking of God as a living, acting being or reciting prayers and blessings. The Farband schools overcame even the ban on God by adopting a "cultural historical" and "ethnological" approach to religious and liturgical texts, which were studied as part of the national literary heritage and for the sake of national unity with religious Jews. The Sholem Aleichem schools adopted a similar approach beginning in 1938.

Given the ideological inconsistencies and ambiguities exhibited by the Yiddish secular educators, it is useful to understand their conflicted relationship to religious tradition not only as an expression of their ideological positions but also as a product of their life experiences. Most Yiddish educators belonged to a single generation. They were born in Eastern Europe toward the end of the nineteenth century and went to traditional heders. They broke with religious faith and observance and joined a Jewish or Russian socialist movement around the time of the 1905 revolution and emigrated to America (or migrated to an East European metropolis) by 1917. Central to their life story was their rebellion against their politically and culturally conservative parents, and against the older generation of their town or street (and later on, their geographic separation from their parents and native communities). Although they identified themselves as social radicals, they had not played an important role in political events or in the labor movement per se. Their initiation into radicalism was the Sabbath day when they joined a gathering of young men and women in the forest outside of town, or in a secluded apartment, and lit a cigarette, talked with members of the opposite sex, exchanged revolutionary pamphlets, and sang revolutionary songs. In short, their rebellion against their religious upbringing was integral to their coming of age. Indeed, their rebellion against religion was a much more vivid and dramatic experience than their adoption of radical political and social ideas.

Years later, in confronting the question of religion and secularism, these Yiddish educators were unconsciously revisiting the most important event in their lives, the time when they broke with their parents. Leybush Lehrer was the only Yiddish educator to openly state that a great collective psychodrama was at work in the secularism of Yiddish educators. Writing in the late 1930s and 1940s, Lehrer called on his fellow Yiddish educators to make their peace with their dead parents and with their childhood communities, which were being destroyed by the Nazis.[44] Writing as a polemicist on behalf of more tradition, Lehrer failed to notice that the Yiddish educators' ambivalence toward their parents and their childhood religious upbringing was greater than for what he gave them credit. They could not part with the stories of the Chumash, even as they threw God out of the text; they could not resist talking about the rituals of the holidays, even as they dismissed them as mere "cultural history." Nevertheless, Lehrer had put his finger on the complex interplay between the ideology and the social psychology of a generation of East European Jews that lay at the heart of Yiddish secularism.

NOTES

1. On the secularizing role of nationalism, see Anthony D. Smith, *National Identity* (Reno: University of Nevada Press, 1991). On the difficult relations between Zionism and Jewish religious orthodoxy, see Ehud Luz, *Parallels Meet: Religion and Nationalism in the Early Zionist Movement* (Philadelphia: Jewish Publication Society of America, 1988), and Gideon Shimoni, *Zionist Ideology* (Hanover: University Press of New England, Brandeis University Press, 1995).

2. This is the subject of my book, *The Rise of Modern Yiddish Culture: Historical Studies* (Pittsburgh: University of Pittsburgh Press, 2006).

3. *Di ershte yidishe shprach-konferents* (Vilna: YIVO, 1931), 86–87.

4. "Vi zol men dertsien undzere kinder do in land?" *Di varhayt*, April 1909, reprinted in *Yoel Entin: Gezamlte shriftn* (New York, 1960), 1:1–4.

5. "Di bildung fun yidishe zin un tekhter," *Di varhayt*, January 13, 1910, reprinted in *Yoel Entin: Gezamlte shriftn*, 10–14.

6. Tzivyon, "Der arbeter ring un zayne kultur-oyfgaben," in *Der arbeter ring: Zamel buch—suvenir* (New York: Workmen's Circle, 1910), 167–187, portions of which are cited by Sh. Niger, *In kamf far a nayer dertsiung* (New York: Educational Department of the Workmen's Circle, 1940), 45–46.

7. Herman Frank, "Di yidishe shul bavegung iber der velt," *Shul-almanach: Di yidishe moderne shul oyf der velt* (Philadelphia: Central Committee of Workman's Circle Schools, 1935), 348–364; see figures on 353, 356; Israel S. Chipkin, *Twenty-Five Years of Jewish Education in the United States* (New York: Jewish Education Association of New York City, 1937), 37, 117.

8. F. Gelibter, "Di Arbeter Ring shuln," *Shul-almanach*, 27–66, see especially 38–39, 57; Frank, "Di yidishe shul."

9. L. Shpizman, "Etapn in der geshichte fun der tsionistisher arbeter-bavegung in di fareynikte shtatn," *Geshichte fun der tsionistisherarbeter-bavegung in amerike* (New York: Yiddisher Kemfer, 1955), 2:408.

10. "Printsipn fun sholem aleichem folk institut (1927)," in *Der derech fun sholem aleichem institute*, ed. Sh. Gutman (New York: Sholem Aleichem Folk Institute, 1972), 117–118.

11. Niger, *In kamf far a nayer dertsiung*, 108. The goals are included in the brochure *Di yidishe arbeiter ring shul*, ed. Jacob (Yankev) Levin (New York: Educational Department of the Workmen's Circle, 1920), 8.

12. *Der yidisher arbeiter ring shul*, 7.

13. The full text of the declaration is printed in *Shul-almanach* (Philadelphia, 1935), 150–151. The IWO schools, which offered antireligious instruction in the 1930s, are not examined in this essay.

14. The exceptions to this rule were the Farband schools, which did teach Bible as a separate subject.

15. See Yudl Mark's evaluation of *Der onfanger* and other textbooks in "Di lernbicher far der yidisher shul in amerike," in *Shul-pinkes*, ed. Shloime Bercovich, M. Brownstone, Yudel Mark, and Chaim Pomerantz (Chicago: Sholem Aleichem Folk Institute, 1948), 260–335.

16. Chaim Lieberman, *Di yidishe religion in der natsyonal-radikaler dertsiung* (New York, 1915), 28.

17. Ch. Be-ni (Bezprozvany), "Nit ratsionalizirn nor primitivizirn," *Shul un lerer*, no. 1 (January–March 1927): 32–36.

18. Jacob (Yankev) Levin, *Mayses un legendes fun der yidisher geshichte*, vol. 1, *Fun Avrom's geburt biz Moyshe's toyt* (*From the birth of Abraham until the death of Moses*) (New York: "Yidishe Shul"/Hebrew Publishing Co., 1928), 4–5.

19. Levin, *Mayses un legendes*, 16, 76, 85.

20. Ibid., 90–91. The seventh commandment against adultery was also changed to read "You shall not act spoiled [*tselozn*]."

21. Ibid., vii–viii.

22. Ch. Bez (Bezprozvany), *Yidn amol* (New York: Max N. Meisel, 1932), 9–14.

23. Ibid., 104–122.

24. Niger, *In kamf far a nayer dertsiung*, 115–116.

25. The omission of certain American holidays was also telling: There was no Washington's Birthday (perhaps because the United States was a capitalist nation) and no Memorial Day (the Workmen's Circle had opposed American entry into the Great War).

26. See the memoirs of teachers Shloyme Berkovitch and Aaron Glants-Leyeles in *Shul-pinkes*, 187–188, 213.

27. See the poignant description by Berkovitch in Ibid, 180–186.

28. Joel Entin, "Our New Jewish Education," in *Gezamlte shriftn*, 90–91.

29. Yudl Mark, "Judaism and Secularism in and around Our Schools," *Shul-pinkes*, 9–68, quote from p. 22.

30. Entin, *Gezamlte shriftn*, 68.

31. *Unzer shul* 2 (January 1932): 31; *Unzer shul* 2 (February 1932): 31. *Unzer shul* was the monthly journal of the Education Department of the Workmen's Circle.

32. In 1935, the pedagogical bulletin of the Sholem Aleichem schools published bibliographies of available Yiddish holiday plays for Chanukah, Purim, Passover, Shavuot, Lag Ba'omer—and May 1. "Der inhalt fun di biz itstike pedagogishe buletenen," *Pedagogisher buleten*, no. 1 (November 1941): 4.

33. Yudl Mark, *Shul-pinkes*, 16–17.

34. See, for example, Leybush Lehrer, "Veltleche yidishkayt" (1937), in *Azoy zenen yidn* (New York: Matones, 1959), 303–312, and his penetrating analysis of the causes leading to a reevaluation of Jewish tradition in Yiddishist circles in "Got, un azoy vayter" (1942), in *Azoy zenen yidn*, 313–318.

35. Leibush Lehrer, *Yidishkayt un andere problemen* (New York: Matones, 1940); idem, *Azoy zenen yidn; Fun dor tsu dor* (New York: Matones, 1959). In English, see his *Symbol and Substance*, with an appreciation by Aaron Zeitlin and translated by Lucy S. Dawidowicz (New York, 1965).

36. Yudl Mark, "Toward a History of the Sholem Aleichem Folk Institute," in *Der derech fun sholem aleychem institute*, 17–30. A year later, in 1939, the Workmen's Circle schools adopted a resolution urging the composition of uniform ritual ceremonies to celebrate Passover, Purim, Chanukah, and May 1 in the schools; Niger, *In kamf far a nayer dertsiung*, 135.

37. Shloyme Simon, comp., *Khumesh far kinder loyt yehoash*, ed. Yudl Mark (New York: Matones, 1940).

38. Shloyme Simon, "The History of One Sholem Aleichem School," *Der derech fun sholem aleychem folk institute*, 73–74. In the postwar years, the recitation of kiddush (in Hebrew) was introduced.

39. I. J. Schwartz, H. Novak, and J. Levin, comps., *A naye hagode shel peysekh* (New York: Educational Committee of the Workmen's Circle, 1946), 11 (not paginated).

40. *A naye hagode shel peysekh*, 12–13, 18–19, 24.

41. Mark, "Toward of History," 19–20.

42. Z. Efroikin and Chaim Bez, *Undzer vort, literarish-gezelshaftlekhe khrestomatye* (New York: Max N. Meisel, 1935).

43. Chaim Bez and Zalmen Efroikin, *Dos yidishe vort: Leyenbukh far der yidisher shul* (New York: Educational Department of the Workmen's Circle, 1947). On Yiddish literature for children and youth in America, see Kh. Sh. Kazhdan's study and bibliography in *Shul-pinkes*, 335–379. The Peretz volume was *Fun Peretz's oytser* (New York: Educational Department of the Workmen's Circle, 1952).

44. See the essays cited in notes 34–35 and Lehrer's group portrait of his generation in *Di tsiln fun kemp boiberik in licht fun zayn geshikhte* (New York, 1962), 7.

6   *Beyond Assimilation*

INTRODUCING SUBJECTIVITY
TO GERMAN-JEWISH HISTORY

SCOTT SPECTOR

In a famous lecture delivered at the World Jewish Congress in Brussels in 1966, Gershom Scholem recalled the history of German Jewish assimilation.[1] It is an astonishing and elegant lecture—piercingly incisive, breathtaking in its synthesis. It tracks the path from the relative autonomy and integrity of a pre-emancipated Jewish community in Germany through the ambitious, idealistic, but fatally wrongheaded project of assimilation. This outline has come in the meantime to be known as the orthodox view of German Jewish history. There are many brilliant insights in Scholem's lecture "Germans and Jews," which also has its share of outrageous and untenable ones; but one of the former that has been little noted is his early disclaimer that his own title forced him onto what he understood to be both epistemologically and ontologically shaky ground. "For not all 'Germans' are Germans and not all 'Jews' are Jews" is the elegant truth forgotten by those citing the lecture, by the historiography it inspired, and, conveniently, by Scholem himself through the rest of his address.[2] To speak of "the Germans" and "the Jews" in this period—the scare quotes are Scholem's—is to descend into the unsustainable realm of generalization worthy of the coarsest anti-Semites. The philosophically trained Scholem did not bring himself to say that the embrace of such "questionable categories" is justified, but rather that one's ability properly to differentiate rather than to use gross categories has been hampered by the memory of a cataclysm executed, after all, by people who saw no use of any such distinctions. This was a sympathetic claim, perhaps, but not an intellectually persuasive one, and one has the sense that Scholem, too, is embarrassed by the lack of rigor.

It seems that to remember assimilation in the way Scholem would like—a way, that is, that would make sense of the catastrophe of German Judaism as well as the hope of the fledgling State of Israel—he had to forget the complex ways in which individual consciousnesses brushed against the grain of abstract collectivities. The poignancy of this gesture derives from the fact that Scholem was speaking not only as an exponent of the first generation of the orthodox school of German Jewish historiography, but also as a member of the last generation of its objects of study. When he spoke of the "emotional confusion of the German Jews between 1820 and 1920"—a confusion, he argued, essential to understand if one is to grasp the fraught phenomenon of "German Jewishness"—the listeners were aware that Scholem was one of those Jews.[3] He was both subject and object of the analysis he offered, and this is the key of a rhetoric which slipped easily from categories of identity at play for assimilated Jews and those available to post-Holocaust historians.

As historian and historical object, Scholem offers an extreme case of a tendency I want to call attention to, and that is the way that histories of German Jewish culture suffer from an excess of empathy with their subjects. By an excess of empathy, I am referring to the ways in which scholars have adopted an assumption of a problematic which might be called the "German Jewish identity crisis," as well as the categories of identity and culture that undergirded it. This empathy, and these assumptions, have been the source of a scholarly production that by any relative measure must be considered large in proportion to the size of the demographic group it focuses upon; furthermore, it has been an interesting literature, and even a critical one. But the limitations of these approaches, I want to argue somewhat polemically, have led to a kind of impasse.[4] That impasse is in provocative ways parallel to the situation of German-speaking Jewish culture producers in the first third of the twentieth century.

As a strategy to get beyond what has been described as a dead end in the historiography, and to open up questions obscured by it so far, the suggestion of this essay is that we begin by forgetting what Scholem chose to remember, and to remember, and expand upon, that which he invoked only to forget. To do so, it will be necessary to speak both of the historiography and of its subjects. "Assimilation" is a problematic both have shared. It is one, however, that needs to be subjected to critical analysis, whereas the categories and concepts sustaining it have with few exceptions been taken for granted by historical subjects as well as historians. Chief among these is a notion of identity inherent in the dominant image of assimilation.

That model of identity is one that assumes a spectrum of possible identifications running from the imagined pole of absolute Jewish identification (what Franz Rosenzweig called "dissimilation") at one end to complete appropriation of German identity at the other.[5] This spectral model was always meant to be flexible in particular ways, not least because the notions of German and Jewish identification were open: "total" assimilation might mean baptism and intermarriage, or else the retention but absolute privatization of Jewish religious adherence; the most extreme pole of Jewish identification could likewise be understood in terms of religious orthodoxy, secular Jewish nationalism, Jewish spiritualism, or some other cultural and intellectual engagement specifically and primarily identified as Jewish. It is often (if not always) assumed that these poles are ideal types, and that actual individuals find themselves somewhere along the spectrum in various combinations. The model hence does seem to offer room for some degree of complexity; it may even have developed as a more nuanced alternative to a simple binary of assimilated and nonassimilated.

Yet, even seen "ideal-typologically," the spectrum of relative assimilation is an inadequate model, and a deceptive one. As the late Amos Funkenstein showed in his 1995 essay "The Dialectics of Assimilation," the long-lived distinctions between "spontaneous" and "acquired" cultural character, accidental adaptation and essential adoption, or stable essence and assimilatory appearance, are all themselves powerfully ideological instruments of segregation, rather than descriptors of a cultural condition. While cultural adaptation has been uneven over time and space, it has nonetheless been universal; what is taken as authentic or traditional is often another example of dynamic interaction with external cultures.[6]

Scholem knew too much to deny this, but he justified his narrative by distinguishing the German influence on the pre-emancipated Jewish community through a "barely conscious process of osmosis" from the indelicate, programmatic force of self-conscious assimilation.[7] The latter process would come to produce a "sinister and dangerous dialectic" whereby Jews were both required to surrender their group identity and despised for the willingness and ability to do so.[8] This analysis of the double-bind of the emancipation-assimilation pact is standard fare in the tradition of historiography represented by Scholem's talk. It is therefore all the more surprising that it is Scholem who points out what in his words "is now often forgotten"—that is, that "assimilating" Jews in practice wished to retain Judaism in some form. While assimilation as an abstraction (or even as a social process promoted by a minority of community leaders) theoretically moves without equivocation toward the dissolution of Jewishness and total absorption of gentile German culture, individuals held on to their Jewishness "as a kind of heritage, as a creed, as an element unknowable and undefinable, yet clearly present in their consciousness."[9] On one level, we are confronted here with the paradox of the secular Jew, who, as Yosef Hayim Yerushalmi reminds us, is both a stranger and a more diverse sort of creature than the "blandly generic term" would seem to indicate.[10] On another level, Scholem's observation brings into view what his own focus on assimilation as a paradigm, a program, and a seemingly inexorable historical process obscures. In their own lives and consciousnesses, actually existing Jews did not experience their relationship to Jewishness (or to Germanness, for that matter) in the zero-sum-game terms of the politics of assimilation. Yerushalmi, taking a skeptical stance toward the uneven and inconsistent positions of these men and women who hovered in an "undefined yet somehow real Jewishness," diagnoses their Judaism/Jewishness as contentless, "pure subjectivity."[11]

Scholem's and Yerushalmi's critiques of the secular Jew, especially the assimilated German Jew, follow familiar lines, identifying the surrender of an integral Judaism as the root of an insoluble confusion, neurosis, or malaise.[12] What has been lacking in the study of secular Judaism has been a sustained analysis of these "troubled subjectivities," rather than the wholesale pathologization of the secular condition. Such a turn to interiority could help answer questions about modern German Jewish cultural production that remain unasked by the paradigms of assimilation in use in the orthodox historiography, as well as by its most articulate critics.

A prominent revision of the orthodox school is represented by the provocative work of David Sorkin, who in several influential contributions has also sought to leave behind the governing concepts of emancipation and assimilation.[13] Working principally in the formative period of German Jewish assimilation, Sorkin has argued that an internal "ideology of emancipation" was the motor of the creation of a German Jewish "subculture" that was by its nature invisible to its own adherents, who only imagined the process they were undergoing as one of abandonment of community. This argument, as Samuel Moyn points out, "sublates" or historicizes the orthodox view, rather than repudiating it—it lifts the veil that assimilation held before its own eyes but preserves the integrity of the categories upon which the ideology of assimilation depended.[14] Sorkin's explanation remains so profoundly structuralist as to leave little room for any subjectivity, or indeed to allow for self-consciousness at any level. As Anthony LaVopa points out, "the irony Sorkin finds is structural, not 'subjective.' "[15] Sorkin is explicit about this distinction at several points, arguing that "the community's invisibility [to itself] thus resulted from a disparity between ideology and social reality. Invisibility was a structural and not a subjective problem."[16] In turning to the concept of ideology, Sorkin relies on an assumption of totalized false consciousness. He recognizes that ideology requires both "a coherent system of ideas and symbols" and also an institutional foundation, but perhaps understandably shies from what I have described elsewhere as the difficult but all important third level of ideology: the contradictory ways in which subjects understand themselves within ideological systems, or how they are "given identity."[17]

Post-Assimilationist Reflections

When the novelist Jakob Wassermann published his memoir, *My Life as German and Jew*, he seemed to be making a new claim for the possibilities and impossibilities contained within the categories "German" and "Jew."[18] Resisting the notion of separate and even opposing racial, ethnic, or cultural identities, his own life story and the aesthetic path of his works was laid out so as to avoid even the term "German Jewish," and to offer an alternative to symbiosis. Instead, Wassermann and his work were at one and the same time "German" and "Jewish," at odds with themselves, and this dialectical rather than dialogical relationship was central to the production of literature.[19] Wassermann's struggle is depicted in his memoir not as the highly individuated experience of an artist with a dual identity, but as a universal condition; his descriptions of German identity sound more like discussions of the "Jewish question"; just as the tangential existence of the struggling writer is merely a sharpened reflection of everyday human existence.[20]

While this memoir is a remarkable document for all of these border crossings, coming as they do just when famously essentialized notions of German Jewish difference were being solidified, it also participates in these discursive processes. Identity in his book is forged by blood and by climate, by insuperable tradition and by inassimilable foreign culture. Wassermann presents himself as German *and* Jew because there are such things as Germans and Jews, collective identities that define their members as similar to all others within and distinct from all those outside of them. Like the anti-Semitic and Zionist challenges to the Jewish participation in German-language culture, Wassermann takes for granted the status of his own self and work as question or problem. For all of its complexity, *My Life as German and Jew*, by virtue of its very appearance, is at the crest of the tide, rather than riding against it. While Gershom Scholem identified Wassermann's text as a "cry into the emptiness, one which recognized itself as such,"[21] calling Scholem to the substance of Palestine, it shares with Scholem's critiques a universe of terms.[22] Within this universe, one could champion or oppose "assimilation," but doing either was a silent concession to the existence of a German Jewish "identity crisis."

The generations I am focusing on in this essay are those that could be called "post-assimilationist." Steven Aschheim has used the term more narrowly to denote those German Jews of the turn of the century, and forward, "second generation" Jewish nationalists and Zionists in particular.[23] But the fact is that whether Zionist or "liberal," the Jews of the generation coming of age at the turn of the century and those after it were all in some sense "post-assimilationist" in that the classical liberal-assimilationist position, with its optimism about a potentially unproblematic fusion of Jewish (private) identities and German public ones, was no longer available. As anyone who has attended to primary sources of the period will testify, liberal and Zionist Jews as well as their non-Jewish counterparts from the Socialists to the anti-Semites had all come to argue their different positions from a shared universe of terms that suggested a different set of assumptions than those of "official" assimilationist discourse.[24]

Post-Assimilationist Historiography

Post-assimilationism can also productively be applied to our historiographical perspectives. Hence I hope that this essay's title, "Beyond Assimilation," may be taken to refer both to the object of study and to the historiography in question. Like other "post-ist" labels (think of "post-structuralist" or "post-Marxist"), post-assimilationism ought not so much suggest a clearly antagonistic relationship to the ideology of assimilation. To the contrary, it should suggest a position that clearly follows from the failed logic of its predecessor; this succession takes place with both an extreme uneasiness about the conclusions of its forerunner and yet with a dependence on it. Hence, the passage from assimilation to post-assimilation might be presumed to be dialectical rather than merely successive or progressive.

Recent historiographical reviews and debates that are relevant to these lines of inquiry have sought to chart the course away from German Jewish historiography from a literature more or less strictly formed along lines mirroring the ideological alternatives of Jewish identity, namely "national" or Zionist and "liberal" (sometimes "cultural," not to be confused with the designation "liberal" internal to German Judaism).[25] Through their sometime disagreement, a clear consensus among these historian-observers is that the stark dichotomy between these histories, like the oppositional stances of Zionist, religious, and liberal figures, is obsolete.

A serious concern of a particular species plagues modern German Jewish cultural and intellectual history in particular. On the one hand, there is nowhere else in modern history where Jews have contributed so massively and so significantly to the general culture. From Moses Mendelssohn to Marx and from Freud to Einstein, Jewish contributions to secular German thought have been both wide-ranging in scope and profound in impact. Indeed, it is hard to imagine what contemporary civilization would look like had it not been for the cultural products of these and a striking number of other less celebrated but variously remarkable thinkers. On the other hand, historians encounter a stumbling block when seeking to discuss these products as manifestations of European Jewish culture. How is such a contribution to be defined as "Jewish"? What relationship is to be drawn between the religious or ethnic identity of the author and the content of his writing? These core questions, of course, immediately reproduce the debates of the post-assimilationist period through the categories in which they are forced to work. Michael Brenner, in his excellent study of Weimar Jewish culture, avoided this problem by focusing on cultural manifestations that defined themselves specifically within a Jewish cultural sphere.[26] Yet, such a strategy necessarily fails to take into account precisely those works produced by German-speaking Jews that have wielded the greatest cultural influence. Steven Beller's study *Vienna and the Jews* displays the contrary tendency, by surveying the landscape of Viennese secular modernism and identifying it as fundamentally "Jewish."[27] To do so, a historian like Beller must engage in the precise diagnoses of those in the period who counted Jewish artists and writers, broadly in spite of their own relationships to Jewish tradition, knowledge of Jewish sources, or religious practice, and who designated their works as inexorably "Jewish." This logic (which I believe fully merits the generally overused label of "essentialist") marks even the thematically Christian aesthetic work of a Hugo von Hofmannsthal or a Gustav Mahler as something apart from German Christian or secular culture; Marx's universalism and his atheism are products of a Jewish background, and on and on. Scholem, in the "Jews and Germans" lecture, falls into this trap when, once again forgetting his bracketed anti-essentialist remark opening the lecture, he turns to the production of secular "Jews" from Marx and Lasalle to Karl Kraus, Gustav Mahler, and Georg Simmel, arguing that "even in their complete estrangement of their awareness from everything 'Jewish,' something is evident in many of them that was felt to be substantially Jewish by Jews as well as Germans— by everyone except themselves!"[28]

This only goes to show that in the post-assimilationist generation, these questions and the assumptions behind them were shared by many of the subjects in question, not merely anti-Semites, although these were the first to bring the connection of Jewish background and modern German cultural production to the forefront of a sociopolitical discussion. Jewish nationalists and Zionists famously shared many of these assumptions, but so in fact (if in a different way) did liberals from the turn of the century through the Holocaust.[29] Not just for Scholem, but for many of the figures of nineteenth- and twentieth-century Jewish central Europe who would make powerful contributions to secular culture, there was a strong consciousness of Jewishness in some sense, but this identification was troubled by deep ambivalence. That is to say, Jewish identity was not a starting point inherited by these figures, or a stable entity that could be taken for granted, but rather a problematic. In other words, the very same difficulty confronting the cultural historian dealing with these figures haunted their own relationship to Jewishness. While the historiography and its subjects share a certain number of common features, these do not overlap precisely. As the example of Wassermann's memoir shows, many of the questions we associate with the problem of "identity" were potentially familiar to members of the post-assimilationist generation; for example, How can I be both Jewish and German? What does it mean to me to be Jewish if I am not religiously observant or believing? Are the products of my creative and intellectual activity inflected by my Jewishness? The category of "identity" as such is another matter. There was a "we," there was an "I," but the collective category was "our/my Judaism" or "our/my Germanness," perhaps even nationality or religion, but not the slate of "identity" to be filled in, discovered, or revealed.

What's more, while historians and contemporary actors share the spectral model of assimilation to some degree, the actual experience or self-experience of people in this period gives the lie to such models of self-identification. In society, German-speaking Jews made judgments about the relative acculturation of them-selves and others in the Jewish communities. Quite a different matter was the com-plex way in which they imagined themselves in relation to Jewish, German, or other collective identities. The German-speaking Jewish writer of this period with whom I am most familiar, Franz Kafka, is arguably an exceptional case, but like many exceptions his example may highlight a condition that is more shared than commonly recognized.[30] While his friend Max Brod argued for an understanding of Kafka as someone who moved from a distant relationship to his own Judaism to ever-increasing identification, and even Zionism, a careful reading of his comments on Jewish and German identity in his diaries and letters reveals above all a powerful ambivalence throughout. Indeed, the most symptomatic comment of all may be the diary entry of January 1914, which reads: "What have I in common with Jews? I have hardly anything in common with myself and should stand very quietly in a corner, content that I can breathe."[31]

Indeed, the swift acceleration of political and social anti-Semitism in German-speaking society from the first decade of the twentieth century through the Shoah constricted the space for being a German and at the same time a Jew to such a point that "German Jewish identity" became less plausibly a grounded subcultural loca-tion than an occasion for the radical critique of identity itself. At any rate, that is what Kafka's reflection anticipates, attacking even the notion of self-identity at the same time as it begs the question of whether this non-self-identical position is not the human condition tout court. This is arguably an eccentric stand to take, but it is worth noting that Kafka was not alone in taking advantage of a situation of "mutual impossibilities" to imagine a way "out" of identity.[32] In the aftermath of the Shoah, the explosive potential of German Jewish subjectivity would not dissi-pate, but rather would be opened to full exposure. The recognition of the magni-tude and existential significance of the holocaust would bring even a man like Theodor Adorno—only "Jewish" by virtue of his somewhat distant father's back-ground, and never Jewish-identified in the boom years of the Frankfurt School—to increasing attention to the question of Jewishness. He found himself, like Kafka before him, drawn ever more into thinking about (his) Jewish identity, but in a way that offered an escape from identity as such. "Auschwitz confirmed the philosopheme of pure identity as death," he wrote in *Negative Dialectics*.[33] In Adorno's conception, heterogeneity, difference, multiplicity—in his own jargon, "non-identity"—was the principle of life, and the cultural marker for nonidentity was the Jew.[34]

Subjectivity, as I mentioned above, has escaped the sophisticated analyses of those discussing the limitations of the concepts of emancipation and assimilation. While these are classically understood to be twin figures, the former describing the "external" conditions offered by the host society, the latter the Jews' "internal" response to those conditions, in fact both describe abstracted structural and collective phenomena.[35] Yet, post-assimilationist Jews such as those invested in the "Jewish Renaissance" consistently identified the "internal" question as one taking place within the consciousnesses of individual German Jews. This is what Martin Buber called "the personal Jewish Question, the root of all Jewish questions, the question that we find in ourselves, and which we must decide within ourselves."[36] Wassermann, echoing Buber from the other side of the assimilation spectrum, used the same language, translating the Jewish "question" to the implied but much sharper term "problem," and transmuting it to within the self: the "tragedy" of each individual Jewish life is the dualism within himself, constituting "the most fundamental, most difficult and most important part of the Jewish problem."[37] All of this points to a tension between an insistent post-assimilationist focus on individual subjectivity and a recurrent translation of this issue into what is recurrently understood as a failed dialogue between hypostatized collectives, "Jewish" and "German." The irony of Scholem's well-known position that the German Jewish symbiosis was a myth was that he himself represented that symbiosis even as he was questioning it; the dialogue that was imagined not to have taken place was in fact the internal, ambivalent "dialogue" within the individual subject.[38] The problem of German Jewishness was in this as in other senses a problem of subjectivity.

Subjectivity as Problem

The chief problem historians have, or should have, with the notion of subjectivity is related to sources. Here, as elsewhere, the difference between identity and subjectivity makes the latter more difficult to access, and requires the critic heavily to rely on interpretation and subtle forms of analysis. Subjectivity refers to the intricate, complex, and self-contradictory ways in which subjects experience their place in the world, *in contrast to* how they are perceived by others, how they are ordered within relatively rigid external systems.[39] These systems (in large part discursive, as we have seen) colonize the means we have of articulating our place in the world. Thus, at the very moment that writers like Wassermann, Stein, or Scholem write a memoir text (or indeed even a diary or letter) to address the "problem" of identity, they conform to a set of rules that might as well have been laid down by the anti-Semitic minority. Where are the sources for how these individuals might really have moved through German, German Jewish, Jewish, or other cultural identifications? As has been noted, the decision to identify as German or as Jewish was obviously one that no one really had to make, and that most never thought to make.[40] What is really required is a sociocultural history that traces practices as well as reflections, an everyday history of interior life.

In other words, there may be a particular set of problems associated with the very sources that have seemed most well suited to investigations of the German Jewish identity crisis—that is, self-reflexive texts on the problem of German Jewish identity such as Wassermann's memoir or Karl Löwith's, Scholem's essays on Germans and Jews, or on the failure of the German Jewish symbiosis, the *Kunstwart* debate, or Victor Klemperer's diaries.[41] In each of these examples, the conditions producing the need for writing about German Jewish identity have governed the terms in which the problem can be articulated (as I said above, the conceptualiza- tion of the existence of a problem in the first place already concedes to these dis- cursive conditions). Yet, these all remain rich sources. If they cannot do what they claim to do (illustrate how German Jews felt about their identities), they provide a mass of material that, as in Wassermann's text above, often illustrates the inver- sions, contradictions, and collusions that characterized German Jewish identities, whether "assimilated" or Jewish-identified.

One admittedly extreme example is that of Edith Stein, the student of Edmund Husserl who left the Jewish faith and then became a Carmelite nun, writing a "Jewish memoir" in the late 1930s.[42] Stein is most well known today because of her controversial canonization as Saint Teresa Benedicta of the Cross by Pope John Paul II. The very complexity regarding German Jewish subjectivity we are now exploring is closely linked to the difficulty of "assimilating" Stein's life and work to various other "canons," such as those of German Jewish and feminist studies in par- ticular. The linear model of understanding identity along a simple spectrum is eas- ier to comprehend than the dialectical one I am proposing, but Stein herself did not see her embrace of Catholicism and entry into the convent as an abandonment of her Jewishness, her philosophical thought, or her feminism. The historian who asks "How assimilated to German culture was my subject?" could in Stein's case, and in many German-speaking Jewish exemplars, find a citation to support a historio- graphical assertion of relative assimilation. Dialectical readings, such as those I am suggesting are required by the subjectivity model, require more expansive analysis. In brief, however, we could point out that Stein's memoir, translated as *Life in a Jewish Family*, is a particularly complex document, working at one and the same time to offer an antidote to the anti-Semitic caricature of the Jew while also reinforcing Jewish stereotypes. The latter are reversed throughout the memoir, where, for example, Jewish faith is portrayed as deep and primordial in opposition to modern secular Christianity; Silesian Jews like Stein's mother are given as emblematic German patriots; Edith herself appears, even in racial terms, as an "Aryan" double of her stereotypically "Jewish" closest sister. In each of these cases (and others, as I have argued), the structure of identification and dis-identification with the figure of "Jewishness" is dialectical: instead of a model of assimilation to a German-Christian context, the memories of a Jewish family figure Jewishness as primordially "Christian" and "German," and this incipient kernel of authenticity is rediscovered in order to be worked through to a higher spiritual level of Christianity. Yet, in order to subvert the stark dichotomies under which she was oppressed by her own historical contexts (German/Jew, Christian/Jew, and also Male/Female), Stein's texts, like Wassermann's, consistently resorted to a restoration of such dichotomies. Her confession of Jewishness documents her own spiritual enlightenment and presages her martyrdom and beatification/canonization.

At the other end of the presumed assimilatory spectrum, we find the case of Martin Buber, raised in Lemberg/Lwów/Lviv and making a career as philosopher, publisher, translator, and popularizer of Hasidic culture in Berlin. Jewish identification saturated all of these activities, certainly, but it is just as certain (and obvious) that each of them represented a deep engagement with German culture. His philosophical work, like Stein's, was written in German and within a largely German phenomenological tradition; his translations of sacred texts no less a German literary project than was Luther's; his journal *Der Jude* a typical exemplar of early-twentieth-century urban German literary culture; the *Tales of Rabbi Nachmann* and *Legend of the Baal-Shem* owe clearly more to a German neoromantic tradition than they do to the font of lore from which they are "collected."

One particular series of texts to offer food for thought in this area are the lectures for the Bar-Kochba association in Prague (1909–1910), taken at the time and in retrospect to be key sources of the Central European "Jewish Renaissance" capturing the hearts and minds of Jewish youth in the years leading up to World War I.[43] These lectures are often cited as the place where Buber's notion of Jewishness appears in its most essentialist form. Steven Aschheim, for example, cites Buber's references to a "community of blood" (rather than an external community of shared experience), "the deepest, most potent stratum of our being."[44] Yet, this deepest, hidden layer of being, evoked by the suspicious metaphor of "blood," cannot be seen as essentialist in any sense parallel to the contemporary *volkish* or otherwise racialist uses of the term. For the central figure in the lectures is not "blood" or Jewish essence, but "choice": Buber exhorted his youthful Jewish audience to choose the path of mining this invisible stratum, to elect Judaism. Clearly, any notion of elective racial belonging would have been anathema to the essentialist nationalist discourses surrounding the Prague lectures, including those of liberal assimilationists who argued for private Jewish identities within a context of public German cultural participation. Yet, it is through a literal invocation of the language of blood that this shared language of essences is ironically subverted.

These far too abbreviated examples are not offered as a solution to the problem of German Jewish subjectivity, but as an incipient outline of its dimensions. Deeper and more extensive readings are required to bring out the dialectical structure that reappears in a multitude of individual forms, differing as much from one another as the examples of Wassermann, Buber, Stein, Kafka, and Scholem diverge among themselves. Getting beyond the assimilation paradigm does not entail dropping the categories subjects used to define their sense of belonging, but it does require a historian's skepticism toward these categories, a sensitivity to the conditions under which they were produced, and painstaking care in following how they were actually lived. There are many examples of textual analysis of German Jewish figures that are compatible with these principles without directly abandoning categories such as identity and assimilation, or focusing explicitly on subjectivity. In Aschheim's 1999 study of Scholem, Hannah Arendt, and Victor Klemperer, in light of the publication of ego-documents by each of these, he presents three thinkers whose place along the "assimilation spectrum" seems clearly differentiated (with Scholem and Klemperer at the poles and Arendt somewhere near the middle). Yet, each of the readings suggests at best a twisted path to these positions.[45] A careful reading of Aschheim's essay on the thinker with whom we began reveals how Scholem's "Jewish self-certitude" emerges out of a deep engagement with German culture, especially Nietzsche (Scholem wishes at one point to write a "Judenzarathustra"), the panoply of German vitalism (*Lebensphilosophie*), and pronounced strains of *volkish* nationalism. Thus is woven an intricate braid of "Jewish" readings of these German sources, along with "German" readings of Jewish ones, producing the staunch position Scholem disavowed in the "Germans and Jews" lecture and then set free into History: an ironclad binary of two incompatible and hostile principles—two "essences" as he called them, the integration of which was "evil" and "impure"—"German" and "Jewish."

The delicately self-contradictory and nonetheless self-affirming subjective experiences of modern German-speaking Jews may have tended to articulate themselves in terms of essential identities, of binary and exclusive oppositionality, and of processes like assimilation, but these vulgar formulas betrayed the subtle chemistry that gave them substance. They were, to put it in Buberian terms, ruined by speech, forced by the process of language to rend those fibers which could not be unraveled from one another. Does it make sense to think of this rarefied position of German Jewish subjects in the early twentieth century as somehow illegitimate or unauthentic? Must (or can) a radically complex subjectivity be equated with false consciousness? Scholem conflated this complexity with a "destructive dialectic," a "liquidation of the Jewish substance by the Jews themselves," and he notoriously linked this process to their ultimate fate.[46] Yet, the dialectics of German Jewish subjectivities might be more justifiably, more productively, and more honestly linked to the cultural contributions that emerged from them than to their catastrophic destruction.

NOTES

1. The lecture was held on August 2, 1966, as part of the plenary session of the World Jewish Congress. Gershom Scholem, "Juden und Deutsche," *Neue Rundschau* 77 (1966): 547–62, reprinted in Gershom Scholem, *Judaica* II (Frankfurt a. M.: Suhrkamp, 1970), 20–46 (page citations below are to this version or, when quoted, the following translation). Translations taken from Gershom Scholem, ed., *On Jews and Judaism in Crisis: Selected Essays*, trans. Werner J. Dannhauser (New York: Schocken, 1976), 71–92.

2. Scholem, "Germans and Jews," see 20–21.

3. Scholem, "Juden und Deutsche," 28.

4. In 1996, Shulamit Volkov suggested that German-Jewish historiography had reached a "dead end," due to the persistence of two tendencies that should now be overcome or synthesized. Both the "National-Zionist" and "Liberal-ethnic" approaches to Jewish history limit the connection of Jewish history/ies to European history more generally. See "Reflections on German-Jewish Historiography. A Dead End or a New Beginning?" *Leo Baeck Institute Year Book [LBIY]* 41 (1996): 309–20. The impasse I refer to here precedes the liberal or Zionist ideological moment in that it refers to assumptions about identity shared by both historiographical schools, as they were by historical actors of both ideological tendencies.

5. On the concept of dissimilation in this sense, see Franz Rosenzweig, *Gesammelte Schriften I. Briefe und Tagebücher*, vol. 2, 1918–1929, ed. Rachel Rosenzweig, Edith Rosenzweig-Scheinmann, and Bernhard Casper (Den Haag: 1979), 770. The more recent revival of the term has yielded inconsistent definitions, but each of these tends to bring out Rosenzweig's intended dialectical tension between the terms "assimilation" and "dissimilation" in more explicit ways, implicitly subverting the spectral paradigm. See especially Shulamit Volkov, "The Dynamics of Dissimilation: *Ostjuden* and German Jews," in *The Jewish Response to German Culture: From the Enlightenment to the Second World War*, ed. Jehuda Reinharz and Walter Schatzberg (Hanover, NH: Dartmouth University Press, 1985), 195–211, and Shulamit Volkov, *Die Juden in Deutschland*, 1780–1918 (Munich, 1994), see esp. pp. 53–56; David Sorkin, "Emancipation and Assimilation: Two Concepts and Their Application to German-Jewish History," *LBIY* 35(1990), pp. 17–33; and Jonathan Skolnik, "Dissimilation and the Historical Novel: Hermann Sinsheimer's *Maria Nunnez*," *LBIY* 43 (1998): 225–237.

6. Amos Funkenstein, "The Dialectics of Assimilation," *Jewish Social Studies* 1.2 (Winter 1995): 1–14.

7. Scholem, "Germans and Jews," 73–74.

8. Ibid., 76–77.

9. Scholem, "Germans and Jews," 83; "Deutsche und Juden," 35: "Sehr breite Schichten der deutschen Juden waren zwar bereit, ihr Volkstum zu liquidieren, wollten aber, in freilich sehr verschiedenen Ausmaßen, ihr Judentum, als Erbe, als Konfession, als ein Ichweißnichtwas, ein undefinierbares und doch im Bewußtsein deutlich vorhandenes Element bewahren."

10. Yosef Hayim Yerushalmi, *Freud's Moses: Judaism Terminable and Interminable* (New Haven: Yale, 1991), 9–10. Steven Aschheim speaks of the "insistence on a Jewishness that resists definition" as a "prevailing ideology of our own times, a way in which countless contemporary secular Jews approach articulating their own persistent but difficult to locate sense of a 'Jewish self.'" See Steven E. Aschheim, "(Con)Fusions of Identity—Germans and Jews," in *In Times of Crisis: Essays on European Culture, Germans, and Jews* (Madison: University of Wisconsin Press, 2001), 72.

11. Yerushalmi, *Freud's Moses*, 10.

12. The *locus classicus* of this critique from the culture-historical perspective is Ahad Ha'am's essay "Slavery within Freedom," where the paradoxical position of the emancipated Jew who must justify his own Jewishness and find meaning in it is laid out. Ahad Ha'am, "Slavery in Freedom," in Leon Simon (ed.), *Selected Essays of Ahad Ha-Am* (New York and Philadelphia, 1962), 171–194. See also Paul Mendes-Flohr, "Cultural Zionism's Image of the Educated Jew: Reflections on Creating a Secular Jewish Culture," *Modern Judaism* 18 (1998): 227–239, esp. 228.

13. David Sorkin, *The Transformation of German Jewry*, 1780–1840 (New York and Oxford: Oxford University Press, 1987); idem, "Emancipation and Assimilation: Two Concepts and Their Application to German-Jewish History," *LBIY* 35 (1990): 17–33; and idem, "The Impact of Emancipation on German Jewry: A Reconsideration," in *Assimilation and Community: The Jews in Nineteenth-Century Europe*, ed. Jonathan Frankel and Steven J. Zipperstein (Cambridge, UK: Cambridge University Press, 1992), 177–198.

14. Samuel Moyn, "German Jewry and the Question of Identity: Historiography and Theory," *LBIY* 41 (1996): 298.

15. Anthony J. La Vopa, "Jews and Germans: Old Quarrels, New Departures," *Journal of the History of Ideas* 54, no. 4 (1993): 688.

16. Sorkin, *Transformation*, 7.

17. Sorkin, "Impact of Emancipation," 187–192, see esp. 187–188. Cf. the discussions of ideology and subjectivity by Zizek and Althusser in Scott Spector, "Was the Third Reich Movie-Made? Interdisciplinarity and the Reframing of 'Ideology,'" *American Historical Review* 106, no. 2 (2001): 4xx.

18. Jakob Wassermann, *Mein Weg als Deutscher und Jude* (Berlin: S. Fischer Verlag, 1921), s.a. English translations Jacob Wassermann, *My Life as German and Jew*, trans. S. N. Brainin (New York: Coward-McCann, 1933) and the revised translation by the British publisher (London: George Allen & Unwin Ltd., 1934).

19. Cf. Amos Funkenstein, "Dialectics of Assimilation," *Jewish Social Studies* 1.2 (Winter 1995): 1–14.

20. See Wassermann, *Mein Weg,* 69. The description here of a "German essence" consisting of "fragmentation," transition and mobility, and lack of center in relation to European cultures proper might be described as a novel form of (Jewish) "German self-hatred."

21. Gershom Scholem, "Wider den Mythos vom deutsch-jüdischen 'Gespräch,'" in *Judaica* 2:10.

22. Cf. Scholem, *Judaica* 2:7–46. Needless to say, the differences of opinion within the shared universe of terms described here were significant and remain of historical importance; focusing on where spokesmen like Wasserman and Scholem silently agreed reveals a *different* history than focusing on where they obviously differed does.

23. Steven E. Aschheim, "Assimilation and Its Impossible Discontents: The Case of Moritz Goldstein," in *Times of Crisis,* 65.

24. LaVopa, "Old Quarrels, New Departures," see esp. 693–94.

25. Besides the Volkov essay cited above, see Evyatar Friesel, "The German-Jewish Encounter: A Reconsideration," *LBIY* 41 (1996): 263–275 and Evyatar Friesel, "Jewish and German-Jewish Historical Views: Problems of a New Synthesis," *LBIY* 43 (1998): 323–336.

26. See Michael Brenner, *The Renaissance of Jewish Culture in Weimar Germany* (New Haven: Yale University Press, 1996).

27. See Steven Beller, *Vienna and the Jews, 1867–1938: A Cultural History* (Cambridge, UK: Cambridge University Press, 1989).

28. Scholem, *On Jews and Judaism in Crisis,* 82.

29. Steven E. Aschheim has eloquently and persuasively tracked the liberal-assimilationist adoption of essentialist terms in his essay "Assimilation and Its Impossible Discontents: The Case of Moritz Goldstein," in *Times of Crisis,* 64–72.

30. The example of Kafka is useful as a reminder that the problematics of German-Jewish assimilation as they unfolded in the nineteenth and early twentieth centuries included German-speaking Jewish Austrians who had no hesitation in identifying themselves as "German-Jews" (*Deutschjuden*), or in some cases simply "Germans," even as they felt themselves in a different situation from Germans from the *Reich* to the North.

31. Franz Kafka, *Tagebücher in der Fassung der Handschrift,* ed. Hans-Gerd Koch, Michael Müller, and Malcolm Pasley (New York and Frankfurt am Main: S. Fischer, 1992), 622.

32. In a letter to Max Brod in reference to the writing of Karl Kraus, Kafka writes that the German-Jewish writers of his generation "lived between three impossibilities . . . The impossibility of not writing, the impossibility of writing German, the impossibility of writing differently." This literature, "impossible from all sides," is in fact the only possibility left for literature. Franz Kafka, *Briefe,* 337–338; see Scott Spector, *Prague Territories: National Conflict and Cultural Innovation in Franz Kafka's Fin de Siècle* (Berkeley: University of California Press, 2000), 89–92.

33. Theodor W. Adorno, *Negative Dialectics,* trans. E. B. Ashton (New York, 1973), 362.

34. The prime source for Adorno's discussion of nonidentity and the privileged example of modern Jewish subjectivity is the *Negative Dialectics.* Cf. Martin Jay, *Adorno* (Cambridge, MA: Harvard University Press, 1984).

35. See Otto Brunner, Werner Conze, Reinhart Koselleck, eds., *Geschichtliche Grundbegriffe. Historisches Lexikon zur politisch-sozialen Sprache in Deutschland,* 2:153–197, see esp. 178–185; Sorkin, "Emancipation and Assimilation," 17–21.

36. Martin Buber, *Drei Reden über das Judentum* (Frankfurt am Main: Rütten & Loening, 1916), 27.

37. Wassermann, *My Life as German and Jew*, 75. The dualism here is the coexistence of twin senses of superiority and inferiority; Buber elsewhere identifies dualism as the essential nature of the Jew.

38. Paul Mendes-Flohr would appear to share this view. Citing Gustav Landauer, Hermann Cohen, Buber, and Rosenzweig, he argues that the imagined symbiosis or cultural dialogue between Germans and Jews was less at issue than "an inner Jewish dialogue—of a dialogue within the souls of individual Jews as well as between themselves." See Paul Mendes-Flohr, *German Jews: A Dual Identity* (New Haven: Yale University Press, 1999), 89–95.

39. There is no room here for a discussion of theories of subjectivity that would be expansive enough to be satisfactory, and the shorthand of identity as more fixed and perceptual in contrast to a more open, complex, and experiential subjectivity is overly schematic, if also useful for us in this context. Nick Mansfield's concise statement is useful here: "Subjectivity is primarily an experience, and remains permanently open to inconsistency, contradiction and unselfconsciousness. Our experience of ourselves remains forever prone to surprising disjunctions that only the fierce light of ideology or theoretical dogma convinces us can be homogenized into a single thing." Nick Mansfield, *Subjectivity: Theories of the Self from Freud to Haraway* (St. Leonards NSW, Australia: Allen & Unwin, 2000), 6–7. Mansfield usefully reviews twentieth-century theoretical models of subjectivity.

40. Samuel Moyn, "German Jewry and Identity," 301.

41. These examples are drawn from very different, if tellingly linked, moments of perceived crisis of German-Jewish relations. The "Kunstwart debate" about Jewish integration into German culture began in 1912 with Moritz Goldstein's provocative essay "Deutsch-jüdischer Parnaß" ("German-Jewish Parnassus"), which challenged the German Jewish assimilationist ideal and suggested that the overwhelming contribution to German culture by Jewish writers was not made by these writers as Germans, but as Jews; see *Der Kunstwart und Kulturwart* 25 (March 1912): 281–294. Assertion and/or questioning of the so-called German-Jewish symbiosis in Wasserman's and Scholem's texts cited earlier is also traceable in Karl Löwith's memoir *Mein Leben in Deutschland vor und nach 1933: Ein Bericht* (Stuttgart: J. B. Metzler, 1986), trans. Elizabeth King, *My Life in Germany Before and After 1933: A Report* (Urbana: University of Illinois Press, 1994), as well as in the recently celebrated diaries of Victor Klemperer, especially *Ich will Zeugnis ablegen bis zum letzten*, ed. Walter Nowojski (Berlin: Aufbau, 1996), trans. Martin Chalmers, *I Will Bear Witness: A Diary of the Nazi Years, 1942–1945* (New York: Random House, 1999).

42. Elsewhere I have offered a detailed reading of this extraordinary life and work and the complex relations of these to each other, and to surrounding historical contexts. Scott Spector, "Edith Stein's Passing Gestures: Intimate Histories, Empathic Portraits," *New German Critique* 75 (Fall 1998): 28–56, reprinted in Joyce Berkman et al., eds., *Contemplating Edith Stein* (South Bend, IN: University of Notre Dame Press, 2005).

43. See the published, albeit reworked, version of the lectures cited earlier. I offer a more detailed discussion of the texts in Spector, *Prague Territories*, 147–151.

44. Aschheim, "Assimilation and Its Discontents," 70.

45. Steven E. Aschheim, *Scholem, Arendt, Klemperer: Intimate Chronicles in Turbulent Times* (Bloomington: Indiana University Press, 2001).

46. Scholem, "Once More: The German-Jewish Dialogue," in *On Jews and Judaism*, 68–69.

7

Jewish Self-Identification and West European Categories of Belonging

FROM THE ENLIGHTENMENT TO WORLD WAR II

TODD ENDELMAN

It is an article of faith in much of the academy that "identity"—everywhere—is fluid, fragmented, and contingent. Whatever the value of this insight with regard to modern Jewish history, it is not helpful in understanding the experience of Jews before the Enlightenment. In medieval and early modern Europe, Jews constituted a well-defined collective unit for whom questions of self-identification—Who are we and what is our place here?—rarely arose. Premodern European Jews differed from their neighbors by virtue of their religion, nationality/ethnicity, legal status, and, in most cases, language, costume, employment, and social and cultural habits. Most lived in quasi-autonomous, self-regulating corporations (*kehillot*), chartered bodies with well-defined privileges and obligations. With the frequent exception of late-medieval Italian and Spanish Jews and those in small isolated communities elsewhere, their contacts with Christians were largely instrumental. Religious traditions (Jewish and Christian alike), social structures, and legal categories defined the borders of the Jewish world, which remained more or less stable throughout the medieval and early modern periods. "Jewishness" was not endlessly constructed and renegotiated. The line between Christian and Jew was clear and stable—not fuzzy and indeterminate—for over one thousand years. Within the Jewish world, the nature of correct belief and practice (what Judaism required) was much disputed, of course. The rabbis clashed over how best to know and serve God and how best to interpret the Law. These were not, however, debates about the boundaries between Jews and non-Jews or about the fundamentals of Jewish self-definition such as origins, chosenness, exile, redemption, and the like.

The one exception to this generalization—the case of former New Christians or *conversos*—is the proverbial exception that proves the proverbial rule. Descendants of Iberian Jews who had converted to Catholicism in the fourteenth and fifteenth centuries under duress, the conversos lived as nominal Christians before resettling in tolerated Jewish communities in the Netherlands, Britain, southwestern France, northern Germany, and the New World. Regardless of the extent to which they harbored a sense of Jewish descent and to which they maintained remnants of Jewish observance, they were educated and socialized as Christians. In Yosef Yerushalmi's now classic formulation, they were "the first considerable group of European Jews to have had their most extensive and direct personal experiences completely outside the organic Jewish community and the spiritual universe of normative Jewish tradition." Before leaving the Iberian Peninsula, and especially afterward, they experienced the tensions that later became characteristic of Jews whose identities were multiple and fragmented as the result of living simultaneously in two or more overlapping worlds. Ex-converso communities confronted the task of collective self-definition, requiring them to balance, reconcile, or negotiate two clusters of traditions: one associated with the normative, rabbinic Judaism of professing Jewish communities; the other with the values, norms, and behavioral traits of Spain and Portugal.[1]

Former conversos, however, were unrepresentative of the European Jewish population, with its roots in Northern and Central Europe (Ashkenaz). The Jewishness of the Ashkenazim (by which I mean both their subjective self-understanding and their objective behavioral and situational distinctiveness, rather than any essential spiritual or biological quality) remained undisturbed until the eighteenth and nineteenth centuries. It became problematic for them—a matter of reflection and debate—only when the structure of state and society that had supported it weakened and then dissolved. When the *ancien régime* gave way, when states ceased to be constituted as clusters of legally structured corporate ranks and orders, and Jews—like others whose civil status previously derived from the collective unit to which they belonged—were incorporated into the emerging liberal order as individuals, only then did Jews turn to forging new self-definitions.

From Emancipation to Integration

The transformation of the Jews, their movement "out of the ghetto" (to use the title of Jacob Katz's well-known account), did not follow a well-defined linear trajectory. It was a complex, multidimensional, messy process with at least four distinct components—emancipation, acculturation, secularization, and integration—which, while interdependent, were also distinct from each other both conceptually and in practice. In Western and Central Europe, the transformation of the Jews entailed the acquisition of citizenship and the rights it bestowed (emancipation); the adoption of new social and cultural values and new modes of deportment, dress, and speech (acculturation); the rejection or neglect of time-honored religious beliefs and practices, including both those sanctioned by custom and those by law (secularization); and the struggle for social acceptance in non-Jewish circles (integration).[2] Their transformation also included far-reaching changes in self-perception, for as Jews moved from exclusion to inclusion, from periphery to mainstream, they found themselves reconsidering and redefining how they saw themselves—and how they wanted others to see them. Formerly, they had viewed themselves—and were viewed by others—as a discrete people, different in kind from other peoples. In the words of the *aleinu* prayer, God had made them different from the other nations of the world and assigned to them a distinct fate. Moreover, they were a people whose national and religious identities were indissolubly linked and whose ties to the Christian peoples among whom they lived were more instrumental than affective. Religion and ethnicity were omnipresent and inseparable, filling the whole of their existence. The integration of Jews into states increasingly built around individual rights rather than collective privileges made the survival of this undifferentiated sense of self-identification difficult if not impossible.[3]

The states that took shape in the West in the eighteenth and nineteenth centuries eliminated or weakened the estates, corporations, chapters, guilds, chartered bodies, and other intermediate units that previously determined the legal status of their members. In particular, they eroded the unity between ecclesiastical community and national identity, replacing it with categories of universal citizenship and individual rights. Religion, in theory, ceased to be a criterion for membership in the nation and became little more than "one feature among others in the diversity of a people, neither more nor less than having different jobs or coming from this or that region." It was reduced to "no more than one of the numerous variables that distinguished between subjects or citizens."[4] This process of civil leveling and homogenizing aimed to impose order, coherence, rationality, and uniformity. Even if Jews had wanted to remain a people apart, with their own distinctive legal niche, the states in which they lived would have been unwilling to tolerate such separatism. There was no room for the anomaly of a legally privileged Jewish corporation exercising authority over its members. As Salo Baron recognized decades ago, "emancipation was an even greater necessity for the modern state than it was for the Jew." Once corporate distinctions were abolished, it would have been "an outright anachronism" to allow the Jews to remain a separate body, with privileges and obligations that were different from those of other citizens.[5]

Both Jewish and Christian supporters of the entry of the Jews into the modern nation-state acknowledged that an undifferentiated sense of Jewishness was an anachronism, a vestige of intolerant epochs when Jews were legally and socially marginalized. In the words of an 1889 editorial in a liberal Hungarian publication, if Jews "want to be regarded as completely equal, they must not differ in any detail from the other inhabitants of the nation." They had to alter "their external appearance, their clothing, their way of life, their occupations."[6] The Jewish component of their identity was to shrink and become compartmentalized as their civil status improved. They reasoned that if Jews continued to consider themselves a separate nation with their own distinct allegiances and hopes, they could not be incorporated into nation-states that no longer recognized corporate or collective membership. (Further to the east, in the multinational Romanov Empire, the survival of a dynastic regime into the early twentieth century allowed an undifferentiated, non-compartmentalized Jewish identity to endure longer.) Jewish peoplehood was to be abandoned, Jewish particularism muted. Judaism was to be transformed into a religion like other religions, adherence to which was to be one among several strands in the identity of emancipated, modern Jews. Inclusion in state and society could occur on no other basis. In the oft-cited declaration of the count of

Clermont-Tonnerre in the debate on Jewish emancipation in France in December 1789: "Il faut refuser tout aux Juifs comme nation et accorder tout aux Juifs comme individus . . . il faut qu'ils ne fassent dans l'Etat ni un corps politique, ni un Ordre; il faut qu'ils soient individuellement citoyens." Jews who refused emancipation on these terms, Clermont-Tonnerre continued, were to be expelled.[7]

While Jewish notables and publicists did not dwell on the consequences of failing to accept the terms of emancipation, they were as adamant as their Christian counterparts that emancipation called for a fundamental shift in Jewish self-identification. Following the emancipation of the Jews of Alsace and Lorraine in September 1791, Berr Isaac Berr, a wealthy *maskil* from Nancy, wrote an open letter to his newly emancipated "co-religionists" reminding them "how absolutely necessary it is for us to divest ourselves entirely of that narrow spirit, of *Corporation* and *Congregation*, in all civil and political matters, not immediately connected with our spiritual laws; in these things we must absolutely appear simply as individuals, as Frenchmen," rather than as "a distinct body of people and a separate community."[8] In the German states, where public debate about the transformation of the Jews was more protracted and charged, *maskilim* and reformers were just as adamant.

From the perspective of the early-twenty-first century academy, with its validation of ethnic diversity and cultural pluralism, the linkage between emancipation and transformation—the demand that Jews refashion their self-definition and behavior—seems harsh, even unreasonable. However, in the context of the period, it represented an advance, a sharp break with the premodern past, when the source of the Jew's defect was a matter of faith, and baptism the sole remedy, the only avenue to integration and acceptance. Moreover, while those Christians who championed emancipation also believed that Jewish morals and customs were in a sorry state and in need of reform, they did not trace this to the basic teachings of Judaism or to any essential trait, spiritual or corporeal, of the Jews. Disciples of the Enlightenment, they rejected the traditional Christian claims of God's eternal damnation and punishment of the Jews and of their ineradicable malevolence. In their view, there was no unchanging Jewish essence. As the English deist John Toland wrote in 1707 (in what may be the earliest statement of this position), whatever "genius" or "bent of mind" reigned among the Jews, it proceeded "from accident and not from nature." He continued: "The different methods of government and education are the true springs and causes of such different inclinations all over the world."[9] If Jews were unsocial, unproductive, devious, and immoral (which was the common Enlightenment view), the reason was that circumstances—bad measures and bad treatment—had made them that way. The Whig historian and essayist Thomas Babington Macaulay was explicit about this in calling for the removal of Jewish disabilities in Britain. If English Jews lacked "patriotic feeling" and viewed Dutch Jews rather than English Christians as their compatriots, it was because an oppressive state had failed to protect them. "If the Jews have not felt towards England like children," he wrote in the *Edinburgh Review* in 1831, "it is because she has treated them like a step-mother." Once treated as equals, they would "know that they owe all their comforts and pleasures to the bond which united them in one community" and would be overcome with feelings of patriotism. In short, the Jews of his day were "precisely what our government has made them."[10]

This belief in the power of environmental influence was central to all Enlightenment and liberal proposals to ameliorate the condition of the Jews. In France, the three prizewinners in the Metz essay contest of 1785–1787 ("Are there means of making the Jews happy and more useful in France?") accepted the premise that persecution was the major cause of Jewish degeneration. In this, they followed the lead of the Prussian civil servant Christian Wilhelm von Dohm, whose *Über die bürgerliche verbesserung der Juden* (1781–1783) was the classic Enlightenment statement of this position. Dohm, for example, traced the concentration of Jews in low-status trades (money-lending, peddling and hawking, trading in secondhand goods) to government measures to regulate their economic activity. For the unfortunate Jew, he wrote, "whose activity is restricted on all sides, whose talents have no scope for free utterance, in whose virtue nobody believes, for whom honor is almost non-existent, to him no other way but commerce is open to acquire means for improving his lot for earning a living." Central to Dohm's argument and that of other reformers was the conviction that human character was universal and plastic and thus subject to environmental influence. Enlightenment and liberal supporters of emancipation were buoyant optimists, firm believers in the oneness of human nature and the perfectibility of human character, confident that toleration would make the Jews more productive and honest and less tribal and superstitious. "A life of normal civil happiness in a well ordered state," wrote Dohm, "would do away with their 'clannish religious opinions.' " Dohm continued by asking, "How would it be possible for [the Jew] not to love a state where he could freely acquire property and freely enjoy it, where his taxes would be no heavier than those of other citizens, where he could reach positions of honor and enjoy general esteem?"[11]

The Meaning of Jewish Emancipation for Jews and Non-Jews

While Jewish reformers and their Christian friends agreed that emancipation and integration required an overhaul of Jewish behavior and identity, they did not agree—nor even discuss—the scope of this transformation. In retrospect, the vagueness of the discussion—its fuzziness, lack of rigor, reliance on catchwords— is striking. What, after all, did those who urged the transformation of the Jews mean when they called for their *régénération, assimilation, rapprochement,* or *fusion sociale*; their *bürgerliche Verbesserung, Veredelung,* or *Reformezirung*; their "complete fusion . . . with their fellow subjects of every other denomination"?[12] At a minimum, they meant that Jews should speak and dress like other citizens, that they should embrace secular education and culture, that they should identify with their country of residence, becoming law-abiding, patriotic, and productive citizens. About these, there was little confusion or disagreement. But more than this was expected. Jewish reformers and Christian critics also targeted the "clannishness" of the Jews (that is, their preference for mixing and marrying among themselves), their concentration in commerce and finance, and their attachment to "backward" or "superstitious" religious customs, including dietary laws that hindered social intercourse. However, while reformers and critics saw these matters as ripe for reform, they failed to specify what constituted sufficient change or to establish criteria to measure it. For example, did the progression of Jews from peddling to shopkeeping meet their expectations? Were Jews expected only to abandon low-status street trades, or were they expected to forsake trade altogether, becoming farm and factory workers, hewers of wood and drawers of water, so that their occupational profile resembled that of the non-Jewish population? They also failed to indicate what they considered a reasonable time for this and other changes to occur. Was the transformation of the Jews a long-term project, stretching over many generations, or was it a change that would occur swiftly in the immediate wake of their emancipation from the restraints of the past?

Expectations about Jewish acculturation and integration—how much and how far—were as fuzzy as those regarding Jewish productivization. Jews and non-Jews alike assumed that Jewish particularism and marginality would diminish following emancipation. Jews would be found in universities, lodges, fraternities, literary and philosophical societies, concert halls, casinos, and clubs. They would drink, carouse, whore, and gamble in pubs, cafes, beer halls, and wine cellars in non-Jewish company. This vision of integration, even if never articulated in these terms, would not have met with opposition from either Jewish or Christian emancipationists. But the problem was more complex than this. Little was said about whether Jews were expected as well to stop choosing their closest friends and marriage partners from among their own community. If the ideal was "a random pattern of interaction, where Jews [were] no more likely to interact with each other than with non-Jews"[13] and the expectation that in time they would seek husbands and wives outside the tribal pond, then the eventual outcome of their integration would be their demographic decline, if not disappearance, as an identifiable or cohesive social unit. Similarly, while even Orthodox Jews in Western countries endorsed the idea of acculturation, there was a point at which the process threatened to erase the most distinctive marks of Jewishness. To what extent were Jews to identify with the dominant culture? Were they to be inconspicuous and even unrecognizable as Jews outside their homes and synagogues? Were they to pursue acculturation to the extent that they embraced the religion of the dominant culture as well and disappeared from the scene by the path of total fusion?

Although those who wanted to reform the Jews were vague about their expectations, some, it is clear, hoped that emancipation and integration would end in the full absorption of the Jews and their disappearance as a collective unit. In Britain, Christian defenders of the Jew Bill of 1753 argued that allowing foreign-born Jews to become naturalized citizens would encourage their conformity to English customs and accelerate their integration into English society, in time preparing the way for their conversion to the Anglican faith. For example, in a sermon to a fashionable London congregation, the Reverend Thomas Winstanley predicted that naturalization would incline the Jews "to cultivate a friendship and familiarity with us; which, of course, must bring them in due season, to a conformity of manners, and an imitation of our ways and customs." Social contact would engender more favorable feelings regarding Christians, and "these more favourable sentiments concerning us may be improved, e'er long, into a more favourable opinion of our religion."[14] In France, the Abbé Grégoire, one of the three co-winners of the Metz essay contest, urged improvements in the socioeconomic status of the Ashkenazim of Alsace and Lorraine for the same reason. The state, he believed, should scatter Jews through-out rural France, thus undermining the influence of their rabbis, while compelling their children to attend state schools, thus exposing them to French culture. This would lead to more interaction between Jews and Christians and in time bring the former to Christianity.[15]

There were Jews as well (not many, of course) who envisioned a future in which Jews qua Jews would disappear and be absorbed into some larger unit of humankind. Baptized Jews presumably held such views—to the extent that they thought about the collective fate of the Jews at all, as distinct from their own personal fortunes. More unusual were those Jewish secularists and deists who dreamed of a future that was neither Jewish nor Christian, who envisioned a world in which divisions among religions, nations, and, in some cases, ranks and classes as well, were effaced. David Friedländer's well-known "dry baptism" letter on behalf of Berlin Jews to Provost Wilhelm Teller in 1799, in which he proposed that Jews who had given up their ancestral rituals be admitted to Protestantism without having to accept its dogmas and mysteries, rested on the premise that there was one rational, natural religion that was the essence of both enlightened Christianity and enlightened Judaism.[16]

A generation later, Jewish Saint-Simonians—Gustave d'Eichthal, Léon Halévy, the Rodrigues and Pereire brothers—spun dreams of a new universal order of one religion, one dogma, one cult, in which Judaism and Jews were to be absorbed. In their vision of the future, which belonged to a larger movement of utopian system-building in the wake of the social upheaval and intellectual confusion engendered by the French Revolution, nations disappeared, religion and politics merged, and universal harmony reigned.[17] In his *Lettres sur la religion et la politique* (1829), for example, the young Eugène Rodrigues, son of a Paris stockbroker, confidently asserted that humanity was advancing toward an immense unity—*la société universelle*—in which nations would disappear, the spiritual and temporal realms of life would merge, and the new religion would include both Christians and Jews within its temples. Church and state would become identical, for religion would absorb all of society within its bosom. The reign of Caesar would cease, the reign of God commence. Although not a Saint-Simonian, their contemporary Joseph Salvador worked out a similar scheme of religious development, culminating in an imminent messianic era in which Mosaism (in effect, ethical monotheism), preserved by the Jews for centuries, provided a foundation for universal organization.[18]

In the German-language cultural orbit, Karl Marx and his Jewish disciples also looked forward to a future in which the categories "Jew" and "Christian" would disappear.[19] The Austrian social democrat Otto Bauer, for example, taught that the Jews were fated to disappear among the nations of Europe because they no longer performed a historical task. Before the rise of capitalism, they pioneered trade and commerce, but with its advent and the "Judaization" of Christianity, they lost their historical role and were condemned to assimilate socially and economically. In imperial Germany, most Jewish advocates of Jewish dissolution saw the future in terms of absorption into the German nation rather than a universalistic utopia transcending particularistic identities. Writing in Maximilian Harden's journal *Die Zukunft* in 1904, the semiticist Jakob Fromer advised Germany's Jews, "Dive under, disappear! Disappear with your oriental physiognomy, with your ways that contrast with your surroundings, with your 'mission,' and, above all, with your exclusively ethical worldview. Take the customs, the values, and the religion of your host people, seek to mix in with them and see to it that you are consumed in them without a trace."[20] The notary and jurist Adolph Weissler, writing in the arch-conservative *Preussische Jahrbücher* in 1900, urged the dissolution of German Jewry through child baptism. Although he believed that Judaism was morally stagnant and inferior to Christianity, he knew that even Jews who agreed with him were unable to believe in the divinity of Jesus and accept baptism. Because he also regarded conversions of convenience as unprincipled but nonetheless wished to see German Jewry disappear, he urged Jewish parents to baptize their children, who, not having been raised as Jews, could not be accused of insincerity and opportunism.[21]

Acculturation and Integration versus Secularization

Views such as these were exceptional by virtue of their radicalism. In addition, they were exceptional—*along with all prescriptive statements about the Jewish future, whatever their tone*—by virtue of their very existence. Few Jews bothered to tell the world what being Jewish meant and what the future of the Jews would or should be. Those who did were public figures (notables, publicists, rabbis) seeking to influence the outcome of Jewish modernization. Their views did not necessarily reflect the sentiments of "ordinary" Jews (traders, clerks, market men, shopkeepers, wholesale merchants, brokers, and their wives and children), who, in the nature of things, were neither pamphleteers nor editorialists. In the absence of survey research for earlier centuries, one of the few ways to know what the "silent majority" felt is to examine what they did and then infer from their behavior, to the extent possible, the sentiments and hopes that motivated them. Doing so makes clear that most emancipated Jews did not imagine a future in which they would renounce or transcend their Jewish attachments. While willing, even eager, to redefine what it meant to be Jewish and to tailor their behavior and views accordingly, there is no evidence, as we will see, that they viewed their disappearance as desirable, necessary, or inevitable, as the final outcome of their integration and acculturation. Nor is there evidence that they even believed that they must shed their collective social attachments and become invisible outside their synagogues and homes. In this regard, their understanding of what was required of them differed from that of Christian emancipationists, who, however vague their expectations, clearly envisioned a more radical and ruthless break with the Jewish past.

Any analysis of changes in Western Jewish behavior between the mid-eighteenth and mid-twentieth centuries must begin with the recognition that while these changes were far-reaching and ubiquitous, they were not uniformly so in all spheres of life or even within the same sphere. Thus, while the practice of many religious traditions declined, key lifecycle rituals continued to be observed even in families otherwise distant from the world of tradition. In Amsterdam, for example, the circumcision of male sons remained almost universal into the twentieth century—though some parents claimed they were doing it for hygienic reasons or for the sake of the grandparents. In 1932, 1933, and 1934, the proportion of boys born to Jewish mothers who were not circumcised was 4 percent, 8 percent, and 10 percent respectively. (Most of those who were not circumcised were from mixed marriages.) Similarly, most marriages between Jews in Amsterdam continued to be solemnized in religious ceremonies: the number between 1901 and 1933 fell only from 97.3 percent to 91.9 percent.[22] Jewish economic activity showed similar patterns of continuity. To take another example: while most Jewish families in the West experienced *embourgeoisement* over two or three generations following the removal of disabilities, their overall occupational profile remained skewed. Most heads of families worked in commerce rather than in heavy industry, agriculture, or the liberal professions. Buying and selling continued to be the chief pillar on which Jewish life rested. The transformation of the Jews, in short, was incomplete, uneven, and irregular.

How irregular becomes clear when one ceases to speak of the transformation of the Jews as an undifferentiated process of "assimilation" and views it in terms of its four constitutive elements—emancipation, acculturation, secularization, and integration. Breaking down the analysis in this way brings into focus the unevenness of the changes that Jews experienced and the problems that this created for them when they needed to define their Jewishness in public debate. For the purpose of this essay, I want to focus in particular on distinguishing secularization from acculturation, and then acculturation from integration.

Curiously, the analytical category of secularization is absent from the standard histories of the entry of the Jews into state and society in Western Europe (in contrast to its prominence in the history of Christianity in modern Europe, where what is known as the secularization thesis functioned as the master narrative for decades after World War II.)[23] Neither Michael A. Meyer's *The Origins of the Modern Jew* (1967) nor Jacob Katz's *Out of the Ghetto* (1973) discusses the secularization of Jewish life as such. Of course, they chart the abandonment of traditional rituals and beliefs, but they do so in the context of acculturation and integration, the changes in belief and behavior that Jews embraced in order to make a place for themselves in European life. Even the later, more conceptually nuanced account of Pierre Birnbaum and Ira Katznelson, their introduction to the collection *Paths of Emancipation* (1995), fails to bring secularization into the equation as a transformative category in its own right. The word itself is also absent from the index to the volume, so presumably its contributors also do not consider secularization qua secularization as a critical part of the story. The most recent surveys of modern Jewish history also take no notice of secularization. David Vital's *A People Apart* (1999) views emancipation as the great agent of change, while Lloyd P. Gartner's *History of the Jews in Modern Times* (2001) speaks more broadly of capitalism, the Enlightenment, and the modern state undermining traditional Jewish life.[24]

The conceptual distinction between secularization and acculturation is not pedantic. Much of the decline in Jewish practice (*kashrut*, family purity, synagogue attendance, festival customs) was the result of currents and influences that were not specific to the historical experience of the Jews. In the eighteenth and nineteenth centuries, religious indifference, anticlericalism, impiety, skepticism, and ignorance of Scripture and doctrine were to be found in all Western societies, among poor and rich alike. Religious doctrine and sentiment guided fewer areas of behavior among Jews and Christians alike (although there is some evidence that this occurred earlier among Jews than among Christians).[25] Historians of European Christianity attribute the growth of irreligion to the economic and intellectual revolutions of the eighteenth and nineteenth centuries (urbanization, industrialization, technological innovation, materialistic theories of the universe, the scientific critique of religion, Darwinism, etc.), and to the political, social, and intellectual conservatism of state churches, which repelled businessmen, intellectuals, and workers alike, depending on the national context. Max Weber set the rise of irreligion in an even longer time frame. He posited a gradual, millennia-long process of disenchantment (*Entzauberung*) of the world, of increasing rationalization and intellectualization, beginning with the rationalization stimulated by Israelite religious prophecy and continuing, during the Reformation, with the elimination of magical ritual. In the nineteenth and twentieth centuries, science, science-oriented technologies, bureaucratization, capitalism, and political centralization accelerated the process, according to Weber, while technical means and calculations banished supernatural, incalculable forces.[26]

Granted, secularization is an elusive concept, the process difficult to describe and, even more, to explain with precision.[27] As the master narrative of modern European religious history (the "big story" into which historians fit their own "small stories" and with which they make sense of their own research), it no longer enjoys the prominence it once did. Nonetheless, the fact remains that Jews were not immune to the impact of the broad, impersonal currents that fueled the decline in Christian belief, affiliation, and worship. In the eighteenth and nineteenth centuries, for example, Western Jewish communities became urban communities. It is an axiom that when West Europeans moved from the country to the city they encountered conditions that "militate[d] against the roots of the familiar and the familial" with which religious beliefs and practices were associated, and that religious institutions were "adversely affected by the increasing size of urban concentrations . . . and corroded by geographical and social mobility," especially when they led to "a relativization of perspectives on the world."[28] Was Judaism exempt from the impact of urbanization? Hardly. It is no coincidence that impiety and indifference were hallmarks of the London and Amsterdam communities, the two largest communities in the West, in the late eighteenth and early nineteenth centuries.

Of course, it is impossible to know how much the decline of Jewish observance was the result of a general cause (the disenchantment of the world) and how much the result of a particular cause (the flight from Jewishness). It is hard even to imagine how to disentangle their respective influence. Nonetheless, it is important to separate them conceptually. Leaving secularization out of the picture suggests that the Jews were immune to general forces of social change and, at the same time, inflates the transformative power of the *haskalah* and other programs of regeneration, leaving the false impression that reason, natural law, and other novel ideas convinced Jews that it was meaningless or unprofitable to separate meat and milk (for example). Owen Chadwick has warned against explaining secularization "by seizing only upon what was expressed in formal propositions, articulately." There are shifts in sentiment and consciousness that run deeper. "That is why the problem of secularization is not the problem of enlightenment. Enlightenment was of the few. Secularization is of the many."[29] Ignoring the impact of broad impersonal currents simply reinforces the old Germano-centric view of the origins of Jewish modernity, in which new ideologies restructured Jewish lives.[30] There is another reason as well to bring in the analytical category of secularization. If one attributes the decline of religious observance solely to the desire to efface Jewish distinctiveness, it is then impossible to explain the survival of Jewish social bonds after this decline, for, if the flight from Jewishness were the key, social cohesion would have declined at the same time as religious observance. But this was not the case. Secularization and integration did not advance in tandem. Social acceptance and mixing lagged behind the decline of belief and practice.

Social Interaction as Evidence of Uneven Transformation

The unevenness of the transformation of the Jews was most pronounced at the level of social relations between Jews and Christians. At first glance, middle-class Jews in Berlin, Paris, London, Amsterdam, Vienna, and Budapest were externally indistinguishable from their non-Jewish counterparts. They wore the same clothes, spoke the same language, visited the same cafés, museums, and concert halls, educated their children at the same schools, enjoyed the same leisure-time activities. To be sure there were subtle differences between the "intimate" culture of the Jews and that of their neighbors. In Imperial Germany, for example, urban, middle-class Jews read different books and newspapers, voted for different parties, responded to "Jewish" jokes in a different manner, and raised their children according to different norms.[31] They clung to the humanistic ideal of *Bildung*, to which the age of Enlightenment and emancipation first gave birth, long after irrationalism and nationalism had weakened its hold among educated Germans. They also killed themselves more frequently per capita than either Protestants or Catholics—which certainly suggests a distinctive sensibility.[32] But, on the surface, to the casual observer, little distinguished Jews from non-Jews in the broad externals of life.

However, while acculturation was well advanced by the turn of the century, integration into non-Jewish social circles and voluntary associations was not. During the nineteenth century, Jews in Western and Central Europe gained access to institutions and organizations that had excluded them in the past: legislatures, municipal councils, the military, the professions, fraternal groups, elite secondary schools, universities, clubs and casinos, charities, athletic and recreational associations. As a rule, English, French, Italian, and Dutch Jews were more successful in doing so than German, Austrian, and Hungarian Jews, although even the latter made their way, however haltingly, into the associational life of middle class society. Yet, despite these advances in institutional integration and social mixing in public forums, Jews remained a people apart in terms of their most fundamental social ties. Most married Jews, formed their closest friendships with other Jews, and relaxed and felt most comfortable in the homes of Jewish friends and relatives. In recalling his upper-middle-class youth in late Imperial Berlin, the fashion photographer Erwin Blumenfeld recalled that his freethinking, atheist parents contentedly lived within "invisible walls," associating exclusively with other Jews, and "were probably not even aware of it themselves." Very rarely "a stray goy happened to find his way into our house," and when one did, "we had no idea how to behave." The absence of social integration also characterized the home of Gershom Scholem. Despite his father's allegiance to liberal integrationism, "no Christian ever set foot in our home," not even Christians who were members of organizations in which his father was active (with the one telling exception of a formal fiftieth birthday visit). The oft-cited autobiographies of famous Jews (musicians, writers, scientists, intellectuals, bohemians), Scholem warned in another context, present a misleading picture. In "an ordinary middle-class bourgeois home, neither rich nor poor," like his, there was no social mixing between Jews and Christians. Richard Lichtheim underlined the awkwardness that arose when these barriers were transgressed. In the 1890s, when he visited the home of a non-Jewish school friend who lived with his uncle, a general, or when his friend visited him, each was aware of entering "enemy territory." No Jew had ever before appeared in the general's house or Christian in the Lichtheim house—although the Lichtheims were unobservant and most of his father's relatives converts to Christianity.[33] Reciprocal home visits, Marion Kaplan has aptly commented, "raised the stakes, announcing an intimacy with which most did not feel comfortable."[34]

The situation was not radically different among the very wealthiest Jewish families. In his exhaustive study of the German Jewish economic elite before World War I, Werner Mosse has concluded that from the late 1870s "unselfconscious and more or less spontaneous social relations between Jew and Gentile virtually ceased."[35] While government ministers, upper civil servants, army officers, and diplomats accepted invitations to lavish entertainments in the homes of Berlin's Jewish bankers and industrialists, they rarely reciprocated. Moreover, while social ambition and "feudalization" (capitulation to aristocratic values) fueled the cultivation of the high born, a very bourgeois motive was at work as well: the Berlin business and financial elite, Jews and Gentiles alike, courted the preindustrial elite for pragmatic reasons. They wanted the government business and privileged information that high office-holders and powerbrokers dispensed while hoping to influence economic and diplomatic policy. Contrary to popular belief, then and now, the highest goal of wealthy Jews was not social acceptance by and intermarriage with the Prussian nobility. Yes, their patterns of sociability were a defensive response to anti-Semitism, but they also reflected "the fact that most Jews of the upper bourgeoisie wanted to associate with Jews."[36] As Marion Kaplan has concluded, "Their starting point was a deep, primary loyalty to their families and a steady allegiance to their religious and ethnic community," both of which "restrained" social interaction with non-Jews.[37]

Outside Berlin, the social lines between wealthy Jews and Gentiles were often firmer. In Hamburg, for example, Jews lived entirely in a private sphere of their own. They did business with non-Jews during the day but at night went their own way. A similar pattern characterized Jewish-Christian interaction in Imperial Königsberg. Jews were welcome in all spheres of public life, including the city council and most voluntary associations, but their social contacts with non-Jews were limited to formal civic occasions and business-related dinners and *Kaffeekränzchen*. Informal, private life "mainly took place in the frame of one's own extended family or within a circle of other Jewish families, with the exception of a small group of Christian and Jewish music-loving families that met regularly." In Breslau, where friendships between Jews and Christians were perhaps more common, Till von Rahden has found it remarkable, in light of the numerous possibilities there were for interaction, "that there were not even more and that in many of these friendships a residue of social distance remained much in evidence."[38] In Prague, Jewish merchants and professionals were well integrated into the institutional life of the German community (largely in response to Czech nationalism). In the last two decades of the nineteenth century, their role as members and officers in the Deutsches Casino and the Deutscher Verein actually increased. But in the most intimate areas of family life Prague Jews remained a group apart. Few married non-Jews before World War I.[39]

From the 1870s on in Central Europe, even baptized Jews remained immersed in Jewish kinship and friendship networks, in which Jews, converted Jews, intermarried Jews, and Jews without religion (those who had formally withdrawn from the *Gemeinde* without converting to another faith) mixed. As social discrimination mounted, converts and those without religion were often forced (or preferred) to choose former Jews like themselves as friends and marriage partners. The close male friends of Gustav Mahler, Maximilian Harden, and countless other celebrated Central European converts were almost entirely Jews and converted Jews. In fin-de-siècle Vienna, the poet André Spire wrote, little changed in the lives of converts after their conversion. "They continued to live apart, in a separate world, among the Jews. . . . Their sons were able to marry only Jews or the daughters of converts." And in Weimar Germany, Hannah Arendt recalled, the convert "only rarely left his family and even more rarely left his Jewish surroundings altogether."[40]

In more liberal states, France and Britain in particular, there was greater social intimacy between Jews and non-Jews, just as there was greater integration at an institutional level.[41] But even in these states, Jewish social solidarity remained more or less firm. Like their German counterparts, French and English Jews kept Jewish company more often than not. The novelist Julia Frankau, a radical assimilationist who raised her children as Christians, noted the same absence of mixing as the German memoirists above. In her novel *Dr. Phillips* (1887), middle-class London Jews live in social isolation, cut off from intimate contact with Christians. In "the heart of a great and cosmopolitan city," she wrote, they constituted "a whole nation dwelling apart in an inviolable seclusion." She continued: "There are houses upon houses in the West Central districts, in Maida Vale, in the City, which are barred to Christians, to which the very name of Jew is an open sesame." To their most common form of social intercourse—card playing in each other's homes—"it was decidedly unusual to invite any but Jews."[42] In seeking to explain the prevalence of marriages between first cousins in late Victorian Anglo-Jewry, the pioneer social scientist Joseph Jacobs cited, inter alia, what he termed "shoolism"—the inclination of London Jews to limit their circle of friends and acquaintances to the members of their own synagogue (*shul*).[43] In France, even those high-ranking judicial and administrative officials whom Pierre Birnbaum has dubbed *"les Juifs d'état,"* graduates of the universities and the *grandes écoles* who zealously served the Third Republic as prefects, subprefects, and as members of the Conseil d'État, the Cour de Cassation, and the Cours d'Appel, tended to marry within the fold, retain membership in Jewish organizations, and establish close social ties with other Jewish state functionaries and politicians. If they had become servants of the universal, laicized state in the public arena, they remained Jewish in their private lives. Marcel Proust captured this kind of social cohesion in describing the Jews who vacationed at the seaside resort Balbec. When they visited the casino, "they formed a solid troop, homogeneous within itself, and utterly dissimilar to the people who watched them go by and found them there again every year without ever exchanging a word or greeting." They presented "a bold front in a compact and closed phalanx into which, as it happened, no one dreamed of trying to force his way."[44]

While distinguishing the secular from the religious in Jewish culture is always risky, it would appear that the bonds linking Western Jews in the half century before the First World War were more secular than religious in character. What made them Jewish was their similar background and descent, common memories and intimate culture, intragroup sociability, and endogamy rather than their religious faith, synagogue attendance, ritual observance, or Hebrew learning. Their Jewishness manifested itself in shared social and cultural practices that were rooted more in the immediate circumstances of their recent history than in the religious culture of traditional belief and practice. In this sense, their Jewishness resembled the ethnicity of the Russian Jews in Zvi Gitelman's chapter in this volume, an ethnicity based on biology and sentiment and defined more by boundaries than by content. Their Jewishness was symbolic ethnicity, a "thin" rather than "thick" culture, which was becoming progressively more "thin" with each generation because high levels of acculturation and secularization weakened its transferability. Unlike secular forms of Jewishness in Eastern Europe and the Yishuv, that of Central European Jews was not expressed in a distinctive and exclusively Jewish language (Yiddish or Hebrew) nor buttressed by a nationalist ideology (Yiddishism or Zionism) or territorial concentration (the Pale of Settlement or the Land of Israel).

Jacob Katz attributed the persistence of Jewish cohesion after the decline of Jewish observance to "the fact—the existential fact, as it were—of Jewish community, which, out of its own inner necessities and traditions, resisted the higher blandishments of emancipation." For him and other nationalist historians, "Jewish existence was a fact, a stubborn fact defying regnant ideology and philosophy."[45] In the early twentieth century, Jewish ethnologists and scientists attributed the persistence of Jewishness to the biological ties of race. The Anglo-Jewish geneticist Redcliffe N. Salaman wrote his fiancée in 1901 that it seemed to him almost self-evident, given the low level of "religious feeling amongst a large majority of the Jews," that "racial feeling" was the chief ingredient in Jewish cohesion: "When I am amongst Christians & the question at all arises of defending one's position as a Jew it is always the racial element that at once appeals—and in that way I feel that the Polish Jew is a brother though we may differ considerably in religion."[46] For the purpose of this essay, knowing the source of Jewish consciousness and cohesion in the aftermath of emancipation is less important than recognizing that it was manifested more frequently in secular than religious ways.

Jewish and Non-Jewish Perceptions of Emancipation

That said, it would be misleading to suggest that Jewish social cohesion in the nineteenth and early twentieth centuries remained rock solid, unshaken by drift and defection. The stigmatization of Jewishness in social and cultural life and the persistence of legal and social barriers to integration took their toll, leading tens of thousands of Jews (especially in Central Europe) to cut their ties to Judaism, through baptism, intermarriage, and other forms of radical disengagement. In Vienna alone, 9,000 Jews formally severed their ties to Judaism (withdrew from the Gemeinde, with or without baptism) between 1868 and 1903—a figure that does not include an unknown but considerable number of children who were baptized by their parents, either at birth or later. In Germany between 1880 and 1919, about 25,000 Jews chose either Protestant or Catholic baptism.[47] The German census of 1939 and the Hungarian census of 1941, both of which defined Jews in racial terms, provide evidence about the cumulative effect of communal secessions over several generations. In Berlin, 8.5 percent of the Jews were not members of the Gemeinde; in Vienna, 12 percent; in Budapest, 17 percent.[48]

Secession figures alone do not express the extent to which the stigmatization of Jewishness eroded its public expression. Among Jews who rejected conversion or secession, for reasons of conscience or otherwise, efforts to mute markers of Jewish difference became increasingly common from the 1870s. The Viennese novelist and satirist Robert Neumann recalled in his memoirs an incident about his mother that encapsulates these efforts. "To be a Jew [in pre–World War I Vienna] was one thing," he wrote, "but to discuss it was as much bad form as it was to swear, and almost as bad as mentioning anything with the functioning of the digestive or sexual organs." Once when his mother had to introduce to her guests a visitor "with the un-gentile name of Cohen . . . she pronounced his name again and again so unrecognizably and so much as if it were some painful infirmity from which he suffered that in the end he withdrew, red-faced."[49] To escape the stigma attached to Jewish family names, German Jews tried to change theirs—a move that officials fought tooth and nail. Some changed even their noses, following the development of cosmetic rhinoplasty by the Berlin Jewish orthopedic surgeon Jacques Joseph in 1898.[50] The pejorative meaning of the word *Jude* caused some to avoid using the word in conversation with other Jews, especially in public. Robert Weltsch, longtime editor of the *Jüdische Rundschau*, recalled that in the bourgeois circles of his youth in pre–World War I Prague it was considered tactless for anyone to say that he was a Jew and that "every Jew of good bourgeois standing avoided doing so," for the word had been "emptied of all positive content" and "shriveled up into a mere name of derision." Ernst Lissauer, author of the World War I "Hate Song against England," recalled that in his parents' Berlin house they would not use the word *Jude* if young girls were present and instead would replace it with "Armenian" or "Abyssinian."[51]

Stigmatization and exclusion were not so pervasive, however, that they stifled all informal social mixing. Social relations between Jews and non-Jews—the young above all—increased gradually, especially in the early twentieth century, weakening, though not dissolving, Jewish social cohesion. The increase in intermarriage from the 1870s through the 1930s indicates that Jews were not confined entirely to their own social ghetto. Intermarriage, then and now, presupposes sustained and more-or-less intimate social contact. In the case of West and Central European Jews, the sites of this social intercourse were the workplace, the university, the voluntary association, the political arena, the dance hall, and the promenade—sites where parents could not monitor their children's friendships and sexual relations. In the Netherlands, the percentage of Jews marrying who took non-Jewish spouses rose from 6.02 percent from 1901 to 1905 to 16.68 percent from 1931 to 1934. In German cities, intermarriage was even more common. In Berlin, from 1905 to 1906, there were 43.8 mixed marriages per 100 pure Jewish marriages; in Hamburg, from 1903 to 1905, 49.5; in Frankfurt, from 1905 to 1909, 24.7. In Breslau, the number jumped from 22.8 during 1874 to 1894, to 64.5 from 1905 to 1920. In Prussia, the rate of intermarriage almost doubled in the last quarter of the nineteenth century, rising from 9.8 intermarriages per 100 all-Jewish marriages from 1875 to 1879 to 18.6 from 1900 to 1903.[52] On the eve of World War I, there were perhaps as many as ten thousand intermarried couples in Prussia. Defection from Judaism in Imperial Germany, whether through intermarriage, conversion, or formal withdrawal from the *Gemeinde* without baptism, was common enough to lead some observers to prophesy that German Jewry was fated to disappear of its own accord. The best-known exposition of this theme was Felix Theilhaber's *Der Untergang der deutschen Juden*, first published in 1911.

Yet, even while informal social contacts were rising, Jews retained a collective social identity wherever they lived, an identity, as we have seen, defined less by their religious practice than by their social behavior. What struck Gentile contemporaries was the persistence of Jewish social separatism ("tribalism"), not its breakdown and decay. Despite their seemingly rapid progress in becoming Germans,

Englishmen, Frenchmen, etc., Jews, the argument went, refused to abandon their cultural and social distinctiveness. In the eyes of their critics, their transformation was stalled and incomplete. They still constituted a well-defined, high-profile social group. Heinrich Treitschke complained that despite their emancipation German Jews rejected "the blood mixing" (intermarriage) that was "the most effective way to equalize tribal differences."[53] To both conservative and liberal critics, this was scandalous: was not the purpose of emancipation to eradicate Jewish tribalism? To remove social and cultural barriers? Moreover, the upward mobility of the Jews, their unparalleled economic and cultural achievements after the removal of old regime restraints—along with their refusal to intermarry en masse or abandon their social cohesion—was an affront to Christian sensibility and pride, fueling fears of Jewish domination and further compounding the scandal. The contrast between their economic and cultural prominence and their marginal demographic status also contributed to Gentile anxiety. In rebutting Treitschke's antisemitic articles in the *Preussische Jahrbücher* in the winter of 1879–1880, the liberal historian Theodor Mommsen scolded Jews for failing to disappear into German society. Just as they had served as a universal element in the Roman Empire, "a force for cohesion shattering particularistic tribal elements, so now they must as '*ein Element der Composition der Stamme.*'" To enable them to carry out their historical task of aiding in German unification, Mommsen instructed them to dissolve their own associations with the same goals as nondenominational integrated ones. In his view, the preservation of Jewish identity for secular reasons was an affront to the Christian character of modern civilization. In the following decade, the Verein zur Abwehr des Antisemitismus, established by Christian liberals and progressives in 1891 to combat the new racial anti-Semitism, denounced the formation of Jewish fraternities and sports clubs because they encouraged Jewish continuity and survival.[54]

While the German case represents an extreme manifestation of liberal intolerance for Jewish continuity, it embodies nonetheless a broader split in Jewish and non-Jewish understandings of the meaning and scope of the transformation of the Jews. In Victorian Britain, where the revocation of Jewish emancipation was not on the table as it was in Central Europe, liberals and radicals still complained about the persistence of Jewish "tribalism." The radical crusader Henry Labouchere, editor of the pro-Gladstonian *Truth*, attacked Jews, beginning in 1878, for resisting "fusion" with Christians. Their endogamy and "clannishness" and their willingness to employ their resources collectively gave them an unfair economic advantage. "It would be desirable," he concluded, "that the state should allow no Jew to marry a Jewess." If the state failed to act and Anglo-Jewry refused to engineer its own voluntary dissolution, then the latter would be responsible for whatever prejudice they faced.[55] In the outburst of Liberal anti-Semitism sparked by Disraeli's Eastern policy, the historian Goldwin Smith attributed the persistence of anti-Jewish hostility to a fundamental misunderstanding in the midcentury emancipation debate. Those Christians who supported emancipation saw Jews as simply another dissenting sect, as persons no different than other citizens, except for their theological opinions, and they assumed that when toleration was extended to them they would become "like other citizens in every respect." The problem was that Jewry was "not a religious sect, but a vast relic of primæval tribalism, with its tribal mark [circumcision], its tribal separation, and its tribal God." "The affinity of Judaism" was "not to nonconformity but to caste." It was not Jewish beliefs that were "the root of the mischief" but the Jews' "peculiar character, habits, and position," which their endogamy preserved.[56]

The Source of Jewish Cohesion

Gentile criticism of the tribalism of the Jews (that is, their failure to intermarry and fade away) created a dilemma for Jewish spokesmen and apologists in the West. Needing to define the character of post-emancipation Jewish cohesion in public debate, they had few options (unless they were Zionists). Once again they restated the conceptual framework for emancipation articulated by Jewish and Christian emancipationists a century before. The Jews were to be integrated into state and society as members of a religious sect who differed from their fellow citizens only in their manner of worship. Their inclusion on this basis meshed with the liberal principle of religious toleration, which first emerged in the wake of early modern Protestant-Catholic violence and then gradually encompassed the toleration of non-Christian faiths as well. Jewish apologists and spokesmen told themselves, their fellow Jews, and the world at large that they were similar to everyone else, except for their religious beliefs and practices. The problem with this strategy was its failure to represent the character of post-emancipation Jewish life accurately.

First, Judaism, even after emancipation, was not a religion in the same way that Christianity was. It retained a collective social dimension and encompassed customs and laws that in Christian eyes were no longer matters of conscience. It regulated behavior in which Christianity took little interest, such as questions of diet and holy day rest. Jewish claims to toleration on the basis of religious difference extended into realms that went beyond conventional Christian understandings of the nature of religion. For example, in Victorian England, university entrance and scholarship examinations were administered on Saturdays, causing considerable distress to those who observed the laws of Sabbath rest. The Board of Deputies of British Jews repeatedly intervened to make alternative arrangements for Jewish candidates.[57] These met with success in most cases, but communal bodies elsewhere did not seek similar exemptions, knowing full well that officials neither understood nor felt sympathetic toward Jewish religious concerns. In the words of David Landes: "If you want a lively debate, try to explain to a group of French people, Jewish or non-Jewish, that the institution of Saturday classes is objectively anti-Jewish. Most Frenchmen cannot even understand the issue."[58]

Second, presenting the Jews as a religious minority misrepresented social reality. When Jewish publicists made religion the basis of Jewish difference, they did so as much from necessity as conviction. They were not blind to the social dimension of Jewish group life, as we will see. They knew full well that emancipation had not dissolved the social ties that bound Jews together and that what united most Jews was the synagogue they did not attend. Their problem was that European states (with the exception of the two multinational empires) endorsed the toleration of religious, not ethnic or national, difference. They conflated citizenship and nationality, leaving no conceptual space for Jewish social cohesion and distinctiveness. For them, citizenship required more than faithful observance of the laws of the land. It expected that those who enjoyed its blessings share the same fundamental ethnic or national identity and the habits, values, and tastes that went along with that identity. This meant that Jews were expected to experience an inner transformation that would reorient their sentiments and affections. Of course, states and societies varied in the degree to which cultural heterogeneity preoccupied them. The more secure they were about their own national greatness, the more content with their place in the world, the less obsessive they were about Jewish distinctiveness. German officialdom, for example, worried more about making Jews German than its British counterpart. But, in general, notions of multiculturalism, ethnic diversity, cultural pluralism, and the like were in the future. Political leaders, social theorists, and cultural spokesmen dreamed of national homogeneity, unity, solidarity, fusion, and integration, leaving religion as the sole basis for defining Jewish difference. As a result, in the face of cries to revoke emancipation and circumscribe their freedoms (which became widespread from the 1870s), Jews insisted ever more zealously in public debate that they were Germans (or whatever), reducing their Jewishness to a mere matter of confessional difference. What they could not do was acknowledge publicly their social cohesion and ethnic distinctiveness. That would have seemed a dangerous move, an invitation to disaster—aside from the question of whether they possessed the conceptual wherewithal to do so. And, when spokesmen for the nascent Zionist movement began to do just that—to define Jews in national terms—communal leaders in the West reacted with alarm, fearing that this endangered their hard-won legal and social achievements.[59] In his presidential address to the Anglo-Jewish Association in 1898, for example, Claude Goldsmid Montefiore warned that in the long run Zionism would be "prejudicial and deleterious to the best interests and truest welfare of the Jews themselves."[60]

It is not clear how conscious Jews (Zionists aside) were of the tension between how they defined themselves in public and how they actually lived their lives in private. To the best of my knowledge, there was no public conversation about this tension, not even an acknowledgement that it existed. And with the advent of Zionism, there was little likelihood that integrationist Jews would pursue the matter. Nonetheless, there is evidence that even those who opposed Zionism were aware that there was a nonreligious collective dimension to their Jewishness. This can be inferred from the willingness of Jews across the political and social spectrums to employ the language of race to describe their collective bonds. John Efron and Mitchell Hart have explained how the pioneers of Jewish social science used the terms and concepts of "race science" to study the sociology, anthropology, demography, and medical pathology of the Jews.[61] However, I have in mind a broader, less ideologically driven phenomenon—the widespread, casual, everyday use of racial language to describe the Jews as a social unit. (Most Jewish "race scientists" were Zionists for whom the racial and national character of the Jews were fused and perhaps inseparable.) Unable to describe their collective ties as national because of the terms of emancipation, emancipated Jews, observant and unobservant alike, borrowed the notion of race, which was ubiquitous from at least the 1870s through the 1940s.

French Jews, perhaps the least observant in Western and Central Europe, commonly and freely spoke of *la race juive*. The radical politician Alfred Naquet, nonpracticing and married to a Catholic, declared in the *Univers Israélite* in 1886 that he was "a Jew by race" but no longer a Jew "by religion."[62] Proust repeatedly ascribed the behavior, looks, and health of his Jewish characters to their racial background. Charles Swann, for example, the son (or grandson—it is not clear) of converted Jews, suffers from "ethnic eczema" and "the constipation of the prophets." When Swann aligned himself with the Dreyfusards, Proust attributed his move to a deep, ineluctable force—"Jewish blood"—that was at work in Swann and others who thought of themselves as emancipated.[63] Although these terms were explicitly biological, those who used them were not biological determinists in the main. Their use of the word *race* was imprecise and often contradictory. By using the word, they wanted to suggest a feeling of community with other Jews, a sense of common historical fate, and a deep emotional bond that transcended religious faith and observance. As Michael Marrus has written in his analysis of French Jewry at the time of the Dreyfus Affair, "the biological terminology of race provided a semantic framework within which all Jews could express these feelings of Jewish identity." Although French culture did not sanction this form of belonging and allegiance, it worked well for Jews, especially unobservant ones. "Only race offered the excuse for a lingering Jewishness among men who had renounced their religion."[64]

In Britain, communal notables, including those who opposed Zionism, freely used the term to describe the nonreligious foundations of Jewish cohesion. In 1871, the founders of the Anglo-Jewish Association, in setting forth the motives for creating an organization to aid unemancipated Jews in other lands, stressed the international, cosmopolitan character of Jewishness, using the language of race. Their aim, they wrote, was "to knit more closely together the bond of brotherhood which united Jew with Jew throughout the world, and which should make its members and fellow-workers sensible of the grand fact that the race of Israel belongs not to England or France alone, but to all the countries of the globe." The Jewish notables and scientists who supported Jewish participation in the Universal Races Congress in London in July 1911 were not Jewish nationalists (with the exception of Israel Zangwill). The only public objection to participation came from the American-born, Cambridge archaeologist and art historian Charles Waldstein, who deplored any manifestation of Jewish separatism and wrote to the *Times* protesting the classification of the Jews as an oriental race in the Congress program. When a reviewer of the memoirs of Lady Battersea (née Constance de Rothschild) implied that she had converted to Christianity, she angrily responded that it was not true, that she was "a Jewess by religion as well as by race."[65] Again, as in France, it was possible for Jewish apologists to both emphasize the ability of Jews to adapt to their surroundings and acknowledge simultaneously the ethnic basis of Jewish solidarity.

For example, in the opening pages of his apologetic volume *Jews As They Are* (1882), the composer and pianist Charles Kensington Salaman repeated the old integrationist chestnut that Jews differed from country to country since they took on the coloration of their surroundings, even quoting Isaac D'Israeli's words to this effect in his *Genius of Judaism*: "After a few generations the Hebrews assimilate with the character, and are actuated by the feelings of the nation of which they become part." But two pages later Salaman asked his readers to reflect on the near-miraculous post-biblical history of the Jewish "nation" and, in particular, on how modern Jews triumphed over "so terrible a state of racial adversity and degradation." He concluded: "None but a divinely-protected people could have done so."[66] Thus, in a mere few lines, Salaman managed to describe Jews as a race, a nation, and a people under divine protection.

In Germany, where defining Jewishness was a more pressing issue, Jews were much less likely to use the language of race in this ambiguous and unfocussed way. Nonetheless, by the Weimar period, there is evidence that even the staunchest liberals were dissatisfied with the old definition of the Jews as a religious group pure and simple. The leaders of the Centralverein deutscher Staatsbürger jüdischen Glaubens, a liberal, integrationist defense agency dating from 1893, used various neologisms that departed from the strictly religious definition of Jewishness that an earlier generation had invoked in the struggle for emancipation. Recognizing that this definition did not encompass the tens of thousands of non-observant Jews who still felt attached to other Jews (and who supported the work of the Centralverein), Ludwig Holländer, who headed the organization from 1921 to 1933, spoke increasingly of the Jews' *Schicksalsgemeinschaft* (community of fate). Words like *Stamm* (tribe) and *Abstammung* (descent) were invoked in sermons, apologia, and Centralverein publications. In seeking to define what was uniquely Jewish, Rabbi Cesar Seligmann told his Frankfurt congregants: "It is not Jewish conviction, not Jewish doctrine, not the Jewish creed that is the leading, the primary, the inspirational; rather, it is Jewish sentiment, the instinctive, call it what you will, call it the community of blood, call it tribal consciousness [*Stammesgefühl*], call it the ethnic soul [*Volksseele*], but best of all call it: the Jewish heart."[67]

Conclusion

The willingness of German Jews to coin new terms to describe the basis of their ties and of Jews in more liberal settings to define them in ambiguous and contradictory ways is symptomatic of a European-wide problem: Jews did not fit in the slot that classical liberalism created for them. Their Jewishness overflowed the narrow framework of religious doctrine and practice to which emancipation theoretically confined it. Liberal and other supporters of emancipation in the late eighteenth and nineteenth centuries envisioned the integration of Jews on the basis of their status as individuals without historical or cultural baggage. During the course of the emancipation debate, Jews agreed with their allies that their integration into state and society required their transformation, especially the differentiation of dimensions of Jewish life that earlier were part of a seamless web of behavior and consciousness. In hindsight, it is clear that both sides were vague, even naive, about what this entailed. It is also clear that, however vague the expectations of Jewish transformation were, Gentile friends of the Jews expected a more radical transformation than occurred following the removal of legal disabilities. Traditional faith and practice eroded; cultural distinctiveness shrunk; but social cohesion remained strong (though not intact). To the extent that Gentile supporters of emancipation thought in concrete terms, this was not an outcome that they foresaw. Their vision was blinded by a naive faith in human perfectibility and plasticity, in the power of laws, institutions, and circumstances to uproot and replace well-entrenched social and cultural traits. Their understanding of the visceral ties—memories, fears, affections, loathings—that bind historical minorities together was equally shallow. The persistence of Jewish ethnicity long after the weakening of Jewish religion frustrated, irritated, and, in some cases, enraged them. For their part, Jews had little ideological space in which to respond to this frustration and anger. Emancipation allowed them to define themselves, at least in public debate, only as a religious minority. What other choice was available? Racial discourse was available before the rise of Nazism, at least in those states where Jews avoided constant scrutiny and were able to talk about themselves in contradictory and ambiguous ways. The inadequacy of defining themselves solely in terms of faith and observance was obvious. Even hard-pressed German Jews struggled to find new terms and expressions to describe the reality of what bound them together. In any case, we can be confident that the construction "German [French, English, Hungarian, etc.] citizens of the Jewish faith" neither exhausted their self-understanding nor captured the social texture of their lives.

NOTES

1. Yosef Hayim Yerushalmi, *From Spanish Court to Italian Ghetto–Isaac Cardoso: A Study in Seventeenth-Century Marranism and Jewish Apologetics* (New York: Columbia University Press, 1971), 44. The most nuanced treatment of this negotiation is Miriam Bodian, *Hebrews of the Portuguese Nation: Conversos and Community in Early Modern Amsterdam* (Bloomington: Indiana University Press, 1997). See also David Graizbord, *Souls in Dispute: Converso Identities in Iberia and the Jewish Diaspora, 1580–1700* (Philadelphia: University of Pennsylvania Press, 2004).

2. On the transformation of the Jews in the eighteenth and nineteenth centuries, see Jacob Katz, *Out of the Ghetto: The Social Background of Jewish Emancipation, 1770–1870* (Cambridge, MA: Harvard University Press, 1973); Todd M. Endelman, *The Jews of Georgian England, 1714–1830: Tradition and Change in a Liberal Society* (Philadelphia: Jewish Publication Society, 1979); Jacob Katz, ed., *Toward Modernity: The European Jewish Model* (New Brunswick, NJ: Transaction Books, 1987); Paula E. Hyman, *The Emancipation of the Jews of Alsace: Acculturation and Tradition in the Nineteenth Century* (New Haven: Yale University Press, 1991); Jonathan Frankel and Steven J. Zipperstein, eds., *Assimilation and Community: The Jews in Nineteenth-Century Europe* (Cambridge: Cambridge University Press, 1992); Steven M. Lowenstein, *The Berlin Jewish Community: Enlightenment, Family, and Crisis, 1770–1830* (New York: Columbia University Press, 1994); Pierre Birnbaum and Ira Katznelson, eds., *Paths of Emancipation: Jews, States, and Citizenship* (Princeton: Princeton University Press, 1995).

3. Some social scientists employ the term *assimilation* to describe the combined process of changing one's culture (what I am calling acculturation) and changing one's subjective identity. For several reasons, I prefer to avoid the term. First, historically, the term was partisan and prescriptive, used to describe a political program for Jewish social and cultural transformation.

The political uses to which it was put in the past still hinder its employment as a value-free, descriptive concept. Second, when used in historical scholarship, it is often deployed without precision or rigor. Historians who write about Jewish modernization frequently fail to distinguish between *assimilation* as a complex of processes and *assimilation* as a cultural and political program. They often fail as well to distinguish between acculturation and integration. Third, *assimilation*, when used to describe subjective identity transformation (becoming Jewish *and* something else), refers to a state of mind rather than concrete practices. While social scientists, armed with the tools of quantitative survey research, can sample the thinking of entire populations, historians must make do with the ideologically driven programmatic statements of elites. The *behavior* of "average" Jews in the nineteenth and twentieth centuries (their acculturation, integration, and secularization) is more accessible than their sense of self-identification.

4. René Rémond, *Religion and Society in Modern Europe*, trans. Antonia Nevell (Oxford: Blackwell Publishers, 1999), 119.

5. Salo W. Baron, "The Modern Age," in *Great Ages and Ideas of the Jewish People*, ed. Leo W. Schwarz (New York: Modern Library, 1956), 317. Baron first advanced this view in the interwar period. See his "Ghetto and Emancipation: Shall We Revise the Traditional View?" *Menorah Journal* 14 (June 1928): 515–526; and his *Social and Religious History of the Jews*, 1st ed. (New York: Columbia University Press, 1937), vol. 2, chap. 11, "Emancipation."

6. "Ujabb tanács" (More Advice), *Egyenlöseg* (Equality), February 10, 1889, quoted in Mary Gluck, "The Budapest Flâneur: Urban Modernity, Popular Culture, and the 'Jewish Question' in Hungary," *Jewish Social Studies*, n.s., 10, no. 3 (2004): 7.

7. *Opinion de M. le comte Stanislas de Clermont-Tonnerre, député de Paris, le 23* décembre 1789 (Paris, 1789), 13, quoted in Patrick Girard, *Les Juifs de France de 1789 à 1860* (Paris: Calmann-Lévy, 1976), 51.

8. Berr Isaac Berr, *Lettre d'un citoyen . . . à ses confrères* (Nancy, 1791), in Diogene Tama, ed., *Transactions of the Parisian Sanhedrin* (London: C. Taylor, 1807), 15–17.

9. John Toland, *Reasons for Naturalizing the Jews in Great Britain and Ireland on the Same Foot with All Other Nations* (London, 1714), 18.

10. Thomas Babington Macaulay, *Critical and Historical Essays*, 2 vols. (London: Longman, Brown, Green, and Longmans, 1854), 1:142–144.

11. Christian Wilhelm von Dohm, *Concerning the Amelioration of the Civil Status of the Jews*, trans. Helen Lederer (Cincinnati: Hebrew Union College; Jewish Institute of Religion, 1957), 3, 14.

12. *The Voice of Jacob*, January 31, 1845.

13. Calvin Goldscheider and Alan S. Zuckerman, *The Transformation of the Jews* (Chicago: University of Chicago Press, 1984), 7.

14. Thomas Winstanley, *A Sermon Preached at the Parish Church of St. George, Hanover Square, Sunday, October 28, 1753* (London, 1753), 12–14.

15. Ruth F. Necheles, *The Abbé Grégoire, 1787–1831: The Odyssey of an Egalitarian* (Westport, CT: Greenwood, 1971).

16. Ellen Littmann, "David Friedländers Sendschreiben an Probst Teller und sein Echo," *Zeitschrift für Geschichte der Juden in Deutschland* 6 (1935): 92–112. Also helpful is Richard Cohen's introduction to the 1975 reprint of the original German text, along with a Hebrew translation, that the Zalman Shazar Center and the Hebrew University published in their *Kuntresim* series, no. 44.

17. On the Jewish Saint-Simonians, see Barrie M. Ratcliffe, "Some Jewish Problems in the Early Careers of Emile and Isaac Pereire," *Jewish Social Studies* 34, 3 (1972): 189–206; Michael Graetz, *Ha-periferyah haytah la-merkaz: Perakim be-toldot yahadut tsorfat ba-meah ha-shmonah esreh mi-Saint-Simon ad li-yessud "kol Yisrael haverim"* (The Periphery Became the Center: Chapters in the History of French Jewry in the Nineteenth Century from Saint Simon to the Founding of the Alliance Israélite Universelle) (Jerusalem: Mosad Bialik, 1982), chap. 4; Perrine Simon Nahum, *La Cité investie: La "Science du judaïsme" français et la République* (Paris: Éditions du Cerf, 1991), 25–39.

18. Graetz, *Ha-periferyah haytah la-merkaz*, chap. 6; Paula E. Hyman, "Joseph Salvador: Proto-Zionist or Apologist for Assimilation?" *Jewish Social Studies* 34, no. 1 (1972): 1–22.

19. The literature on this topic is enormous. See in particular Edmund Silberner, *Sozialisten zur Judenfrage* (Berlin: Colloquium Verlag, 1962); Robert S. Wistrich, *Socialism and the Jews: The Dilemmas of Assimilation in Germany and Austria-Hungary* (Rutherford, NJ: Fairleigh Dickinson University Press, 1982); Isaiah Berlin, "Benjamin Disraeli, Karl Marx and the Search for Identity," in *Against the Current: Essays in the History of Ideas*, ed. Clarendon Paperback (Oxford: Oxford University Press, 1991).

20. Quoted in Alan Levenson, "Jewish Reactions to Intermarriage in Nineteenth-Century Germany" (Ph.D. diss., Ohio State University, 1990), 136. Levenson discusses a number of advocates of Jewish dissolution in chapter 4 and in "The Conversionary Impulse in Fin-de-Siècle Germany," *Leo Baeck Institute Year Book* 40 (1995): 107–122.

21. Levenson, "The Conversionary Impulse," 112; Alan Levenson, "Radical Assimilation and Radical Assimilationists in Imperial Germany," in *What Is Modern about the Modern Jewish Experience?* ed. Marc Lee Raphael (Williamsburg, VA: Department of Religion, College of William and Mary, 1997), 40.

22. J. C. H. Blom and J. J. Cahen, "Jewish Netherlanders, Netherlands Jews, and Jews in the Netherlands, 1870–1940," in *The History of the Jews in the Netherlands*, ed. J. C. H. Blom et al., trans. Arnold J. Pomerans and Erica Pomerans (Oxford: Littman Library of Jewish Civilization, 2002), 249.

23. Callum G. Brown, "The Secularisation Decade: What the 1960s Have Done to the Study of Religious History," and Jeffrey Cox, "Master Narratives of Long-Term Religious Change," in *The Decline of Christendom in Western Europe, 1750–2000*, ed. Hugh McLeod and Werner Ustorf (Cambridge: Cambridge University Press, 2003).

24. Michael Meyer has briefly discussed the relationship between modernization and secularization in his contribution to the Yosef Yerushalmi *Festschrift*. While acknowledging that Jews expanded "the secular spheres of their existence" and devoted "less time and concentration to specifically religious matters," he has preferred to describe this change as "a displacement of the sacred rather than its abandonment." Thus, when Jews performed tasks to further "universal progress," he believes that those activities were cloaked in "the mantle of sanctity." Perhaps. But this interpretive move may also express an unwillingness to confront the decline of Jewish belief and practice in the modern period. See "Reflections on Jewish Modernization," in *Jewish History and Jewish Memory: Essays in Honor of Yosef Hayim Yerushalmi*, ed. Elisheva Carlebach et al. (Hanover, NH: University Press of New England, 1998), 372–373.

25. Steven Lowenstein found that in nineteenth-century Germany, small-town Jews often embraced a secular outlook before moving to the city. See his collection *The Mechanics of Change: Essays in the Social History of German Jewry* (Atlanta: Scholars Press, 1992).

26. Max Weber, "Science as a Vocation," in *From Max Weber: Essays in Sociology*, trans. and ed. H. H. Gerth and C. Wright Mills (New York: Oxford University Press, 1946), 139.

27. The best working definition of secularization with which I am familiar is that of David Ellenson: "If the attitude of the premodern traditionalist is captured in the words of the Psalmist, 'I have placed the Eternal before me always,' the paraphrase uttered even by the religious traditionalist in a secularized world is, 'I place the Eternal before me, but not all the time'"; *After Emancipation: Jewish Religious Responses to Modernity* (Cincinnati: Hebrew Union College Press, 2004), 239.

28. David Martin, *A General Theory of Secularization*, ed. Harper Colophon (New York: Harper & Row, 1979), 83, 160.

29. Owen Chadwick, *The Secularization of the European Mind in the Nineteenth Century* (Cambridge: Cambridge University Press, 1975), 8–9.

30. This is the central theme of Goldscheider and Zuckerman, *The Transformation of the Jews*. For example: "Religious decline resulted neither from the inability of old ideas to adapt to new conditions nor from the less demanding nature of some of the new religious ideologies, but

from transformations in social conditions" (64). More broadly, they argue that "most—but not all—of the transformations that have occurred among Jews during the processes of modernization relate to general forces of social change" (ix). The problem with their account is that in seeking to undermine explanations that emphasize the unique and the particular in the transformation of the Jews they take an equally unbalanced view and throw out the baby with the bathwater—that is, they fail to give due recognition as well to the transformative pressures that Jews qua Jews experienced as Christendom's quintessential outsiders.

31. Henry Wassermann, "Tarbutam ha-intimit shel yehudei-germanyah" (The Intimate Culture of German Jewry), in *Crises of German National Consciousness in the 19th and 20th Centuries*, ed. Moshe Zimmermann (Jerusalem: Magnes Press, Hebrew University, 1983), 187–198; Shulamit Volkov, "Yihud u-temiyah: Paradoks ha-zehut ha-yehudit ba-reich ha-sheni" (Unity and Assimilation: The Paradox of Jewish Identity in the Second Empire), in *Crises of German National Consciousness*, 169–185; Shulamit Volkov, "Yehudai germanyah ba-meah ha-tesha-esrei: Sheaftanut, hatslakhah, temiyah" (The Jews of Germany in the Nineteenth Century: Ambition, Success, Assimilation), in *Hitbolelut u-temiyah: Hemshekhiyyut u-temurah be-tarbut ha-amim u-ve-yisrael* (Acculturation and Assimilation: Continuity and Change in Jewish and Non-Jewish Culture), ed. Yosef Kaplan and Menahem Stern (Jerusalem: Zalman Shazar Center for Jewish History, 1989), 173–188; Jacob Katz, "German Culture and the Jews," in *The Jewish Response to German Culture from the Enlightenment to the Second World War*, ed. Jehuda Reinharz and Walter Schatzberg (Hanover, NH: University Press of New England, 1985), 58–99.

32. Konrad Kwiet, "The Ultimate Refuge: Suicide in the Jewish Community under the Nazis," *Leo Baeck Institute Year Book* 29 (1984): 140, table 1. On the ideal of *Bildung* in German Jewish culture, see George L. Mosse, *German Jews beyond Judaism* (Bloomington: Indiana University Press, 1985).

33. Erwin Blumenfeld, *Eye to I: The Autobiography of a Photographer*, trans. Mike Mitchell and Brian Murdoch (London: Thames and Hudson, 1999), 52; Gershom Scholem, "With Gershom Scholem: An Interview," in *On Jews and Judaism in Crisis: Selected Essays*, ed. Werner J. Dannhauser (New York: Schocken, 1976), 4–6; Gershom Scholem, "On the Social Psychology of the Jews in Germany, 1900–1933," in *Jews and Germans from 1860 to 1933: The Problematic Symbiosis*, ed. David Bronsen (Heidelberg: Winter, 1979), 18–19; Richard Lichtheim, *She'ar yashuv: Zichronot tsiyoni mi-germanyah* (A Remnant Shall Return: Memoirs of a Zionist from Germany) (Jerusalem: Ha-Histadrut Ha-Tsiyonit, 1953), 37.

34. Marion Kaplan, "Friendship on the Margins: Jewish Social Relations in Imperial Germany," *Central European History* 34, no. 4 (2001): 481. Georg Simmel's distinction between *friends* and *acquaintances* is helpful in understanding the character of German-Jewish social relations. Ties between *friends* are rooted in the total personality, while mutual acquaintance, such as we find in the German-Jewish case, "involves no actual insight into the individual nature of the personality." *Acquaintance* "depends upon the knowledge of the *that* of the personality, not of its *what*. After all, by saying that one is acquainted, even well acquainted, with a particular person, one characterizes quite clearly the lack of really intimate relations. Under the rubric of acquaintance, one knows of the other only what he is toward the outside. . . . The degree of knowledge covered . . . refers not to the other *per se*; not to what is essential in him, intrinsically, but only to what is significant for that aspect of him which is turned towards others and the world." *The Sociology of Georg Simmel*, trans. and ed. Kurt H. Wolff (Glencoe, IL: Free Press, 1950), 320. Simmel's own fate—baptized at birth, he, as well as his work, was labeled and scorned as Jewish—may have contributed to his thinking.

35. Werner E. Mosse, *The German-Jewish Economic Elite, 1820–1935: A Socio-Cultural Profile* (Oxford: Clarendon Press, 1989), 93, 95.

36. Dolores L. Augustine, *Patricians and Parvenus: Wealth and High Society in Wilhelmine Germany* (Oxford: Berg, 1994), 240.

37. Kaplan, "Friendship on the Margins," 274.

38. Augustine, *Patricians and Parvenus*, 194–195; Stefanie Schüler-Springorum, "Assimilation and Community Reconsidered: The Jewish Community in Königsberg, 1871–1914," *Jewish Social*

Studies, n.s., 5, no. 3 (1999): 105–106, 110; Till van Rahden, *Juden und andere Breslauer: Die Beziehungen zwischen Juden, Protestanten und Katholiken in einer deutschen Grossstadt von 1860 bis 1925* (Göttingen: Vandenhoeck & Ruprecht, 2000), 132.

39. Gary B. Cohen, *The Politics of Ethnic Survival: Germans in Prague, 1861–1914* (Princeton: Princeton University Press, 1981), 136, 177–179.

40. Norman Lebrecht, *Mahler Remembered* (London: Faber and Faber, 1987), xix–xx, n. 53; Mosse, *The German-Jewish Economic Elite,* 130; André Spire, *Quelques Juifs,* 2nd ed. (Paris: Société du Mercure de France, 1913), 195; Hannah Arendt, *The Origins of Totalitarianism,* part 1, *Anti-Semitism* (New York: Harcourt, Brace & World, 1966), 64 n. 23.

41. Todd M. Endelman, *Radical Assimilation in English Jewish History, 1656–1945* (Bloomington: Indiana University Press, 1990), chaps. 3–4. There is no parallel work on Jewish social integration in other liberal, western states in the nineteenth century.

42. Julia Frankau [Frank Danby], *Dr. Phillips: A Maida Vale Idyll* (London: Vizetelly, 1887), 55, 168. See also Todd M. Endelman, "The Frankaus of London: A Study in Radical Assimilation, 1837–1967," *Jewish History* 8, nos. 1–2 (1994): 117–154.

43. Joseph Jacobs, *Studies in Jewish Statistics: Social, Vital and Anthropometric* (London: D. Nutt, 1891), 6.

44. Pierre Birnbaum, *Les Fous de la République: Histoire politique des Juifs d'état de Gambetta à Vichy* (Paris: Fayard, 1992); Marcel Proust, *In Search of Lost Time,* trans. C. K. Scott Moncrieff and Terence Kilmartin, rev. D. J. Enright (New York: Random House, 1992–1993), 2:434–435.

45. Jacob Katz, "Emancipation and Jewish Studies," in *Jewish Emancipation and Self-Emancipation,* 81–82.

46. Redcliffe N. Salaman to Nina Davis, July 16, 1901, MS 8171/97, Redcliffe Nathan Salaman Papers, Cambridge University Library.

47. Jakob Thon, *Die Juden in Oesterreich* (Berlin: L. Lamm, 1908), 69–70; Monika Richarz, "Demographic Developments," in *German-Jewish History in Modern Times,* ed. Michael A. Meyer, vol. 3, *Integration in Dispute, 1871–1918* (New York: Columbia University Press, 1997), 15–16.

48. Peter Honigmann, "Jewish Conversions—A Measure of Assimilation? A Discussion of the Berlin Secession Statistics of 1770–1941," *Leo Baeck Institute Year Book* 34 (1989): 5. Honigmann acknowledges that these figures are not precise and "at best give no more than the order of magnitude" of formal defection. This is because the considerable emigration that occurred after 1933 might have changed the balance between the two groups (Jews by virtue of their formal communal membership and Jews by virtue of their racial background).

49. Robert Neumann, *The Plague House Papers* (London: Hutchinson, 1959), 85–86.

50. Dietz Bering, *The Stigma of Names: Anti-Semitism in German Daily Life, 1812–1933,* trans. Neville Plaice (Ann Arbor: University of Michigan Press, 1992); Sander Gilman, *The Jew's Body* (London: Routledge, 1991), 181–188.

51. Robert Weltsch, introduction to Martin Buber, *Der Jude under sein Judentum: Gesammelte Aufsätze und Reden,* 2nd ed. (Gerlingen: L. Schneider, 1993), xv; Ernst Lissauer, "Bemerkungen über mein Leben," *Bulletin des Leo Baeck Instituts* 20 (December 1962): 297.

52. E. Boekman, *Demographie van de Joden in Nederland* (Amsterdam: M. Hertzberger, 1936), 59; Arthur Ruppin, *The Jews of To-Day,* trans. Margery Bentwich (New York: Henry Holt, 1913), 163; Yaakov Lestschinsky, "Ha-shemad be aratsot shonot" (Apostasy in Different Lands), *Ha-olam* 5, no. 9 (1911): 4; Van Rahden, *Juden und andere Breslauer,* 149, table 27.

53. Quoted in Walter Boehlich, ed., *Der Berliner Anti-Semitismusstreit* (Frankfurt a. Main: Insel-Verlag, 1965), 79.

54. Uriel Tal, *Yahadut ve-natsrut ba-"reich ha-sheni"* (1870–1914) (Jews and Christians in the "Second Reich") (Jerusalem: Magnes Press, Hebrew University, 1969), 26–27; Ismar Schorsch, *Jewish Reactions to German Anti-Semitism, 1870–1914* (New York: Columbia University Press, 1972), 63, 95–97. Earlier in the century the abbé Grégoire expressed his frustration with French Jews for refusing to regenerate themselves, like their "enlightened brethren" in Germany, in the

wake of emancipation. Alyssa Goldstein Sepinwall, "Strategic Friendships: Jewish Intellectuals, the Abbé Grégoire, and the French Revolution," in *Renewing the Past, Reconfiguring Jewish Culture: From Al-Andalus to the Haskalah*, ed. Ross Brann and Adam Sutcliffe (Philadelphia: University of Pennsylvania Press, 2004), 192.

55. Claire Hirshfield, "The Tenacity of Tradition: *Truth* and the Jews, 1877–1957," *Patterns of Prejudice* 28, nos. 3–4 (1994): 69.

56. Goldwin Smith, "The Jewish Question," *The Nineteenth Century* 10 (1881): 495, 497, 499.

57. Charles H. L. Emanuel, *A Century and a Half of Jewish History Extracted from the Minute Books of the London Committee of Deputies of the British Jews* (London: George Routledge & Sons, 1910); David C. Itzkowitz, "Cultural Pluralism and the Board of Deputies of British Jews," in *Religion and Irreligion in Victorian Society: Essays in Honor of R. K. Webb*, ed. R. W. Davis and R. J. Helmstadter (London: Routledge, 1992), 85–101.

58. David S. Landes, "Two Cheers for Emancipation," in *The Jews in Modern France*, ed. Frances Malino and Bernard Wasserstein (Hanover, NH: University Press of New England, 1985), 291 n. 4.

59. Stuart A. Cohen, *English Zionists and British Jews: The Communal Politics of Anglo-Jewry, 1895–1920* (Princeton: Princeton University Press, 1982), chaps. 5–8; Jehuda Reinharz, *Fatherland or Promised Land: The Dilemma of the German Jew, 1893–1914* (Ann Arbor: University of Michigan Press, 1975), chap. 5; Paula Hyman, *From Dreyfus to Vichy: The Remaking of French Jewry, 1906–1939* (New York: Columbia University Press, 1979), 155–169.

60. *Jewish Chronicle*, July 8, 1898.

61. John M. Efron, *Defenders of the Race: Jewish Doctors and Race Science in Fin-de-Siècle Europe* (New Haven: Yale University Press, 1994); Mitchell B. Hart, *Social Science and the Politics of Modern Jewish Identity* (Stanford: Stanford University Press, 2000).

62. Quoted in Michael R. Marrus, *The Politics of Assimilation: A Study of the French Jewish Community at the Time of the Dreyfus Affair* (Oxford: Clarendon Press, 1971), 20.

63. Proust, *In Search of Lost Time*, 1:571, 2:643–644.

64. Marrus, *The Politics of Assimilation*, 26.

65. *Report of the Anglo-Jewish Association, 1871–1872* (London, 1872), 8; *Jewish Chronicle*, May 12, 1911; *Jewish Guardian*, December 1, 1922.

66. Charles Kensington Salaman, *Jews As They Are* (London: Simpkin, Marshall, 1882), 7, 9.

67. Donald L. Niewyk, *The Jews in Weimar Germany* (Baton Rouge: University of Louisiana Press, 1980), 103–106; Ruth Louise Pierson, "German Jewish Identity in the Weimar Republic" (Ph.D. diss., Yale University, 1970), chap. 1.

People of the (Secular) Book

LITERARY ANTHOLOGIES AND THE
MAKING OF JEWISH IDENTITY IN
POSTWAR AMERICA

JULIAN LEVINSON

*Reb Hersh, you say that I have forsaken a fountain of
living waters for a broken cistern. I must tell you you're
wrong. I draw water from the same pure fountain as
you, only I use a different vessel.*
—Chaim Grade, "My Quarrel With Hersh Rasseyner"

If secular Jewish culture exists, then it would seem to possess identifiable content. It should be possible, that is, to find practices, ideas, or texts that might be defined at once as Jewish and nonreligious. This is obvious, perhaps, and yet little agreement exists on how to define the content of secular Jewish culture. One possibility, suggested over the years by various scholars and intellectuals, has been through literature—not in the sense of rabbinic commentary, ethical literature (e.g., *musar*), or any other genre sanctioned by religious tradition—but rather in the sense of Jewish belles lettres.[1] If the religious Jew reads the rabbinic *Pirke Avot* on Shabbat afternoon, the argument goes, his or her secular counterpart would spend the same time with a novel by Saul Bellow. Jewish literature conceived along these lines is notoriously difficult to define, but it is generally understood to include novels, stories, plays, or poems by Jews on Jewish themes or possessing an identifiable relation to ideas, images, or values associated with Judaism.[2] Unlike religious texts, however, these texts do not derive sanction for their views or values from divine revelation or any communally sanctioned tradition of commentary. They are considered to be solely products of human creativity, expressing the subjective opinions, outlook, or "vision" of the author. According to this definition, a novel by an American Jew about a man struggling to understand his place in the modern world (such as Bellow's *Herzog*) might well qualify as secular Jewish culture. Part of the appeal of this notion of secular Jewish literature, we might add, is that it preserves the traditional image of Jews as the "people of the book," while broadening the definition of "the book."

No sooner are such propositions put forth, however, than a host of definitional problems appear. What qualities must a work include before it is accepted as "Jewish"? Must it be written by a Jew? Must it be explicitly about Jews? How might one demonstrate that a work derives from a specifically Jewish sensibility rather than some other source? (To return to the above example, Saul Bellow has humorously disparaged those who would pin him with the label "Jewish writer": "I am well aware of being Jewish and also of being American and also of being a writer. But I'm also a hockey fan, a fact which nobody ever mentions."[3]) Moreover, to get to the heart of our concerns here, even if a given work seems close enough to Jewish life to qualify as *Jewish* literature, how can we confidently place it under the *secular* rubric? Allen Ginsberg's autobiographical poem about his mother, "Kaddish," includes transliterated passages from the Aramaic prayer. But its primary theme is his mother's descent into schizophrenia and his personal development as a poet. Henry Roth's *Call It Sleep* features a protagonist obsessed with the Book of Isaiah, and yet the text continually reminds the reader that he is but a young, vulnerable boy. The novel's style and overall aims share much more with the High Modernism of James Joyce than any Jewish source. E. L. Doctorow's *The Book of Daniel* also pivots around allusions to biblical prophets, even though Doctorow's main point is to retell the story of the Rosenbergs' trial and execution. None of these works would generally be classified among Judaism's religious texts. If they contain some religious sentiments or yearnings, these are more properly associated with "religiosity" (vague feelings connected with the supernatural) than with Judaism proper. Thus their Judaic motifs seem only to function metaphorically: the Kaddish becomes a type of lament, and the figure of the prophet stands for the defiant critic of the status quo.

And yet this seems too easy. A religious allusion does not get automatically separated from the traditions of Judaism simply because of the ostensibly (secular) purpose of the work. After all, the meaning of any metaphor derives from its original context, which remains present even in the new context as a tacit frame of reference (a "trace," in the language of deconstruction. At the very least, the use of a motif borrowed from Judaism would complicate any simple assignation of a text to the realm of the secular. Nor are the avowed attitudes of authors sufficient as a final arbiter of a text's meaning. As D. H. Lawrence wrote, "Trust the tale, not the teller.") And, finally, were one to argue that, allusions and motifs notwithstanding, a form like the novel is somehow inherently secular, one would have to contend with the fact that for every theory of the novel as a secular or at least agnostic form (recall Mikhail Bakhtin's claim that the novel "denies the absolutism of a single and unitary language"),[4] countless readers have found religious teachings encoded within novels (consider, for example, Gershom Scholem's argument that Kafka's *The Trial* allegorically recapitulates key insights of the Kabbalah).[5] Thus one would be hard pressed to determine the status of a given work as secular or religious solely on the basis of its internal, formal characteristics.

A further complication is introduced when we consider the institutional contexts in which works are presented. Countless examples abound of texts being brought into liturgical or other sacral contexts even though their religious content is debatable. A classic case is the Song of Songs, which is considered appropriate for the biblical canon only when its erotic motif is read allegorically to recount the love affair between Israel and God. Similarly, poems or other kinds of writing that might be read as secular in one context can be introduced into religious services, where they are suddenly read with an eye toward their religious significance. One example is a liturgy recently compiled for Yom Hashoah by the literary scholar David Roskies. The liturgy *Nightwords* is comprised of a number of radically different sources, ranging from the Hebrew Bible to the Talmud and the Midrash to modern literary texts, most (but not all) by Jewish writers. What makes this example particularly complex is that one impulse behind the liturgy is to bear witness to the experience of the eclipse of God. One of the included poems is Yehuda Amichai's "El Male Rachamim" (God Full of Compassion), which evokes the traditional prayer only to subvert its meaning. In the lines "I . . . Who brought fallen bodies down from the hills / Can swear that the world is devoid of compassion," Amichai challenges the idea of a God who intervenes mercifully in human affairs. Here, then, is a poem written in defiance of religious tradition but inserted into a liturgical context.[6]

On the other hand, texts generally used in religious contexts may be brought into secular contexts, where once again they take on different meanings. Perhaps the most unambiguously religious Jewish text is the Pentateuch, traditionally ascribed to Moses' authorship under God's direction. Indeed, to bolster its status as divine scripture, the Talmud provides lengthy explanations of the ontological division separating words of Torah from mere works of poetry.[7] And yet, beginning as early as Longinus's first century treatise *On the Sublime*, we observe an approach to the Bible "as literature," namely as a body of writing studied primarily for its stylistic devices and patterns of imagery.[8] Erich Auerbach's "Ulysses' scar" (1946) reflects a similar approach. Auerbach contrasted the story of the binding of Isaac from Genesis to the account of Odysseus's homecoming in *The Odyssey* to illuminate two "basic types" of narrative style. Auerbach argued that these types serve as "a starting point for an investigation into the *literary representation* of reality in European literature" (19; emphasis added).[9] In addition to the creation of a subfield within biblical research, the idea of the Bible as literature has flourished in American universities since the mid twentieth century, where the Bible is routinely taught as world literature.[10] When the Bible is introduced in the context of a nonsectarian classroom, its traditional significance for religious Jews is defined as but one aspect to be considered.

These problems are abrogated, perhaps, if the discussion is limited to works written in a Jewish language, such as Hebrew, Yiddish, or Ladino. In "Secularity and the Tradition of Hebrew Verse," Robert Alter has argued that religious and secular elements have existed side by side in Hebrew poetry, beginning with medieval poets like Judah Halevi and Solomon Ibn Gvirol. Juxtaposing liturgical poems (*piyyutim*) with works focusing on this-worldly themes such as nature, erotic love, and drinking, Alter pointed to "the vigor with which a secular sensibility could flourish in the heart of an officially religious culture."[11] For Alter, the Jewishness of these latter works is guaranteed by virtue of being written in Hebrew; their secularity derives from their this-worldly focus. This would seem a plausible argument. But when we turn to writers who use non-Jewish languages, Alter's argument provides little help, because it is more problematic to insist that a given work maintain a close focus on things Jewish as well as a sufficient distance from things religious to qualify as both Jewish and secular.

It would appear, then, that the search for secular Jewish literature as a sui generis discourse is doomed to an arbitrary process of abstract definition and imprecise measurement. The lines separating the secular from the religious are hazy at best, and in any case, the context in which a work is read seems to trump any formal criteria in determining its status as secular or religious. Moreover, individual readers are inevitably affected by their own backgrounds and interests as they read, once again introducing an element of indeterminacy. But if these considerations lead us away from the study of individual works (i.e., away from asking whether the work is secular or religious), they also introduce secondary questions about when and how literature has been used to promote the agenda of secular Jewish culture. For the fact remains that many who have supported the idea of secular Jewishness have looked to literature as a touchstone for this form of identity. Thus secularism need not be looked for in the literary work itself; it can be seen instead as a project that might use literature in defining Jewish identity.

To proceed along these lines, we can examine different anthologies of Jewish literature that have been compiled with some view of Jewish secularity in mind. A literary anthology typically leads to the construction of a "canon," a list of works proffered as the embodiment or metonymic representation (i.e., a part standing for the whole) of a tradition. In Jewish history, we might add, anthologies have played an especially prominent role in redefining textual tradition at various historical junctures (for example, medieval anthologies such as *Yalqut shim'oni*, the *Maysebukh*, and the *Tsena u're'na*, or modern collections such as *Sefer ha'agadah* or *Mimkor yisrael*).[12] Behind every anthology it is possible to find some premise, implicitly or explicitly stated, about the meaning of Jewishness.[13] Different forms of Jewish identity, including secular forms, can thus be tracked by analyzing literary anthologies.

In the following discussion, I will consider three anthologies published since the end of World War II. The period in question has witnessed an increase in the production of anthologies of Jewish writing, prompted, among other reasons, by an impulse to reconstitute some sort of Jewish culture in the wake of the Holocaust. The anthologies I will examine include *Jewish Short Stories* (1945), edited by Ludwig Lewisohn; *A Treasury of Yiddish Stories* (1954), edited by Irving Howe and Eliezer Greenberg; and *Jewish American Literature: A Norton Anthology* (2001), edited by Jules Chametzky, John Felstiner, Hilene Flanzbaum, and Kathryn Hellerstein. Broadly speaking, these anthologies may be linked respectively with the agendas of Cultural Zionism, Yiddishism and/or Bundism, and American multiculturalism. To understand how these anthologies construct versions of Jewish identity, we must consider the specific contexts in which they were produced, their targeted audiences, and the vocabularies available for defining individual and group identities.

Jewish Short Stories (1945)

This anthology was commissioned in 1945, just as World War II was ending, by the National Jewish Welfare Board (JWB) for distribution through the United Service Organization (USO). Formed in 1941, the mandate of the USO was and continues to be to "provide morale, welfare, and recreation-type services to military personnel . . . extending a touch of home to the military." Their activities include organizing concerts, providing cafes and other meeting places, and distributing reading materials such as novels, popular magazines, and religious books for military personnel. The JWB was known primarily as a religious organization, as were five of the other six service agencies that formed the USO: the YMCA, the YWCA, the National Catholic Community Service, and the Salvation Army. Yet their mandate clearly extended beyond any narrowly defined religious function, as is evident in *Jewish Short Stories*. This anthology is geared toward an audience, both non-Jews and Jews, espousing any number of perspectives. The iconography displayed on the cover evokes religious practice—an open book with a tassel, suggesting a prayer book—and yet the volume itself, which contains works of fiction, could hardly be confused with liturgy. Nevertheless, the implication is that this too is a "Jewish book," and that short stories might embody the essence of Jewishness as well, if not better, than a prayer book.

The editor of *Jewish Short Stories*, Ludwig Lewisohn, was the most prominent Jewish novelist and all around "man of letters" in America from the 1920s through the 1940s. He became widely known after the publication of *Up Stream* (1922), in which he railed against the incipient anti-Semitism spreading throughout the country. He also became one of America's most outspoken proponents of Zionism. After being encouraged by Chaim Weizmann to visit the Yishuv in Palestine, he published a series of glowing reports in *The Nation* (ultimately collected in the volume *Israel* [1925]). His recurrent message to his American Jewish readers was that assimilation was neither possible, given the intractable anti-Semitism of Christian societies, nor desirable, given the violence it inflicts on the Jewish psyche. He looked to Zionism as a therapeutic antidote to the misguided impulse among modern Western Jews to be "just like everybody else." However, joining the pioneers in Palestine was not as crucial for him as the sheer act of asserting one's Jewishness, which he insisted one could do even in the Diaspora.

In his introduction to *Jewish Short Stories*, the polemical tone of most of Lewisohn's writing is muted. He seems to have had in mind a readership not only consisting of Jewish GIs but also non-Jews, presumably American soldiers who may have known nothing about the Jews with whom they served or about those whom they had just liberated from concentration camps. He cast the Jewish people as a personable bunch whose stories reflect their internal nature: "No people has been more inveterate in the telling of tales than the Jewish people," he asserted. "And it is known to all Jews and to all who have had friendly dealings with Jews that it has always been and is to this day their habit to relate stories and to 'swap' anecdotes in all the languages which they speak."[14] Here the Jews are not so much the people of "The Book" as a people of multiple stories, some oral, some written. Lewisohn has described the works in the anthology as products of this basic storytelling impulse. He has also linked the stories in the anthology, all written in the modern period, to the "tales concerning the prophets and heroes and kings of ancient Israel" (1). This mimics the idea of the "Bible as literature" we have already explored. By connecting modern stories written by Jewish authors to the Bible, Lewisohn has suggested that the sensibility of modern Jews can be traced back to that of their antecedents in the biblical period. All are moved by "tales" about the heroism of their people. Incidentally, no explicit concept from Judaism, such as chosenness, commandment, or covenant, is mentioned. "Tales," not Torah, comprise Judaism.

Lewisohn explained that these stories are Jewish "in quite the same sense in which stories written by Swedes are Swedish or, to use a better example, the sense in which a story written by a Frenchman is a French story, whether the story was written in Montreal or in Paris or in Algiers or in Indo-China" (4). His equivocation here suggests the difficulty in finding a perfect analogy, but it is evident that Lewisohn's purpose is to place the Jews amongst other nationalities. But while Jews comprise a distinct national culture, Lewisohn suggested that this should make them familiar rather than foreign in the eyes of other Americans. Moreover, he insisted that loyalty to nation and love of freedom are equally Jewish and American values. This view is echoed in the prefatory note by JWB president Frank Weil, who asserted that while the stories come from different historical periods "their significance is the same—men and women must be eternally vigilant in defense of freedom" (i). This familiar American rhetoric thus linked the essence of Jewish literature directly to American self-understanding.

The stories included in the anthology bear out the assertion that Jewish culture spans multiple languages. Three of the stories were originally written in Yiddish (I. L. Peretz's "Bontche Shweig" [sic], Sholem Aleichem's "Fishel the Teacher," and Sholem Asch's "A Peculiar Gift"); two in German (Arnold Zweig's "Jerusalem Delivered" and Karl Emil Franzos's "The Savior of Barnow"); one in Hebrew (Moshe Smilansky's "Latifa"); and four in English (Israel Zangwill's "Tug of Love," Edna Ferber's "No Room at the Inn," Ben Hecht's "God Is Good to a Jew," and Howard Fast's "The Price of Liberty"). The theme of freedom is most prevalent in the stories by Hecht and Fast, which epitomize Lewisohn's intentions for the collection.

In Hecht's "God Is Good to a Jew," a Jewish survivor of the Lublin ghetto, Aaron Sholomas, has made his way as a broken and traumatized man to an unnamed American city, where he boards with distant family members. In this new context, he becomes a mysterious figure, a symbol of the Jewish world of Europe which now lies in ruins. Walking in a daze through the streets one night, he encounters a building on fire, which he imagines to be a Nazi attack that will finally take his life: "This was death, the homeland of the Jews. . . . Where fire burned there Jews died" (136). Much to his surprise, the benevolent American crowd comes to his rescue just as he is collapsing in agony. His life cannot be saved, but the benevolence shown to him at the scene of his death becomes a redemptive closure to a life of suffering. "Here was the street he had never found in the history of the Jews, the shining street in which faces smiled on the tribe of Abraham. . . . After many years and after a long journey, I have found goodness that does not vanish where the Jew stands. I have found a home. God is good!" (138). Hecht's story connects the Holocaust to a familiar motif from immigrant Jewish writing, namely that of America as the true home for the Jews (consider, for example, Mary Antin's 1912 autobiography, *The Promised Land*). What is striking here (in both Hecht's and Antin's work) is that America appears to displace the Jewish God as the force of salvation. Sholomas sees his fate as controlled by God, but in the story it is the American crowd that comes to his aid. While this leaves open the possibility that the American crowd may be an agent of God, the point of the story, at least as presented in Lewisohn's anthology, seems to be that America has provided the first real home for the Jews in their two thousand years of wandering. The implication is that the dying Orthodox Jew will be superceded by a new kind of Jew, at once loyal to Jewish tradition and to American civic culture.

As if to answer this story about Jewish vulnerability, the anthology ends with an assertion of Jewish military might. Howard Fast's "The Price of Liberty" features a figure who stands outside of the tradition of the "schlemiel" that has been a common feature of Jewish American literature since the war: Johnny Ordonaux is an American Jew of French descent who becomes a naval hero in the War of 1812. Ordonaux descends from a line of rabbis ("And all Cohanim," the narrator adds), yet he exchanges the role of religious leader for that of a naval captain. He assembles a preternaturally brave, multiethnic crew with an ad that reads: "I sail for liberty, equality, independence, I offer shares or wages, I will take Irish, Jews, Negroes, Germans, Portuguese, Frenchmen: Any who own the name American" (152). After an epic battle in which Ordonaux's outnumbered crew overpowers a British warship, Ordonaux and his Negro officer are the only men left standing. The story ends with Ordonaux delivering a triumphant quasi-sermon in a synagogue: "The price of liberty is in the blood of brave men, and it was never bought otherwise. That should be written down by the scribe in the record-book of the synagogue" (157). Courage in battle emerges as the highest virtue, displacing more traditional notions of religious piety. Like Hecht's piece, Fast's story forces a rethinking of the idea of a providential God, suggesting that human powers take precedence over God. Ordonaux's orders are written down in the synagogue record book as if to symbolize the notion of a new kind of scripture, one that offers testimony to human tenacity and courage.

In the introduction, Lewisohn evoked the question of Zionism, noting that "significant stories are again being written in Hebrew by the older and younger writers who live in Jewish Palestine" (4). Literary creativity is thus seen as an index of national vitality. Zionism emerges in Sholem Asch's story, which traces a portrait of an East European Jew who has become a farmer in Palestine. The hero of the story, Reb Noah (a survivor of the "flood" of European anti-Semitism), attributes his self-transformation to the fact that he is "gifted for Palestine," a quality that one would have hardly expected from an East European Jew. The unnamed narrator concludes by speculating: "Perhaps that gift belongs not only to some Jews, but to all. Perhaps the gift for Palestine slumbers in the whole Jewish people" (53). Jews possess an inchoate identity waiting for the proper time and, by implication, the very message contained in these stories.

Considered together, the collection presents an image of Jews as simultaneously loyal to basic American principles as well as committed to a surging national movement. In the hands of non-Jewish GIs, these stories offered reassurance of the patriotism of Jewish GIs, as well as preparation for the eventuality of a Jewish State. For Jewish GIs, the stories may have generated pride and a renewed impulse to identify as a Jew. Raising the flag of Jewish nationality, Lewisohn has drawn a connection between modern Jewish culture and biblical literature. The quintessential expression of Jewishness, he argued, remains loyalty to the nation. In Lewisohn's own words and in the stories themselves, the role of God recedes from view.

A Treasury of Yiddish Stories (1954)

An anthology of an entirely different sort, published less than ten years later by Viking Press, is *A Treasury of Yiddish Stories*. Viking Press was known at this time as the publisher of highbrow works, ranging from *The Portable William Blake* (1946) to Lionel Trilling's essay novel, *The Middle of the Journey* (1947). To bring out a selection of Yiddish stories in this context was to assert that these works had something to offer the serious, "intellectual" reader. Edited by the American literary critic and socialist writer Irving Howe along with the Yiddish poet Eliezer Greenberg, the collection contains fifty-two stories by writers such as Mendele Mocher Sforim (1836–1917) and Chaim Grade (1910–1982). It provides a broad sampling of works by I. L. Peretz and Sholem Aleichem and includes first-time translated works by writers such as Lamed Shapiro and Abraham Reisen. Howe and Greenberg anticipated a readership that knew no Yiddish other than a few expressions and that had little if any familiarity with Yiddish writers. One premise behind the volume is that given the distinctiveness of the East European Jewish experience, Yiddish literature emerges most clearly when viewed alone, not alongside writings by American, French, German, or Israeli Jews. Another premise, which remains largely tacit, is that Yiddish literature distills out a worldview that is more authentically and uncompromisingly Jewish than what one finds elsewhere, particularly in postwar American Jewish life. In this sense, the anthology questions the idea expressed in Lewisohn's work of a single Jewish nation capable of preserving its identity in different eras, different places, and different languages. To ensure that readers will properly register what he calls the "qualitatively unique . . . cultural aura of Yiddish,"[15] Howe has provided an extensive ninety-three-page introduction, presenting the social and intellectual life of East European Jewry. The anthology also contains a glossary, in which a number of Yiddish terms are translated into English. Both aspects of the anthology help code the stories as an expression of a foreign world, a world populated, so to speak, by "real Jews" who have yet to compromise their identities. The introduction begins with a broad description of the shtetl, which thanks to works such as Marc Zborowski and Elizabeth Herzog's ethnography *Life Is with People* (1954) and Abraham Joshua Heschel's *The Earth Is the Lord's* (1949), was being mythologized at this time as the essential geography of prewar Jewish life, the site of what Heschel called "the golden period in Jewish history, in the history of the Jewish soul."[16] Howe agreed with this view, celebrating the shtetl for its religious intensity, typified by a feeling of relatedness to the transcendent God: "God was a living force, a Presence, something more than a name or desire. . . . Toward Him the Jews could feel a peculiar sense of intimacy" (8).

But unlike Zborowski and Heschel, Howe was not chiefly concerned with delineating the religious life of East European Jews. Instead, he was most interested in what happened when, toward the end of the nineteenth century, the combined pressures of anti-Semitism, urbanization, and the spread of secular ideologies began to erode the foundations of shtetl life. He has argued that as the traditional structures of East European Jewish life came apart, a uniquely productive and dynamic period in Jewish history emerged, a period in which a secular culture began to take shape. The distinctive mark of this culture was its "precarious balance" (28) between the folk world and the modern world, its familiarity with shtetl life, and its ability to reflect critically on that life. One characteristic dimension of this new culture is socialism, as well as other types of political radicalism; another is formal—that is, secular—literature. "Formal Yiddish literature," he asserted, emerged during a "wonderful interregnum" when East European Jews were no longer within the grip of the traditional religious order, but had yet to lose their distinctiveness through acculturation to non-Jewish norms. Thus he has characterized Yiddish literature as a necessary temporary cultural form, improvised under duress, to negotiate the crisis of modernity. "Yiddish reaches its climax of expressive power," he asserted, "as the world it portrays begins to fall apart" (28). Howe calls this culture "Yiddishkeit," a misleading term, perhaps, since contemporary Orthodox Jews use it as synonymous with religious Judaism, but one that has also gained broad currency with Howe's definition.[17]

Howe's account of the birth of Yiddish literature at a moment of social upheaval echoes Hegel's dictum that "the Owl of Minerva flies at twilight," meaning that true insight becomes available when the structures of society break down and their inner nature is laid bare. Indeed, Howe was most drawn to stories that dealt with the conflict between an older order and some new way of life yet to be fully articulated. Unlike the stories in Lewisohn's collection, the stories in Howe and Greenberg's *Treasury* emphasize conflict and alienation. The pieces that frame the collection—Mendele's "The Calf" and Chaim Grade's "My Quarrel with Hersh Rasseyner"—address this conflict with particular clarity and poignancy. "The Calf," at once humorous and tragic, is about a boy whose affections and imaginative life can no longer be contained by the traditional contours of religious life. Instead he is drawn to the natural world, specifically to a single calf that has been born to the family cow. The calf becomes the center of his affective life: "The Talmud lay open before me, but all I could see was the calf: small chin, tiny perked-up ears, delicate neck." (99). Although the boy is sent away to yeshiva, an "Evil Spirit" continues to beckon him, pointing him toward the beauties of nature. The story itself would appear to side with this Evil Spirit and with the boy who cannot tolerate yeshiva life. Nevertheless, tradition remains too powerful. At the story's end, the boy learns that his calf has died, symbolically crushing the boy's bid for self-liberation. He then collapses in misery. Positioned as the first story in the anthology, Mendele's tale reinforces Howe's point that Yiddish literature arises as a critique of traditional forms of piety.

The final story in the anthology, "My Quarrel with Hersh Rasseyner," revisits the conflict between Jewish tradition and the impulse to escape in the context of the post-Holocaust world. Grade's story takes the form of a philosophical dialogue between Chaim Vilner, a former Yeshiva student who has become a secular (veltlekh) Yiddish writer, and Hersh Rasseyner, his former classmate from the Novaredok Yeshiva of the Musar movement. The dialogue begins on the streets of Bialystok on the eve of World War II and resumes after the war in Paris, where they meet as if drawn by destiny to deliberate on the status of their attitudes in the wake of the Holocaust. Rasseyner attacks Vilner, and by extension all secularists, for having betrayed the only true path for a Jew: strict observance of mitsvot. He sees Jewish belles lettres as an oxymoron; he calls Vilner's poetry "godless verses." Secularism, he maintains, necessarily equals assimilationism. And if any further evidence was ever required to testify to the bankruptcy of a life without God, he finds it in the Holocaust, which he attributes to the moral anarchy of the world at large. As for his own faith, the Holocaust has made him more, not less, resolute. "How could I stand it," he asks, "without Him in this murderous world?" (629).

In his riposte, Vilner questions Rasseyner's tidily constructed opposition between Jewish tradition and secular thought. He sees greatness not in blind submission to a readymade worldview, but in tolerating doubt and seeking to uncover "the hidden root of the human race" (632). He has not abandoned the Jews so much as he has accepted a double responsibility, toward Jewish tradition and toward secular culture. He adds that Jewish secularists have been at the forefront of the struggle against tyranny, testifying to their moral seriousness. But finally, Vilner's prime concern now that a third of the Jewish people have been killed is to make a truce with Rasseyner and everything he stands for:

> That's what has changed for me, and for all Jewish writers. Our love for Jews has become deeper and more sensitive. I don't renounce the world, but in all honesty I must tell you we want to incorporate into ourselves the hidden inheritance of our people's strength, so that we can continue to live (650).

Having rejected the premises of Orthodoxy, Vilner refuses to abandon his ambiguous position between worlds. Yet he has found a renewed inclination to identify himself as a Jew, not by performing mitsvot, but by laying claim to a cultural memory, what he calls the "hidden inheritance of our people's strength." It is memory, instead of commandments, which he embraces as the essence of Jewishness.

Here Vilner articulates a new mandate for Jewish literary culture after the Holocaust, namely to shore up a form of Jewish identity by redoubling the effort to understand oneself in relation to Judaism and the Jewish past. Literature becomes a forum for precisely this operation. Indeed, the attitude he expresses resonates powerfully with Howe's own, and by extension Vilner's speech may be read as a motto for Howe's anthology as a whole. To be sure, there is an awareness of the difficulty inherent in seeking to embrace a tradition he cannot believe in. "We have not silenced our doubts," he insists, "and perhaps we will never be able to silence them" (650). But the emphasis lies on reestablishing a relation to Judaism, even if it is one of struggle and antagonism. That this seems to be Grade's view as well is evident from the fact that he uses the form of dialogue in this work not only to express his ideas, but also as a metaphor for Jewish identity itself. Finally, the view of Jewish secularism that emerges here is not of some stable worldview, but a shuttling between positions, an effort to honor the life of faith while remaining committed to doubt.

A Treasury of Yiddish Stories proved enormously successful. After its original appearance in 1954, it was reprinted a total of six times, and five additional volumes of Yiddish writing translated into English followed: *A Treasury of Yiddish Poetry* (1969), *Voices from the Yiddish: Essays, Memoirs, Diaries* (1972), *Selected Stories: I. L. Peretz* (1974), *Yiddish Stories Old and New* (1974), and *Ashes Out of Hope: Fiction by Soviet-Yiddish Writers* (1977). It seems that Howe and Greenberg's vision of "literary Judaism" offered at least a semblance of a "usable past" for postwar American Jews searching for their bearings. At the same time, Howe himself was less than convinced that the troubled path of Jewish secularism outlined in Grade's story could really be an option for Jews who did not come from the same intensely religious background as Vilner. A few months before his death in 1994, Howe delivered a speech at Hunter College titled "The End of Jewish Secularism." He argued that Jewish secularism is bound up with a specific period in Jewish history and with the Yiddish language itself, which preserves in its nature the dialogue with tradition that Grade valued. Howe despaired of the possibility of transferring a vital Jewish secularism into English. The period of the "wonderful interregnum," he feared, was over: the traditions of the past no longer figured prominently enough to lend any meaning to rebellion. Seen from this standpoint, Howe and Greenberg's *Treasury* may be read not as a project of sustaining a model of Jewishness, as in Lewisohn's case, but as one of commemoration. We are left, in Howe's view, with a memory of Jewish secularism much less than a vibrant way of life.

Jewish American Literature: A Norton Anthology (2001)

The recent *Jewish American Literature: A Norton Anthology*, edited by four literature professors at American universities (Jules Chametzky, John Felstiner, Hilene Flanzbaum, and Kathryn Hellerstein), builds on Howe and Greenberg's work, reprinting several of its works, including "Gimpel the Fool" and "My Quarrel with Hersh Rasseyner." But it embraces the much more hopeful vision that a Jewish literary culture, including pronounced secular currents, can sustain itself in English in modern America. Unlike Howe, who perceived American society as a leveling force, the editors of the Norton anthology have described America as a vibrant pluralistic society in which multiple ethnic identities and cultures can sustain themselves.

Published primarily for use in college literature classes, the Norton anthologies are typically lengthy volumes with generous annotations by noted specialists. Among the many anthologies in print, at least two—the *Norton Anthology of Women's Literature* (edited by Susan Gubar and Sandra Gilbert) and the *Norton Anthology of African American Literature* (edited by Henry Louis Gates)—have been instrumental in codifying subtraditions defined according to specific group identities. These volumes have justified and enabled the inclusion of classes on women's and African American literature in college curricula. While courses of study on Jewish American literature are, for a variety of reasons, less common on college campuses than other courses, the Norton volume suggests—explicitly in its introduction and implicitly by its sheer presence—that Jewish American literature deserves the same consideration as other fields. The significance of the Norton anthology, then, lies in its claim that Jewish culture deserves to be welcomed under the banner of academic multiculturalism.[18]

The introduction's thesis is that American Jews constitute an ethnic group, one of many structurally analogous groups that constitute the pluralistic society of the United States. To explain the formulation "Jewish American literature" (as opposed to, say, American Jewish literature), the editors have emphasized that " 'Jewish American literature' sounds nicely congruent with 'African American literature,' 'Mexican American literature,' 'Asian American literature,' and 'Native American literature,' filling a multiethnic and multicultural paradigm for what America has come to be."[19] The term "ethnicity" tends to have a positive valence in American academic discourse; it has offered an alternative to the suspect category of "race"— downplaying the role of biology and emphasizing the role of culture. In discussions of Jews, "ethnicity" tends to designate a category that includes religion but is not reducible to it. For the editors of the Norton anthology, ethnicity is shaped in dialogue with Judaism and Jewish collective memory within the larger cauldron of surrounding non-Jewish culture. Thus they deemphasize the question of common features that might link Jewish American literature with, for example, Australian Jewish literature or German Jewish literature. If the USO edition of Jewish stories defines Jews as a transnational, multilingual peoplehood, and if *A Treasury of Yiddish Stories* emphasizes the uniqueness of modern Yiddish culture, the Norton anthology assumes that the American experience has produced a self-contained Jewish American cultural heritage, crossing linguistic boundaries (by including entries from English, Yiddish, and Hebrew language writers) and generic boundaries (including fiction, autobiography, drama, poetry, criticism, and even sermons) but remaining in one geographical space.

To be sure, this notion of ethnicity does not translate into some unchanging essence. The editors have shied away from making the sort of broad claims about a Jewish temperament or a Jewish sensibility that Lewisohn seemed happy to make.

Instead, they have understood Jewish identity as a product of ongoing, dynamic interaction with changing historical circumstances. As in Grade's story, the operative concept is dialogue and debate, though the debate is often with America as much as with Judaism. The anthology is organized chronologically into five sections, telling the story of Jewish life in America: "Literature of Arrival, 1654–1880"; "The Great Tide, 1881–1924"; "From Margin to Mainstream in Difficult Times, 1924–1945"; "Achievement and Ambivalence, 1945–1973"; and "Wandering and Return: Literature since 1973." These headings invite us to imagine two poles: a Jewish margin and an American mainstream. In the movement between these two poles of experience, Jewish American ethnicity develops. As the editors have noted in an instructive formulation: "Despite the pressures to 'make it' in a relatively tolerant American society and to divest themselves of 'foreign' or 'ethnic' qualities, Jews as a whole did not 'melt.' Traditional values held out (to some degree) against or alongside Americanization and modernization. Yet most Jewish Americans adapted to the new culture—not necessarily abandoning tradition, but transforming it, learning to live as Jews and Americans (11)." The motif of a journey between some prior Jewish sphere and America is symbolized by the image on the cover, a painting by the immigrant artist Raphael Soyer titled "The Bridge." It depicts figures moving across what seems to be the Williamsburg Bridge, shuttling between Brooklyn and Manhattan as if embodying the movement between Jewish tradition and American society. Just as the Yiddish writers in Howe and Greenberg's collection are said to exist in a space between the disintegrating shtetl and the greater world, the writers in this collection are portrayed as figures in transition. The crucial difference is that the transition is now imagined as a continual process, indeed as the essence of an ongoing Jewish American identity. While there has been talk of American Jews having entered a "post-ethnic" stage, given the dispersal of Jews from recognizable urban enclaves and the decline of Yiddish, the Norton editors have asserted that a distinctive Jewish culture has persisted.

When the editors assert that the texts in the volume contain a vital connection to "traditional values," they do not understand this tradition in a limited religious sense. Rather, they have included the traditions of leftist political activism that Howe linked with Yiddishkeit. The two longest works printed in their entirety—Clifford Odets's play *Arise and Sing!* and Tillie Olsen's novella *Tell Me a Riddle*—make negligible references to Jewish themes, and yet are called emblematic Jewish American works by virtue of their connection to the world of political radicalism. Both writers associated with socialist circles, particularly in the 1930s, and both texts explore the problem of transmitting a radical political outlook between generations in America. As the editors have written about Olsen: "Although her writing is not marked overtly by Jewishness as such, [her] radical background shapes her whole outlook. And *Yiddishkeit* permeates *Tell Me a Riddle*, her finest story, in both spirit and language." Thus the editors have suggested that a dedication to political radicalism can be a sufficient basis for Jewish identity.

Interestingly, *Arise and Sing!* and *Tell Me a Riddle* follow similar narrative patterns. Both feature immigrant grandparents who embody the political idealism of turn-of-the-century East European radicalism, and both show how upon their deaths the grandparents transfer their idealism to their American-born grandchildren. In Odets's play, the patriarch Jacob, described in the notes as "an old Jew with living eyes in his tired face," inspires his grandson Ralph to fight so that "life won't be printed on dollar bills" (493). In Olsen's novella, the dying Eva, active as a youth in the 1905 revolution, passes on her iconoclasm to her granddaughter Jeannie, who resolves at the conclusion of the story to leave her job as a nurse and start over as an art student in San Francisco. The resolution of these narratives reinforces the premise of the anthology itself: a cultural sensibility, linked to the Jewish past, *can* be translated into an American context.

Jewish Culture and Jewish Anthologies

Each of these anthologies is premised on the idea that a definable Jewish culture, not reducible to religion, exists. Each works with a master category that displaces religion as the primary definition of Jewish identity: Lewisohn described Jewishness as a nationality; Howe introduced the idea of a "culture of Yiddishkeit"; and the Norton editors have characterized Jewishness in America as "ethnicity," wrought in the interchange between the Jewish margins and the American center. For Howe, the possibilities of a form of Jewish identity expressed in and centered on literature are dim, but for Lewisohn and the Norton editors prospects appear brighter. As for the question of secularism proper, we might note that in each of these models religion figures prominently, though generally as historical background, as a frame of reference, or even a force of antagonism. In other words, religion is not absent, but neither is it regarded as normative in any way.

It also appears that the different perspectives embodied in these three anthologies represent a progression of prevailing understandings of Jewish identity. The idea expressed by the Norton anthology that Jewish identity exists within an exchange between a (variously defined) Jewish sphere and a local, non-Jewish culture appears to be gaining ascendancy. This view may be seen in a variety of other recently published anthologies, all devoted to localized manifestations of Jewish culture: *Argentine Jewish Theater: A Critical Anthology* (1996, edited by Nora Glickman and Gloria Waldman), *Enough Already: An Anthology of Australian-Jewish Writing* (1999, edited by Alan Jacobs), and *King David's Harp: Autobiographical Essays by Latin American Jewish Writers* (1999, edited by Stephen Sadow). Even more striking, in 2001 the University of Nebraska Press initiated a series called *Jewish Writing in the Contemporary World*, which already includes volumes devoted to Jewish writing in Germany, Austria, Hungary, South Africa, and Canada. As in the Norton collection, these definitions depend upon the idea of a bridge that connects Jews to a broader national culture without permanently wrestling them away from their Jewish base. This turn toward highly localized versions of Jewish identity suggests that we have seen the dilution of the grand ideological projects formerly aligned with models of secular Jewish identity. Zionism, Bundism, and Territorialism each announced broad programs for social and political change when they first emerged. The model endorsed by the Norton anthology points instead to the idea of maintaining a balance between two spheres: a national culture (which provides a language and context for daily life) and a Jewish culture (which provides a range of references and what the Norton editors have called "traditional values").

Why, we might ask, does imaginative literature figure so centrally in this model of Jewishness as "ethnicity" or "culture"? What do stories and poems offer that other kinds of Jewish texts do not? The answer may lie in the association of literature with individual subjectivity. If the central metaphors for Jewishness are the debate, the struggle, and the bridge, and if the authority of the normative religious tradition has been unseated, the only remaining mediating force becomes human consciousness, which itself becomes the final arbiter of meaning. And imaginative literature, we might say, specializes in the representation of individual consciousness and subjective response. Grade's "My Quarrel with Hersh Rasseyner" stages a confrontation between conflicting voices, but it possesses no authority to adjudicate between them. The reader may be tacitly enjoined to submit his or her vote, but this, once again, is but another response. Finally, it appears that a Jewish identity supported by literature may not be necessarily secular, but neither can it ever be truly religious, since its proposals will be inevitably mutable.

NOTES

I would like to thank Jeremy Dauber, Jeremy Shere, Alvin Rosenfeld, and Lisa Makman for their thoughtful responses to previous drafts of this chapter.

1. See Ruth Wisse, *I. L. Peretz and the Making of Modern Jewish Culture* (Seattle: University of Washington Press, 1991).

2. The problem of defining Jewish literature has long preoccupied scholars, and it seems unlikely that any consensus on a solution will soon emerge. For the purposes of this essay, I begin with the premise that "Jewish literature" exists, at least as an operational category, and I explore distinct meanings that have been linked to this term. For a review of the dominant views of this question, see Hana Wirth-Nesher, ed., *What Is Jewish Literature?* (Philadelphia: Jewish Publication Society, 1994).

3. Gloria Cronin and Ben Siegel, eds., *Conversations with Saul Bellow* (Jackson: University of Mississippi Press, 1994), 32.

4. Mikhail Bakhtin, "Discourse in the Novel," in *The Dialogic Imagination: Four Essays*, ed. Michael Holquist, trans. Caryl Emerson and Michael Holquist (Austin: Texas University Press, 1981), 366.

5. To Scholem, the celebrated historian of Jewish mysticism, Kafka was a "Jewish writer" in a purely religious sense—that is, because he grappled with the problem of revelation and the meaning of revealed law. In Kafka's depictions of an agonized quest to understand the hidden bureaucratic workings of modern society, Scholem perceived "[certain] mystical theses which walked the fine line between religion and nihilism." Quoted in David Biale, *Gershom Scholem: Kabbalah and Counter-History* (Cambridge: Harvard University Press, 1979), 31. In his book *Walter Benjamin, The Story of a Friendship* (Philadelphia: Jewish Publication Society, 1982), Scholem noted the pedagogic uses to which Kafka's writings can be put: "I said then . . . that one would have to read the works of Franz Kafka before one could understand the Kabbalah today, and particularly *The Trial*" (158).

6. The *Nightwords* liturgy (copyright David Roskies) has been used in many synagogues, including the Conservative Anshe Chesed synagogue in New York City.

7. See, for example, the following discussion from Sotah 35b: "Raba expounded: 'Why was David punished? Because he called the words of Torah songs, as it is said: 'Thy statutes have been my songs in the house of my pilgrimage (Ps. 119:54). The Holy One, blessed be He, said

to him: 'Words of Torah, of which it is written (Prov. 23:6): When your eyes light upon it, it is gone [the Torah is beyond human comprehension], you call songs!'" For an extended discussion of the relationship between poetry and prophecy in rabbinic, Christian, and philosophical thought, see Abraham Joshua Heschel, *The Prophets* (New York: HarperCollins, 2001), 468–497.

8. In a discussion of literary style, Longinus compared the book of Genesis to Homer, judging the former superior to the latter in certain aspects. See W. R. Roberts, *Longinus on Style* (Cambridge, 1899), 209.

9. Auerbach's approach should be distinguished not only from a reading from the standpoint of religious faith but also from modern German biblical scholarship, with its emphasis on the multiple sources behind the biblical text.

10. A case in point is the Literature Humanities curriculum at Columbia College. When it was first conceived and instituted in the 1920s, the only ancient works students read were Greek and Latin literature. Gradually, instructors began to incorporate biblical literature as well, prompted by an impulse toward inclusion. If Western civilization can be said to derive from Jerusalem as well as Athens, the argument went, why not consider representative works from both cultures in a survey course on literature? For a useful anthology of essays on the Bible as literature, see Robert Alter and Frank Kermode, eds., *The Literary Guide to the Bible* (Cambridge: Belknap Press, 1987).

11. Robert Alter, *Hebrew and Modernity* (Bloomington: Indiana University Press, 1994).

12. See the double special issue of *Prooftexts* devoted to "The Jewish Anthological Imagination," *Prooftexts* 17, nos. 1, 2 (1997).

13. The phenomenon I am considering—the effort to define groups via their literary expressions—is not restricted to Jews, of course. The process of nation building or ethnic self-assertion has commonly involved the recovery and celebration of certain writers, who become viewed as "classics" and whose work is meant to stand metonymically for the qualities of the group as a whole (e.g., Goethe for Germans, Pushkin for Russians, Shevchenko for Ukrainians, etc.). There are several factors, however, which make the Jewish case somewhat more complex than these examples. First, because Jews have been spread out geographically and have written literature in different languages, the effort to define a unified and coherent literary tradition has presented singular challenges. Second, given the variability of definitions of Jewishness, any effort to nominate a literary canon in support of one identity will involve a process of exclusion that is more dramatic than in the case of other literatures. Finally, there is the problem we have already noted of distinguishing between secular and religious works: is there a place for "religious" texts in a canon that purports to underwrite a version of secular identity? How are such texts accounted for, framed, or reinterpreted?

14. Ludwig Lewisohn, introduction to *Jewish Short Stories* (New York: Berman House, 1945), 5. Subsequent references will be cited in the text.

15. Irving Howe and Eliezer Greenberg, *A Treasury of Yiddish Stories* (New York: Viking Press, 1954), 3. Subsequent references will be cited in the text.

16. Abraham Joshua Heschel, *The Earth Is the Lord's* (New York: Farrar, Strauss & Giroux, 1949), 18.

17. Howe used the spelling "Yiddishkeit," adhering to the rules of German orthography, while YIVO dictates the spelling, "yidishkayt." However, I will keep Howe's spelling, since I use his specific meaning of the term.

18. The relationship between Jews and multiculturalism is a vexed topic. In brief, it might be said that Jews in America have been seen as a privileged, white group rather than among the unprivileged minorities whom multiculturalism was meant to address. Seen in this light, the Norton anthology is making a more polemical statement than might seem apparent. See Andrew Furman, *Contemporary Jewish American Writers and the Multicultural Dilemma: The Return of the Exiled* (Syracuse: Syracuse University Press, 2000).

19. Jules Chametzky, et al., *Jewish American Literature: A Norton Anthology* (New York: Norton, 2001), 1. Subsequent references will be cited in the text.

PART III

SECULAR JEWISHNESS
IN ISRAEL TODAY

In Israel the relationship of ethnicity and religion is even more complex. It is different from that in diaspora situations such as those described by Spector, Endelman, and Fishman, partly because the relationship is played out in a self-described "Jewish state." Israelis do not have to be even nominally religious in order to be Jewish—as citizens of a Jewish state, their ethnicity is bound up with their citizenship. The late Charles Liebman and his colleague, Yaacov Yadgar, explore the outlooks and behavior of secular Jews in Israel. Using survey data, their own observations, and a series of in-depth interviews, the authors differentiate between those who are nonobservant (secular by default) and those who are committed antireligionists. The authors ask whether secular Jewishness has a future in the Jewish state. They point to the "enormous dependence of secular Judaism on the public arena, of the inability of the secular to generate private structures of life that are Jewish, or to compete with the consumer culture that does create such structures." Secular Jewishness has failed outside of Israel, but its viability in Israel is still an open question.

Liebman and Yadgar then show that Israeli society cannot be divided simply into "religious" and "secular," as is often done. As much as a third of the Jewish population defines itself as *Masorti*, or "traditional," meaning partly observant religiously. As with "religious" and "secular," the identity of Masorti is not absolute but dependent on context, time, and place. It continually evolves as it confronts competing mosaics of identities and changing social and political conditions. Masorti is a distinctly modern identity because, whereas the traditionalist does not consciously choose his or her identity, Masorti identity is not forced upon a person. The authors conclude that "the traditionalist option may yet reveal itself as a solution to the continuing tension inherent in the Jewish national enterprise—the tension between a universal and a particularistic identity, between a state which is 'democratic' and one which is 'Jewish.'"

As an officially Jewish state, Israel is challenged to define the roles of religion and Jewish ethnicity in its multireligious and multiethnic society. Mark Tessler examines Israeli attitudes toward the role of Judaism in Israel and sentiments about Jewishness and how they affect Israel's non-Jewish (mainly Arab) citizenry. Tessler then makes some comparison to the issues Islam raises in the very different polities of the Arab world, using survey data from Jordan and Egypt to illustrate his points.

Shachar Pinsker turns to Hebrew literature, observing that the lines between religious and secular in literature are highly imprecise. He analyzes attempts by leading Hebrew writers of the early twentieth century (Chaim Nachman Bialik and Michah Yosef Berdichevsky) to transform rabbinic texts into secular modern Jewish texts. The struggle to do so became a hallmark of modern Hebrew culture. The relationship between religion, tradition, and modernity continues to occupy Israeli literature.

9

Secular-Jewish Identity and the Condition of Secular Judaism in Israel

CHARLES S. LIEBMAN

AND YAACOV YADGAR

The term *hiloni*[1] (secular) is commonplace in Israel as a means of identifying a type of Jew, a type of Jewish identity, and a type of Judaism. It carries different meanings to different people depending on the context. This chapter is devoted to seeking to understand the different meanings, or at least the major meanings, that the term *secular* carries in Israel. We will look at this from the perspective of those who use the term in a positive or a neutral fashion. We refer only by indirection to the meaning of the term in hostile circles. Very often, especially but not exclusively in extreme religious circles, the term evokes an image of libertinism (*prikat ol*), at the moral, especially sexual level, and an absence of any commitment to Judaism or the Jewish people or to family values. Many traditionalists (*masortim*) whom we describe in an accompanying essay associate the term hiloni with emptiness, a vacuum (*reykanut*). The leaders of secular organizations dedicated to a Jewish renaissance (there are probably close to one hundred such organizations in Israel), find that among their potential audience the term *secular* bears negative connotations, although evidence presented in this essay points in the opposite direction.[2] The term certainly bears negative connotations among many secular intellectuals, which may point to the intellectuals' idiosyncratic nature. More on this below.

We are concerned with secular Judaism in Israel. Our topic is the *secular* Jew, not the *secularization* of Judaism. By secularization we mean the rationalization and the differentiation of the nonreligious realm from the religious realm. Secularization has taken place in the transformation of the Hebrew language (formerly "the holy tongue") of Jewish culture, Jewish politics, in the thought processes of Jewish leaders, and, indeed, to a varying extent within the Jewish religion itself. Secularization has affected Orthodoxy from the modern-Orthodox and religious-Zionist camp to the *haredi* camp.[3] It is a topic that has engaged scholars, complicated as it is fascinating, but it is not the topic of this essay.[4]

We will use the terms *secular* or *hiloni* (plural *hilonim*) and *secularism* or *hiloniut* interchangeably. After a brief historical excursus, we turn to a description of the Jewish practices and beliefs of Israelis who define themselves as secular (hiloni), as distinct from Israeli Jews who define themselves as "religious" (*dati*) or "traditional" (masorti). This section relies primarily on survey data, but it is informed, as are the remaining sections, by our own interviews and impressions and by the transcripts of eleven interviews of secular students in Rupin College conducted by Hadas Franco.

We distinguish two meanings of the term *secular*. Defining oneself as secular may simply be the way one who observes little or nothing of the Jewish tradition defines oneself, but it may also be a way of distancing oneself from the rabbis or the religious establishment. When such Jews define themselves as secular (or "non-religious," in the terminology of the Guttman study), they are saying, at least in part, that they reject that establishment or its demands. We call such Jews "secular by default." There are also those who, as a matter of ideology, define themselves as secular. Among those who define themselves as secular by ideology we can distinguish two groups at end points on a hypothetical continuum. At one extreme are those who consciously observe some rituals and some Jewish traditions and even seek to enhance them even though they themselves are not religious (dati), and/or do not believe in God, and/or believe that Judaism is a culture and not a religion, and/or believe that religion is a constraint on the ideal society they envision. We call them secular Judaists and distinguish them from secular Universalists. The latter adhere exclusively to a Universalist humanist vision. Although born Jewish, Judaism and Jewishness are irrelevant to their lives. At the extreme, they believe that Judaism is an impediment to the creation of a society in which no political distinctions are drawn between Jews and Arabs. Most of those who fall into this category are post- or anti-Zionists about whom much has been written.[5] Although they are not a subject for this essay, we believe that some of what they say merits the attention of the other camp of ideologists.[6] Since our topic is secular Jewish identity in Israel, we are not concerned with the Universalists who are hostile to the Jewish nature of the state and are generally indifferent to Judaism itself. Between the two groups of secular intellectuals, one finds others of different stripes. Some are antagonistic to religion and indifferent to Judaism. As Israeli nationalists they favor a Jewish state, but one in which Judaism and Jewishness do not interfere with their lives. One also finds, as one does in the public at large, those who are enraged by what they perceive as religious coercion, by the behavior of the religious parties and the ultra-Orthodox public whom they view as parasites on the public coffers. This is the public that comprises the core of the Shinui electorate, which sent fifteen representatives (about 13 percent of the total votes) to the 2003 Knesset. But they continue to affirm their commitment to aspects of the Jewish tradition, arguing that it is the religious establishment that has misappropriated it.

A Historical Note

There is an important historical dimension to our discussion. Until the late 1940s–1950s the Hebrew term for a nonreligious Jew was *hofshi*, literally "free." The term developed during the nineteenth century with the advent of the *haskalah* (Jewish enlightenment), when the classical term for a nonreligious Jew, *kofer* or *apikores*—that is, a heretic—was no longer appropriate. According to Zvi Zameret, hofshi was the standard appellation in the *Yishuv* (the Jewish settlement in Palestine before the creation of the state), but it carried a far more positive meaning there than it had amongst the *maskilim* (enlighteners) who first used the term. To the maskilim it meant "free from religion." But to the Zionist settlers it meant "free to choose"—to choose not to observe the *halacha* but also free to attend synagogue, or light candles on Friday night, etc. Hofshi, as used by the Zionist settlers, did *not* mean the denial of religion and tradition.[7]

The term *hiloni*, or *huloni*, according to Zameret, was used as early as the nineteenth century. It appears among other places in the writing of Micha Joseph Berdichevsky. It implied materialism (*homranut*) and this-worldliness, a term which at that time had very positive connotations. In the eyes of the *maskilim* and the early Zionists, Jews were obliged to embrace the material rather than just the spiritual. This was essential in the creation of the "new" Jew, distinguished from the "old" Jew, who was dissociated from the real world. (The early Zionists used the term *ivry* (Hebrew) to distinguish the "new Jew" from the "old Jew.") Only later was the term *hiloni* transformed into meaning nonreligious. *Hofshi*, as a synonym for nonreligious, gradually disappeared around the time of the creation of the state. But by then it had also lost its positive valence. Zameret explains this as part of the general loss of a specific hiloni identity amongst the early settlers.

The relatively recent usage of the term *hiloni* as a synonym for *nonreligious* or *nonobservant* is further attested to by the late Moshe Goshen-Gottstein, the prominent linguist who conducted a weekly language column on the pages of the daily newspaper *Ha'aretz*.[8] The author introduced a column in June 1965 with a quote concerning a young girl who is hiloni. Goshen-Gottstein wonders if the term *hiloni* would have been so readily understood ten years earlier. Until recently, he says, the term used was either *hofshi* or *lo-dati* (not-religious). He goes on to explore the classical meaning of the term *hiloni*, noting that in the *Targum Onkelos*, the semi-canonical translation of the Pentateuch, *hiloni* is a rendition of the Hebrew word *zar* (stranger). Goshen-Gottstein finds the term *hiloni* objectionable but has no suggestions for a substitute.

Dissatisfaction with the term remains. The Shenhar commission created in 1991 to offer recommendations to the Ministry of Education on the teaching of Jewish subjects in the state (nonreligious) schools expressed its discomfort with the term *hiloni*, but absent an alternative term it used the word *hiloni* to identify students in nonreligious schools.[9] The chair of the commission, Aliza Shenhar, told us that in her public appearances she has returned to the term *hofshi*.[10] The problem is not so much a matter of appropriate usage. Goshen-Gottstein already noted that the term *hiloni* is properly translated as profane and one can speak of a profane literature, of profane professions, of profane values, but not of a profane person. The problem is that because the term has come to mean nonreligious, it carries a negative, not a positive, resonance. It tells you what somebody is not, rather than what somebody is. As the reader will note, many of the authors cited below use the term *hofshi* (plural *hofshiim*) to refer to secular Jews, and we are at a loss of how to translate the term. Hence, we retain the original Hebrew in order to provide an appreciation of the large number of Israeli intellectuals who shun the term *hiloni*.

The second historical point to be noted is that a thriving form of secular Judaism existed in the recent past. The secular Yiddish culture of Eastern Europe is well known, but it is easy to forget that a strong positive secular Jewish culture existed in the Yishuv and in the early years of statehood. Among the pioneer settlers who came to Palestine in the first decades of the last century there was, generally speaking, a positive attitude toward Jewish ethnicity—that is, membership in the Jewish people and concern for Jews throughout the world, a nostalgia for many traditional Jewish practices, but a principled objection to "religion" and hence to the observance of Jewish ritual in its traditional form. The Yishuv, therefore, adapted traditional ritual, transforming and transvaluing it in secular terms at the national level as well as at the local and private level.[11] Intensive efforts in this direction took place within the kibbutz movement.[12] However, the historical record is heavily skewed in favor of the ideology, practices, and beliefs of the working class and intellectuals within the labor movement. We suspect that among the urban middle and lower middle classes many aspects of traditional Judaism were simply incorporated into their lives without ideological passion, without misgivings, and with less of a need to transform and transvalue them.

The creation of the state of Israel, along with the influx of new immigrants breathed new life into secular Judaism. Jewish symbols were now adapted to build and to strengthen national identity and loyalty and to zionize the new immigrants, many of whom were tied to traditional religious practice. Israel's civil religion, however manipulative and distorting it might have been, was built upon traditional Jewish symbols and still is. The problem is that the civil religion itself no longer evokes the allegiance and the emotion that it did in the past, and the older secular rituals have been largely forgotten. Furthermore, in most cases, as is true of other innovative rituals, they lose relevance very rapidly, especially in a changing society. What is important to note, a point to which we return in subsequent sections, is that the Zionist enterprise, Zionist ideology, and Zionist commitment were inextricably tied to Jewish ethnicity and a sensitivity to Jewish history and Jewish symbols. It is fair to say that Zionism sought to nationalize Judaism. It succeeded to a great extent, but this, we will suggest, has also been the undoing of secular Judaism in Israel.

Practices and Beliefs of Hilonim

According to the 1999 survey of the Jewish population of Israel by the Guttman Institute,[13] 43 percent of Israeli Jews (N=1,272, out of a total of 2,717 respondents) define themselves as nonreligious, and an additional 5 percent define themselves as antireligious (N=115). The Guttman Report uses the term *nonreligious* rather than *secular*. This is unfortunate since a traditionalist (*masorti*) Jew is also nonreligious— that is, does not define him- or herself as *dati* (a religious Jew). Perhaps to remedy this confusion the report lists the term *secular* in parenthesis following the label "nonreligious." The Guttman Report is also misleading by distinguishing those who define themselves as "antireligious" from the "nonreligious (secular)," despite the fact that almost all the antireligious report that they are totally nonobservant of the tradition. We have chosen to label both those whom the Guttman Report calls nonreligious and those whom they call antireligious and observe no part of the tradition as secular.[14] Together these two groups constitute 48 percent of the Guttman sample. Assuming this is a representative sample, it means that secular Jews comprise almost half of the Jewish population of Israel. Respondents were also asked about their observance of the tradition. Looking only at the secular, and recalculating the Guttman Report data, we find that 57 percent of the secular report they observe a small part of the tradition; 34 percent of the secular report they do not observe any part of the tradition (as we shall see, this is questionable), and 8 percent of the secular report they are antireligious and did not observe any part of the tradition.[15] These three groups are the subject of our essay.

Ethnicity played a major role in our study of masortim, and its impact is equally evident among the secular. Based on Guttman Report data, we find that 17 percent of the total sample was Israeli born with fathers also born in Israel. They are not identified by ethnic origin. The remainder is composed of Mizrahim (those born in Moslem countries or those whose fathers were born there), who constitute 46 percent of the total sample, or Ashkenazim (those born in Christian countries or those whose fathers were born in Christian countries), who constitute 36 percent of the total sample. Looking only at the secular portion of the population, we find that Mizrahim constitute 28 percent of the secular who observe something, 15 percent of the secular who observe nothing, and 12 percent of the antireligious who observe nothing. By contrast, Ashkenazim constitute 56 percent of the secular who observe something, 65 percent of the secular who observe nothing, and 60 percent of the antireligious. (The remainder, those born in Israel whose fathers were also born in Israel, constitute 16 percent of those secular who observe something, 20 percent of those secular who observe nothing, and 28 percent of the antireligious who observe nothing.)[16]

In other words, Mizrahim are dramatically underrepresented among secular Jews in Israel. In addition, the less traditional the secular group is, the fewer Mizrahim are to be found in it. In figure 9.1, we report on observance and belief by secular groups.

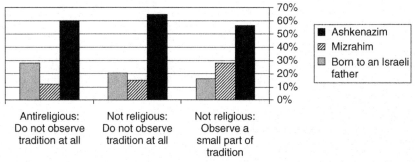

Fig. 9.1   Ethnicity among Secular Israeli Jews
Source: Levy, Levinson, and Katz, *Israeli Jews.*

We must bear in mind that these figures include the data for recent Russian Jewish immigrants—those who have arrived since 1989. Seventy-three percent of the Russians describe themselves as either secular or antireligious, and they constitute 19 percent of the total sample of secular Jews (21 percent of the antireligious). Everything we know about them suggests that their religious practice and belief is lower than that of the remainder of the Jewish population in Israel. This is confirmed in a study by Daphna Canetti who sampled over 2,200 college and university students from most institutions of higher education in Israel. We may assume that even if the proportion of students from the Former Soviet Union among them is the same as the proportion of Israelis who immigrated from the Former Soviet Union in the general population, these students are more highly socialized to patterns of Israeli Jewish behavior than other immigrants from the Former Soviet Union. Eighty percent of Canetti's sample reported they were secular.[17] But she found an even higher incidence of traditional observance and belief among her sample of secular Jews than did the Guttman report. For example, 43 percent reported that they believed in God, and 36 percent believed that the soul continues to exist after death.[18] Over a quarter believed that the Jews were a chosen people, that the Torah was given at Sinai, and that Jewish history is guided by a supernatural force. Forty-three percent refrained from eating bread on Passover, and 35 percent lit Sabbath candles with a blessing.

The conclusion from the Guttman study, the Canetti study, and other studies to be mentioned below, is that a sizable minority of Israeli secular Jews observe at least some Jewish traditions, share to some extent the basic beliefs of the religiously observant, and feel strong ties to the Jewish people. Thus, we wonder why so many Israelis define themselves as secular when they might instead have defined themselves as traditional (masorti) and why so many secular Jews report that they do not observe any aspects of the tradition when this is clearly contrary to their own reported behavior. Perhaps this stems from negative feelings about the rabbinic establishment and/or the religious tradition, but we suspect that much of it has to do with the fact that when many secular Jews report their observance or their belief they are not thinking in terms of Judaism but in terms of Israeliness. In other words, when some secular Jews light Sabbath candles, even with a blessing, or fast on Yom Kippur, they think of themselves as performing an Israeli as much as a Jewish act. A sense of Jewishness is very weak among many secular. Indeed, as we see from the last two items in table 9.1, the less traditionally observant the group, the more tenuous their ties to the Jewish people. This finding is consistent with the larger finding of the Guttman study and with every other study that looks at the ties of different groups of Israeli Jews with the Jewish people. Therefore, it ought not to surprise us if, indeed, the secular Israeli has incorporated his Jewishness into his Israeli identity and hardly distinguishes between them.

Elsewhere we have written about other recent studies of Israeli Jewish identity.[19] All of them yield similar if not identical conclusions and two points serve us here as a convenient review.[20] First, although there are significant differences between groups of Israeli Jews in their Israeli identity and their Jewish identity, the

Table 9.1   Percentage of Secular Jews Affirming Traditional Judaism and Jewish Ties

	Partially Observing Seculars N = 793	Nonobserving Seculars N = 479	Antireligious Seculars N = 115	Total of All Seculars N = 1387
Special meal on Sabbath	29	16	8	23
Lighting Sabbath candles with a blessing	25	7	4	17
Avoiding nonkosher meat	38	15	8	28
Participating or leading a Seder in accordance with halacha	50	26	12	38
Fasting on Yom Kippur	55	19	4	38
Using special dishes on Passover	30	11	8	22
Has a mezuzah in every room in the house	65	44	39	56
Believes there is a God	45	20	9	33
Wants a state that is Jewish, not necessarily halachic	88	80	79	84
Wants more Jewish study in state (nonreligious) schools	47	24	10	36
Wants more Jewish content on Israeli television	48	29	22	39
Feels part of worldwide Jewish people	57	43	34	50
If reborn would want very much to be reborn as a Jew	45	29	22	38

Source: Levy, Levinson, and Katz, Israeli Jews.

two identities are positively related except in the case of the ultra-Orthodox (haredim). But, as Yair Auron found, the attitudes of the secular toward the Jewish people and the self image of the secular as part of the Jewish people is much less meaningful to them than other identity components, such as their attitudes toward the State of Israel or to the Land of Israel.[21]

The correlation between the strength of the Israeli and Jewish identities suggests the second major finding. Respondents who define themselves as religious (dati) have stronger Jewish and Israeli identities than respondents who define themselves as traditional (masorti), and they, in turn, have stronger Jewish and Israeli identities than those who define themselves as secular. And all the studies report on a minority of young secular Jews who express negative attitudes toward religion and the Jewish tradition and alienation from Diaspora Jews.

When we try to get behind the labels and ask what they really mean to the respondents themselves, the survey data is less helpful. Yair Auron, whose studies of students in teachers' seminaries is most instructive, feels that for his secular respondents, the Holocaust is the central element in their Jewish identity. Attitudes toward the Jewish people, he says, are mediated by way of the Holocaust, and the tie to the Jewish people is a tie to a dead people.[22] His analysis recalls that of Amos Elon, who, in the 1970s stressed the importance of suffering and victimhood in the Jewish identity of Israelis.[23] Laura Zarembski describes this crisis in terms of a lost sense of defining characteristics—what it means to be an Israeli. She contrasts the insecurity of the secular community to the self-confidence of the religious community.[24] This reinforces our suspicion that weakened ties to a sense of Jewish peoplehood may not stem from the dissociation from religion or from tradition but from a loss of belief, by significant numbers of secular Israelis, in the values of secular Zionism—an ideology that until now had nourished their sense of identity with Judaism and the Jewish people.

Types of Secular Jews

What does it mean to be a secular Jew in Israel? As we suggested at the outset, some distinctions should be made in trying to fathom the meaning of secularism (hiloniut) in Israel. First, the distinction between those who are ideologically secular— that is, those to whom their secularism is a matter of conviction and a way of life—and those whose secularism is a kind of default position. By "secular by default" we refer to persons who label themselves secular because they are neither dati nor masorti, they keep few if any of traditional observances, the vast majority if not all their friends consider themselves secular, and they probably do not like the rabbinical establishment. We suspect that these are individuals whose identity is primarily Israeli and who observe some Jewish traditions because they have become Israeli-Jewish traditions. All this makes them secular by default. The term secular, or hiloni, bears no positive meaning; it is not an ideology or a belief system. Secularism is not part of the identity of the Jew who is secular by default in contrast to the ideologically secular Jew—and certainly in contrast to the religious (dati) Jew for whom the fact of his being dati is basic to his identity. The line distinguishing ideologically secular Jews from secular Jews by default is not always sharp, and there are surely those who fall very close to either side of the line. But in our judgment it is a fair and important distinction because it reminds us that when we turn to hearing how secular intellectuals describe their secularism, we are hearing the voices of a group who constitute only a small part of the secular public.

Those who are ideologically secular are in turn divided into those whom we call secular Judaists and those whom we call secular Universalists. The former feel strongly Jewish; their secular identity is tied to their Jewishness, and they are anxious to retain and even strengthen the Jewish components of the state and society of Israel. On the other side of the divide is a smaller group of ideologically secular to whom Judaism is at best trivial and at worst a barrier to their aspirations for a state based on liberal universalistic principles in which distinctions between Jews and non-Jews have no bearing. The lines distinguishing these two groups are also not hermetic. There are some who find themselves on one side of the line in terms of their political preferences and on the other side of the line in terms of their negative attitudes toward the religious tradition. Some have shifted back and forth between the two orientations. But we believe that most of those who are ideologically secular can be categorized as being closer to either the Jewish or Universalist positions. As noted earlier, the latter fall outside the purview of our essay.

Jews Who Are Secular by Default

The majority of Israeli seculars fall into the category of secular by default. A statement of the organization Ma'agal Tov is instructive in this regard. Ma'agal Tov identifies itself as a secular institution addressing students, parents, youth group leaders, and young teachers in the spirit of the labor movement. Its concern is that secular Israeli society is turning its back on its Jewish heritage.[25] The leaders of Ma'agal Tov are quoted as follows: "In the present reality, the overwhelming majority of the secular public is not aware of what it does not have. For most young secular people in Israel, the word 'Judaism' generally produces a feeling of repulsion."[26]

This may be overstated, and that which is true of young people is not necessarily true of an older generation. But the point is not without validity. The secular by default, most of whom observe a bare minimum of Jewish tradition, are not embarrassed by the fact of their Jewishness. Although most of them do not feel strongly that they are a part of the Jewish people and do not feel strong ties to the Diaspora, they do have some sense of their Jewishness; they do have some feeling, weak as it may be, that they are part of the Jewish people. As table 9.1 shows, the vast majority do want a state that is Jewish, though not one governed by Jewish law. In a more speculative vein, as noted, we suspect that the Jewish orientations these Jews do possess, however weak they may be, stem primarily from the fact that in the minds of most Israelis, being Israeli and being Jewish are inseparable. In a more specific sense, this is attributable to the culture of Israel and the folk customs of the society; to historical memories, of which the memory of the Holocaust is the most powerful; and to the educational system, where Jewish content is severely diluted, but the notion that one ought to honor the tradition and Jewish peoplehood is present.

We believe that a significant portion of the secular by default think of their Jewishness, probably unconsciously, as an accident of birth. Judaism, in their view, seems to be a biological-ethnic fact. To be Jewish in Israel has traditionally meant that one was not an Arab. The sense of Jewishness is tied to the notion that Israel should be a Jewish state. Jewish and Arab were mirror images of one another. A Jewish state was a state where Jews outnumbered Arabs. Beginning in the 1990s, as the percentage of non-Jewish non-Arab immigrants and foreign workers rose dramatically, the prevalent notion in Israeli secular society was to think of the immigrants as part of the non-Arab majority, which in some sense made them part of the Jewish collective.[27] This was especially true of those immigrants who served in the army. In other words, one's contribution and display of loyalty to the state incorporated one into the Jewish people. Hence, it is not surprising that secular Jewish society never encouraged the Russian non-Jews to convert. Today, as the proportion of those who are non-Jewish and non-Arab grows dramatically, older conceptions are under challenge, and it is too early to tell where they will lead.

The secular by default are also influenced by currents prevalent in Western culture. Consumerism may be the strongest of such currents. Guy Ben-Porat suggests that secular Jews who spend Shabbat with their families at shopping malls may bear no animus to religion, no radical opinion on issues of religion-state relations, and may even cherish the Shabbat.[28] But Shabbat at a shopping mall is their choice of leisure-time activity. The atrophying of Jewish and Judaic commitment, a process that has been taking place for at least two decades, seems to proceed from the natural rhythms of life. It is too early to determine what long-term effect the second intifada has had on secular Israelis, but it is our impression that the immediate result has been the strengthening of the sense of Israeliness and its identification with Jewishness. The perception of being engaged in a national conflict between Arabs and Israeli Jews has, we believe, strengthened Jewishness in its national, Zionist, some might say neo-Zionist, sense. The perception of the Arab as the "other" was strengthened, but this did little to strengthen Jewishness in its religious, or halakhic, sense.

The Ideologically Secular Judaists

The ideological Jewish-seculars, like the secular organizations concerned with Jewish identity, are troubled by the state of Judaism among the secular public. Dedi Zucker edited a book published in 1999 titled *We the Jewish Seculars: What Is Secular Jewish Identity?* Written and edited against the background of what has been called "the culture war between religious and secular," this book is a kind of self-conscious effort by prominent representatives of the Israeli cultural elite to identify for themselves and their readers the significance and meaning of an identity that was, in the recent past, simply taken for granted, in no need of any kind of textual support.[29] The lack of clarity in the meaning of a secular identity, or indeed in the meaning of the term "secular Jew," that led to the writing of the book was also behind the decision of those who conducted the Guttman Report to substitute the term "not religious" for the term "secular."[30] At the time Zucker edited the book he was a member of the Knesset representing Meretz, the most left wing and—along with the Shinui party—the most outspokenly secular of the Zionist parties. Zucker, however, was uneasy with the absence of a Jewish component in his party's secularism. He writes of the secular public:

> [This public] has been pulling in a universalistic direction in order to express its secularism. Expressions of empathy and identification with traditional Jewish concepts and with the Jewish history of the various diasporas has lessened. . . . .The non-religious Israeli knows only a banal Judaism or a fanatical Judaism enclosed in its own world. Against this he sees an Israel almost totally cleansed of any Jewish concepts. . . . Too many Israeli seculars are left stammering when asked to define their Judaism. Secular identity has based itself far too much on hostility to religion and the religious. A secular humanist identity must gather its courage and enter the Jewish (Judaic) territory without abandoning an iota of the universalistic tradition. . . . Only such a Jew can enter into a real dialogue with the other Jewish tribes. Only such Jews can prevent a cleavage from the traditional-*mizrahi* tribe. The alternative is to stand on the fringes of Israeliness.[31]

The volume is comprised of contributions from twenty Israeli intellectuals— some of them, like A. B. Yehoshua, are quite well known, others less so. A wide variety of opinions found expression, and all that really united the contributors was the fact that to be a secular Jew meant that one was not a religiously observant Jew. A few of the contributions were primarily expressions of hostility toward the religious establishment, especially its stance on political issues. A few, at the opposite extreme, were concerned with the secular-religious divide and the need to find a basis for unity and consensus. Many, like Zucker in his introduction, bemoaned the ignorance and indifference of secular Jews toward Jewish history and the Jewish heritage and noted that secular Jews are often confused about Judaism. Indeed, a few contributors dissociated themselves from secular Judaism for that very reason. A number of them preferred to identify themselves as *hofshiim* (see our historical excurses) rather than seculars (*hilonim*). One contributor noted that, whereas the real secular Jews sought the normalization of the Jewish people, he feared that normalization would lead to assimilation. He sought instead the construction of a society built on the vision of the prophets.[32] Another contributor, expressing what we earlier called a biological-ethnic perception of Jewishness, thought that "there are Jews but no Judaism," but he was one of the few who expressed the notion.[33] A few years earlier it was more common to hear from secular Jewish intellectuals that whatever Jews (presumably Israeli Jews) do, is Judaism.[34] In contrast, another contributor suggested the equation of religion and Judaism.[35]

Two points about the volume were especially striking to us. First, whereas the title and subtitle of the volume make no mention of Israel and speak only of secular Judaism, the authors all write as though the topic was secular Judaism *in Israel*. A. B. Yehoshua is only the most extreme in this respect. He writes, "If asked to present my identity card as a secular Jew I would answer that I don't employ the concept 'secular Jew' at all but the concept 'Israeli.' I suggest . . . a return to the simple concept 'Israeli' as the primary concept of identity, without any unnecessary additions. I am an Israeli. And if the religious Israeli wants to identify as a religious person, let him say, 'I am a religious Israeli.' I don't ask him to do that."[36]

We attribute great significance to this statement. On its face it is nonsensical. The statement would make sense if Yehoshua, instead of saying that he identifies himself as an Israeli had said that he identifies himself as a "Jew," not a "secular-Jew," and that if religious Jews choose to identify themselves as religious, it is their choice to hyphenate their Jewish identity. But this is not what Yehoshua said. He simply confused the term *Jewish* with the term *Israeli*. This confusion, we have already suggested, goes to the heart of Israeli secularism. It also ignores the fact that over 20 percent of the population is non-Jewish and that there are non-observant Jews outside of Israel. We are arguing here for a subconscious interpretation that extends to many of those who are secular by default as well. At least until recently, to be a Jew in Israel meant, for many secular Jews, not to be an Arab. For many secular Jews, being Jewish had little content other than pointing to the fact that they were not Arab. But since Arabs, at the conscious level were never present as part of the "us" collective, the confusion between Jew and Israeli was natural.

In many of the other essays, the seeds of the equation, Israeli equals Jew, are to be found. The most prominent academic among the contributors, Professor (and sometimes minister of education) Yael Tamir, notes that only in Israel can one be a secular Jew because only in Israel do the Jewish tradition and the Jewish heritage exist in education, the media, literature, museums, etc.[37] The assumption here is that there are no private structures for secular Judaism, an assumption with which others agree. Professor Ruth Gavison, outspoken and secular, makes a similar point. She often notes in her public lectures that, whereas the religious public does not need the state and society to express their Judaism, the secular public, in the absence of the public acknowledgment of the Jewish tradition, would be hard pressed to find ways to express their Jewishness. "Israel," she writes, "is the only place where the public culture is Hebrew-Jewish. From this point of view, Israel allows people like me—Jews who are not at all religious—to lead a Jewish life in which our Jewish identity has a central place. It is possible that it is the only place where Jews can survive without the observance of commandments for more than two generations."[38]

Gavison and Tamir's points, we believe, are well taken. We agree with them. But they also suggest how dependent the Jewish identity of these seculars is on their Israeliness.

The second striking aspect of the Zucker volume is how few of the contributors defined, even in broad outline, what they meant by secular Judaism in other than negative terms (i.e., it is not religion, it is not authoritative, it is not ritual). Those who did so—for example, Yael Tamir, Yaron London, and Ruth Calderon—viewed secularism as embedded in the Jewish tradition but offering a new interpretation and model in which the tradition is transmitted.[39] But this, as all the contributors pointed out, was yet to be done. Indeed, Tamir is unsure if the secular public can meet the challenge of constructing "a new prayer book, a new reading of the sources, and a new interpretation of Jewish holidays."[40] The overwhelming conclusion with which the reader is left, a conclusion with which the majority of contributors would surely concur, is that secular Judaism in Israel, when defined in a positive way rather than simply as a negation of religion, is pretty thin both in practice and in intellectual content. It appears to us that none of the contributors, with the exception of Yair Tzaban,[41] believe that the ideology of Israeli secularism, at the present time, amounts to much. It has little to offer and has few advocates. Under the circumstances, one can resort to one of two strategies. Either concede the point, as most of the authors do, and point to the direction in which things might get better (i.e., renewed interest in and a new interpretation of the Jewish tradition) or argue that whatever Israeli Jews do is by definition secular Judaism. Our own opinion is that the pessimism most of the contributors exhibit is premature.

The Meanings of Secular Judaism

It would seem that secular Judaism has at least three meanings in the minds of most Israelis. The most common meaning, one that survey researchers simply assume to be *the* meaning, is a Jewish person who is not observant of religious commandments. As already suggested, many if not most Israeli Jews who call themselves secular do observe quite a few commandments, and the question (in that case) is why they call themselves secular rather than masorti.[42] The differences are very basic. The secular who do observe some religious commandments do not think of themselves as observing *religious* commandments. They are acting out Jewish or Israeli folk customs or performing acts out of deference to parents, other family members, or friends. Furthermore, even if they do recognize that a few of the rituals that they perform are religious acts—for example, kissing a mezuzah or fasting on Yom Kippur—the basis may well be a superstitious placating of spirits. We have also heard secular Jews rationalizing their behavior in New Age terminology (that is, fasting is good for the soul).

A second definition of secular, one that many intellectuals seem to favor, is the absence of a belief in God.[43] As we have seen, many Israeli Jews who define themselves as secular report that they believe in God. (Forty-three percent of secular college students, according to Daphna Canetti's survey). While it seems to us that this is the least useful or accurate way of describing a secular Jew, the fact remains that it is the definition used by a few secular and is a central tenet of secularism in Yaakov Malkin's *What Do Secular Jews Believe?*[44]

A third definition of secular Jew refers to one who has a nonreligious conception of Judaism—the notion that Judaism is a culture or a civilization of which religious practice and belief is a only a part. This would contrast to a religious conception of Judaism that argues Judaism is constituted by Jewish law. This notion of secular Judaism was basic to the Jewish enlightenment of Eastern Europe in the nineteenth century and a critical component in the thinking of such luminaries as Ahad Ha'am and Mordecai Kaplan.[45] This basic notion, however, is shared by virtually every student of Judaism, including many religiously observant Jews.

The problem, therefore, with defining a secular Jew in this manner is that all it does is distinguish between those who are familiar with Judaism and Jewish history and those who are not. Our own preference is the definition offered by the Moroccan-born Israeli musician Shlomo Bar. Judaism, he feels, "isn't a religion but 'a way to live,'"[46] but not many of those whom we studied echo this sentiment.

Prospects for Secular Judaism

What are the prospects for secular Judaism in Israel? Will secular Jews in Israel succeed in developing a meaningful Jewish culture? We have discussed this problem elsewhere and have concluded, as we do now, that the verdict is not yet in.[47] The evidence is mixed. The ideologically Secular-Judaists, as we have seen, fear the growing ignorance of and indifference toward the Jewish tradition. It is easy to blame the religious establishment itself for this state of affairs, and to their credit most of the secular intellectuals in the Zucker volume refrain from doing so. It would have been easy for them to argue, as only a few did, that the erosion of tradition in the lives of so many Israelis is a consequence of the Orthodox elite appropriating Judaism and interpreting the traditional text and traditional values in a xenophobic, sexist manner overlooking or rejecting values within the Jewish tradition, which could have provided a vision and a model of moral behavior for all Israelis. But even if the religious house of Israel is morally rotten, most of the secular-Jewish ideologists whom we read do not find this sufficient in explaining the feeble character of secular Judaism in Israel. And we agree with them. Because blaming the religious establishment would not account for the easy manner in which seculars surrendered the battle over defining the nature of Judaism. That we suspect, stems from the lack of passion and commitment secular Judaism engenders. This passion and commitment once existed not because of the nature of secular Judaism, but rather because it was anchored in a Zionist vision and ideology. As that vision diminishes in importance, so does the Jewish tradition. The Guttman Report is instructive in this regard as well. On all the measures of Zionist-Israeli loyalty and identity, the seculars score lower than the masortim, and indeed lower than non-haredi religious. For example, in response to the question "Would you want very much to be born again as an Israeli?" 85 percent of the non-haredi religious responded "yes"; 73 percent of the masortim said "yes"; but among the secular, 42 percent of those who kept something of the tradition, 31 percent of those who kept none of the tradition, and 30 percent of the antireligious who kept none of the tradition answered "yes." Similar proportions are found in response to the question "Do you feel yourself Israeli?"[48] Respondents were asked about components that were very influential in shaping their Jewish identity. Some of these components were of a religious nature (i.e., lighting Shabbat candles), some of them were of a general Jewish nature (i.e., the Holocaust or the Warsaw ghetto uprising), and some of were of an Israeli nature (i.e., the establishment of the state or the wars that Israel underwent). In all cases these components, even the Israeli components, were weaker among the secular than among the masortim or religious.[49] This finding makes sense only if we assume that as far as many (not all) secular Jews are concerned, both the Jewish and Israeli identity are so weak that respondents are reluctant to credit any factor as being "very influential" in the shaping of their Jewish identity.[50]

On the other hand, the situation is not as bleak as some would have it. And here we must distinguish between secular Judaism as an interpretation of the tradition and secular Judaism as a Jewish way of life.

Secular Judaism as Interpretation

The interpretive or homiletic enterprise that authors such as Yaron London, Yael Tamir, and Ruth Calderon called for has been taking place for a number of decades in Israel with great urgency and intensity since the beginning of the nineties. This takes place in various secular institutions of learning (Oranim and Alma are outstanding examples) but also among the modern Orthodox. There are scores of study groups all over Israel where both secular and modern Orthodox Jews study together and undertake the interpretation of text together.[51] It may well be that little of what they produce is of lasting importance, but the most significant aspect of the enterprise is that Israelis are making the interpretive effort. What do we mean by interpretation? We mean looking anew at traditional Jewish texts to see how they can relate to one's own life, to the joys, to the tragedies, to the journeys and the passages from one status to another. Secondly, how they can be understood as illustrating and explaining such values as human reason, acting justly to non-Jews as well as Jews, tolerance of a variety of opinions, eschewing violence, responsibility to society, and the requirements and parameters of ethical behavior. In other words, values that are likely to make a liberal humanist proud to be a Jew rather than cringe at the mention of Judaism; values which demonstrate the compatibility of Judaism and humanism and only in that context project the value of Jewish particularism.[52] Interestingly, one of the lessons of all or at least most of the groups where secular and Orthodox Jews study together is that the secular need the help of religious Jews in accessing the text.

The non-Orthodox, even the best educated among them, are generally ignorant of the Jewish sources. They have much to contribute once they understand the simple meaning of the texts, but they need the Orthodox to serve as their basic guides. Once the simple meaning of the text is uncovered, differences between Orthodox and secular, so we are told, tend to disappear. And the differences that remain provide sources of stimulation for both sides. But how much better off secular Judaism would be if seculars were knowledgeable and secure enough to engage in the study of Jewish texts on their own.

If, as the evidence suggests, such groups are emerging all over Israel, how do we explain the negative assessments of secular intellectuals regarding the state of Jewish understanding and Jewish study? The answer is that one can judge the same cup as half full or half empty. It is also a matter of judgments by insiders versus those by outsiders. For example, for those who look at the status of Jewish study from the inside, one finds that "in the last few decades, the secular population of Israel has been undergoing a revival of interest in all matters related to Hebrew culture and Jewish identity. The organizations and societies which have arisen as a reflection of this revival have . . . exchanged the academic-disciplinary approach for a holistic approach which perceives the engagement in and study of Judaism as a doctrine, a source of inspiration and a way of life for secular Israelis Jews as well."[53]

The symbolic expression of this renewal is the term "a return to the Jewish bookshelf," a play on words taken from a poem by Israel's great national poet H. N. Bialik. One can find evidence in other areas as well. In a most illuminating article, basic we think to understanding contemporary Israeli art, David Sperber writes about the emergence of Jewish themes, a process that he dates to the eighties of the last century.[54] Sperber notes other manifestations of this Jewish renaissance. He writes the following:

> In this spiritual climate the "Jewish" artists of today, who in the past were pushed to the margins of the Israeli art world, are warmly embraced. The great change with regard to Judaism that began more than two decades ago, is not unique to the world of art but is influenced, of course, by the dominant current among the Israeli cultural elite and by the transformation of the "Jewish bookshelf" to a dominant topic of discourse. Even a movement as singularly secular as Hashomer Hatzair participates in this. . . . The goals of that movement have been revised to include "educating a person to be involved in Jewish culture."[55]

He goes on to say that when twenty thousand members of Hashomer Hatzair meet at the end of July 2003 for the Shomria, a gathering held once every ten years, they will be treated to an event unimaginable in the past, a dramatic presentation of portions of the Talmud.[56]

As we said, if one follows development in Israeli culture closely, one finds evidence for a renewed interest in Judaism.[57] But to an outsider with no stake in demonstrating a renewed interest in Jewish matters or in exploring the margins of mainstream Israeli culture (margins that may, of course, become mainstream themselves at some future time), the condition of secular Jewish culture is not as rosy. Sperber himself assesses the Jewish content of the art upon which he reports as shallow and simplistic with an overemphasis on anti-Semitism and the Holocaust. Secondly, he suggests that much of the renewed interest in Jewish matters in art is related to sense of post-Zionist ennui, if not hostility toward the Israeli past and the manner in which it was portrayed in mainstream Israeli culture. This, in turn, leads to the search for new foci of identity. Jewish renewal among Israeli seculars, the study groups, and the interpretive effort described above, is funded in good part by private foundations, mostly in the United States and the United Kingdom, and a few Jewish Federations in the United States. Israeli government funding has been severely cut in recent years. The Jewish renewal itself receives little attention in the media and, most significantly, relatively little encouragement or reinforcement in Israeli schools despite the demands of the Shenhar Report. It does not seem to touch the day-to-day lives of the vast majority of secular Israeli Jews, although according to the Guttman Report, most Israelis would like more Jewish emphasis in both the media and the schools.

Conclusion: Secular Judaism and the Rhythms of Life

The confusion in the minds of many Israeli seculars between Jew and Israeli is understandable, and where it exists it is obviously at the subconscious level. The notion that only Israel affords an opportunity for the secular Jew to live a life in which Judaism and Jewish identity are central to one's identity is not without foundation. But if living in Israel is a necessary condition, it is by no means a sufficient one. One cannot ignore the impact of Western consumer culture and assume that the present level of Jewish practice and commitment guarantees the survival of a substantive rather than a nominal Jewish culture in Israel. The possibility exists because, as both Yael Tamir and Ruth Gavison pointed out, only in Israel is the public arena Jewish, and this Jewishness is reflected in the minds and lives of at least some seculars. When Ilan Ramon, the first Israeli astronaut, embarked into space on the ill-fated Columbia shuttle, he brought aboard a Hebrew Bible; a Kiddush cup for the blessing over sacramental wine; a *mezuzah*, which he borrowed from the Israeli air force; and a picture drawn by a child during the Holocaust. Ramon, according to family members with whom we spoke, did not observe any of the laws of kashrut, but he requested and was provided with kosher meals by NASA. Ramon saw himself as a representative of Israel (not of the Jewish people), and these were the symbols he chose to represent his nation. It tells us a great deal about the power of Jewish secularism in Israel. But it also suggests its weakness.

At the risk of generalizing and oversimplifying—for countertendencies, as we have noted, are present—what is suggested here is the enormous dependence of secular Judaism on the public arena, of the inability of the secular to generate private structures of life that are Jewish, or to compete with the consumer culture that does create such structures. Does secular Judaism succeed in doing so elsewhere? It does not. This is the great problem that confronts the vast majority of European Jewry, Jews of both Western but especially Eastern Europe. Has it ever done so? The example of the nineteenth-century Jewish enlightenment, especially in Eastern Europe, and the early Zionist settlers in Palestine offers a ray of hope. But in many respects the rich presence of Jewish tradition in the lives of the early *maskilim* and the Zionist settlers was a debt to their own childhood—a taken-for-granted way of life that was inconsistent with their own ideological emphases and was not successfully transmitted to future generations.

For most Jews, ritual is the central aspect of Judaism. It is what comes to mind when they think of what it means to be a Jew. It is that which makes Judaism distinctive. It is interesting that in *What Do Secular Jews Believe?* Yaakov Malkin is also concerned with what the ritual and ceremonial implications of being secular are. Perhaps all that God demands of the Jew is to do justice, love mercy, and walk humbly in his path, but that is not what sets the Jew apart from non-Jews. Can Judaism in Israel be lived exclusively at the public level and/or by incorporating Jewish folk customs (a Passover Seder, Shabbat meals, even a blessing over candles) into one's private life? According to Table 9.1, roughly a quarter of secular Israeli Jews do incorporate religious commandments into their private lives, although they do not think of them as commandments. Are they likely to be retained if the performance of the "commandment" or ritual lacks the mantle of authority, if one does not feel *obligated* to perform them? We do not know. What is clear, however, is that secular Judaism does not generate the commitment, the passion, and the confidence that religion generates in the hearts of its adherents. Perhaps if more Israeli Jews thought of Judaism as "a way of life," as the masortim do, it would generate the kind of commitment that is required if Judaism is to survive in the face of the challenge of Western culture. Jewish practice would then become authoritative, not because God commanded it, but because that is what it means to be Jewish. As it now stands, the passivity of secular Jews with regard to issues of Judaic meaning and Jewish commitment coupled with their antagonism to the rabbis and religious parties, who are perceived as coercive and intolerant, and the assimilatory pressures of a global postmodern culture are difficult hurdles to overcome.[58]

There is another alternative. Perhaps secular Jews in Israel can generate new rituals or transform older ones so that they become more meaningful than traditional ones. There has been a lot of activity in this regard, and a number of organizations have developed in the last few years to help secular Jews think through and perform rituals and *rites de passage* in a "secular" manner. Needless to say there is a Web site as well. The interesting questions are to what extent the new secular rituals incorporate traditional ritual and how widespread have they become. We have no answer to the first question. We believe secular ritual in Israel incorporates a good deal of traditional ritual. (For example, we interviewed a number of rabbis who perform marriages for secular couples, laypeople who facilitate or conduct secular marriages, and the author of a doctoral dissertation on the topic. All of them report that in every instance the secular couple wants a bridal canopy and the ceremonial breaking of a glass. The variation from tradition is that in many cases the bride as well as the groom will smash the glass.) The differences between secular and religious ritual might in many cases be the interpretation given to the ritual rather than the ritual itself. The subject merits study. As to the second question, we are skeptical about the prospects for secular ritual. The kibbutz movement invested energy and resources in devising secular rituals, and they have all but vanished today. This topic also merits careful investigation. In many instances the secular have not replaced one ritual with another but have incorporated tradition into their lives by changing the rhythm or pattern of their lives in conformity with tradition. The Sabbath and the Jewish holidays are set apart by special meals, reading special books, listening to special music.

In Israel, unlike the Diaspora, the opportunity for recovery of the tradition and of secular Judaism is always close at hand. But it is also possible that Jewish renewal in Israel will come only with some dissociation from Zionism and Israeli nationalism. In a period where national and even ethnic loyalties are increasingly frayed among the Westernized middle-class Jews of Israel, Judaism must represent something beyond an expression of national identity. Israel, as we have seen in the case of intellectuals, serves too readily as a synonym for Judaism. The decline of national allegiance, which is far more pronounced amongst the secular than amongst the traditional or the religious, bodes ill for secular Judaism as well.

NOTES

We are grateful to Riv-Ellen Prell for her comments on an earlier draft.

1. The Hebrew letter "khet" is variously transliterated as "kh" or "h." The first variant is used in most chapters in this volume; however, the other variant is used in this chapter.

2. Interview with Meir Yoffe, September 27, 2002. Yoffe is the Director of *Panim*, an umbrella and service organization for a variety of Israeli groups dedicated to strengthening Jewish identity and knowledge among Israelis. Many, if not most, of the organizations are de facto secular. They cooperate with one another regardless of their religious orientations so that, whereas some of the organizations define themselves as Orthodox, they are of a decidedly moderate variety that acknowledges the Jewish legitimacy of non-Orthodox groups. Yoffe was basing himself on his own observations and on remarks in the text of the Shenhar Report.

3. A dramatic example of the secularization of modern Orthodox and religious Zionist thought is found in Yoske Achituv, "Towards an Illusion-free Religious Zionism," *A Hundred Years of Religious Zionism*, vol. 3, "Philosophical Aspects" (Ramat Gan, Israel: Bar-Ilan University Press, 2002), 7–30. Achituv, in our opinion the most brilliant and creative Orthodox-Zionist thinker, says that religious Zionism must rid itself of four illusions. They are a meta-historical and metaphysical conception of history; incorporating mystical foundations in the term "beginning of redemption"; incorporating promises of the prophets and the sages in cultural, historical, and social projections; and, finally, the vision of a renewal of ancient times and the possibility of a state conducted in accordance with Jewish law.

A forthcoming study by Kimmy Kaplan is devoted to the topic of the Israelization, by which he means the secularization of the *haredim*.

4. See, for example, Yaacov Shavit, "The Status of Culture in the Process of Creating a National Society in Eretz-Israel: Basic Attitudes and Concepts," in Zohar Shavit, ed., *The Construction of Hebrew Culture in Eretz-Israel* in the series *The History of the Jewish Community in Eretz-Israel Since 1882* (Jerusalem: Israel Academy for Sciences and Humanities and Bialik Institute, 1998), 9–29 (in Hebrew), and the extensive literature cited therein. In our opinion, however, the topic has not been exhausted.

5. On post-Zionism and its relation to radical secularism, see Bernard Susser and Charles S. Liebman, *Choosing Survival: Strategies for a Jewish Future* (New York: Oxford University Press, 1999), 127–134, and Charles S. Liebman, "Reconceptualizing the Culture Conflict among Israeli Jews," *Israel Studies* 2 (Fall 1997): 172–189. Reprinted with some revision in Anita Shapira, ed., *A State in the Making: Israeli Society in the First Decades* (Jerusalem: Zalman Shazar Center for Jewish History, 2001), 249–264 (in Hebrew).

6. We are thinking particularly of an article by Zvi Bekerman and Marc Silverman, "The Corruption of Culture and Education by the Nation State: The Case of Liberal Jews' Discourse on Jewish Continuity," *Journal of Modern Jewish Studies* 2 (2003): 1–18. The authors strike us as benign post-Zionists, a label they themselves might reject. While we demur from their conclusions, we find their critique of the ideological foundation of secular Judaism in Israel and of the inconsistency between liberalism and national identity of much merit.

7. Interview, November 4, 2002.

8. Moshe Goshen-Gottstein, "Society, Culture and Language: Secular and Religious," *Ha'aretz*, June 11, 1965, and "Secular and Religious," *Ha'aretz*, June 18, 1965. We are indebted to Anita Shapira for bringing these columns to our attention.

9. *People and World: Jewish Culture in a Changing World: Recommendations of the Committee to Examine Jewish Studies in the General Educational System* (Jerusalem: Ministry of Education, 2002). The report itself was submitted in December 1993.

10. Interview, October 31, 2002.

11. On the role of religion and the use of traditional symbols in the *Yishuv*, and on the role of religious symbols in the strengthening of national identity, see Charles S. Liebman and Eliezer Don-Yehiya, *Civil Religion in Israel: Traditional Judaism and Political Culture in the Jewish State* (Berkeley: University of California Press, 1983); Anita Shapira, "Religious Notions of the Labor

Movement," in *Zionism and Religion*, ed. Shmuel Almog, Jehuda Reinharz, and Anita Shapira (Jerusalem: Mercaz Zalman Shazar, 1994), 301–327 (in Hebrew); Shmuel Almog, "Religious Values in the Second Aliyah," in Almog, *Zionism and Religion*, 285–300; Moti Zeira, *Rural Collective Settlement and Jewish Culture in Eretz Israel during the 1920's* (Jerusalem: Yad Yitzhak Ben Zvi, 2000) (in Hebrew); and Nili Aryeh-Sapir, *Shaping an Urban Culture: Rituals and Celebrations in Tel-Aviv in Its Early Years* (Ph.D. diss., Tel Aviv University, 2000) (in Hebrew).

12. Shalom Lilker, *Kibbutz Judaism: A New Tradition in the Making* (New York: Herzl Press, 1982).

13. Shlomit Levy, Hanna Levinsohn, and Elihu Katz, *Beliefs, Observance of the Traditions and the Values of Israeli Jews—2000* (Jerusalem: Avi Chai Foundation and the Israel Democracy Institute, 2002).

14. There are a handful of antireligious who do report that they observe some of the tradition. The Guttman Report eliminated them from their analyses. As we shall see in Table 9.1, even a few of those who report that they are antireligious and observe no part of the tradition do indeed observe some traditional practices.

15. The antireligious category includes not only those who are hostile to the religious establishment, but those who really are opposed to religious practice. For example, in our own interviews we spoke to a kindergarten teacher in a secular school. The curriculum in such schools includes a ceremony, each Friday, of lighting candles and welcoming the Shabbat. Our respondent reported that some parents objected to any religious ceremony.

16. Levy, Levinsohn, and Katz, *Israeli Jews*, 14.

17. Daphna Canetti, *Democracy and Religious and Parareligious Beliefs in Israel: Theoretical and Empirical Perspectives* (Ph.D. diss., University of Haifa, 2002) (in Hebrew). We are grateful to Dr. Canetti for providing us with a breakdown of her data.

18. Riv-Ellen Prell has suggested to us that the high proportion of believers among secular Jews, and the especially high proportion among college students, may be due to the influence of Eastern religion that has penetrated Israeli youth culture. This is a postmodern phenomena strengthened by the few months or longer that so many Israelis spend in India and other Eastern countries following completion of their army service. Daphna Canetti finds confirmation for this in her interviews, adding that it is not only trips to the East but also participation in periodic "spiritual festivals" that have become popular among young Israeli Jews.

19. Charles S. Liebman and Yaacov Yadgar, "Israeli Identity: The Jewish Component," in *Israeli Identity in Transition* ed. Anita Shapira (Connecticut: Praeger Press, 2004).

20. In addition to the Guttman Report 2000, the studies include Shlomit Levy, Hanna Levinsohn, and Elihu Katz, *Beliefs, Observances and Social Interaction among Israeli Jews* (Jerusalem: Louis Guttman Institute of Applied Social Research, 1993) [the highlights of that report are reprinted in Charles Liebman and Elihu Katz, eds., *The Jewishness of Israelis* (Albany: SUNY Press, 1997), which also includes an analysis of the 1993 Report]; Yair Auron, *Jewish-Israeli Identity* (Tel Aviv: Sifriat Poalim Publishing House, 1993); Michal Shamir and Asher Arian, "Collective Identity and Electoral Competition in Israel," *American Political Science Review* 93 (June 1999): 265–277; Uri Farago, "The Jewish Identity of Israeli Youth, 1965–1985," *Yahadut Zmanenu* 5 (1989): 259–285; Uri Farago, "National Identity and Regional Identity in Israel," in *Between I and We*, ed. Azmi Bashara (Tel Aviv: Van Leer Institute and the Kibbutz Hameuchad, 1999), 153–168; Eliezer Ben-Rafael and Stephen Sharot, *Ethnicity, Religion, and Class in Israeli Society* (Cambridge: Cambridge University Press, 1991); Yochanan Peres and Ephraim Yuchtman-Yaar, *Between Consent and Dissent: Democracy and Peace in the Israeli Mind* (Jerusalem: Israel Democracy Institute, 1998); an unpublished study by Ezra Kopelowitz and Hadas Franco of 160 students in Rupin college in 2001 (for a report of the study with a summary of the findings see *Ha'aretz*, September 12, 2002, p. 3B); Jacob Shamir and Michal Shamir, *The Anatomy of Public Opinion* (Ann Arbor: University of Michigan Press, 2000); Stephen Sharot, "Jewish and Other National and Ethnic Identities of Israeli Jews," in *National Variations in Jewish Identity*, ed. Steven M. Cohen and Gabriel Horenczyk (Albany: SUNY Press, 1999), 299–316; Eliezer Leshem, "The Aliyah from the Former Soviet Union and the Religious-Secular Cleavage in Israeli

Society," in *From Russia to Israel: Identity and Culture In Transition*, ed. Moshe Lisak and Eliezer Leshem (Tel Aviv: Hakkibutz Hameuchad, 2001), 125–148; and Alec Epstein, "Continuity and Change in the Characteristics of the Identity of Russian Speaking Jews in Israel," *Gesher* 147 (Summer 2003): 19–33.

21. Yair Auron, *Jewish-Israeli Identity* (Tel Aviv: Sifriat Poalim Publishing House, 1993).

22. Ibid.

23. Amos Elon, *The Israelis* (London: Penguin, 1971).

24. Laura Zarembski, *The Religious-Secular Divide in the Eyes of Israel's Leaders and Opinion Makers* (Jerusalem: Floersheimer Institute for Policy Studies, 2002).

25. This description of Ma'agal Tov, provided by the institution itself, is found in Meir Yoffe's report *Mapping Programs That Promote Tolerance and Unity in the Israeli Jewish Public* (Jerusalem: Jewish Agency for Israel, June 2001), 105 (in Hebrew).

26. Alma College, *Center for Secular Judaism: Submitted by the Think Tank on the Issue of the Jewish People* (Tel Aviv: Alma College, December 2001), 26.

27. Israel's Central Bureau of Statistics records the Jewish population as those living in Israel less Arabs. In fact, the "Jews" as they appear in the Bureau's publications includes non-Jews who are not Arab.

28. Guy Ben-Porat, "Between Consumerism and Tradition, Israelis and Saturday Shopping Centers," forthcoming. On the association between Western values in general and consumerism in particular, and Israeli secularism, see Liebman, "Reconceptualizing the Culture Conflict."

29. The book appeared as part of the series *Judaism Here and Now*, published by Yediot Aharonot, Israeli's largest selling newspaper. The series is an interesting test case of the effort to provide contemporary texts whose purpose is the creation (strengthening) of a secular Israeli Jewish identity.

30. This was confirmed in private correspondence.

31. Dedi Zucker, ed., *We the Secular Jews: What Is Secular Jewish Identity?* (Tel-Aviv: Yediot Aharonot, 1999), 9–12. Another edited volume of importance is Yehoshua Rash, ed., *Regard and Revere—Renew without Fear: The Secular Jew and His Heritage* (Tel Aviv: Sifriat Poalim, 1987). This is the English title of the volume. The Hebrew title uses the term *hofshi* rather than *hiloni* for secular. Another relevant volume is Yaakov Malkin, *What Do Secular Jews Believe? Beliefs and Values of Hofshiim* (Tel-Aviv: Poalim, 2000).

32. Eli Ben Gal, "Between *Hofshiim* and *Hilonim*," in Zucker, *We the Secular Jews*, 167–173.

33. Nissim Calderon, "The Bells of the Jubilee," in Zucker, *We the Secular Jews*, 74.

34. This notion has its origins among the more antireligious (antitradition) Zionist thinkers in the late nineteenth century, continuing through the work of Y. H. Brenner, a literary figure of enormous significance to radical Zionists.

35. Amnon Denkner, "To Live with Internal Contradiction," in Zucker, *We the Secular Jews*, esp. p. 82.

36. A. B. Yehoshua, "Life as Paradox," in Zucker, *We the Secular Jews*, 19.

37. Yael Tamir, "Revolution and Tradition," in Zucker, *We the Secular Jews*, 174–183.

38. See her personal statement in the document prepared by Gavison and Rabbi Yaacov Amidan, *Foundation for a New Social Contract between Those Who Observe Commandments and Hofshiim in Israel* (n.p.: Shalom Hartman Institute and the Yitzhak Rabin Center, 2001), 39.

39. Yaron London, *Datiim v'hofshiim*," in Zucker, *We the Secular Jews*, 23–39; Ruth Calderon, "A Time for Homiletics," in Zucker, *We the Secular Jews*, 194–198.

40. Tamir, "Revolution and Tradition," 183.

41. Yair Tzaban, "An Unashamed Secularist," in Zucker, *We the Secular Jews*, 111–131. This article was translated into English and appears under the title "An Unabashed Secular Jew," in the annual *Contemplate: The International Journal of Cultural Jewish Thought* 2 (2003): 5–14 (continued in the following issue).

42. See Yaacov Yadgar and Charles Liebman, "Beyond the Religious-Secular Dichotomoy: Masortim in Israel," this volume.

43. For example, Tom Segev writes that "anyone who says that he believes in God cannot be considered totally secular"; Tom Segev, "Who Is Secular?" *Ha'aretz*, September 25, 1996.

44. Yaakov Malkin, *What Do Secular Jews Believe?* (Tel-Aviv: Sifriat Poalim, in Hebrew, 2000). Although his book is of little intellectual value, what Malkin says is important for our purposes because he is probably the best-known "professional" secularist in Israel. Malkin edits the Hebrew language quarterly *Secular Judaism* and is the academic director of Meitar, the College of Judaism as Culture. He is co-dean of the International Institute for Secular Humanistic Judaism, which ordains Humanistic rabbis.

45. Immanuel Etkes, ed., *The East European Jewish Enlightenment* (Jerusalem: Zalman Shazar Center for Jewish History, 1993), and the extensive bibliography listed in the appendix.

46. Tamara Novis, "Raising the Bar," *Jerusalem Post, City Lights*, August 1, 2002, 10.

47. Liebman, "Secular Judaism and Its Prospects."

48. Levy, Levinson and Katz, *Israeli Jews*, 82.

49. Ibid., 85.

50. The reader must bear in mind that this figure, like all others, includes Jews from the Former Soviet Union. As noted, they constitute 19 percent of the secular sample and may have skewed the results somewhat by weakening the Jewish identity of the secular sample as well as weakening the Israeli components of that identity. We were unable to obtain the information that would have allowed us to do a secondary analysis of the Guttman data and corroborate if and to what extent this is the case.

51. For a detailed description of these institutions and organizations, see the report by Meir Yoffe, *Mapping Programs That Promote Tolerance and Unity.*

52. Bekerman and Silverman, "The Corruption of Culture," would argue that this is impossible as long as Judaism is associated with the national state.

53. Alma College, *Center for Secular Judaism*, 1.

54. David Sperber, "Yiddishkeit: Oil on Canvass, 2002," *De'ot* (June 2003): 30–33.

55. Ibid., 30.

56. For more detail on what one might call the Judaization of Hashomer Hatzair and its effort to attract religiously traditional youth, see *Ha'aretz*, "Hashomer Hatzair Observes the Sabbath," March 17, 2003.

57. But it is important to note that Israeli culture and identity in the last few decades has swung back and forth between two extremes of national identity: a particularistic-Jewish extreme on the one the hand and a universalistic-secular extreme on the other.

58. On the other hand, a number of factors moderate this tendency. The violent struggle against Israel in the second intifada is the most important. But another factor of great importance is the postmodernist orientation that encourages the individual to explore and identify his- or herself and the particular groups through which one is defined. This, the postmodernists believe, is necessary in the context of globalization. This may encourage the effort to rediscover aspects of Judaism viewed through a contemporary prism—first and foremost among them, aspects which are identified as spiritual or mystical.

10 Beyond the Religious-Secular Dichotomy

MASORTIM IN ISRAEL

YAACOV YADGAR AND
CHARLES S. LIEBMAN

In this chapter, our concern is Israeli Jews who, when asked to categorize their religious behavior, define themselves as "traditional" (*masorti*, plural *masortim*).[1] Their religious behavior is defined as "traditionalism" (*masortiut*), and they constitute about one-third of the Israeli Jewish population. By comparison, less than 20 percent of Israeli Jews define themselves as either "religious" (*dati*, a synonym for Orthodox in the Israeli context) or ultra-Orthodox (*haredi*). The remaining Jews define themselves as secular (*hiloni*).[2]

The meaning of and differences between these categories are not entirely clear. The "traditional" category is the most enigmatic. Even among those who have stressed its demographic importance, many dismiss this category as no more than an inconsistent cocktail of beliefs and practices characterized by lack of clarity. Academic analyses and popular discussion of religious identity among Israeli Jews often refer to this category. Both academic and popular discourse draw a distinction between "secular" and "religious," and the category "traditional" is often applied to a very different typology, one that was so popular among social scientists until recently—that between "traditional," meaning one who had not undergone modernization, and "modern," referring to one who had.[3] Indeed, the very birth of the category "traditional" to mark a kind of intermediate category between the "completely secular" and the "really religious" marks it as a problematic form of identity. It renders traditionalism or traditional identity as a kind of artificial category located between two ideal types and lacking any meaning independently of the two other categories. Nonetheless, with all our reservations about these terms, we will continue to employ them (or the Hebrew equivalents, masorti and masortiut), as we attempt to establish the foundations for further research that will explore the content and sociopolitical implications of a masorti identity. We will use the terms *traditionalist* or *traditionalism* to refer to the general phenomenon. We will most often use the Hebrew terms *masorti* and *masortiut* when referring to the specific Israeli manifestation. We will sometimes revert to English terminology for the sake of linguistic niceties where the meaning is clear. As we shall see, masortiut is actually a special form of traditionalism.

As in every form of individual identity, including hiloni and dati identities, the identity of masortim is not absolute but dependent on context, time, and place. It continually evolves as it confronts competing mosaics of identities and changing social and political conditions. We also believe that it is possible to distinguish a variety of masorti identities that range from a positive and independent definition of *masorti* (i.e., one that is not substantially dependent on other types of identity to define itself), to a negative understanding of one's own traditional identity (i.e., one that does indeed see itself as straddling the secular-religious dichotomy and locates itself in between them). Ethnicity and age also play a role in the choice of religious identity. Gender, as far as we can tell, does not.

Research on Traditionalism: The Dominance of the Modernization-Secularism Paradigm

In 1984 the distinguished anthropologist Moshe Shokeid summarized the relationship of academic research to traditionalism in Israel as developing in three stages. In the first stage, masortiut was met with dismissal by the academy as "part of the general category of characteristics comprising traditional culture that never garnered much esteem in veteran Israel society—in its secular as in its Orthodox [variety]."[4] This contempt has deep roots. Yaacov Shavit has noted that the cultural elite of the early Zionist movement was both contemptuous of and bitterly hostile toward the Jewish folk culture of Eastern Europe. Incredibly, the elite thought they could prevent the emergence of folk culture, except under their tutelage, in the Yishuv.[5] The second stage, according to Shokeid, was characterized by ignoring masorti Jews whose behavior was now viewed as an expression of folklore and unworthy of serious academic interest. The third stage, in which Shokeid together with his research partner Shlomo Deshen were outstanding exemplars, was characterized by a renewed interest in masortiut, an interest that was primarily anthropological and sociological.[6]

Much of the research on and discussions about traditionalists and traditionalism took place within the framework of the modernization-secularization paradigm. Within this framework, science is posed as an alternative to religion, and religion is moved from the public arena to the arena of private practice and belief. At its extreme, this theory suggests that the modernized and secularized human is freed from theological and metaphysical discourse. It is the only route whereby the individual can free himself from the constraints imposed by religious modes of thought. As a consequence of being secularized, people become self-conscious actors who create their own history. There is no longer a space for religion as an overarching system of meaning. The central theme in the secularization discourse argues that in the modern world, religion is so weakened that it must choose between rejection of modernity and acceptance of a reduced role in the dominant secular order. The implications of this are the abandonment of the public arena (cultural, social, and political) for the private arena, if not for an eventual disappearance.[7]

In this general frame of mind (though not always in this extreme form), the terms *tradition* or *traditionalism* (*masoret* and *masortiut*) were discussed in studies of

Israeli society. These studies provided evidence of the presence of traditionalism among Israeli Jews, especially among Mizrahim (Jews who originate or whose families originated in Muslim societies), whose religion was thought to be virtually synonymous with traditionalism. The distinction between a modern and a traditional society served the authors as a kind of paradigm through which the studies of the religion of Mizrahim as an expression of "pre-modern Judaism" were undertaken.[8]

As a consequence, they found little prospect for the survival of traditionalism in the context of a modern, secular, Westernized Israel. Masortim will have to choose between one of two mutually exclusive alternatives: secularism (i.e., completing the process of modernization and integration into the modern-Western-secular culture), or the strengthening of religion, of what we will describe below as "scripturalism," which includes at least the partial rejection of modernity and a strong measure of isolation within the confines of the community and the culture of the religious. Thus, Mizrahi traditionalism was portrayed as a temporary phenomenon, though it served the Mizrahim in their competition for public resources.[9] Some of these studies also pointed to factors slowing the process of modernization-secularization. Two factors—the central role of the family and the special place accorded rabbis in traditional Mizrahi society—are mentioned in this regard.[10]

Much of the description of masortiut was located in the context of a discussion of ethnicity and ethnic identification in Israel.[11] Special attention was devoted to some of the prominent expressions of religious traditionalism among Mizrahim, first and foremost among them being the pilgrimages to the graves of saints.[12] Another direction this research has taken is the role of gender in the process of modernization and secularization. Susan Sered, for example, has observed that even though modernization opens up new possibilities for the religious participation of women, "the religion of women" is most vulnerable to the forces of modernization. This vulnerability stems from the personal, somewhat hidden, home nature of women's religion.[13]

We are not prepared to dismiss the secular/modern versus the traditional/religious paradigm as wrong, although we are not comfortable with it intuitively, and contemporary scholarship rejects it.[14] But we are also anxious to pursue an alternative line of inquiry, which Shokeid himself has suggested. He has recognized that a third alternative besides secularization or integration into the established Orthodoxy of Israel also exists. This is the transformation of Mizrahi traditionalism into a form of ethnic identification in which traditionalism would play a more important role than is otherwise accorded to it. Shokeid has noted that "the *masoret* religiosity adopted and proclaimed by Middle Eastern Jews . . . may under certain circumstances develop into a symbolic linkage with the more dominant cultural stream. With the growing disparity between the expanding Ashkenazi orthodoxy and the dominant secular sector, on the one hand, and the growing notion of cultural need concerning the symbolic realm of Jewish identity in the secular sector, on the other hand, *masoret* religiosity may be more than an ethnic peculiarity."[15]

In line with this observation, we wish to propose the possibility that traditionalism is in fact a modern response—a method of coping with modernization rather than simply rejecting or accepting it. Following this reasoning, it may be more accurate to see masortiut as an expression of multiple modernities—an expression born of a discomfort with the older modernization discourse that instead emphasizes the simultaneous existence of a variety of modernity models that influence one another. Modernization in the Western sense is understood in this context as one expression of a variety of modernities.[16] Which of these paradigms is better suited to the condition of Israel and especially Mizrahi traditionalism is a key question of our larger study, one that remains unanswered for the moment.

Traditionalism Defined

We understand the term *traditionalism* to refer to a life lived, at least in part, in accordance with tradition—for example, conduct learned from the immediate environment, particularly the extended family. It is religious because so much of it refers to matters of religious concern. The term *traditionalism* is best understood by its mirror concept—scripturalism. Clifford Geertz has applied the label *scripturalism* to religious developments in two Muslim societies, Indonesia and Morocco.[17] Haym Soloveitchik has expanded Geertz's theoretical insight to a description of scripturalism in Orthodox Judaism (though he did not use the term).[18] Among traditionalists, religious conduct is the product of social custom. In the scripturalist form of religion, conduct is the product of conscious, reflective behavior. Among traditionalists, religious life is governed by habit and by what "seems" right; among scripturalists, by rules. Authority in the world of traditionalists is rooted in customs in the home, in the culture; it is transmitted mimetically. Authority in the world of religious scripturalism is rooted in texts as they are interpreted by the learned masters of the texts (in Judaism: *talmidei hakhamim*), and the heads of the advanced religious academies (in Judaism: *roshei yeshivot*). In the world of traditional religion and among traditionalists, the division between the masses and the elite is fixed. In the world of religious scripturalism, to use a Weberian concept, all should strive to become religious virtuosi. The last point is crucial because characteristics centered on the primacy of text are by no means modern.[19]

Both Geertz and Soloveitchik are sympathetic to what we call traditionalism, but for both authors, traditionalism emerges as a thing of the past. Both authors explain, most convincingly, why scripturalism has become the religious norm, at least in Indonesia and Morocco (which Geertz studied), and within American Orthodox Judaism (to which Soloveitchik devoted his attention). We are less certain that this is true of our case. Masortiut faces challenges from both the religious right and the secular left; its future is problematical, but by no means certain. We will argue that it has not disappeared because it is tied to other sources of legitimacy.

Some of the explanations that Geertz and Soloveitchik have offered for the rise of scripturalism and the decline of traditionalism are particular to the societies they studied; some of them are applicable to a variety of societies, indeed to the modern world in general. Although the authors do not say so, their analysis hints at one general reason for the decline of traditionalism: the dissociation of religion and culture. We believe that traditionalism continues to feed upon another source—its tie to ethnic or national identity. But masortiut is, as we shall see, a peculiarly modern phenomenon in other respects.

Traditionalism flourished when religion and culture were united. The dissociation of religion and culture rendered religion "unnatural," artificial, its practices no longer part of the normal rhythms of life. Haym Soloveitchik has provided the telling example of an undergarment, which Jewish law commands the Jew to wear. But, Soloveitchik has emphasized, today when it is "worn not as a matter of course but as a matter of belief then it becomes a ritual object. A ritual can no more be approximated than an incantation can be summarized. Its essence lies in its accuracy. It is that accuracy the haredim are seeking. The flood of works on *halachic* prerequisites and correct religious performance accurately reflects the ritualization of what have previously been simply components of the given world and parts of the repertoire of daily living."[20]

Scripturalist religion faces the challenge of living in a culture that is no longer conducive to, indeed which may even threaten, its religious mandates. It meets this challenge through a number of strategies.[21] One is by withdrawal from the culture and, insofar as possible, the creation of a new culture. Another is one in which religion conquers the culture and imposes its mandates. A third strategy is to seek some accommodation with the culture through the reinterpretation of the religious tradition. Among Orthodox Jews in Israel, as elsewhere, one finds accommodationist rabbis. They will accept the norms and values of modern culture where their interpretation of Scripture permits them to do so. But even these "modern" rabbis and their followers accept the basic spirit of scripturalism—the supreme authority of the text. They differ from other rabbis only in their more lenient and permissive interpretations of the text. There is a fourth strategy that is most common among the religious laity—compartmentalization (the notion that certain forms of behavior or behavior in certain areas of life are subject to religious demands, whereas others areas of behavior are religiously irrelevant). Traditionalism falls outside this paradigm (although it does adopt a form of compartmentalization) perhaps because it is a *sense* or a *feeling* rather than an ideology. It includes a sense that the choices described above are unnecessary because the religious observance that one incorporates into one's life is perfectly natural.

However masortiut, as we describe it, is not at all premodern. The masorti is thoroughly modern in the sense that he is self-conscious of his masortiut. As a consequence, two important differences distinguish the masorti from the classical traditionalist: first, the recognition that what he or she finds natural may not be natural for others, and, second, an acknowledgment that scripturalism is synonymous with the proper observance of religious commands. Hence, the masorti does not reject scripturalism, so much as he or she chooses what to observe and not observe. This choice, however, is strongly influenced by the tradition to which the masorti has been socialized. Does this make masortiut a variety of popular religion or, more likely, to use David Hall's felicitous term, "lived religion"?[22]

The traditionalist's recognition of the religious authority of the scripturalist necessarily renders him or her conscious of the complexity of his or her values and behavior and to what appears as the absence of consistency. In everything touching upon ideology, it would appear that the traditionalist is unable to project a coherent and consistent ideology. As Moshe Shokeid summarized the ethnographic description of Moroccan immigrants to Israel, these traditional Jews "never developed a consistent set of behavioral rules or philosophical justifications to their mixed secularist-religious style. In retrospect they view themselves as continuing the tradition of their father, adapted to their present condition."[23] This absence of ideology is expressed in their stubborn refusal to impose the traditional way of life, or for that matter the religious scripturalist way of life, on others or on the environment.[24] (It is important to note that in Judaism, the demand that the public arena be conducted in a certain manner is an integral part of one's religious obligation.) The difficulty or the conscious refusal to articulate a traditionalist ideology stems from the acceptance of the scripturalists' religious authority. In other words, traditionalists accept the scripturalist point that the latter represent the ideal and have exclusive claim to a religious ideology. The traditionalist chooses, therefore, not to intervene in this arena.

Therefore, traditionalism is intimately related to scripturalism. Traditionalists are aware of their own ignorance of the scriptural tradition and are sometimes prepared to amend some of their practices when informed by those more knowledgeable than themselves that they are not practicing this or that rule properly. They accept the organizational structure and are relatively indifferent to the belief structure of the elite religion. Of course, the rituals and symbols that are important to them imply a belief system, but one tending to be mythical rather than rational and ideational, and hence not in opposition to the more complex theological or legalistic elaboration of the elite religion. (Of course, the mythical dimensions of ritual also play a central role among the religious scripturalists.) Therefore, in the eyes of the elite religion, folk religion or, in our case, traditionalism, is not a movement but at best an error, or set of errors, shared by many people. At worst, it is understood as avoiding basic decisions, as a kind of halfway house to heresy.

Masortiut, the modern Israeli variety of traditionalism, is a coalescence of different traditions under the impact of a similar environment and of similar pressures—both the pressure from the religious elite who adamantly insist on traditionalism's lack of religious legitimacy and from the pressures of modern culture and the secularist camp. The big differences that remain are those between Ashkenazim (those who originate or whose families originate from predominantly Christian societies) and Mizrahim (those, as we noted, who originate or whose families originate from predominantly Muslim societies). The latter constitute a much higher proportion of traditionalists. Only a minority of Ashkenazim define themselves as traditionalists rather than as religious or nonreligious (secular).

According to the most comprehensive survey on the subject (the Guttman Center Survey) 50 percent of all Israeli Mizrahim identified themselves as masortim, whereas only 19 percent of Ashkenazim so identified themselves. In general the survey found that whereas Mizrahim in Israel were far more observant of the tradition than Ashkenazim, their religious identity was more moderate. Israeli scripturalists are, by and large, Ashkenazi. The same is true at the other extreme. Only 9 percent of the Mizrahim identify themselves as either nonreligious (i.e., do not maintain any traditional observances) or antireligious, whereas 34 percent of the Ashkenazim define themselves in this manner.[25] Moreover, both the Guttman survey and our own interviews suggest that the gap between Mizrahim and Ashkenazim is also expressed in the manner in which traditional rituals are observed. As a rule, Mizrahim are far more careful in observing the tradition in accordance with Jewish law than are Ashkenazim. Among the Ashkenazi tradition-alists, not only is the observance of religious practices less intense, but we suspect that unlike their parents, they have a fairly weak sense of traditionalism. Much of their religious observance is trivial in their own minds and abandoned with relative ease. The remainder of our discussion focuses primarily on Mizrahim, since they not only constitute the bulk of masortim, but we know a good deal more about them. However, our interviews that included Ashkenazim allow us to introduce a comparative dimension as well.

The Phenomenology of Mizrahi Traditionalism

There is a rich secondary literature on Mizrahim, but few scholars have analyzed Mizrahi traditionalism as a self-conscious alternative to strict observance.[26] The most common explanation for what is viewed as religious laxity in the behavior of many Mizrahim is to tie this laxity to the religious traditions of the Mizrahim that, as Zvi Zohar has demonstrated, are more pragmatic and in that sense more relaxed than those of the Ashkenazim.[27] But this would not explain why some traditions that are retained are rather difficult to observe (for example, fasting on Yom Kippur or not smoking on Shabbat), whereas some traditions that are easier to observe (such as males covering their head at meal times) have been abandoned.[28]

The image of the Mizrahi traditionalist that more than any other symbolizes his or her anomalous behavior is of one who "prays in the synagogue on Shabbat and then travels by car to the beach" or to a soccer game.[29] This religious-secular compromise generates both unease and a measure of contempt among both datiim and hilonim. Ethnographic studies and our interviews provide a series of similar, ostensibly anomalous examples, including wearing a yarmulke during prayer in the synagogue or during the reciting of Kiddush at the Sabbath table and punctiliously removing it afterward; participating in a family meal on Friday evening that includes reciting Kiddush but ignoring almost all the remaining Sabbath injunctions; or the punctilious observance of dietary laws, including two sets of dishes in the home, but exercising much greater leniency outside the home.[30] We were espe-cially interested to find a great gap between observance within and outside the home. Many of our female respondents reported on their rigid observance of the laws of family purity while ignoring laws pertaining to modesty of dress out-side the home. A number of male respondents reported that whereas they put on t'filin (phylacteries) every day (Jewish men are commanded to don phylacteries prior to reciting the morning prayers), they did not recite morning prayers. They neither attended synagogue on a daily basis nor even prayed in their own home. Many of our respondents reported that they regularly read chapters from the biblical Book of Psalms or at least carried the book around with them. Many also reported that they not only fast on Yom Kippur but on the ninth of Av as well, although they do not attend synagogue on that day. Some even reported that they washed their hands ritually before every meal, generally without saying the blessing that Jewish law prescribes. All our respondents carefully refrain from eating forbidden foods on Pesach and are very strict in observing all the prohibitions in addition to fasting that are associated with Yom Kippur.

A distinguishing characteristic of traditionalists seems to be their solution to the tension between religion and modernity. Unlike the scripturalists who insist that all of life is governed by Jewish law (among the most extreme is the governing of bodily movement),[31] in a sense sacralizing every aspect of life, masortim incorporate that which they consider religious or holy into the regular pattern of their otherwise modern lives. There are holy days, holy people, and holy events. Holiness demands very special behavior and makes very special demands. For some masortim, if one cannot meet these demands, then he "exits" or leaves the realm of the sacred or holy. If on a particular Sabbath one cannot or chooses not to meet the demands for Sabbath observance, then the Sabbath loses its holiness for that person. Perhaps it is more correct to say that the masorti loses the merit of Shabbat and its sanctity. The masorti chooses to violate the Sabbath, and therefore has no right to enjoy its sanctity. The sanctity of the Sabbath is always present, and the masorti must choose whether to enter into this world or remain outside.

Religious demands are sometimes weighed against personal considerations of comfort, convenience, and the doable and are chosen accordingly. The "comfort" to which our respondents referred was often the ability to observe a modern style of life. In other words, in many cases the choice takes place in the effort to resolve the tension between the world of religious observance and modernity. The decision is made by weighing reality against what is desirable.

Religious demands are deemed absolute, but "not for me." That is, the masorti accepts the principle—the same principle according to which the scripturalist conducts his life—but the principle remains at the level of the abstract and the general, whereas life takes place in the real world of the individual. And here the demands of religion lose their absolute status and compete with other values, notions, and customs with which they are not always compatible.

The religious laws that come closest to being absolute in practice are those laws concerned with proper respect for a dead family member, a parent in particular. What distinguishes masortim from datiim is not the manner in which these laws are observed, but in the hierarchical importance given to these laws. For example, Mizrahi traditionalists will observe the laws and customs of mourning quite punctiliously, although they may be quite lackadaisical in their observance of laws such as Sabbath observance, laws to which religious authorities accord greater importance. Indeed, the custom among Mizrahim is that when observing laws of mourning in this intense manner, the male signals himself as dati by wearing a yarmulke not only for the week of shiva but for the full thirty days of mourning.

The attitude of the Mizrahi-masorti to the yarmulke is of special interest because it symbolizes the complex attitude of the masorti to the whole world of religion. From our interviews we understand that the wearing of a yarmulke is a symbolic act signaling the division between the world of holiness and religion, and the world of the secular and mundane.[32] In donning the yarmulke the masorti identifies himself as one who has entered temporarily the arena of religion, of the holy. Removal of the yarmulke signals his return to the everyday, where holiness is absent. By wearing the yarmulke and removing it (or not wearing it), the masorti signals to himself the boundaries of the holy and the different set of rules demanded of him. This symbolic meaning of the yarmulke constitutes a central component in the tendency of the masorti to compartmentalize the Jewish religion, to limit its sanctity, and to draw the distinction between holy and profane. This symbolism is reinforced in the context of Israeli society, where the wearing of a yarmulke denotes membership in the community of the religious. In this context, not wearing a yarmulke is of great significance for the masorti because it distinguishes him from the dati. Amongst our respondents, there was general agreement that one who always wears a yarmulke and does not maintain a religious life is a charlatan.

In Israel, the yarmulke's style (whether it is knitted, black, velvet, colored, large, or small), alludes to the religio-political group with which the wearer is identified. Hence we asked ourselves whether the choice of yarmulke style among masortim also expressed some kind of group identity. To the best of our understanding, it does not. In synagogues in which the majority of the worshipers are masortim, one is struck by the range of yarmulke styles. Our general impression is that the masorti chooses his yarmulke according to subjective notions of aesthetics and what is or is not available, not in accordance with "political" criteria. However, our observations also suggest that on those occasions when the masorti did switch his yarmulke style, it was done self-consciously. The switch reflected the type of scripturalist authority that he now accepted. In other words, the masorti chooses the yarmulke that marks the rabbinic stream that he, the masorti, sees as his religious model of emulation.

Holy people, or saints, play a major role among some but not all Mizrahi traditionalists. Mizrahi traditionalists are not the only group to believe that certain persons (alive or dead) are endowed with special relations toward God. Such beliefs are found to a greater or lesser degree among all religious Jews, find special emphasis among one brand of Ashkenazi ultra-Orthodox, and are rooted in the Jewish tradition. Nevertheless, the veneration of saints, the special festivities that mark the day of their death, the magical power accorded to the blessings of the living saints, and the "excesses" that accompany all this find some resistance and a desire to restrict its expansion among the Mizrahi scripturalist leaders. They take exception (albeit with care) to what they consider to be the excessive adoration of holy people. Tension between the leaders of the official or elite religion and the practice of popular religion in Islam and in the Catholic Church is well documented. Likewise, studying how this tension plays itself out among the religious elite and the traditionalist masses of Mizrahim may suggest new theoretical insights. We must also explore whether traditionalists observe customs that are totally foreign to the Jewish tradition and which, for example, find their origin in Islamic custom. Much research remains to be undertaken.

Our attention was also engaged by the question of how masortim viewed "morality" and its relationship to religion. We phrased our questions in terms of "who is a good Jew?" The vast majority of our respondents denied emphatically that a Jew who observed religious law punctiliously was a better Jew or a better person. Instead, they defined morality, ethics, and humanitarianism as the criteria by which to judge a good Jew. In other words, our respondents refused to identify religiosity with morality.

It is instructive to compare the masortim we studied with those whom Nancy Ammerman has called "Golden Rule Christians."[33] Ammerman has distinguished Golden Rule Christians from "Evangelical Christians" and "Activist Christians." The evangelicals and activists emphasize social action and working for justice. For Golden Rule Christians, "'meaning' is not found in cognitive or ideological structures, not in answers to life's great questions, but in practices that cohere into something the person calls a 'good life.'"[34] Ammerman quotes one church member as saying, "I think all He [God] stands for makes you hope that you could be a better person." Another, when asked to describe the essence of God, answered that it's "the way you live your life. By that I mean, what good is it to know God if—you can study, you can be an excellent Bible student but if you don't practice what you have learned, then you aren't making a better world for yourself or for anyone."[35]

Our masortim have also described what they call "a good person," which is comparable to the good person as described by Golden Rule Christians. It is a person who cares for and helps others without regard to who those other persons are. Our respondents claim that they strive to be such people, that such people rank very highly in their eyes. But—and here is the big difference with what Ammerman found—our respondents deny that there is a connection between being such a good person and being a religious Jew or fulfilling one's religious obligations. Were we to press our respondents we probably could have elicited agreement that Judaism does demand one of the qualities that make for a good person. But that is not their intuitive sense, which is that religion has to do with punctiliously fulfilling ritual demands and acquiring knowledge of sacred text. They know too many rabbis and have too many acquaintances that meet the requirements necessary to call oneself dati, yet they are not good people. On the other hand, they have acquaintances who are good people, but they clearly are not datiim. Indeed, in one interview the respondent hinted at the fact that although she was "only" masorti, she was a better person than religious women of her acquaintance. Her husband, sitting in the room while the interview took place, then related a story in greater detail that demonstrated that his wife behaved, in a specific situation, in a more ethical and honorable manner than religious women.

Nevertheless, we suspect that what our respondents told us is not the whole story. In the course of many of our interviews we "heard" our respondents identifying religiosity and morality. Indeed, on a number of occasions the passion with which our respondents insisted that there was no relationship between how religious a person was and whether he was a good person reflected an opposite position. They expressed disappointment when they found fully observing Jews wanting from a moral point of view. In other words, we suspect that in many cases one could deduce (indirectly and not openly), that our respondents anticipated that the religious Jew would act in a more ethical and humane manner than others. But the expectation that the religious Jew would serve as a kind of exemplary model for Judaism, for the Jewish way of life, was often met with disappointment.

The identification between Judaism or a Jewish way of life, and ethics and morality, is also evident in the attitudes of masortim toward hilonim. Our respondents tended to identify hiloniut (a secular way of life) with *reykanut* (literally emptiness, an absence of values) and a kind of absence of humanity. The absence of belief in God (which is the mark of the hiloni in their eyes) is understood by Mizrahi (though not by Ashkenazi) masortim we interviewed as signaling egoism and unbridled hedonism. The hiloni was described by some as concerned only with him- or herself at the expense of others and at the expense of national as well as universal values and principles. If we think in terms of mirror images, hiloniut is the mirror image of datiut (being religious), but hiloniut is also the mirror image of principled, altruistic, moral behavior. By extension, therefore, religiosity does signal moral and ethical principles.

Conflicting Pressures on Masortim

Amongst the three categories of Israeli Jews grouped by religious identity (dati, hiloni, and masorti), only the percentage of masortim declined (by 7 percent) between 1990 and 1999. The proportion of the other two groups within the Jewish population either remained constant or grew.[36] The influx of Russian immigrants is a partial explanation for the decline in the proportion of masortim, but we believe that the major explanation is the absence of socializing agents, in addition to the family circle and close friends, that reinforce masortiut. There are no schools or voluntary organizations that encourage traditional behavior. In addition, as we argued elsewhere, the Israeli media ignore the masorti as distinct from the hiloni or the dati way of life and hardly offer it any form of representation.[37] As a result, masortim live under constant cross pressures with no reinforcement outside their family or immediate circle of friends and the complexity of traditionalist practice—a complexity stemming from its idiosyncratic solution to the tension between modernity and religion—which hinders its growth.

The masorti's identity problems are compounded by the sense of many masortim that the manner in which they conduct their religious life is almost unique. Some of our respondents believed that most Israeli Jews behaved like them. But most believed they were a small minority. One of the problems in sustaining a masorti identity is the sense that one is "peculiar" and different. The dati Jew easily identifies other datiim. Since datiim tend to live in dati neighborhoods, their religious identity is reinforced by those they see around them. The same is true of hiloni Jews. Religious and secular readily recognize one another by their public mannerisms but especially by their dress. Masortim, however, who dress like secular Jews and who practice their Judaism in the confines of the home and family do not readily identify one another. Many of our respondents were shocked when told that masortim constituted over 30 percent of Israel's Jewish population. They live with the sense that they are alone, making the temptations to join the ranks of either the secular or the religious that much more pronounced.

The major source of pressures on masortim is the demand for coherence and consistency. In the eyes of datiim and hilonim the behavior of the masorti seems inconsistent if not hypocritical. This pressure comes not only from datiim. Hilonim, at least by implication but sometimes explicitly, demand that the masorti decide to which side he or she belongs and act accordingly.

The cultural context of Israeli life plays an important role in this regard. The demand of both sides that the masorti choose where he or she belongs is a demand to leave that liminal state of "neither here nor there." Choosing one of the two sides requires the masorti to identify the other side as "other" and to structure his or her behavior in opposition to the other. We will begin by describing some of the pressures that arise from the religious side.

Religious Pressures

As noted, scripturalists see masorti behavior as flawed, because it reflects a weakness of character, if not a choice of sin, rather than religious compliance. Masortiut is seen as partial heresy. Rabbis play a word game with the etymology of the term *masorti* to deny its legitimacy. "Masorti," they say, comes from the word *masor* (saw) and *nisur* (sawing) and not from the words *masoret* (tradition) and *mesira* (handing over). The masorti saws off a piece of Judaism for himself, chooses what is easy for him, and throws away that which denies him the pleasures that secular culture offers. Rav Yosef Azran, a former Knesset representative from Shas (the bulk of Shas voters are Mizrahi masortim), expressed this idea in a television panel that was discussing the last Guttman Report. Azran reserved his criticism for the bulk of masortim, those who, in his opinion, were distancing themselves from the world of religion. (He excluded those who were originally secular and were now becoming more religious). In his words: "Why masortim? Because it was hard for them to bear the yoke of religion, so they created an easy Judaism, whatever was easy for them. They keep cutting off more and more until all will be gone."[38] From the point of view of Azran and his fellow scripturalists, masortiut is not an error stemming, for example, from ignorance, but rather a self-conscious transgression stemming from a weak spirit, from a search for personal comfort at the expense of halachic truth.

This critical stance toward the masortim is not confined to haredim. It can be found in the camp of religious Zionism, a more open and modern camp than that of the haredim. A new television channel, one devoted entirely to the interests of the religious, was scheduled to begin airing in the spring of 2003. One of the stars of this channel spoke to the press about the nature of the satiric program he was preparing. "I intend to devote a lot of time to the religiosity of the non-religious Israeli. They wear yarmulkes at funerals, seek counsel from mystics, and don't observe the Sabbath but fast on Yom Kippur. The *hiloni-dati* [a secularist who adopts some religious practices] is pathetic in my eyes. He wants very much to be politically correct—both an Israeli and progressive and a little bit of a Jew . . . this is an internal contradiction."[39]

This attitude is found in most religious schools, whether they are run by haredim or religious Zionists. The journalist Daniel Ben Simon came to Israel from Morocco at the age of sixteen.[40] The traditionalist style of Jewish life is all he knew—that is, riding to the beach or swimming pool in summer after attending Shabbat services. He came to Israel through the Youth Aliyah Department of the Jewish Agency and was placed in a religious-Zionist boarding school, where the principal explained that he would have to wear a *kippah* and pray three times a day. When the youngster explained that in Morocco he was accustomed to praying only on Shabbat and holidays, the principal interrupted him and said he must decide if he was dati or hiloni. Ben Simon replied that he knew what dati was, but he did not understand hiloni. The principal explained that a hiloni is someone who does not believe in God and does not see the Torah as the supreme heritage of the Jewish people. "Either you are *dati* or you are *hiloni*," he added. "I'm a Jew," Ben Simon stammered. After some more prodding, Ben Simon said, "I think I am both *dati* and *hiloni*." "There is no such thing" the principal said, "You are either *dati* or *hiloni*. There is nothing in the middle."[41]

This delegitimation of the masorti contrasts with the attitude of Sephardic (Mizrahi) rabbis in the past. Their attitude was characterized by relative tolerance through a lenient interpretation of the halacha, aimed at preventing the exclusion of masortim from the community of the faithful, an exclusion that was the fate of the totally secular. The attitude of Ovadia Yosef, the most important halachic decisor and unquestioned religious leader of Mizrahi Jews in our generation, is a model for this type of tolerance. Studies of his halachic decisions point to his manipulation of the law to preserve a place for masortim within the community. As one example of many, Yosef distinguished between the two separate commandments to observe the Sabbath. One insists that the Jew *"observe* the Sabbath day," the other that he *"remember* the Sabbath day." According to Yosef, if the Jew "remembers" (e.g., by reciting Kiddush), even if he does not "observe," he has fulfilled the basic commandment and is not subject to the sanctions imposed on a Sabbath violator (for example, not being given any ritual honor in the synagogue).[42] Meir Buzaglo has concurred by citing other examples to illustrate the same point that older Mizrahi rabbis were lenient with regard to masortim. But he has noted that these halachic solutions are not answers to the masorti's dilemma. The basic tensions between the halachic demands, which the masorti recognizes as legitimate, and the masorti's own behavior remain core tensions in the rhythms of the masorti's life.[43] Furthermore, we sense that as the strength of the scripturalists within the camp of Israeli Mizrahim has grown, attitudes toward masortim have become less accepting.

A central component in these tensions is the conception of the hiloni in the eyes of the rabbis and the attraction of the modern-secular way of life for the masorti. Scripturalist spokesmen portray the hiloni as the opposite of all that is good and proper. The hiloni is vacuous, irresponsible, and immoral. Even when they show an understanding toward the masorti and try to draw him closer to them, the Mizrahi scripturalists continue to voice their total rejection of "modern" life, which they often identify with democracy. Even when he escapes this criticism, the masorti is, as it were, infected with the disease of secularism.

Finally, we must recall that as a rule, even the positive attitude of the older generation of Mizrahi rabbis toward the masortim was based on the expectation that in the end, perhaps as a consequence of the rabbis' lenient and open attitude, the masorti would adopt an Orthodox way of life. In other words, the masorti is accepted, but under the condition that the masorti recognize the flaw in his behavior and inconsistency, and admit that he is mistaken.

In the last three decades, with the emergence of Shas, a haredi-scripturalist movement, the pressures on the masorti have become more institutionalized. Nissim Leon has described it as "the reorganization of *Mizrahi* religion under the hegemony of Sephardic masters of learning,"[44] which is expressed in the appointment of haredi-Mizrahi rabbis to head synagogues whose congregants are primarily masortim. This leads to a kind of religious extremism or, in our terms, scripturalist values replacing traditional ones. Leon has described this as "a move from a lenient religious culture to a strict religious culture expressed in strict adherence to the *halachic* text, at whose center stands the local rabbi transformed from a community leader to an *halachic* leader whose charisma doesn't stem from his image as a mystic but as one learned in sacred text."[45]

Secular Pressures

The secular side also demands consistency. However, in this case the rhetoric is less one-sided. The hiloni demands that the masorti "make himself clear," that he choose one of two coherent paths: secularism (hiloniut) or religion (datiut). The hiloni acknowledges the right of the individual to live as he or she chooses. But sometimes without realizing it, the hiloni confines the choice to the two end points of the continuum. The dominance of this end-point discourse finds expression in the demand for choosing a pure model. This is a discourse that confirms itself in its very presentation. When political, social, and cultural discussion concentrates on the differences and tensions between datiim and hilonim, everyone is naturally expected to identify themselves with one of the two sides, leaving no room for an intermediate position. This, at least, is how it appears in the eyes of the masorti.

It is also worth recalling the distinction, at least within academic circles, between traditional and modern. One of the characteristics of the non-modern ("primitive" in the pre-politically correct era) is religion. This distinction between the modern and traditional, which also guided social and educational policy, demanded that the masorti modernize himself or herself. The need was felt to de-socialize the Mizrahim (undermine traditional society) and then resocialize them into modern Israeli society.[46] A major component in modernization was the aban-donment of religion. That demand was implied in the political and academic estab-lishment's insistence on consistency and coherence for locating oneself in one of the two dichotomous categories and abandoning "primitive" traditionalism for the sake of modernity.[47]

Masortiut threatens both extreme positions—secularism, on the one hand, and religion, on the other. Masortim provide a living example of the possibility that there is an alternative to rejecting either modernity or religion. This is true of Reform and Conservative Judaism as well, but their presence in Israel is too weak to constitute a threat. The dichotomy of religious-secular builds the identity of each side. Each benefits from this binary image. The religious camp is crowned with a monopoly on the definition of the Jewish religion; the secular, on the defini-tion of freedom and progress. Recognition of the presence of the traditionalist undermines all this. We do not really believe that more than a few of the protago-nists are conscious of this. But we suspect that it is nonetheless a factor in their resistance and even more so in their ignoring the phenomenon of masortiut.

One of the fields where cross pressures on the masorti are most pronounced is in education. There are very few schools that provide a place for the expression and reinforcement of a child's identity as a masorti (primarily a result of a sympathetic principal and/or teachers), and there is no school system that does so. Most chil-dren from masorti homes attend state schools with a hiloni environment, or state-religious schools with a dati environment. In both types of schools, even when masortim constitute a majority of the student population, masortiut, if it receives any attention at all, is treated as a peripheral phenomenon. Curricula in both types of schools have no place for the system of beliefs and rituals or the hierarchical structure of masorti practices. The attitude of both school systems reflects the same discomfort with the hybrid nature of masortiut noted above. By implication, if not design, they press students to adjust themselves to the way of life the school itself projects.[48]

Internal Pressures

Up to this point we have described some of the external pressures on masortim to conform to either the secular or the religious way of life. But there are pressures, no less strong, generated by masortim themselves. These are naturally more com-plex, not as straightforward, and generally functioning at the subconscious level. They result from the internalization of external pressures; the masorti internalizes the demand for consistency, and these demands become part of his or her internal world. From a psychological point of view, we suspect that these are the most important pressures.

These pressures emerged in our discussions with respondents, especially Mizrahi respondents. Some painted a religious way of life as the ideal and their own religious life as falling short, as flawed, as something they hoped to correct.

Other respondents did not express themselves so directly, some even denied that their behavior was religiously flawed, but nevertheless expressed the basic hope that they would become "stronger" religiously. Many reported that they expected that they would be more observant in the future, although in some cases the expectations were for a slow process of "strengthening." Not a single Mizrahi respondent expected to be less religious in the future. We interpreted this as an affirmation of the conception that the religious way of life was a better life. However, this was not true of our Ashkenazi respondents.

The internal pressures stem from a sense of guilt the Mizrahi masorti bears. The scripturalist demand for "religious perfection" has been internalized by the masorti. He accepts the notion that the religious Jew represents authentic Judaism and the desirable way of living a Jewish life. When asked to explain why the respondent's own behavior falls short of the ideal, we were offered a variety of reasons—but the feeling of guilt remained. Nevertheless, as we indicate in the concluding section, this sense of guilt is concomitant to a consciously chosen way of life.

Hiloni pressure also leads to self-denigration. In this respect, too, the masorti views himself as flawed, not from a religious but from a modernizing point of view. The negative self-image of the masorti, the association of masorti and *primitivi* (primitive) is in some cases so pronounced that, as the Guttman Reports shows, many who live a masorti life choose not to identify themselves as such and identify themselves as hilonim.[49] It is also important to recall the identification of masortiut with Mizrahim in the minds of many Israelis. The cultural and socioeconomic status of the Mizrahi renders Mizrahi identity peripheral. Considering the generally peripheral image of a religious identity in Israeli society, masortiut combines two stigmatized identities: Mizrahi and quasi-religious. No wonder that some masortim prefer to be identified as something other than masorti.

Another sort of pressure the masorti confronts is the temptation that the liberal-hiloni style of life accords. It is viewed as a liberated life in which the individual's basic responsibility is to oneself, a life relatively free of strong communal and collective constraints and free from the responsibility to history and the archaic demands of religion. These responsibilities are often described in terms of coercion, as coercing or imposing themselves on the individual, whereas the secular-liberal life frees one from these constraints. One manner of confronting these temptations is for the masorti to privatize his or her own conceptions of what is Judaically proper. Thus, as we indicated above, the masortim, regardless of how observant they may be in their own lives, refuse to impose religious observance on the Israeli public,[50] although many express the hope that the Israeli "street" will bear a religiously distinctive character.

Masortiut and Multiple Modernities

In rereading the interviews we conducted (a continuing process) and in reconsidering what we have learned, we feel that the concept *multiple modernities* is most appropriate in seeking to fit the phenomenon of Israeli masortiut into some wider framework. The most important respect in which masortiut is a decidedly modern phenomenon is that the traditionalist consciously chooses his identity. It is not forced upon him; nor, in light of the pressures from both the secularists and the scripturalists, can it by any stretch of the imagination be taken for granted. The masorti is quite familiar with the other, culturally dominant alternatives. He hears their demands, is aware of their system of values, and conscious of the fact that both secularism and scripturalism offer a consistent way of life that imbues the follower with a sense of confidence in his or her own identity—a quality that many of the traditionalists with whom we speak admit they lack. Nonetheless, the masorti chooses to be masorti. He is conscious of his identity, of its special character, of its advantages (as he or she sees them, of course), and of its unique place on the map of sociopolitical identities in Israel.

The element of choice, the importance of which we cannot overemphasize in any discussion of the modern face of traditionalism, arose in our interviews in a most direct manner, most often at the initiative of the respondents themselves. All our Mizrahi respondents noted that they had learned traditionalist behavior from their homes. They all recognize the importance of the manner in which they were raised, but they also reported that at a certain stage in their lives, generally between the ages of eighteen and twenty-one, while performing compulsory army service, they consciously chose to adopt the masorti identity they had learned at home. Most often they mentioned that an important factor was their own commitment to the state of Israel, to the Jewish people, to religion, to Jewish history, to their families, or to some combination of these factors. Here, for example, is how one female respondent phrased it: "You can say that it is a commitment to family, to parents, and also a commitment of a larger nature (*b'gadol*), to all of Judaism. . . . The tradition is like an umbilical cord. This is where you come from. It's rational as well as emotional." Our respondent told us about the moment when she became conscious of this rational choice while recognizing the social cost involved: "After matriculation, in the army, after leaving home I was stationed in a base far from home . . . you don't live in the circle of parents, so you set the rules for yourself. You decide what you are going to do on Shabbat, you decide what you will eat and not eat, you go out with friends and decide on your behavior, and I decided to isolate myself from my surroundings."

We do not doubt that many secular and religious Israeli Jews see their identity as a matter of choice. But a comparison of the choice of masortiut with that of secularism on the one hand and scripturalism on the other demonstrates the greater complexity of the first. We argue that the masorti identity is based on a choice that is of greater significance than the alternative choices, because in most cases the secular and the religious Jew never really have the identity options of the masortim. In many respects the scripturalist and the secularist identities, to the extent that they are matters of choice and not simply givens from the home and the cultural environment, are formed as mirror images of their polar opposites.

It is our sense that the dominant alternatives from which most of those born into scripturalist and secularist homes can choose is to either remain as they are or totally transform their identities. Not surprisingly, they tend to become extreme in these new identities (at least so we are told anecdotally). The masorti identity, on the other hand, is always of a mixed, hesitant, tempered nature. It must always, so it seems, justify itself and, as we have noted, is often accompanied by feelings of guilt. The possibility of alternate choices is always present because the options are always present and fairly easy to adopt.

In conclusion, the notion of "multiple modernities"—the idea that modernity is arrived at in a variety of ways—seems to provide a more useful theoretical paradigm than the secular modernization paradigm. Multiple modernities and our example of masortiut provides far richer opportunities to explore the relationships between modernization and religious, ethnic, national, and collective identity.[51] In the Israeli context, in the context of the discourse concerning a "Jewish State" or a "State for the Jews," the relationship of religion, nationalism, ethnicity, and modernity is complex. The relationship between national symbols, ceremonies, and values (the civil religion), and the system of Jewish-religious values, beliefs, and ceremonies troubled the Zionist enterprise from its very outset, underwent many changes, and has been the topic of research in recent years.[52] But the modernity-secularism discourse renders masortiut and masortim into something of an anomaly, requiring a solution rather than an identity expression that sheds light on new ways to view Israeli society. In the context of a Jewish national state, the traditionalist option may yet reveal itself as a solution to the continuing tension inherent in the Jewish national enterprise—the tension between a universal and a particularistic identity, between a state that is "democratic" and one that is "Jewish."

NOTES

Our thanks to Carol Liebman for a critical reading of an early draft and some poignant criticisms.

1. We chose to use here the noun form of *masortim*—which should be translated as "traditionalists"—instead of the adjective *masortiyim* (which in English would be translated as "traditional"). As will be elaborated below, we believe that this is a small step in the direction of stressing that the label "masorti" signifies an identity category rather than a sociological property of being "premodern."

2. In the latest Guttman Report (see note 3), not one respondent who identified him- or herself as Conservative or Reform also identified him- or herself as dati. Most categorized themselves as either "masorti" or as "not dati." A few Reform identified themselves as "anti-dati."

3. Meir Buzaglo, "The New Traditionalist: A Phenomenology," in *Collected Essays on the Heritage of North African Jewry*, ed. Ephraim Hazan and Haym Saadon (in Hebrew) (Ramat-Gan: Bar-Ilan University, in press). For a summary presentation of the distinction between modern and traditional societies, see Yaacov Katz, "Traditional Society and Modern Society," in *Jews of the Middle East: Anthropological Perspectives on Past and Present*, ed. Shlomo Deshen and Moshe Shokeid (in Hebrew) (Tel-Aviv: Schocken, 1984), 27–34.

4. Moshe Shokeid, "New Directions in the Religiosity of Middle Eastern Jews," in *Jews of the Middle East*, 78–91, quote from 79.

5. Yaacov Shavit, "Supplying a Missing System—Between Official and Unofficial Popular Culture in the Hebrew National Culture in Eretz-Israel," in *The Folk Culture*, ed. Benjamin Z. Kedar (Jerusalem: Zalman Shazar Center for Jewish History, 1996), 327–345.

6. Shokeid, "New Directions," 79–80.

7. Peter van der Veer and Hartmut Lehman, introduction to *Nation and Religion: Perspectives of Europe and Asia*, ed. Peter van der Veer and Hartmut Lehman (Princeton, NJ: Princeton

University Press, 1999), 1–14; Talal Asad, "Religion, Nation-State, and Secularism," in van der Veer and Lehman, *Nation and Religion*, 178–196; Ernest Gellner, *Postmodernism, Reason and Religion* (London: Routledge, 1992).

8. The term *premodern* appears in an introduction by Shlomo Deshen and Moshe Shokeid to an article by Yaakov Katz, "Traditional Society and Modern Society," reprinted in a collection edited by Deshen and Shokeid. The choice by the editors of this article, which is a summary of modernization, of an introduction to a volume dealing with Mizrahi Judaism with special emphasis on the religion of Mizrahim, is instructive as to the theoretical framework in which traditionalism was studied. See also Shlomo Deshen, "The Religiosity of Middle Easterners in the Crises of Immigration," in *Jews of the Middle East*, 71–77.

9. See Moshe Shokeid, "The Religiosity of Middle Eastern Jews," in *Israeli Judaism: The Sociology of Religion in Israel*, ed. Shlomo Deshen, Charles S. Liebman, and Moshe Shokeid (New Brunswick, NJ: Transaction Publishers, 1995), 236–237.

10. See Shlomo Deshen, "The Religiosity of the Mizrahim: Public, Rabbis, and Belief," *Alpayim* 9 (1994): 44–58 (in Hebrew); Shokeid, "New Directions"; Stephen Sharot, "Judaism in Pre-modern Societies," in *Jews of the Middle East*, 35–50; Mordechai Bar-Lev and Peri Kedem, "Ethnicity and Religiosity of Students: Does College Education Necessarily Cause the Abandoning of Religious Tradition?" *Megamot* 28, nos. 2–3 (1984): 265–279 (in Hebrew); Shokeid, "The Religiosity of Middle Eastern Jews," 213–237; Hannah Ayalon, Eliezer Ben-Rafael, and Stephen Sharot, "The Costs and Benefits of Ethnic Identification," *British Journal of Sociology* 37 (December 1986): 550–568; Shlomo Deshen, "On Religious Change: The Situational Analysis of Symbolic Action," *Comparative Studies in Society and History* 12 (July 1970): 260–274; Shlomo Deshen, "Israeli Judaism: Introduction to the Major Patterns," *International Journal of Middle East Studies* 9 (April 1978): 141–169; Harvey Goldberg and Claudio G. Segre, "Holding on to Both Ends: Religious Continuity and Changes in the Libyan Jewish Community, 1860–1949," *Maghreb Review* 14, nos. 3–4 (1989): 161–186; Harvey Goldberg, "Religious Responses among North African Jews in the Nineteenth and Twentieth Centuries," in *The Uses of Tradition: Jewish Continuity in the Modern Era*, ed. Jack Wertheimer (New York: Jewish Theological Seminary and Harvard University Press, 1993), 119–144; Harvey Goldberg, "Religious Responses to Modernity among the Jews of Jerba and of Tripoli: A Comparative Study," *Journal of Mediterranean Studies* 4 (1994): 278–299; Harvey Goldberg, "A Tradition of Invention: Family and Educational Institutions among Contemporary Traditionalizing Jews," *Conservative Judaism* 47, no. 2 (1995): 69–84.

11. See, for example, Harvey Goldberg, "Historical and Cultural Dimensions of Ethnic Phenomena in Israel," in *Studies in Israeli Ethnicity*, ed. Alex Weingrod (New York: Gordon and Breach, 1985), 179–200; Eliezer Ben-Rafael, *The Emergence of Ethnicity: Cultural Groups and Social Conflict in Israel* (London: Greenwood Press, 1982); Eliezer Ben-Rafael and Stephen Sharot, *Ethnicity, Religion, and Class in Israeli Society* (Cambridge: Cambridge University Press, 1991); Harvey Goldberg, "The Changing Meaning of Ethnic Affiliation," *Jerusalem Quarterly* 44 (1987): 39–50; Harvey Goldberg, "Ethnic and Religious Dilemmas of a Jewish State: A Cultural and Historical Perspective," in *State Formation and Ethnic Relations in the Middle East*, ed. Akira Usuki (Osaka: Japan Center for Area Studies, 2001), 47–64.

12. Yoram Bilu and Eyal Ben-Ari, "The Making of Modern Saints: Manufactured Charisma and the Abu-Hatseiras of Israel," *American Ethnologist* 19 (February 1992): 29–44; Yoram Bilu, "Moroccan Jews and the Shaping of Israel's Sacred Geography," in *Divergent Jewish Cultures: Israel and America*, ed. Deborah Dash Moore and S. Ilan Troen (New Haven: Yale University Press, 2001), 72–86; Yoram Bilu, "Dreams and the Wishes of the Saint," in *Judaism Viewed from Within and from Without: Anthropological Studies*, ed. Harvey Goldberg (Albany: State University of New York Press, 1987), 285–313; Eyal Ben-Ari and Yoram Bilu, "Saint Sanctuaries in Israeli Development Towns: On a Mechanism of Urban Transformation," *Urban Anthropology* 16 (1987): 234–272; Harvey Goldberg, "Potential Polities: Jewish Saints in the Moroccan Countryside and in Israel," in *Faith and Polity: Essays on Religion and Politics*, ed. M. Bax, P. Kloos, and A. Koster (Amsterdam: Vrije Universiteit University Press, 1984), 235–250; Alex Weingrod, *The Saint of Beersheba* (Albany: State University of New York Press, 1990).

13. Susan Sered, "Women, Religion, and Modernization: Tradition and Transformation among Elderly Jews in Israel," *American Anthropologist* 92 (June 1990): 306–318; see also idem, "Women and Religious Change in Israel: Rebellion or Revolution," *Sociology of Religion* 58 (Spring 1997): 1–24.

14. See, for example, Bjorn Wittrock, "Rethinking Modernity," in *Identity, Culture and Globalization*, ed. Eliezer Ben-Rafael with Yitzhak Sternberg, *The Annals of the International Institute of Sociology* 8 (2002): 51–73, and most of the articles in *Daedalus* 129 (Winter 2000).

15. Shokeid, "The Religiosity of Middle Eastern Jews," 237.

16. For a detailed presentation of the idea of multiple modernities, see *Daedalus* 129 (Winter 2000). See especially S. N. Eisenstadt, "Multiple Modernities," 1–29.

17. Clifford Geertz, *Islam Observed* (New Haven: Yale University Press, 1968). Ernest Gellner, addressing the same phenomenon (even using the term *scripturalism*), prefers to label it as "fundamentalism." See Gellner, *Postmodernism, Reason and Religion*.

18. Haym Soloveitchik, "Migration, Acculturation, and the New Role of Texts in the Haredi World," in *Accounting for Fundamentalism*, ed. Martin Marty and R. Scott Appleby (Chicago: University of Chicago Press, 1994), 197–235.

19. For example, the early historian of Hasidism, Simon Dubnov, attributes the bitter conflict from the late eighteenth through the early nineteenth century between Hasidism and its opponents to the former's rejection of the primacy of text. S. M. Dubnov, *Toldot Ha-Hasidut* (Tel Aviv: Dvir, 1975).

20. Ibid., 201.

21. For an extended discussion of these options, see Charles S. Liebman, "Religion and the Chaos of Modernity: The Case of Contemporary Judaism," *Take Judaism for Example: Studies toward the Comparison of Religions*, ed. Jacob Neusner (Chicago: University of Chicago Press, 1983), 147–164.

22. That is a question to which we hope to turn in a future essay. David Hall, ed., *Lived Religion in America* (Princeton: Princeton University Press, 1997).

23. Shokeid, "New Directions," 88.

24. This characteristic recurs time and again in our interviews as well as in all the opinion surveys of Israelis on the topic of religion and the public arena. Traditionalists are characterized by their moderation on the topic of imposing Jewish law in the public arena. See, for example, Shlomo Hasson and Amiram Gonen, *The Cultural Tension within Jerusalem's Jewish Population* (in Hebrew) (Jerusalem: Floersheimer Institute for Policy Studies, 1997).

25. Levy, Levinsohn, and Katz, *Jewish Israelis: A Portrait*, 14–15.

26. One exception is Harvey Goldberg, "Ethnic and Religious Dilemmas of a Jewish State."

27. Zvi Zohar, *Tradition and Change: Halachic Responses of Middle Eastern Rabbis to Legal and Technological Change (Egypt and Syria, 1880–1920)* (in Hebrew) (Jerusalem: Ben-Zvi Institute, 1993).

28. Buzaglo cites other examples in "The New Traditionalist: A Phenomenology."

29. Shokeid, "New Directions," 88.

30. See especially Shokeid, "New Directions"; Shokeid, "The Religiosity of Middle Eastern Jews"; and Deshen, "The Religiosity of the Mizrahim."

31. Gideon Aran, "The Haredi Body: Chapters from an Ethnography in Preparation," in *Text, Rhetoric, and Behavior: Collected Articles on Haredi Society in Israel*, ed. Emanuel Sivan and Kimmy Kaplan (in Hebrew) (Jerusalem: Van Leer Institute and the Kibbutz Hameuchad, forthcoming).

32. See also Shokeid, "New Directions."

33. Nancy Ammerman, "Golden Rule Christianity," in *Lived Religion in America*, ed. David Hall (Princeton: Princeton University Press, 1997), 196–216.

34. Ibid., 202.

35. Ibid., 202–203.

36. Levi, Levinsohn, and Katz, *Jewish Israelis*, 5.

37. Yaacov Yadgar and Yeshayahu (Charles) Liebman, "Jewish Traditionalism and Popular Culture in Israel," *Iyunim* 13 (in Hebrew) (forthcoming).

38. Rav Yosef Azran, interview by Aliza Lavi, *Shavua Tov*, Israeli TV Channel 1, May 4, 2002. We are grateful to Dr. Aliza Lavi for securing this quotation for us.

39. Kobi Ariel's quotation cited in Aviv Lavi, "Rating's Judaism," *Haaretz-Musaf*, November 1, 2002.

40. The story is related in Daniel Ben Simon, "Dati or Hiloni," *We the Secular Jews: What Is Secular Jewish Identity?* ed. Dedi Zucker (in Hebrew) (Tel-Aviv: Yediot Aharonot, 1999), 102–110.

41. The attitude of the young Ben Simon is echoed in a recent interview with another Moroccan, this one aged sixty. Shlomo Bar, a popular vocalist and drummer, has become "observant—in his own style. . . . Often he mentions God and quotes from Jewish sources. . . . But if you ask him whether he's observant, he says, simply 'I'm a Jew.'" The treatment of masortiut and masortim in religious schools merits a separate study, although we discuss it briefly below. Tamara Novis, "Raising the Bar," *Jerusalem Post, City Lights*, August 1, 2003.

42. Benny Lau, "Defining the *Masorti* Jew" (paper presented at Conference on Jewish Approaches to Conflict Resolution, Bar Ilan University, November 11, 2002). See also Ariel Picard, "Rabbi Ovadia Yosef and His Struggle with 'the Generation of Freedom'" (in Hebrew) (forthcoming).

43. Buzaglo, "The New Traditionalist: A Phemonology."

44. Nissim Leon, "Sephardim and Haredim: An Ethnographic Inquiry of Shas Movement's Influence on the Identity Discourse in Israel" (master's thesis, Tel Aviv University, 1999), 1.

45. Ibid.

46. Rivka Bar Yoseph, "Desocialization and Resocialization: The Adjustment Process of Immigrants" in *Immigration, Ethnicity and Community*, ed. Ernest Krausz (New Jersey: Transaction Books, Studies of Israeli Society, 1980), 19–27.

47. Some of the more brutal applications of this philosophy to the area of education are found in Reuven Feuerstein, *Children of the Melah: Cultural Underdevelopment among Children of Morocco and Its Educational Implications* (in Hebrew) (Jerusalem: Machon Szold and the Department of Children's Immigration of the Jewish Agency, 1965). For an analysis of this approach, see Meir Bozaglo, "Mizrahiut, Tradition, and the Melting Pot: Toward an Alternate Narrative," in *Zion and Zionism*, ed. Z. Harvey, G. Hazon-Rokem, and Y. Shiloach (in Hebrew) (Jerusalem: Misgav, forthcoming).

48. For a critical review of educational ideologies and their attitudes toward Mizrahi traditionalism, see Meir Buzaglo, "Educational Ideologies: The Mizrahi Point of View," in *Crossroads: Values and Education in Israeli Society*, ed. Yaacov Iram, et al. (Jerusalem: Israeli Ministry of Education, 2001), 480–521. Further evidence is found in the deliberations of a recent conference published in the *Zohar* journal. Zohar consists of a group of young Orthodox rabbis at the liberal end of the religious continuum who made a mark for themselves in their willingness to accommodate marriages of non-Orthodox Jews within the broadest limits of Jewish law. The Avi Chai Foundation invited Zohar rabbis to a meeting in which they were to assess the desirability of creating an educational system for *masortim* (*Zohar* 12 [September 2002]: 111–126). Many of the participants, even as they expressed their basic support for such a move, also expressed their fears about the creation of the system. Among the fears they expressed were that such a system would encourage absence of knowledge and an unwillingness to be observant, and that it would end up with "a bit of yiddishkeit; but this is not enough." The rabbis all agreed, however, that there was a great opportunity to draw the masorti public closer to full-fledged religion (i.e., Orthodoxy). See also Eldad Cohen, "Religious Zionism–Between National Haredism and Liberal Religion: The Socio-Religious Split within Religious Zionism in the Educational System" (master's thesis, Bar Ilan University, 2003).

49. There are additional reasons for this identification, some of which are discussed in our chapter on secularism in Israel.

50. In addition to the evidence from our own interviews, see Hasson and Gonen, *The Cultural Tension*, and Levy, Levinsohn, and Katz, *Jewish Israelis*.

51. Van der Veer and Lehman, "Introduction"; Asad, "Religion, Nation-State, and Secularism." For a critical assessment of the secularization thesis, see Rodney Stark, "Secularization R.I.P.," *Sociology of Religion* 60 (Fall 1999): 249–273.

52. See, for example, Charles S. Liebman and Eliezer Don-Yehiya, *Civil Religion in Israel: Traditional Judaism and Political Culture in the Jewish State* (Berkeley: University of California Press, 1983).

11

What Kind of Jewish State Do Israelis Want?

ISRAELI AND ARAB ATTITUDES TOWARD RELIGION AND POLITICS

MARK TESSLER

What does it mean to be a Jewish state? Can the state of Israel be both Jewish and secular? At least partly, of course, the answer to these questions depends on how secularism is defined.[1] The most basic element in Zionist political thought and the Zionist project is that there should be an independent and sovereign political community with a Jewish majority in some part of the historic Land of Israel. But whether more than a Jewish majority is needed to make this political community properly "Jewish" is not something on which there has been agreement among Jews and Israelis, even today.

An obvious question with which to begin thinking about secularism concerns the degree to which the State of Israel should be governed by Jewish law. While there may be a need for civil law in some areas, Israelis have often clashed over whether the state should enact and enforce legislation—for example, banning public transportation on the Sabbath, requiring the observance of *kashrut* in state enterprises, disallowing civil marriage, and so forth. Similarly, what role, if any, should rabbinical councils and men of religious learning play in the affairs of state? To the extent one believes that Jewish laws and religious institutions should be given preponderant or at least very significant influence in political affairs and public life, he or she favors a model of governance that departs from secularism and moves in the direction of theocracy. Alternatively, one who favors secularism believes that religion should be a personal affair and should not guide the affairs of state in any formal or institutionalized manner.

There is a second way in which questions about secularism are relevant, which may be less self-evident, since it focuses on ethnicity and nationalism rather than religion. If in any political community there exists a distinction—based on a criterion other than citizenship—between who can and cannot identify fully with the state, then it would seem that there is a limit on the degree to which the state can be considered secular. A state may serve the interests of all of its citizens to a meaningful degree. Nevertheless, secularism is absent—or at least compromised—if that state additionally defines its identity and mission with respect to a particular subset of its citizens, whether that subset is defined in terms of religion, race, ethnicity, caste, or otherwise. The situation may be further complicated if some members of the group with a privileged claim on the identity and resources of the state are not citizens of that state.

There is thus a sociological as well as a religious dimension to secularism, and both dimensions apply to Israel, although not to Israel alone.[2] Non-Jewish citizens of Israel have full legal rights. Moreover, to the extent that a measure of discrimination—state-sanctioned as well as private—exists nevertheless, some is a by-product of the Arab-Israeli conflict rather than the result of Israel's Jewish identity. Some discrimination also results from divisions within the Israeli Arab community and from political weakness associated with minority status. Nevertheless, these considerations are not the whole story, perhaps not even the most important part of the story. Israel's identity as a Jewish state, with a priority concern for the needs, aspirations, and welfare of the Jewish people, wherever its members may reside and whatever the country of which they are citizens, is reflected in state policy in numerous symbolic, legal, and institutional ways. This unavoidably gives distinct and ultimately inferior political status to the country's non-Jewish citizens. In this way, Israel willingly and self-consciously departs, to at least some degree, from the secular ideal that, however imperfectly realized, guides polities like the United States and France.

None of this is unfamiliar to students of politics and society in Israel. Nor is there likely to be disagreement about the issues that are central to an inquiry into the prospects for secularism in a country with an official Jewish identity. There have been many important and instructive studies of the relationship between religion and politics in Israel, with attention given to legislative battles, judicial decisions, the role and influence of religious parties, and public policy in areas ranging from education to military service.[3] In all of these areas, there have also been clashes among Israelis with differing views about the desired character of their state and society.

Arab and Jewish scholars have conducted valuable studies of the political circumstances of Israel's Palestinian Arab citizens.[4] Among the issues examined in these works are the allocation of state resources and benefits, local government, the development and influence of Arab political institutions, including the participation of Arab parties in government coalitions, education, housing and land policy, and the ties to Israel of Jews who are citizens of other countries. From the perspective of many and probably most of Israel's Arab citizens, favoritism toward Jews is both institutionalized and legally sanctioned in these and other areas. This compromises Israeli democracy, in their view, and makes the equality associated with "true secularism" their overriding political demand.

Against this background, my analysis will use public opinion data to investigate the following questions about Israeli attitudes and orientations pertaining to these two dimensions of secularism:

1. What is the distribution of attitudes held by Israeli Jews about issues associated with both the religious and sociological dimensions of secularism?

2. What is the relationship between attitudes toward these two dimensions of secularism, and are certain normative orientations based on the two dimensions taken together particularly common?
3. What factors and experiences account for individual level variance in attitudes toward the religious and sociological dimension of secularism, both separately and taken together?

To what extent, if any, do relevant attitudes appear to have changed during the last ten to fifteen years, and what hypotheses may be advanced about the causes and consequences of any discernible aggregate change?

To put these questions into comparative perspective, I also analyze public opinion data from Jordan and Egypt to assess the nature and determinants of Arab attitudes pertaining to secularism. While the situation in the Arab world is not identical to that in Israel, the relationship between religion and politics is an important issue in many Arab societies. Islam is the official state religion in most Arab countries, raising questions about whether Christian citizens, who are Arabs but not Muslims, can identify with and be served by the state to the same degree as citizens who *are* Muslim. Even more important, there are vigorous debates, as in Israel, about the extent to which society should be governed by Islamic law and about whether or not men of religious learning should play an important role in political affairs.[5]

These questions play out differently in different Arab societies, and attitudes about them vary at the individual level of analysis. Christian Arabs are full citizens in Jordan and Egypt, where in both instances the country is officially Arab as well as Muslim. There is no officially sanctioned discrimination against Christians or in favor of Muslims. But while these religious minorities certainly identify with the mission of the country and would probably also say that Islamic civilization is their own civilization, Muslim extremists have attacked Christians in Egypt, Jordanians who have emigrated from their country are disproportionately likely to be Christian, and there have been debates in both countries about whether Christians should have the same legal rights as Muslims. As a result, issues associated with the sociological dimension of secularism are salient concerns in Jordan and Egypt, though perhaps less so than in Israel.

Likewise, issues associated with the religious dimension of secularism are no less salient in Jordan, Egypt, and other Arab countries than they are in Israel. If anything, the political struggles and policy debates surrounding these issues are even more intense than they are in the Jewish state. The most important questions concern the degree to which society should be governed by Islamic law, particularly but not exclusively in areas pertaining to women and the family. Issues pertaining to the political status and role of Islamist movements and leaders are also discussed. Noting that these questions are addressed and debated within a democratic context in Israel, with religious parties and leaders active and influential but nonetheless forced to compete for support with those who reject their conception of what it means to be a Jewish state, there have occasionally been suggestions in the Arab and Muslim world that Israel might offer a model for managing disagreements about the relationship between Islam and politics.

In light of the salient issues in Jordan, Egypt, and some other Arab and Muslim countries, and with the possibilities for instructive comparative analysis in mind, the following question may be added to those listed above:

4. To what extent are the nature and demographic correlates of Israeli Jewish attitudes toward the religious and sociological dimensions of secularism similar to or different than those in Arab countries with an official Muslim identity, specifically in Jordan and Egypt?

Answers to these questions will shed light on what it means to be a Jewish state in the Jewish Israeli conception, and about the degree to which these conceptions embrace or reject secular values. My analysis will also provide evidence about the factors shaping relevant attitudes and about whether these orientations are or are not changing. Finally, this research will lay a foundation for informed discussion about whether the nature, distribution, and determinants of attitudes associated with secularism in a state with an official Jewish identity are or are not similar to the nature, distribution, and determinants of attitudes associated with secularism in states with an official Muslim identity.

Survey Data and Analysis

The Israeli data analyzed for this report was gathered by the Israel National Election Study (INES), directed by Professors Asher Arian and Michal Shamir. Arian has been conducting election surveys and publishing the results since 1969; Shamir has been codirector of the INES since 1984. The reports of this research are among the most prominent and thorough analyses of Israeli electoral behavior.[6] The INES data are based on representative national samples and thus provide a meaningful basis for drawing general conclusions about the Israeli public. This includes Arab as well as Jewish citizens of Israel, although only the latter are considered in this study. The data also permit a comparison of Israeli attitudes and values at different points in time. The only limitation is that the interview schedules in various surveys are not entirely identical, and therefore in some instances it is necessary to compare attitudes and values that are conceptually equivalent but measured with different indicators. The present study uses the INES surveys from 2001, 1999, and 1988.

The 2001 Survey

A sample of 1,237 Israeli Jews was interviewed for the 2001 survey, and among the questions on the interview schedule are several that pertain to the dimensions of secularism discussed earlier. The two items that ask most directly about the religious dimension of secularism are (1) Should public life be guided by *halacha*? and (2) Do you have a stronger preference for democracy, for halacha, or an equal preference for both? These two items are strongly intercorrelated. Both are also strongly correlated with a ten-point "hate-love" scale that asks about attitudes

Table 11.1   Attitudes of Israeli Jews About Secular Issues

	Public life should not be guided by halacha (%)	Preference for democracy over halacha (%)	Arab political parties should participate in governing coalitions (%)	Important political decisions should be made by both Jews and Arabs (%)
Strongly agree (most secular)	26.2	55.6	6.5	8.8
Agree	24.9		29.5	28.0
Maybe/both equal	22.7	23.0		
Disagree			31.3	26.3
Strongly disagree (least secular)	26.2	21.4	32.7	36.9
	(N=1,237)	(N=1,237)	(N=1,237)	(N=1,237)

toward "religious people." The two items that ask most directly about the socio-logical dimension of secularism are (1) Should Arab political parties participate in government coalitions? and (2) Should important political decisions be made by both Jews and Arabs or only by Jews? Again, the two items are strongly intercorre-lated, and both also correlate strongly with a ten-point "hate-love" scale that asks about attitudes toward "Arabs." Although all of the questions possess "face valid-ity" and are unlikely to be misunderstood by respondents, these inter-item correla-tions offer additional evidence that the data provide valid and reliable measures.

Table 11.1 presents the distribution of responses by Jewish respondents to each of the four questions listed above. With regard to both questions about halacha, it shows that responses are skewed in the direction of secularism, but a significant minority gives primacy to halacha. These findings, which will not be surprising to those familiar with Israel, show that there is substantial division among Israelis with regard to both religious and sociological dimensions of secularism. What may be less well known is that while a slight majority favors secularism in the religious domain, only a minority favors secularism in the sociological domain, at least as this pertains to political equality for Jewish and Arab citizens.

Table 11.2 compares the attitudes of different subsets of the Israeli Jewish pop-ulation. More specifically, it contrasts the attitudes pertaining to religious and soci-ological aspects of secularism of respondents who differ on five demographic attributes: age, educational level, sex, ethnicity, and religious orientation. For pur-poses of parsimony, only one of the two attitudinal items associated with each dimension of secularism is included, and responses in each case are dichotomized.

Table 11.2   Demographic Attributes of Secular Israeli Jews, 2001

	Believe public life should not be guided by halacha (%)	Believe Arab political parties should participate in governing coalitions (%)
Age		
Under 30	47.6	34.3
30–44	46.0	31.6
46–59	51.4	38.8
60 and over	61.5	38.6
Education		
Less than high school	46.7	25.9
High school	49.5	33.8
University	52.0	38.2
Postgraduate	61.9	48.6
Sex		
Female	55.0	38.4
Male	47.3	33.6
Ethnicity		
Ashkenazi	61.0	38.4
Sephardi	37.2	25.4
Religious Orientation		
Secular	70.0	46.2
Traditional	41.8	25.7
Orthodox	14.5	23.6
Ultra-orthodox (haredi)	1.9	18.5
All Respondents	51.1	36.0

The table thus compares across the categories of each demographic attribute the proportion of respondents who answered either "no" or "certainly not," as opposed to either "definitely" or "maybe," when asked whether halacha should guide public life; and the proportion who answered either "yes" or "certainly yes," as opposed to either "no" or "certainly not," when asked whether Arab political parties should participate in government coalitions.

Table 11.2 shows that secular attitudes in the religious domain are much more common among Ashkenazim than Sephardim, and among Jews who describe their

Table 11.3   Religious and sociological attitudes among Israeli Jews, 2001

		Public life should not be guided by halacha	
		YES	No
Arab political parties should participate in governing coalitions	Yes	23.6% secular on both dimensions	12.5% secular only on sociological dimension
	No	27.5% secular only on religious dimension	36.4% not secular on either dimension

personal religious orientation as secular as opposed to orthodox, ultra-orthodox, or traditional. Secular attitudes are also somewhat more likely among those who are older, better educated, and female. Except that differences associated with age are much less pronounced, the same pattern pertains with respect to attitudes about whether Arab political parties should participate in governing coalitions. The view that they should participate is much more common among Ashkenazim, less religious Jews, better educated individuals, and women.

The relationship between religious and sociological dimensions of secularism is explored in table 11.3. There is a statistically significant correlation ($r = .213$, $p < .001$) between attitudes toward halacha and attitudes toward Arab political involvement. Thus, to a degree, attitudes and values relating to secularism may be considered unidimensional. Israeli Jews who embrace (or reject) secular values relating to the religious dimension of secularism also tend to embrace (or reject) such values with respect to the sociological dimension of secularism.

Table 11.3 shows that a unidimensional conceptualization of secularism is only partially justified, that a significant proportion of respondents do not have the same orientation toward both dimensions of secularism, and that in the Israeli case this is more likely to involve the embrace of religious secularism than sociological secularism.

Table 11.4 completes the analysis of data from the 2001 survey. It compares respondents in each of the four attitudinal categories shown in table 11.3 with respect to the five demographic variables employed in table 11.2, when the religious and sociological dimensions of secularism were considered separately rather than in combination. As expected, given the findings in table 11.2, those who express secular values on both dimensions and those who express such values on neither dimension differ with respect to age, sex, educational level, religious orientation, and ethnicity. Specifically, the former are the most likely of all respondents and the latter are the least likely of all respondents to be neither orthodox, ultra-orthodox, nor traditional in religious orientation, to identify themselves as Ashkenazi, to be older, and to be better educated. Respondents who reject secular values in both the religious and the sociological domain are also more likely than all other respondents to be male.

The pattern is somewhat different among respondents who express secular values in one domain but not the other. Those who reject secularism in the religious

Table 11.4   Religious and Sociological Attitudes Among Israeli Jews,
by Demographic, 2001

| | Respondents (%) who express secular views on | | | | |
	RELIGIOUS AND SECULAR DIMENSIONS	RELIGIOUS DIMENSIONS ONLY	SOCIOLOGICAL DIMENSION ONLY	NEITHER DIMENSION	ALL RESPONDENTS
Age					
Under 30	18.8	23.5	28.4	22.8	22.7
30–44	25.3	26.9	25.7	34.3	29.2
46–59	30.3	25.4	29.1	26.7	27.4
60 and over	25.6	24.2	16.9	16.1	20.7
					100.0
Education					
Less than high school	7.8	16.7	14.2	15.7	14.0
High school	39.4	39.8	36.5	44.7	40.8
University	35.8	31.9	38.8	31.9	33.3
Postgraduate	17.0	11.6	13.5	7.6	11.9
					100.0
Sex					
Female	53.7	55.1	54.6	43.7	50.6
Male	46.3	44.9	45.4	56.3	49.4
					100.0
Ethnicity					
Ashkenazi	78.6	68.7	58.6	48.3	62.3
Sephardi	21.4	31.3	41.4	51.7	37.7
					100.0
Religious Orientation					
Secular	79.3	70.2	51.3	26.6	54.2
Traditional	17.2	27.4	25.0	36.4	27.8
Orthodox	3.5	1.8	10.5	17.7	0.0
Ultra-orthodox	0.0	.6	13.2	19.3	8.8
					100.0

domain alone are more likely than those who reject secularism in the sociological domain alone to be older, Ashkenazi, and neither orthodox nor ultra-orthodox in religious orientation. The two groups of respondents do not differ measurably with respect to sex, educational level, or traditional religious orientation.

The results of this analysis of survey data collected in 2001 may be summarized as follows:

- There is substantial division among Jewish Israelis with respect to both religious and sociological dimensions of secularism. Those with a strong preference for secularism in the religious domain constitute a very slight majority. Well under half, 36 percent, favor secularism in the sociological domain.
- A more secular orientation in either the religious domain, the sociological domain, or both domains is, with few exceptions, more common among Israeli Jews who are Ashkenazi, less personally religious, older, better educated, and female.
- Despite a significant correlation between attitudes and values associated with the religious dimension of secularism and those associated with the sociological dimension, the concept of secularism does not appear to be unidimensional. Roughly 40 percent of Israeli Jews express secular values in only one of the two domains. Of these, two-thirds embrace secularism in the domain of religion and one-third embrace secularism in the domain of sociology.
- Israeli Jews who embrace secularism in the religious domain and those who embrace secularism in the sociological domain have slightly different demographic profiles. The former are more likely to be older, Ashkenazi, and neither orthodox nor ultra-orthodox in religious orientation. The two groups differ little with respect to sex and educational level.

These findings lay a foundation for informed speculation about whether support for secularism is likely to increase or decrease in the years ahead. The contrast between the views of Sephardim and Ashkenazim and between those of religious and nonreligious Jews suggests that support may decrease, given that in each case the former demographic category is growing more rapidly than the latter. A decrease in the support for secularism is also suggested by the relationship between older age and support for secularism, especially the religious dimension of secularism. This means that distribution of Israeli Jewish attitudes toward issues associated with secularism may shift as older persons retire or pass away and as younger individuals come into the mainstream of adult life.

If these projections are correct, it is likely that the country will become more equally divided on issues pertaining to the religious dimension of secularism and that these issues will steadily become more salient and a source of increasing tension. These demographic trends also have the potential to diminish the proportion of Jewish Israelis, already a minority, who embrace secular values in the sociological domain. Should this occur, full equality for Israel's Arab citizens would be increasingly unlikely, intensifying their alienation from the state.

Table 11.5   Attitudes of Israeli Jews About Secular Issues, 1999

	Public life should not be guided by halacha (%)	Preference for democracy over halacha (%)	Arab political parties should participate in governing coalitions (%)	Important political decisions should be made by both Jews and Arabs (%)
Strongly agree (most secular)	28.5	44.4	11.0	13.7
Agree	38.7	21.5	38.8	35.4
Maybe/unsure	17.8	16.8		
Disagree		10.2	26.7	25.9
Strongly disagree (least secular)	14.9	7.1	23.5	25.0
	(N=1,075)	(N=1,075)	(N=1,075)	(N=1,075)

These projections, offered to stimulate reflection about the future of secularism in Israel, should be considered with caution. Countervailing trends may also be at work. The expansion of education, especially among Sephardim, could increase support for secularism. Given the important role of mothers in early childhood socialization, this may also be a possible consequence of the fact that women are more likely than men to hold secular values. Beyond this, the distribution of Israeli Jewish attitudes relevant to secularism will almost certainly be shaped in the years ahead not only by demographic trends but also by changing patterns of immigration, by developments associated with the Israeli-Palestinian conflict, and by other domestic, regional, and international factors. Nevertheless, the need for caution notwithstanding, it seems reasonable at present to hypothesize that the course of events is likely to intensify rather than offset societal dynamics that portend diminished support for secularism in both the religious and the sociological domains.

The 1999 Survey

This examination of Jewish Israeli attitudes and values pertaining to secularism can also be informed by an analysis of older survey data. One data set available for this purpose was collected just prior to the 1999 elections and is based on a sample of 1,075 Israeli Jews. The results of an analysis of these data, comparable to that carried out with the 2001 data and using the same questions from the interview schedule, are presented in tables 11.5–11.7. Table 11.5 shows the responses of Jewish Israelis to the four questions considered earlier. Table 11.6 shows the relationship between items measuring the two different dimensions of secularism. Table 11.7 compares, with respect to the demographic characteristics listed earlier,

Table 11.6   Religious and Sociological Attitudes Among Israeli Jews, 1999

		Public life should not be guided by halacha	
		YES	No
Arab political parties should participate in governing coalitions	Yes	37.3 secular on both dimensions	12.7 secular only on sociological dimension
	No	30.4 secular only on religious dimension	19.6 not secular on either dimension

respondents who express secular values in both domains, in the religious domain alone, in the sociological domain alone, and in neither domain.

There is some variation in the aggregate demographic profiles of the 1999 and 2001 samples, perhaps resulting from the vagaries of probability sampling. A comparison of findings from the two surveys is nonetheless instructive. Given the relative proximity of the two surveys, similar findings will increase confidence in observed patterns and suggest that these patterns are indeed a part of the Israeli experience at the present historical moment. Different findings, by contrast, will suggest that recent developments may have affected attitudes and values pertaining to secularism and strengthen the foundation for informed speculation about the future. Given the outbreak of the al-Aqsa intifada in 2000 and the collapse of the Israeli-Palestinian peace process more generally, a comparison of patterns observed in 1999 and 2001 will shed light on whether, and if so how, the evolution of the conflict influences the views related to secularism held by Jewish Israelis.

Four conclusions are suggested by a comparison of the 1999 and 2001 surveys. First, table 11.5 shows that on all four items selected for analysis, support for secularism declined significantly between 1999 and 2001. These findings are consistent with projections about the direction of attitudinal change offered on the basis of the 2001 data. They also suggest that deterioration in Israeli-Palestinian relations tends to diminish support for secularism.

There are both similarities and differences in the demographic attributes that correlate with attitudes toward secularism in 1999 and 2001. In both years, not surprisingly, a more secular perspective in both the religious and sociological domains is disproportionately likely among Ashkenazim and those whose religious orientation is neither orthodox, ultra-orthodox, nor traditional. What can be added is that attitudinal differences associated with ethnicity and religious orientation are not quite as strong in 1999, suggesting among Sephardim and more religious Jews support for secularism declined the most between 1999 and 2001. Attitudinal differences associated with age, education, and sex, by contrast, were much less important in 1999 than they were in 2001. This suggests that the patterns observed in 2001 are not necessarily enduring and, also, although some of the differences are not large, that a secular perspective on political and social issues declined to the greatest degree among younger individuals, less well-educated individuals, and men.

Table 11.7   Religious and Sociological Attitudes Among Israeli Jews,
by Demographic, 1999

| | Respondents (%) who express secular views on | | | | |
	RELIGIOUS AND SECULAR DIMENSION	RELIGIOUS DIMENSION ONLY	SOCIOLOGICAL DIMENSIONS ONLY	NEITHER DIMENSION	ALL RESPONDENTS
Age					
Under 30	36.0	40.9	44.4	36.1	38.2
30–44	20.3	24.6	17.8	28.8	22.8
46–59	21.1	17.6	14.5	22.0	19.9
60 and over	22.6	16.9	23.4	13.1	19.1
					100.0
Education					
Less than high school	12.0	13.0	9.8	7.8	11.2
High school	50.5	63.2	69.1	69.3	59.8
University	29.0	19.8	17.8	19.8	23.5
Postgraduate	8.5	4.0	3.3	3.1	5.5
					100.0
Sex					
Female	52.4	49.2	52.8	47.7	50.8
Male	47.6	50.8	47.2	52.4	49.2
					100.0
Ethnicity					
Ashkenazi	63.5	47.7	45.5	37.7	50.8
Sephardi	36.5	52.3	54.5	62.3	49.2
					100.0
Religious Orientation					
Secular	81.1	61.5	44.8	23.3	59.4
Traditional	17.6	35.1	44.0	37.3	29.9
Orthodox	.8	3.0	9.6	32.2	8.8
Ultra-orthodox	.5	.3	1.6	6.2	1.9
					100.0

Table 11.6 shows that the relationship between attitudes pertaining to the two dimensions of secularism was no stronger in 1999 than it was in 2001. The proportion of respondents who either embrace or reject both is roughly the same in both years. All that has changed, as suggested by the preceding discussion, is that many fewer respondents embrace secularism in both domains and many more reject it in both domains. In addition, the ratio of those who embrace secularism only in the religious domain to those who embrace it only in the sociological domain is also about the same in 1999 and 2001.

The similarity of the distributions shown in table 11.7 to those shown in table 11.3 thus provides additional support for the assessment offered earlier about the dimensionality of the concept of secularism. The concept is at best only somewhat unidimensional at the individual level of analysis and, accordingly, a proper understanding requires attention to the sociological as well as the religious dimension.

As seen in table 11.7, the demographic profiles of Israeli Jews who embrace secularism only on the religious dimension and those who embrace secularism only on the sociological dimension are not very different. The former are more likely than the latter to be secular in their personal religious orientation, which is not surprising. Otherwise, the profiles of respondents in the two categories differ only in minor respects. This departs somewhat from the pattern observed in 2001, as shown in table 11.4, in that in 2001 those embracing secularism only on the religious dimension were more likely than those embracing secularism only on the sociological dimension to be Ashkenazi and older, as well as less personally religious.

The 1988 Survey

It is interesting to compare this picture of Jewish Israeli attitudes around the turn of the present century to those of Israeli Jews a decade earlier, which can be evaluated with data from the INES election survey of 1988. The survey is based on a sample that contained 873 Jews. It would also have been instructive to examine data from the 1984 election survey, which preceded the first Palestinian intifada; however this survey did not ask the necessary questions. Indeed, although the 1988 survey asked questions pertaining to both the religious and sociological dimensions of secularism, questions pertaining to the latter dimension were not the same as those asked in later surveys. Caution must thus be exercised when comparing aggregate distributions at different points in time.

Although it does specifically ask about halacha, the 1988 survey asks respondents whether or not they agree that public life should be "run according to Jewish tradition." The distribution of responses is shown in table 11.8. With respect to the sociological dimension of secularism, there are many questions that ask about the rights and status of Israel's Arab citizens but none that is fully comparable to those asked in 2001 and 1999. The most relevant questions from the 1988 survey ask respondents whether or not they would "object to an Arab prime minister of Israel," whether or not they think "Arabs should be allowed to hold political demonstrations," and whether or not they agree that "Jews who hurt Arabs should

Table 11.8   Attitudes of Israeli Jews About Secular Issues, 1988

	Public life should not be run according to Jewish tradition (%)	Would not object to an Arab prime minister of Israel (%)	Arabs should be allowed to hold political demonstrations (%)	Jews who hurt Arabs should not receive lesser punishments (%)
Strongly agree (most secular)	26.9	3.2	9.6	12.7
Agree	29.3	6.9	34.0	28.0
Maybe/unsure		8.3	22.6	22.8
Disagree	24.6	27.6	21.9	23.4
Strongly disagree (least secular)	19.1	55.0	11.9	13.2
	(N=873)	(N=873)	(N=873)	(N=873)

receive lesser punishments." Table 11.8 also presents the distribution of Jewish Israeli responses to each of these questions.

This table shows that about 56 percent of the Israeli Jews surveyed in 1988 agree or agree strongly that public life should not be run according to Jewish tradition. This is less than in 1999 but more than in 2001. The proportion that agrees strongly and thus rejects secular principles is about the same as in 2001. Taken as a whole, this pattern suggest much more continuity than change and indicates—recent developments and projections about the future notwithstanding—that a division of opinion on the religious dimension of secularism has been fairly constant over the last decade or so. This will be no surprise to those familiar with Israel.

Attitudes pertaining to the sociological dimension are more difficult to summarize. Although the three items included in table 11.8 are highly intercorrelated, they differ in terms of the kind of policy favoring Jews or disadvantaging Arabs about which they ask, and they thus have different response distributions. A reasonable assessment is that the level of support for Jewish-Arab equality in 1988 was roughly similar to that observed in 2001, perhaps marginally higher. If this assessment is correct, the data suggest that a solid majority of Jewish Israelis has historically been opposed to secularism in the sociological domain, that this opposition lessened somewhat in the 1990s, presumably as a result of the Israeli-Palestinian peace process, and that it has returned to its traditional and for the most part low level following the collapse of the peace process.

Table 11.9, like tables 11.2 and 11.4, compares different subsets of the Israeli Jewish population with respect to attitudes pertaining to secularism. Respondents classified as having secular attitudes in the religious domain are, again, those who

Table 11.9   Israeli Jews with Secular Values, by Demographic, 1988

	Public life should not be run according to Jewish tradition (%)	Jews who hurt Arabs should not receive lesser punishments (%)
Age		
Under 30	52.8	36.5
30–44	56.3	45.8
46–59	58.5	36.8
60 and over	65.3	47.0
Education		
Less than high school	54.8	33.6
High school	56.6	39.4
University	55.6	48.6
Postgraduate	63.3	56.0
Sex		
Female	52.0	35.1
Male	59.8	45.7
Ethnicity[1]		
Ashkenazi	65.6	56.3
Sephardi	49.9	31.7
Religious observance[2]		
Not at all	82.4	53.2
A little	62.5	40.1
To a great extent	32.8	33.0
Fully	15.2	26.6
All respondents	56.2	40.7

[1] Twenty-four percent responded "both" or "none" to the question about ethnicity and are excluded from the calculations in the table.

[2] The categories of secular, traditional, orthodox, and ultra-orthodox were not used in the 1988 survey.

either agree or agree strongly that public life should not be run according to Jewish tradition. Respondents classified as having secular attitudes in the sociological domain are those who either disagree or disagree strongly that Jews who hurt Arabs should receive lesser punishment.[7] The table shows that secular attitudes in

Table 11.10   Religious and Sociological Attitudes Among Israeli Jews, 1988

| | | Public life should not be run according to Jewish tradition | |
		Yes	No
Jews who hurt Arabs should not receive lesser punishments	Yes	27.4% secular on both dimensions	13.3% secular only on sociological dimension
	No	28.6% secular only on religious dimension	30.7% not secular on either dimension

the religious domain are more likely among respondents who are older, highly educated, male, Ashkenazi, and less personally religious. This is consistent with the patterns observed in 2001 and 1999, indicating continuity with respect to the demographic correlates of secular attitudes. The only notable difference concerns sex. Secular attitudes were more common among men in 1988, there was no difference between men and women in 1999, and secular attitudes were more common among women in 2001. The pattern is very similar with respect to secular attitudes in the sociological domain, the only differences being that the correlation with education is noticeably stronger and the correlation with age is somewhat weaker.

Table 11.10 shows that the relationship between attitudes pertaining to the two dimensions is very similar to that observed in later years. As in 1999 and 2001, approximately 60 percent of the respondents either embrace or reject secular values in both domains and about 40 percent embrace such attitudes in one domain but not the other. The distribution across the four categories shown in table 11.10 is different in one respect and similar in another respect to the patterns observed in 1999 and 2001. On the one hand, those who embrace secularism on both dimensions are less numerous than in 1999 but more numerous than in 2001, and those who reject secularism on both dimensions are more numerous than in 1999 but less numerous than in 2001. This is consistent with the pattern noted above, when the dimensions of secularism were considered separately. Support for secular norms increased in the 1990s and then subsequently declined to a level lower than in the past, due in part, perhaps, to the rise and fall of the peace process. On the other hand, the 2:1 ratio of respondents who express secular attitudes only in the religious domain to those who express secular attitudes only in the sociological domain is almost identical to the ratio in both 1999 and 2001. Accordingly, this appears to be an enduring pattern.

In table 11.11 we compare respondents with respect to age, education, sex, ethnicity, and degree of religious orientation. Ethnicity excludes the 24 percent who answered "both" or "none" and only compares respondents who identified themselves as either Ashkenazi or Sephardi. With respect to religious orientation, the 1988 survey did not use the categories of secular, traditional, orthodox, and ultra-orthodox but instead asked about degree of religious observance. Consistent with the findings shown in table 11.9, and as expected since the demographic correlates

Table 11.11   Religious and Sociological Attitudes Among Israeli Jews,
by Demographic, 1988

	Respondents (%) who express secular views on				
	RELIGIOUS AND SECULAR DIMENSIONS	RELIGIOUS DIMENSION ONLY	SOCIOLOGICAL DIMENSION ONLY	NEITHER DIMENSION	ALL RESPONDENTS
Age					
Under 30	33.3	42.4	42.3	44.1	40.4
30–44	35.5	30.5	40.5	30.3	33.2
46–59	15.4	15.9	9.0	15.7	14.6
60 and over	15.6	11.9	8.1	9.8	11.8
Education					
Less than high school	24.0	32.6	23.9	32.5	29.0
High school	35.1	42.2	39.4	37.8	38.5
University	31.6	20.9	31.2	24.9	26.5
Postgraduate	9.3	4.3	5.5	4.9	6.0
Sex					
Female	37.0	51.1	49.5	53.1	47.7
Male	63.0	49.9	50.5	46.9	52.3
Ethnicity[1]					
Ashkenazi	61.6	32.3	38.3	28.5	40.3
Sephardi	38.4	67.7	61.7	71.5	59.7
Religious observance[2]					
Not at all	40.1	29.0	12.0	8.7	23.6
A little	49.8	51.3	35.2	41.1	45.6
To a great extent	7.9	16.8	38.0	30.8	21.4
Fully	2.2	2.9	14.8	19.4	9.9

[1] Twenty-four percent responded "both" or "none" to the question about ethnicity and are excluded from the calculations in the table.

[2] The categories of secular, traditional, orthodox, and ultra-orthodox were not used in the 1988 survey.

of attitudes in the religious domain and the sociological domain were almost identical, Israeli Jews who embrace secularism in both domains are disproportionately likely to be older, highly educated, male, Ashkenazi, and less personally religious, and those who embrace secularism in neither domain are disproportionately likely to be younger, less well-educated, female, Sephardi, and more personally religious. So far as respondents who express support for secular principles on only one dimension are concerned, those with secular attitudes in the religious domain are more likely than those with secular attitudes in the sociological domain to be younger than forty-five, less well-educated, and not religiously observant. Perhaps the most interesting of these latter findings is that respondents who reject secularism in the sociological domain but embrace it in the religious domain are disproportionately *unlikely* to be either very poorly educated or to report that they are not at all or only a little religiously observant.

Survey Data from Jordan and Egypt

Although parallels between Israel and Arab countries should not be overstated, almost all of the latter officially proclaim Islam to be the religion of state and have institutions that give Islamic leaders a role in governance not found in more secular polities. As one author has stated, "Islam plays a pivotal role in all aspects of Muslim societies. . . . Even during periods of quietism, Islam has played a determining role in Arab politics."[8] Perhaps this puts the matter too strongly. At the very least, however, Islam is an inevitable point of departure and ideological referent for most Muslim Arabs when thinking about issues of governance and political identity. To this extent, at minimum, Arab countries, like Israel, are not secular political communities.

Further, and also like Israel, the issues raised by a strong connection between religion and politics are ones about which Muslims in the Arab world and elsewhere often disagree, sometimes very strongly. The tension between "profane and sacred politics" is described by a prominent scholar of Islam, who has written, "on the one hand, most Muslim politicians are only politicians; on the other, Islam has become almost an obsession in political debate for the past two decades."[9] In this connection, there are intense debates not only about the extent to which Islamic law should be the law of the land, but also about how Muslim legal codes should be interpreted and applied in a wide range of areas. Among these are the role and authority of national assemblies, the political status of non-Muslim citizens, banking practices and regulations, criminal law and court proceedings, and matters of personal status ranging from marriage and divorce to inheritance. In these and other areas, there are questions about whether a more strict and narrow or a more liberal and contextualized interpretation of Islam should prevail.

All of this gives Islam not only an accepted and legitimate but indeed a necessary and unavoidably central role in political life and the construction of political identity, and this in turn makes it entirely relevant to ask what kind of "Islamic" state is desired by the Muslim citizens of Arab countries. The parallels with Israel need not be overstated. But those familiar with issues of religion and politics in the

Jewish state will probably recognize, notwithstanding differences on many specifics, that Israeli Jews and Muslim Arabs are both addressing the same fundamental questions: to what extent, if at all, and in what way, should the political character and identity of their countries be shaped by the religion of the majority rather than by a political formula inspired by secularism?

Data for addressing questions about secularism are available from two Arab countries, Jordan and Egypt. The Jordanian data are based on a representative national sample of 1,000 adult citizens, 96.4 percent of whom are Muslim, carried out in 2001 by scholars at the University of Jordan in Amman. The Egyptian data are based on a representative national sample of 3,000 adult citizens, 94.3 percent of whom are Muslim, carried out in 2000 as part of the University of Michigan-based World Values Survey. Both surveys ask about the role of Islam and Islamic leaders in political affairs. The Jordanian survey also asks about the political rights of Jordanian citizens who are Christian rather than Muslim. Only the responses of Muslim respondents are examined in the present analysis.

The Jordanian survey contains a series of highly intercorrelated items that ask about issues pertaining to the religious dimension of secularism. Two of these are considered in the present analysis: "Should religious leaders be involved in political decision-making or restrict themselves to providing religious guidance?" and "Should political leaders be selected solely by Islamic clerics or elected solely by the people?" The Jordanian survey also asks respondents whether or not they agree that "Non-Muslims should have the same legal rights as Muslims in our country" and that "Non-Muslims should be allowed to hold high government positions." The Egyptian survey contains one question that pertains to the religious dimension of secularism: "Should religious leaders exercise influence in political affairs?"

Table 11.12 presents the responses of Jordanian and Egyptian Muslims to the five questions listed above. It shows there is considerable support for secularist principles in both countries. In the case of Jordan, three-quarters of the Muslim respondents express the view that political leaders should not be selected solely by Islamic clerics, 30 percent believe Islamic leaders should not be involved in politics at all, and a majority favors political equality for the country's non-Muslim citizens. In Egypt, a majority also states that religious leaders should not exercise political influence. Since substantial numbers of respondents take the opposite position on each of these issues, however, it may be concluded that, as in Israel, questions about the relationship between religion and politics are contested in the Arab world and divide citizens with different views about the kind of state in which they want to live.

Comparisons with Israel must be advanced with caution since identical questions were not asked in the different surveys and, more generally, there are important differences in political context. For example, views about the rights of Israel's non-Jewish citizens are shaped at least in part by the Israeli-Palestinian conflict, something that is not the case with respect to non-Muslim citizens of Jordan and Egypt. Nonetheless, with due caution, some observations based on a comparison of the Israeli and Arab cases may be instructive. Moreover, differences among the

Table 11.12   Attitudes of Jordanian and Egyptian Muslims About Secular Issues

	Jordan				Egypt
	RELIGIOUS LEADERS SHOULD NOT BE INVOLVED IN POLITICAL DECISION-MAKING (%)	POLITICAL LEADERS SHOULD NOT BE SELECTED SOLELY BY ISLAMIC CLERICS (%)	NON-MUSLIMS SHOULD HAVE THE SAME LEGAL RIGHTS AS MUSLIMS (%)	NON-MUSLIMS SHOULD BE ALLOWED TO HOLD HIGH GOVERNMENT OFFICE (%)	RELIGIOUS LEADERS SHOULD NOT EXERCISE INFLUENCE IN POLITICAL AFFAIRS (%)
Strongly agree (most secular)			46.3	23.1	31.5
Agree	30.0	74.1	34.3	24.6	24.8
Maybe/unsure	11.6	10.8			11.9
Disagree	58.4	15.1	14.1	35.5	22.0
Strongly disagree (least secular)			4.3	16.8	9.7
	(N=964)	(N=964)	(N=964)	(N=964)	(N=2,830)

cases give this comparison the advantages of a "most different systems" research design. Similarities will shed light on patterns and relationships that are not country-specific and may thus apply to other countries with an official and institutionalized connection between religion and politics. Differences will help to identify conditionalities, suggesting hypotheses about country-level attributes and experiences that define the locus of applicability of particular patterns and relationships.

There is considerable division of opinion among ordinary citizens in all three countries considered in the present study, meaning that the political and conceptual divide flowing from Israel's identity as a Jewish state finds a counterpart in Arab countries where Islam is tied to the state's identity. Further, the proportions on each side of the conceptual divide are fairly similar in Israel and the two Arab countries. Findings pertaining to the religious dimension of secularism are in the same general range, although support for secularist principles in this domain appears to be somewhat higher in Israel. On the other hand, there appears to be a higher level of support for the equality of Muslim and non-Muslim citizens in Jordan than for the equality of Jewish and non-Jewish citizens in Israel, although at least some of this difference, as noted, results from the Israeli-Palestinian conflict rather than Israel's Jewish character. Overall, differences and cautions notwithstanding, the Israeli and Arab cases are more similar than might have been

Table 11.13 Demographic Attributes of Secular Jordanian and Egyptian Muslims, 2000

	Jordan		Egypt
	BELIEVE RELIGIOUS LEADERS SHOULD NOT BE INVOLVED IN POLITICAL DECISION-MAKING (%)	BELIEVE NON-MUSLIMS SHOULD BE ALLOWED TO HOLD HIGH GOVERNMENT OFFICE (%)	BELIEVE RELIGIOUS LEADERS SHOULD NOT EXERCISE INFLUENCE IN POLITICAL AFFAIRS (%)
Age			
Under 30	29.9	43.4	52.2
30–44	26.7	45.2	59.0
46–59	38.7	58.8	59.3
60 and over	28.4	56.9	55.4
Education			
Less than high school	32.9	47.2	55.5
High school	28.2	47.4	57.1
University	26.2	47.2	54.7
Postgraduate	41.8	63.2	59.7
Sex			
Female	35.0	54.3	59.3
Male	25.0	41.6	53.1
Religious observance			
Not at all	33.9	52.4	58.3
A little	27.7	45.7	54.2
Some			55.9
Considerable	33.3	43.2	60.6
Fully	22.7	43.6	55.8
All respondents	30.0	47.7	56.3

expected, which suggests that there may be some common themes and attitudinal patterns in countries where the religion of the majority is also the religion of state.

This last table compares attitudes pertaining to the religious and sociological aspects of secularism of Arab respondents who differ with respect to age, educational level, sex, and religious observance. It shows that in almost all cases, attitudes consistent with secular principles are held most frequently by individuals who are

Table 11.14   Religious and Sociological Attitudes Among Jordanians, 2001

		Religious leaders should not be involved in political decision making	
		Yes	No
Non-Muslims should be allowed to hold high government office	Yes	17.2% secular on both dimensions	30.4% secular only on sociological dimension
	No	13.4% secular only on religious dimension	39.0% not secular on either dimension

better educated, male, and not religiously observant. They are also held most frequently by older individuals in the case of Jordanian attitudes toward the sociological dimension of secularism. With the exception of findings pertaining to sex, this
pattern is similar to that observed in Israel in 2001, which in turn suggests that findings about the demographic correlates of secular attitudes in nonsecular societies
can be somewhat generalized. On the other hand, differences between the Arab
and Israeli cases are also significant. It is men in the former and women in the latter who were disproportionately likely to hold secular values in 2001. Further, the
relationships involving age and education are neither as strong nor as consistent as
in the Israeli case, although in that case, too, these relationships are not extremely
strong.

Most important, perhaps, the correlation with personal religiosity is much
weaker than in the Israeli case. This suggests that in the Arab world, or at least in
Jordan and Egypt, judgments pertaining to the relationship between religion and
politics are influenced by temporal considerations almost as often as by religious
conviction, something that appears to be much less true in Israel. This is consistent
with findings from other studies based on survey research in the Arab world. These
studies show that support for Islamic leaders and movements does not necessarily
indicate a rejection of secular values and a corresponding desire for an Islamic
state, but rather is frequently a statement of protest against governments judged to
be authoritarian, corrupt, and uninterested in the welfare of ordinary citizens.[10]
The comparison of Israel and the two Arab cases thus suggests the following
hypothesis: in states with an official connection between religion and politics, attitudes toward secularism are shaped by religiosity to a much greater degree in
democratic and developed countries than in those that are less democratic and less
developed.

Table 11.14 examines the relationship between the religious and sociological
dimensions of secularism with data from the Jordanian survey. Questions pertaining to the sociological dimension of secularism were not included in the Egyptian
survey. As in the Israeli case, the proportion of Jordanian respondents in each cell
of this table is affected by the choice of items and cutting points. The distribution
of percentages across the cells shows a pattern that is unlike that observed in Israel

in any of the three years examined. It is probably unwise to compare the proportion of respondents who either embrace or reject secularism in both the religious and sociological domains. These percentages are affected directly by the items selected for analysis. Also, they were not the same in Israel in the different years examined, which suggests that combinations of attitudes, like individual attitudes, vary considerably in response to circumstance and context. But the ratio of those who embrace secularism in the religious domain alone to those who embrace secularism in the sociological domain alone may offer a more instructive comparison. A 2:1 ratio, or slightly higher, was observed in Israel in all three years, and the ratio was about the same in Jordan in 2001. The difference, however, is that support for secularism in the religious domain alone is greater in the Israeli case, and support for secularism in the sociological domain is greater in the Jordanian case. Is this a pattern that holds true more generally, and if so, does it perhaps reflect the influence of the Arab-Israeli conflict? Or rather is it due to different understandings of what it means to be a Jewish state and what it means to be an Islamic state? These are questions for future research.

Table 11.15 examines the demographic correlates of attitudes toward the two dimensions of secularism considered in combination. Jordanian Muslims who hold attitudes consistent with secularism in both domains are disproportionately likely to be older and male but differ little from other respondents with respect to education and religious observance. Those who hold attitudes consistent with secularism in the religious domain alone are disproportionately likely to be poorly educated but otherwise have a demographic profile similar to that of other respondents. Those who hold attitudes consistent with secularism in the sociological domain alone do not differ noticeably from other respondents on any of the attributes examined. Finally, respondents whose attitudes are not consistent with secularism in either domain are slightly more likely to be younger, to be women, and to be more religious. This differs from patterns observed in Israel in several respects, the most important being the limited explanatory power of personal religiosity. As noted earlier, this suggests that in states with an official connection between religion and politics, the degree to which personal religiosity accounts for variance in attitudes toward secularism may depend on the country's level of democracy and development. The most notable similarity between the Arab countries and Israel is that support for secularism, in both the religious and the sociological domains, is disproportionately high among older individuals. This suggests a pattern that may be generalized to other nonsecular states. It also suggests, other things being equal, that generational change may reduce support for secular values both in Israel and in the Arab world, perhaps with implications for Arab-Israeli relations.

The Nature of the Jewish State

Most Jews in Israel, like most Jews elsewhere, want Israel to be a Jewish state. But there is much less agreement about what this means. Can and *should* the state be secular as well as Jewish? Can the country maintain a Jewish identity and mission

Table 11.15   Religious and Sociological Attitudes Among Jordanian Muslims,
by Demographic, 2001

	Respondents (%) who express secular views on				
	RELIGIOUS AND SECULAR DIMENSIONS	RELIGIOUS DIMENSION ONLY	SOCIOLOGICAL DIMENSION ONLY	NEITHER DIMENSION	ALL RESPONDENTS
Age					
Under 30	33.1	40.5	33.2	39.3	36.5
30–44	31.3	34.8	40.0	42.8	38.9
46–59	24.7	17.2	16.9	10.9	15.9
60 and over	11.0	7.5	10.0	7.0	8.6
Education					
Less than high school	41.8	47.2	37.0	37.1	39.2
High school	29.5	30.8	33.4	33.0	32.2
University	23.2	22.0	28.3	27.9	26.4
Postgraduate	5.5		1.3	2.0	2.1
Sex					
Female	36.0	53.6	50.7	59.5	52.0
Male	64.0	46.4	49.3	40.5	48.0
Religious observance					
Not at all	23.8	23.3	21.7	14.9	19.5
A little	11.2	10.4	12.0	11.9	11.6
To a great extent	36.1	45.2	32.8	34.4	35.7
Fully	29.0	21.1	33.5	38.8	33.2

without privileging Jewish citizens, Jewish institutions, and Jewish law? If not, must it of necessity deviate from the principles of secularism to remain faithful to the Zionist vocation? The debates to which this situation gives rise have been prominent features of Israeli politics and society since the country became independent in 1948. Particularly central have been questions about the place of Jewish law and religious institutions in government and public life and about the rights to be accorded to non-Jewish citizens.

As the data presented in this analysis demonstrate, these are questions about which Israeli Jews are deeply divided. A majority supports secular principles in what has been termed the religious domain, in matters pertaining to the enactment of legislation based on Jewish law and giving religious leaders and institutions a formal and significant role in political affairs. But Israeli Jews who hold secular attitudes in this domain may not be in the majority much longer. Support for the positions they espouse has declined in recent years and is diminished by regional developments and demographic trends that portend a further decline in the future. In 2001, only 51 percent of Israeli Jews agreed that public life should not be guided by halacha.

In matters involving the status and rights of Israel's non-Jewish citizens, almost all of whom are Palestinian Arabs, support for secularism is even lower in what has been termed the "sociological domain." Survey data suggest that true and complete equality for Jewish and non-Jewish citizens may never have been advocated by more than half of Israel's Jewish population, and the proportion that supports this degree of equality has also declined in recent years and appears likely to decline even further in the years ahead. Thus, if secularism means that the state represents and serves all of its citizens in equal measure, with no group able to identify with the mission of the state more than any other, then only about one-third of Israeli Jews can be said to have a favorable attitude toward secularism.

Attitudes pertaining to the religious dimension of secularism and those pertaining to the sociological dimension of secularism are not independent of one another. In about 60 percent of the cases, respondents either embrace secular principles in both domains or reject these principles in both domains. This is the case in Israel for all three of the years examined, which is itself surprising given time-related differences in other attitudinal distributions. Nevertheless, the correlation between attitudes in the religious and sociological domains is not so strong that the notion of secularism lends itself to a unidimensional conceptualization in the Israeli case, and data from Jordan suggests that this may not be unique to Israel.

It turns out to be important to consider the dimensions of secularism in combination as well as separately. Support for secularism is at best incomplete if citizens embrace it in one domain but not the other, and so "true" secularists are those who express secular attitudes in both the religious and the sociological domain. Many express such attitudes pertaining to only one dimension, however, and these individuals might be described as partial, or perhaps "compromised" or "incomplete," secularists. As noted, such individuals have been and remain about 40 percent of Israel's Jewish population. It is thus significant that the trends and projections noted above apply when attitudes are considered in combinations as well as separately. The proportion of Israeli Jews supporting secularism on both dimensions, those who are "true" secularists, rose between 1988 and 1999 and thereafter declined, just as the proportion opposing secularism on both dimensions fell and then rose over the same period, apparently influenced by the political and demographic factors noted earlier. This is important because it means that a change in support for secularism in one domain is not balanced by continuity in the other domain, making the impact of previously noted trends that much greater.

Whether one hopes that Israel's future will be guided by secular principles or believes that secularism is not the right model for the Jewish state, certainly issues and concerns raised by the question of secularism will remain central and passionately debated aspects of Israeli political life. The present study seeks to shed light on the way that ordinary men and women in Israel think about these issues and concerns. It presents and analyzes attitudinal data in an effort to respond to the question, "What kind of Jewish state do Israelis want?" Additional research is needed, of course, to determine whether current trends persist and whether projections about the influence of regional and demographic factors are correct. Survey research is well developed in Israel, and future election and other surveys will certainly provide the data needed for such investigations.

A final line of inquiry concerns the uniqueness of Israel with respect to issues of secularism. Israel is not the only country with an official connection between religion and politics. The Arab and Islamic world is full of countries that proclaim Islam to be the state religion. Many also have legal systems based at least partly on Islamic law and political systems that give religious leaders and institutions an influential role in political life. While these countries obviously differ from Israel in important respects, they share with the Jewish state a rejection of Western-style secularism. Moreover, data from Jordan, and to some extent Egypt, suggest that there may be interesting similarities between the nature and distribution of attitudes pertaining to secularism held by Muslim Arabs and Israeli Jews. More research is needed to provide a fuller account of these similarities and differences. Likewise, research that examines the attitudes of Christians in Arab countries and of Muslims and Christians in Israel would be instructive. Based on the Jordanian and Egyptian data considered in this study, one can conclude that similarities in the attitudes held by ordinary citizens in Israel and the Arab world may be greater than might have been expected. Or, more generally, the weight of available evidence shows that the Israeli situation is not unique in so far as the views of ordinary citizens are concerned.

A related point, offered in conclusion, is that the way Israeli society evolves with respect to the question of secularism may hold lessons for Muslim Arab societies, and developments in the latter may in some instances be instructive for Israel as well. As noted, Israeli Jews and Muslim Arabs are asking and struggling to answer the same basic question: to what extent should the political character and identity of their countries be shaped by the religion of the majority rather than by a political formula inspired by secularism? Israeli Jews are asking what kind of Jewish state they want and what it means to be a Jewish state at the present historical moment. Muslim Arabs are similarly asking what it means to be a Muslim state, and which among the various and competing answers to this question that are regularly advanced is most appropriate. In neither the Israeli nor the Arab case are these issues likely to become less salient in the years ahead. Accordingly, given that each is dealing with the same underlying concerns, information about the experiences of one may offer the other insights possessing explanatory power as well as guides and cautions relating to public policy.

NOTES

1. Tom Segev, "Who Is a Secularist?" *Haaretz*, September 25, 1996, quoted in Charles Liebman and Bernard Susser, "Judaism and Jewishness in the Jewish State," *Annals* 555 (January 1998): 20. The Summer 2003 issue of *Daedalus* is devoted to the theme "Religion Still Matters" and contains many useful articles pertaining to secularism. See in particular Nikki Keddie, "Secularism and Its Discontents." Keddie, a Middle East specialist, has written that, "The Western path to secularism, and indeed the Western definition of secularism, may not be fully applicable in all parts of the world, because of religious differences" (30). For a useful cross-national overview of consensus and controversies regarding the place of religion in political and public affairs, with chapters on Israeli, Muslim, and many other societies, see Ted Jelen and Clyde Wilcox, eds., *Religion and Politics in Comparative Perspective* (Cambridge: Cambridge University Press, 2002).

2. I have explored this issue from both a conceptual and an empirical perspective in several earlier studies. See, for example, Mark Tessler, "Secularism in Israel: Religious and Sociological Dimensions," *Discourse* 19 (Fall 1996): 160–178; Mark Tessler, "The Identity of Religious Minorities in Non-secular States: Jews in Tunisia and Morocco and Arabs in Israel," *Comparative Studies in Society and History* 20 (July 1978): 359–373; Mark Tessler, "Secularism in the Middle East: Reflections on Recent Palestinian Proposals," *Ethnicity* (July 1975): 178–203.

3. The following works provide a useful overview of these issues: Naftali Rothenberg and Eliezer Schweid, eds., *Jewish Identity in Modern Israel: Proceedings on Secular Judaism and Democracy* (New York: Urim, 2002); Alan Dowty, *The Jewish State: A Century Later* (Berkeley: University of California Press, 1998), esp. chap. 8, "Religion and Politics"; Charles Liebman and Bernard Susser, "Judaism and Jewishness in the Jewish State," *Annals* 555 (January 1998): 15–25; Charles Liebman, *Religion, Democracy and Israeli Society* (London: Routledge, 1997); Zvi Sobel and Benjamin Beit-Hallahmi, eds., *Tradition, Innovation, Conflict: Jewishness and Judaism in Contemporary Israel* (Albany: State University of New York Press, 1991).

4. The following works provide a useful overview of these issues: As'ad Ghanem, *The Palestinian-Arab Minority in Israel, 1948–2000: A Political Study* (Albany: State University of New York Press, 2001); Alan Dowty, *The Jewish State: A Century Later* (Berkeley: University of California Press, 1998), esp. chap. 9, "Arabs in Israel"; Mark Tessler and Audra Grant, "Israel's Arab Citizens: The Continuing Struggle," *Annals* 555 (January 1998): 97–113; Nadim Rouhana, *Palestinian Citizens in an Ethnic Jewish State: Identities in Conflict* (New Haven: Yale, 1997); Majid Al Haj, *Education, Empowerment, and Control: The Case of the Arabs in Israel* (Albany: SUNY Press, 1995); Elie Rekhess, Binyamin Neuberger, and Boaz Shapira, eds., *Arab Politics in Israel at a Crossroads* (Tel Aviv: Proceedings of a Conference Held at Tel Aviv University, October 1994); Jacob Landau, *Arabs in Israel: A Political Study* (London: Oxford University Press, 1992).

5. For a useful discussion of similarities between Judaism and Islam with respect to issues of secularism, see William Galston, "Jews, Muslims, and the Prospects for Pluralism," *Daedalus* 132 (Summer 2003): 73–77. Galston has noted, "Acceptance of pluralism comes more easily to religions that emphasize inner conviction. . . . By contrast, religions that take the form of law, as do traditional forms [and interpretations] of Judaism and Islam, are forced to take seriously the content of public law" (73–74).

6. See, for example, Asher Arian and Michal Shamir, eds., *The Elections in Israel: 1999* (Albany: State University of New York Press, 2002); Asher Arian and Michal Shamir, eds., *The Elections in Israel: 1996* (Albany: State University of New York Press, 1999). See also Asher Arian and Michal Shamir, eds., *The Elections in Israel: 2003* (New Brunswick and Jerusalem: Transaction Books and Israel Democracy Institute, 2004).

7. Had the item asking about Arab political demonstrations been used instead, the demographic profile of those who express secular values would have been almost identical.

8. Mehran Tamadanfar, "Islamism in Contemporary Arab Politics," in *Religion and Politics in Comparative Perspective*, ed. Ted Jelen and Clyde Wilcox (Cambridge: Cambridge University Press, 2002), 141. Readers seeking a fuller exposition of the relationship between Islam and politics are directed to Dale Eickelman and James Piscatori, *Muslim Politics* (Princeton: Princeton

University Press, 1996); and John Esposito, *Islam: The Straight Path* (Oxford: Oxford University Press, 1997).

9. R. Stephen Humphreys, *Between Memory and Desire: The Middle East in a Troubled Age* (Berkeley: University of California Press, 1999), 131–132.

10. See, for example, Mark Tessler, "The Origins of Popular Support for Islamist Movements: A Political Economy Analysis," in *Islam, Democracy, and the State in North Africa*, ed. John Entelis (Bloomington: Indiana University Press, 1997); and Jodi Nachtwey and Mark Tessler, "Explaining Women's Support for Political Islam: Contributions from Feminist Theory," in *Area Studies and Social Science: Strategies for Understanding Middle East Politics*, ed. Mark Tessler, Jodi Nachtwey, and Anne Banda (Bloomington: Indiana University Press, 1999). The finding that support for political Islam in Arab countries is often motivated by temporal concerns rather than the desire for an Islamic state is to some degree similar to the situation in Israel among Shas supporters who are not ultra-orthodox.

12

The Construction of Secular and Religious in Modern Hebrew Literature

SHACHAR PINSKER

How to define, or even recognize, modern Jewish literature is one of the most vexing and contested questions that faces a scholar in this field.[1] Yet naturally, and almost automatically, nearly everyone seems to assume that everything written in Hebrew over the last two centuries is Jewish, regardless of its content.[2] This tendency apparently derives from the view that modern Hebrew literature epitomizes secular national Jewish culture. In fact, many Zionist writers and thinkers argue that modern Hebrew literature is the single most important manifestation of Jewish *secular* culture that stretches continuously from its origins in the nineteenth century to contemporary Israel.[3]

The problematic term here may be *secular*. While scholars and critics freely use the terms *secular* and *religious*, it is far from clear how they go about placing any given Hebrew literary text in either category. One would be hard-pressed to define a given text as secular or religious according to its formal literary characteristics. What, after all, makes a poem, a story, or a novel religious or secular? Does a religious motif or traditional Jewish language cease to be of religious significance at the moment it is used in a modern form, such as the novel?

If *secular* and *religious* cannot qualify as formal or purely literary categories, perhaps then these are categories of representation in which a secular or religious literary text represents socially and politically distinct groups. If so, are these stable categories? Do they change in different contexts, times, and locations? Are secular literary texts written (presumably in Hebrew) in Israel similar in any way to secular Jewish literature written in other languages around the world? Did the meaning of these categories change from the nineteenth century to the beginning of the twenty-first century? How did the changing sociopolitical environment in Jewish and Israeli society affect the possibility that modern Hebrew literature could be the scaffolding of a secular Jewish culture, a Hebrew literature that is "the watchman of the house of Israel"?

Considering the central position of modern Hebrew literature in any conception of Jewish secular culture, these problems are crucial to the larger question of defining secularism, or more specifically, "Jewish secularism." Is this "Jewish secularism" merely a negation of religion, or is it a coherent system of beliefs, values, and practices that is secular, yet Jewish?

These are difficult questions to answer, mainly because there is hardly agreement on the meaning of the terms *religious* and *secular* in general, let alone what we might consider a religious or secular poem or novel. The problem seems to be especially acute in the case of Hebrew, the "holy tongue." In a letter to Franz Rosenzweig, Gershom Scholem wrote, "The secularization of the [Hebrew] language is only a figure of speech, no more than a slogan. It is impossible to empty the words that are filled to the point of bursting with meaning, save at the expense of the language itself."[4] In contrast, Chaim Nachman Bialik wrote, "Let us not be afraid to see Agadah as a secular literature like every other world literature. Perhaps by doing so, we will enable Agadah to enter into a sphere of a different sanctity, the sanctity of a national creation."[5] These quotations demonstrate two seemingly opposing views: one affirms and celebrates the transformation of traditional Jewish texts into a modern, national, and secular culture; the other questions the very possibility of the secularization of Hebrew. The fact that these seemingly conflicting views are expressed by two major writers and intellectuals who saw themselves as Zionists, and the fact that they both use theological imagery in their utterances, give important testimony to the complexity of these matters.

The history of modern Hebrew literature from the end of the eighteenth century to contemporary Israel provides many fascinating examples of literary texts and critical debates that touch upon these questions—from the literature of the *Haskalah* in Germany and Eastern Europe, to the literature of the *tehiya* (revival) period at the turn of the twentieth century, through the literature created in Israel immediately after its establishment, and the recent resurgence of *Shira Emunit* (best translated as "faith poetry" or "poetry of religiosity") in the last decade in Israel. In this chapter, I focus on what might be the most complex test case to examine these issues—the attempts by Bialik, Berdichevsky, and others at the turn of the twentieth century to transform rabbinic and Midrashic texts into secular modern Jewish texts. The ambiguities and internal struggles that characterized these creative endeavors became the hallmark of modern Hebrew culture. They shaped and prefigured the ruptures that surfaced in the early 1950s and that have erupted again in recent years in a totally different political and sociocultural context.

The Early Modern Revival of Hebrew Literature: Bialik and Berdichevsky

Some of the main figures of early modern Hebrew literature in Eastern Europe were adherents of what was called "cultural Zionism," the movement whose most well-known spokesman was Ahad-Ha'am. These writers and intellectuals sought to transform Judaism's traditional symbols, values, and beliefs into a modern, national, and essentially secular system. This is especially important in the context of the tehiya, the "revival" of Hebrew language and literature that accompanied the birth of the Jewish national movement. Perhaps because traditional Jewish culture in Eastern Europe was defined by its relation to religious texts,[6] the transformation was supposed to happen first in the textual domain. This transformation was to occur as part of the creation of original Hebrew poetry, prose, and essays, as well as in the anthological and editorial projects (like *Sefer Ha'agadah* and *Tzfunot va' agadot*), which sought to gather and rework rabbinic texts into a form befitting a modern nation. These Zionist writers believed that this transformation required nothing less than a total revolution. The revolution had to be double: a transformation of religious texts into secular literature, and then a transformation of secular literature back into the "sacred realm" of the national, where it would take on the aura of being the product of the nation's collective genius.

This is one of the most important components of what Benjamin Harshav described as "the modern Jewish revolution." Harshav defined this revolution, which began in the 1880s and lasted for several decades, as a multidirectional, centrifugal movement away from an old and into a new existence, a move of immigration and assimilation that negated the old nation and created a new Jewish secular nation in its place. The concept of "Jew" itself shifted. It ceased to be a religious category and came to designate either a culture and nation, or a racial-ethnic affiliation. This revolution was, according to Harshav, based on the force of negation ("not here, not like now, not as we are"), as well as on the positive force of creating a new modern "cultural cluster" of ideology, literature, and social network that redefined the very notion of being Jewish.[7]

The main figures in the revival of Hebrew culture—Bialik, Ahad-Ha'am, Berdichevsky, and Brenner—all attempted in their own, often conflicting ways to redefine the notion of Jewishness and to transform the religious system of values, beliefs, and canonical texts into a secular-national one. The producers and consumers of Hebrew literature from the 1880s until at least the 1930s did not come from the secular Jewish intelligentsia or the circle of the Maskilim. The Hebrew literary community of writers, readers, editors, and critics were almost exclusively drawn from a reservoir of young people who had followed very similar paths: childhood schooling in the traditional *heder*, further studies as adolescents in a yeshiva, and exposure to *Haskalah* through reading Hebrew and Yiddish literature.[8] Even the most committed Zionists among them took this path, and were only later influenced by Jewish nationalism and by the various strands of Zionism.[9]

The Hebrew poet Chaim Nachman Bialik is probably the single most important figure in this literary and intellectual movement. Bialik shared with Ahad-Ha'am and many of his contemporaries a concern that if the primal spiritual sensibilities of the Jews were not respected, the new Hebrew culture would stray from its goal. To secure what Bialik called "the spirit of the nation," he sought to establish a new canon, one that replaced the rabbinic curriculum of sacred texts while maintaining some kind of continuity with it. Bialik, deeply influenced by nineteenth-century European romanticism and nationalism, believed that the Hebrew renaissance must be firmly rooted in works of the past that embodied "the holy spirit of the nation." He maintained that Hebrew writers and readers no longer had ready access to this literature because it was "buried" in the "graveyards" of rabbinic legalism and the convoluted rabbinic commentaries and homilies. Thus, Bialik insisted that a radical process of selection must be made: "In order to build a new synagogue the old one must be destroyed."[10]

Bialik's notion of canonization (*hatima ve-genizah*) is essentially linked to his notion of ingathering (*kinus*). Kinus was the name that Bialik and other cultural Zionists gave the enterprise of ingathering the most important works of the Jewish past that appeared destined to be forgotten in the modern world.[11] The works were to be preserved by collecting them into modern anthologies in a new time and a new place (Palestine). For Bialik, this mission was urgent, and he seemed at times very confident that the practitioners of Zionist Hebrew culture could create a "new Talmud" to replace the old one.[12] Bialik devoted a remarkable amount of attention and labor to this task, editing several ambitious anthologies of ancient and medieval Jewish texts. The most impressive and well known of these projects is *Sefer HaAgadah*, which he undertook together with Y. H. Ravnitzki from 1906 to 1910.

In this monumental work, Bialik sought to transform what he described as the "messy," indiscernible Agadic material "buried" in the Babylonian and Palestinian Talmuds and in various Midrashic works into a crystallized "folk literature of the Jews," a well-structured monument that would express "the spirit of the Nation."[13] Agadah, the nonlegal part of rabbinic literature, has always been part of the traditional study of the Talmud and Midrash, but it was never the center of attention. Bialik wanted to change this by focusing on Agadah, or what he considered the "folk" element in rabbinic literature. The romantic and national elements in Bialik's perspective clearly constituted his understanding of the rabbinic material. Bialik's most important and radical innovation was to regard these fragments of rabbinic texts as belles-lettres—a literature in the secular, modern sense. In his understanding, the Agadah was the Jewish people's belletristic work during the long period of Jewish history that followed the canonization of the Bible. Bialik was well aware of the radical nature of this claim. He argued time and again that to recognize the aesthetic and literary qualities of Agadah, it had to be "redeemed" from the religious, studious atmosphere of the traditional house of study, heder and yeshiva. "There is a need to redeem the Agadah from its traditional limited domain and open it to the public domain of secular belletristic literature."[14]

As Midrash scholars such as Yosef Heineman, Efraim Urbach, and David Stern have shown, selection and rearrangement of Agadic material came at a price.[15] Bialik was troubled by many elements of the Agadah as it had been preserved for centuries in the Talmuds and various collections of Midrash. He was disturbed by the fragmentation of Agadah and by the fact that the Talmud and Midrash contain no large-scale epic narratives. In Bialik's assessment, when compared with Homeric epic, the Agadah in his time was nothing but "crumbs, a jumble of broken stones and ruins." However, without giving much historical or philological evidence to support his view, Bialik seemed to believe that in the distant past, the Agadah was more epic in nature, and the process of fragmentation occurred due to the nature of its dissemination and the corruption of its materials. Bialik strove to correct this "historical accident," not by philological and academic study, but by what can be called "a creative restoration." Crucial for Bialik was the new structural and compositional arrangement: "fragments of stones, joined into layers, layers into walls, a complete fortress in which everything is arranged and installed in its proper place, restoring the ruined palace to its original glory."[16]

Another feature of the Agadah that disturbed Bialik's aesthetic and ideological sensibilities was that most of the Agadic texts are written not in Hebrew but in Aramaic. He and Ravnitzki translated all Aramaic texts into a homogeneous, synthetic Hebrew of the type being used in modern Hebrew fiction of their time. Even more significantly, Bialik and Ravnitzki edited and compiled the narratives so as to divorce them from their original homiletical and exegetical setting. Instead they created a new arrangement of the material, which is historical, thematic, and literary. This new arrangement produced unity and narrative closure, but this form was entirely their own creation, aimed at molding Agadah into something like their idea of literature.

Anyone who reads Agadah in its original context in the Talmud and Midrash knows that, to a large extent, the essence of this kind of literature is its relation to the biblical text on which it comments. Most of the Agadah's narratives and dicta were not related for their own sake but rather as interpretation of the Bible. Bialik thought that, "Agadah has a bad tendency . . . to employ the Biblical text as a proof-text." He maintained that "the verse is a distraction; it stands between us and the Agadah."[17]

There are many Agadot that were part of homilies (whether real sermons or literary homilies). Moreover, the bulk of Agadah in the Talmud appears in the context of debates and discussions that are legal in nature. The Agadic narratives often comment upon a legal assertion, either supporting or disputing it. All these elements—the essence of rabbinic literature—invoked for Bialik the stifling environment of the yeshiva or Beit Midrash (House of Study):

> I would like to remove from the hearts of our people the notion that Agadah is a specific phenomenon within the parochial context of the Beit-Midrash that has nothing to do with literature as such. I would say that there is an urgent need to secularize Agadah and remove it from the specific context and atmosphere, so it can be born into the world, society and our modern literature not just as a religious literature. The problem is in the fact that the Agadah is within the legal, halachic texts, annexed to it like an appendix. The other reason for our doubts about the creative merit and literary value of the Agadah is its relationship with the Biblical verse. The Biblical verse interrupts. . . . There is a need to extract that verse from the Agadah the way one takes a bone out of one's throat.[18]

Despite the dramatic changes he made in this literary form, Bialik did not seem to recognize that something was being lost. On the contrary, he felt that he and Ravnitzki were not only faithful to Agadah, but were actually restoring to it something of its original glory.[19]

More or less contemporary with Bialik's project, another prominent Hebrew prose writer and intellectual, M. Y. Berdichevsky, was engaged in a similar yet different task of collecting rabbinic and Agadic materials. During his lifetime, Berdichevsky collected and published (in Hebrew and in German) several such anthologies, such as *MeOtsar Ha'Agadah* (1913) and *MiMekor Yisrael* (posthumously published in 1939).

The main difference between the two compilers was that Berdichevsky was mainly interested in recovering Agadah as folklore and limited himself to what he considered folkloric material. Berdichevsky understood folklore in the same way as most early-twentieth-century intellectuals and scholars (especially in Central Europe and Germany, where he obtained his doctorate). The result was that Berdichevsky included in his anthologies a large amount of material from texts other than the Talmud, Midrash, or other canonical Jewish texts: some from late antiquity, others from the twelfth through sixteenth centuries. On the other hand, Berdichevsky did not include in his anthologies Talmudic and Midrashic materials that did not fall into the folkloric niche. Although Bialik also wanted to recover Agadah as folkloric literature, he used the term *folklore* in a very different way, because for him, folklore was the literary essence of what the spirit of the nation created.[20]

In spite of these important differences, Berdichevsky's literary and intellectual project was, like Bialik's, driven by his romantic (or neo-romantic) and national quest. He wished to explore what he perceived as the psychological and social forces that generated the "national spirit," before it became subjugated by the pressures of normative religious Judaism. Berdichevsky viewed Jewish society and thought not as a cohesive, integrated social and philosophical system, but rather as an arena for conflicting forces and tendencies. He rejected what he considered to be the religious synthesis that the rabbis constructed and sanctioned (and this caused a bitter dispute with Ahad-Ha'am and his unified system of cultural Zionism). This diffusing rather than unifying approach also marked his conception of the anthologies. In his introduction to the collection *MeOtsar Ha'Agadah*, Berdichevsky wrote that his intention was to create "not a whole book, which was made according to one mold or one overarching design is given here to the readers, but a certain collection of Agadot, that were chosen and written in different times and different contexts. . . . The redactor did not have a specific goal to create a unified book of Agadah. . . . The Hebrews did not have one single literature, with one spirit that was given by one Shepherd, but a variety of fragments of literature, that were born and developed in different periods, under different spiritual conditions."[21]

Where Bialik was striving to achieve unity and harmony in his editing, Berdichevsky was seeking diversity and heterogeneity. And yet, there is something similar in their rebellious quest for a modern secular-national conception of Jewishness that these new books would enable or even generate. Bialik, Berdichevsky, and others involved in *kinus* projects were well versed in the textual world of rabbinic and other traditional Jewish texts. They knew very well that they were making radical changes and creating something totally new. Nevertheless, they thought they were not inventing but preserving, not breaking but building, even restoring something that had been lost.

How can we explain this seemingly contradictory impulse? Bialik, Berdichevsky, and other cultural Zionists emphasized the overarching significance of the Hebrew language in the kinus project—the ingathering of Jewish traditional texts in new, modern, and secular forms. For Bialik, kinus was the act of rendering those works touched by "the spirit of the people" in Hebrew because the Hebrew language had for Bialik almost a mystical force. Therefore, the translation of Rabbinic and other works into the synthetic Hebrew that Abramovitz and other writers in this period were creating was not just a technical issue—making the texts more accessible—but one of the main goals. He believed that this act of translation would not only "nationalize" and "secularize" the texts, but paradoxically would also make them "sacred" in a new way and render their Jewishness manifest. Bialik and other Hebrew writers from his generation believed that speaking, reading, and, of course, writing Hebrew would bring the Jew, no matter how secular or assimilated into Western culture, in tune with Judaism. It is as if the very flow of the sacred language through the lips of the Jews assured that their creative and spiritual sensibilities would have a distinctly Jewish tonality and texture. One of the most important paradoxes in the creation of Hebrew secularism is the fact that Bialik, like many figures of his generation, was a confirmed secularist—yet he did not shy away from religious, even mystical, terminology.[22]

This can be seen very well in Bialik's term *Nusah*. Bialik used it as both a descriptive and prescriptive label for the synthetic style that his generation artificially created to produce flexible, realist fiction that was able to represent the world of East European Jewry in Hebrew. He first used it in 1910 in a well-known essay on Abramovitz.[23] For Bialik, the Nusah style was the perfect literary means for mimetic representation (or a desire to create such a mimetic representation) of the Jewish national collective.

Clearly, Bialik's new usage of "Nusah" plays on the traditional meaning of the term as a conventional melody for chanting prayers that anyone could follow and emulate, as well as the notion of Ashkenazi and Sefardi Nusah (the traditional order of prayers in the two major Jewish communities). Thus, Bialik understood the Nusah as a collective resource that could and should be adapted and transmitted. According to Bialik, Abramovitz "took, drop by drop, whatever he found in the treasure-house of the people's creative spirit and gave it back, and in a refined form, to the same treasure-house." In typically romantic fashion, Bialik saw the Nusah as expressing "the essence of the national genius," and Abramovitz as "the first national artist in our literature."[24]

Similar issues and problems I have identified in the creation of a modern-secular conception of Agaddah were also involved in the Nusah—both the concept itself and the actual literary style that it attempted to describe. Despite its stylistic richness, the modes of intertextuality in the Nusah style are limited and create mainly mimetic and ironic effects.[25] As a public intellectual committed to the ideology of cultural Zionism, Bialik could not see these problems, because for him, both the project of kinus and the creation of Nusah were tropes for the "ingathering" of the scattered Jewish people who could recapture their glory by being reassembled in their "palace"—the national territory.[26]

Creativity and Ambivalence in Bialik's Poetry

Bialik's tone in articulating the process of canonization and ingathering the Agadah as well in the creation of the Nusah style was confident, even triumphant. But in reading his poetry, one discovers deep doubts and painful, even tragic awareness of the impossibility of achieving what he advocated.[27] Over the course of his life, Bialik wrote several poems that touch on the subject of the Agadah, the Talmud, and the world of traditional yeshiva study: "El HaAgadah" (*To the Agadah*, 1882), "Al saf beit HaMidrash" (*On the Threshold of the House of Study*, 1904), and "Lifnei aron hasefarim" (*Before the Bookcase*, 1910).

"El HaAgadah" is one of the first poems that Bialik ever published. Bialik wrote two different versions, one entitled "Ha'agadah" and the other "El-Ha'agadah." The title of the second version (which was the one he chose to publish in all subsequent collections of his poetry) emphasizes the fact that the poem is written in the tradition and genre of the ode—a lyric poem written in the form of rhetorical evocation. In this case, the object of the apostrophe is the Talmud.

The poem begins with a description of a heavily conflicted subject-speaker. He is described as someone who just returned after a period of absence and alienation to the Talmud, which he studied in his youth. The return is not accidental—he returns to the sacred book because of his harsh experiences during his attempt to enter the world of European culture and enlightenment.

The speaker describes his attempt to escape from the "darkness" of Talmud study in the traditional yeshiva to a new place of "light," in which he moved like a mouse or a worm.[28] He endured blows and suffering and gave up, returning to the same "hole" from which he originally fled. He now hopes it will be a refuge: "there lived and found safety a worm."[29] The speaker opens a volume of Talmud, pores over the old, rustling pages, and tries to find there some comfort for his weary soul. He hopes to find solace not in the main legal part of the text, but rather in the "ancient, kind Agadot" that are scattered throughout.

The speaker's negative attitude toward the Talmud and its traditional study is manifest not only in its description as "a hole in ground" and "a crack in the rock," but also in the metaphor for the pages of the Talmud—*alim balim*, which can mean both "worn pages" and "withered leaves." According to this metaphor, the Talmud is like a plant that has not yet died, but which is wasted and dry.

The poem's two versions give different answers to the speaker's question: can he find revitalization and consolation in the pages of the lifeless Talmud and especially in the Agadah? The early version of the poem ("H'agadah"—the one that Bialik did not republish) gives a very pessimistic and doubtful answer. It ends with a feeling of disappointment and failure at what seems to be an undesirable, even forced, return of the speaker to the world of the house of study from which he fled to the domain of the secular, European enlightenment:

> You exist, and like headstones on graves
> You bear witness to the loss of our joy
> You bear witness to the loss of all that is holy and dear

That our enemies seized and robbed.
And I, the miserable, with head bowed to the ground
Will cry with the weeping of an owl in the ruins
I wail in my plaint until I am consumed by tears
I wail on the graves of the fathers.[30]

The second and more optimistic version suggests that although the consolation that the speaker finds in the Talmud and the Agadah will not come fully and immediately, it will surely arrive in the foreseeable future, and not just for the speaker as an individual, but also as a representative of the experience of an entire generation. Indeed, it is essential to understand that Bialik, even in his most intimate and personal poems, also represents a generation of young people who studied at heder and yeshiva and left them to find some kind of social and cultural renewal in the world of liberal Europe. Since the 1880s, a large part of this generation in Eastern Europe was totally disillusioned with the attempt to assimilate into a non-Jewish society and culture, which rejected the "enlightened" Jew just as it had previously rejected the "primitive" Jew. The traumatic realization that came in the early 1880s finds a clear expression in Bialik's poem, which reaches far beyond Bialik's own experience in Volozhin, Zhitomir, and Odessa.

As the poem progresses, the reader discovers that Bialik's speaker does not represent himself or even his generation. Rather, his individual story parallels a national historical narrative of the Jewish people. The speaker's present situation metonymically stands for the Jewish nation in the state of exile. In this scheme Bialik presents us with a grand unfolding historical narrative:

I had a harp too, and hung it on the willows
Of a stream where I once sat;
And I wept much weeping and in the rivers of my tears the harp I let go from
    my hand.
O harp of Yeshurun, sweetest of the songs of Israel,
This was the harp of Solomon and David; in you David saw God,
and Solomon in holiness Saw in you a dream of Shulamit.
And from then till now there is no king in Yeshurun
No king–no harp and no music.
My lyre is the sound of weeping,
My harp like a dove sighs on the riverbeds of Babylon.[31]

Building upon the familiar Psalm 137, Bialik recites the story of the tragic fall from the grand and glorious biblical days, which are associated with the poetry of King David and Solomon, to the lowly, limited writings of the rabbis of the Babylonian exile, where the Talmud was composed. In the narrative Bialik constructs in this poem, there is clearly a direct link between national and political sovereignty and the possibility of creating a genuine national literature and culture. The state of exile of the Jewish people does not allow the creation of either a national or personal literature. This was true in the Talmudic period and is equally true at the end of the nineteenth century. The attempt of the Jewish enlightenment to assimilate and participate in European culture failed. In 1882, the only partial solution Bialik's speaker puts forth is to use the Agadah as a sort of limited substitute. Particularly in lieu of a living national literature, the Agadah can serve as a linguistic and poetic source for creating poetry:

> And from then till now when I think sad thoughts
> The Agadah as a harp I raise up—
> In it I weep the lowliness of my people, in it I sing consolations—
> I play and I have relief.[32]

For Bialik, both the problem and its partial solution lie at all three levels: the personal, the poetic, and the national. Only by being a poet can the speaker find consolation in the lifeless Talmud, and only using the Talmud as a source for a new poetic expression conveys the sorrows of the nation that there can be personal and national regeneration. This poetic and ideological solution is the reason for the triumphal ending of the second version:

> I understand, finally, that though this people is worms
> It will yet cope with and bring down giants.

This defiant ending to the poem is not the conclusion of Bialik's struggle with these questions; rather it is the earliest expression of one of the main problems with which Bialik grappled his entire life. In 1894, Bialik returned to the topic of the Talmud and the traditional house of study in a poem entitled "On the Threshold of the House of Study." Like "To the Agadah," this poem is also an ode, but the differences between this and the earlier poem are striking. Instead of the ambivalent position of the speaker in the earlier poem, here the speaker puts forward a clear and certain poetic and ideological position. In this poem too, the house of study and the rabbinic texts are described as "ruins" without much hope of revival in even stronger terms than the earlier poem. The speaker constructs the house of study as an old institution of his lost youth. In a romantic manner, the speaker and the house of study of his youth mirror each other, and the destruction of the house of study is also the downfall of the poet. Therefore, he mourns both of them:

> Once more, my House of Study, with head downcast and bent,
> I tread your threshold, desolate like you.
> Shall I lament your ruin or mine,
> Or mourn the twain?[33]

Because of this total identification, in this poem the speaker does not bitterly accuse the house of study or the Talmud of being a lifeless entity, as he did in the earlier poem, nor does he attempt to find consolation in "the old ruins." He recognizes that there is neither good reason nor real ability to return to the religious traditions that the speaker abandoned. However, perhaps because of this realization, the speaker finds within himself the confidence that he can bring something from the "light" of modernity and enlightenment to cure and rebuild the ruins of religious traditions, by turning it into a secular modern Hebrew culture:

> The sanctuary of God will not collapse! I will yet build you and it will be built
> From the heaps of your dust I will restore your walls;
> Temples will yet crumble, as you crumbled
> On a day of great destruction, when towers fell,
> And in my healing of the destroyed Temple of God—
> I will widen its walls and tear open a window
> And the light will drive out the broad darkness of its shadow.[34]

One can easily connect this idea of restoration and optimistic mood about the future of Jewish culture in its modern national form with Bialik's notion of kinus. Indeed, a few years after writing this poem, Bialik began to contemplate the idea of devoting his own time and creative energies to this project of restoration and rebuilding. In the following decade, Bialik devoted many years to the project of *Sefer Ha'agadah*, and the book became a great success. It won critical acclaim and was something of a bestseller (in early-twentieth-century Hebrew terms). However, with his rare sense of self-criticism, in his poetry Bialik did not describe these efforts of renewal and restoration as great accomplishments.

In 1910, shortly after the publication of *Sefer Ha'agadah*, Bialik wrote and published one of his greatest and most ambitious poems, "In Front of the Bookcase." It is also one of the most autobiographical poems of a poet renowned for his ability to fuse the national and the personal, and to turn his own biography into a collective spiritual and emotional portrait. Like Bialik's entire poetic oeuvre, this poem extends from the personal, to the poetic and national.

However, against all expectations, Bialik did not celebrate the great achievement of the publication of his anthology. On the contrary, the celebratory mood was replaced by a ruthless sense of disappointment and failure. Bialik felt not only that the attempt to find personal happiness and consolation in the traditional Jewish books was mistaken and bound to fail, but also that it was wrong to project his own fantasies onto the books and the religious Jewish tradition they represented. These "aging, elderly" books always promised and could promise only one thing—the values and traditions of religious Judaism. Any effort to find anything else was totally irrelevant, especially the attempt to find in them the Nietzschean *liebesspruch* of life philosophy that Bialik and others projected onto them.

> I look, I see—and I do not recognize you, old folk,
> From within your letters no won't gaze
> Any longer to the depths of my soul opened eyes
> That stir in a forgotten grave in the distance . . .
> Has my eye dimmed or my ear grown faint?
> Or are you decay, you eternal dead
> With no survivor in the land of life . . .[35]

What, then, did Bialik come out with after working so intensely in "the grave-yards of the nation, and the ruins of the spirit?" According to the poem, he found nothing but the "dagger" and "dust" that those who engage in "burial" and in "archeological digs" find. In his own poetic account, Bialik attempted to revive Judaism as a living modern-secular culture, but he failed and accomplished some-thing akin to the scholars of *Wissenschaft des Judentums*, who embarked on a mis-sion of giving Judaism "a proper burial."

> And who knows,
> If when I go out again to the rule of night
> From digging in graves of people and ruins of spirit
> And nothing remains with me and nothing is saved
> Apart from this spade that cleaves to my hand
> And this ancient dust grooved in my fingers—
> If not poorer and emptier than I was
> To the glory of the night I'll not spread my hands . . .[36]

As Dan Miron and other scholars have demonstrated, this sense of failure was to a certain degree due to Bialik's sense that the more attention he gave to *Sefer Ha'agadah* and the entire project of kinus, the less he wrote poetry.[37] However, Bialik's writer's block does not sum up the larger issue with which Bialik struggled all of his life. The feeling of failure is to a large degree a result of conflicted ambiva-lence and a painful, tragic realization that it was impossible to transform the entire range of religious Jewish experience into a secular national Hebrew system.

The producers and consumers of Hebrew literature and culture in the forma-tive period of Zionism and the Hebrew revival came almost entirely from the yeshiva world, and almost all tried, later in life, to flee it. However, in order to pro-duce the desired new secular Hebrew culture, there was a need to go deeper and deeper into the religious system and its language. The transformation was never as successful or complete as they had hoped. Bialik himself realized this, and he gave this sense of simultaneous hope and disappointment, successes and failure, an astonishingly honest expression in his poetry. Writers like Berdichevsky and Brenner expressed similar tortuous and ambivalent attitudes in their prose fiction and in their essays.

Afterward, or Back to the Future

These inherent contradictions in the nature of modern Jewish national culture and the difficulty (perhaps impossibility) of creating a truly secular or "normal" litera-ture in Hebrew were recognized by critics such as Baruch Kurzweil, Dov Sadan, and Yonatan Ratosh, who were active in the Yishuv and the young state of Israel during the 1940s and 1950s.[38] In their judgment, with the establishment of the state and with the rise of a new generation of writers (known as the *Palmah* or the Sabra generation) who were born in Palestine and educated in the Hebrew secular system of the Labor Zionist movement, the transformation Bialik and others hoped for began to materialize. For sure, these critics had a different assessment of these developments. For Yonatan Ratosh (the poet, founder, and ideologue of a movement called the Young Hebrews, better known as the Canaanite movement) it was a sign of great success that signaled the beginning of a Hebrew literature that was separating itself from its Jewish sources and traditions.[39] The critic Baruch Kurzweil identified the same developments, but he saw them as a colossal failure that must lead Hebrew literature and culture to an artistic and spiritual dead end.[40] Dov Sadan, another major critic and a prominent professor of Yiddish and Hebrew literature at the Hebrew University, found in these developments a reason for hope for the future. Since Sadan was a committed Zionist, he viewed the establishment of the state of Israel as a miraculous event. But he also believed that secular nationalism, which had been necessary for the fulfillment of the Zionist vision, would decline quickly without a renewed encounter with traditional Jewish religious experience. He was convinced that a reconciliation of the two must happen and would happen very quickly.[41]

In his discussion of Zionist hopes and Israeli realities, Dan Miron, one of the most important contemporary Israeli scholars of Hebrew literature, claims that Sadan, Kurzweil, and Ratosh were wrong in their predictions about the development of Israeli literature. Miron claims that Kurzweil's ideology prevented him from seeing some of the most interesting writers and texts in Isreali literature of the 1960s and 1970s. At the same time, Miron has asserted, the overwhelming majority of Israeli writers did not follow Ratosh's "Canaanite" program, and the "Semitic space" he envisioned did not become the main cultural influence on Israeli literature. According to Miron, Israeli literature also exposed Sadan's vision of reconciliation with tradition as wishful thinking. Instead, he claimed:

> Israeli literature became the vanguard of the battle against the reconciliation that Sadan predicted [between secularism and Jewish religious tradition]. It is no doubt in a defensive position, but if it fails in this battle, and reconciliation in its contemporary Israeli version takes over our cultural life, it is probable that Hebrew literature, instead of reaching a synthesis of the best of the past and the present, will decline and maybe even disappear. . . . In the face of the neo-Judaic ascendance, which inevitably nowadays goes hand in hand with extreme right-wing politics, most Israeli writers see not a resurrected father, but a frightening hybrid—an enemy whose cultural victory would be the downfall of everything for which they stand.[42]

Instead of the reconcilation that Sadan envisioned, Miron and many other Israeli writers and critics of his generation spoke of a secular-religious culture war, with Hebrew literature as a key player on the battleground. It should be clear what side Hebrew literature was on, in Miron's view. Moreover, Miron is candid about his identification of religion (or "neo-Judaism," in his words) with nationalistic right-wing politics, which is of course opposed to "enlightened," "moderate," left-wing secular culture.

Is this an accurate picture of Hebrew literature in Israel? Is Miron right about the failure of Kurzweil, Ratosh, and Sadan to predict the future developments in

Israeli literature? Is Hebrew literature really the secular "vanguard" in the culture war? Although these kind of assessments are necessarily based on generalizations (to which there are always some exceptions), Miron's analysis is indeed quite accurate for the literature that was produced in Israel in the 1940s, 1950s, and even most of the 1960s and 1970s. In spite of its variety and achievements, this literature is surprisingly homogeneous. The overwhelming majority of the writers in this period were products of secular socialist Zionism. Their stories and novels were not only usually set in a kibbutz, the army, or in youth movements, but these settings were also their main themes. The language aspired to capture the colloquial speech of young people in these institutions. This style precluded the intertextual dialogue with rabbinic literature and other traditional Jewish texts that typifies Hebrew fiction and poetry of the early twentieth century, and it did not leave much room for religious themes or concerns.

Yet one can hardly describe Hebrew literature of the 1980s, or especially the 1990s, without noting religious themes and concerns. Clearly, contemporary writers have shattered the facade of what was seen as a "monolithic" Israeli culture. Recent Israeli literature can be described as a battle of conflicting narratives—narratives of national, religious, gender, and ethnic identity—all struggling to make themselves heard in their own voices and in their own ways. Over the past decades there has been an explosion of writing by and about Mizrahi Jews, Holocaust survivors, Arabs, religious Jews, and other groups that together bear witness to the diversity of Israeli society and culture.

Many sociologists and other social scientists who study the changing face of Israeli society observe that what is defined as "Israel's hegemonic secular Ashkenazi labor Zionist culture" has waned, and a different social and cultural order is in formation. A new system of subcultures and countercultures are now engaged in an escalating culture war with the fading but still-powerful secular Zionist culture, which is rapidly losing its hegemonic position. Some critics and scholars, such as sociologist Baruch Kimmerling, have attributed this crisis to the decline of the hegemonic secular-Zionist Ashkenazi cultural and social elite, while others, like Charles Liebman, have argued that it is the product of the polarization of Israeli politics, and of Israeli society's metaphysical and spiritual view of the world. Still others, such as Eliezer Schweid, believe the crisis signals the decline of a secular movement that has nearly exhausted its cultural resources.[43]

It is quite clear that in recent years, parallel with the process of rapid Westernization (sometimes referred to as "Americanization") of Israeli society, the automatic identification of Israeli culture (even high culture) with secular-national culture might be eroding with the collapse of the political and cultural hegemony of the Ashkenazi-secular elite group. What replaces this model of Israeli literature and culture? Everything in the recent developments and debates about religious and secular elements in Israeli literature indicates that these have become, for better or worse, categories of representation in which "religious," "secular," and also "traditional" (*masorti*) represent distinct social and political groups. The founders of Hebrew literature would certainly not be at ease with this notion of Hebrew literature and culture, but this seems to be the meaning of these categories in recent years in the political, social, and even literary systems.

The question that remains unanswered is this: Which narrative of cultural change really describes these shifts? On one hand, there is a narrative of an ever-growing and expanding multicultural Israeli identity that now embraces all the groups not represented in the Zionist ideal of the melting pot (Arabs, women, and orthodox and traditional Jews from European as well as Arab countries). On the other hand, an alternative narrative describes an escalating cultural war between these conflicting subcultures or countercultures. Surprisingly—at least for those who identify revolution with innovation—these countercultures are not necessarily based on new and radical ideas, rituals, or practices. In fact, most of them are not new at all. They are the current incarnations of streams of thought and literature that have been part of Zionism and Hebrew culture since its inception. Perhaps what we are seeing is a new and quite unexpected return to the questions and concerns that preoccupied modern Hebrew literature and culture at its birth.

Nothing illustrates this shift and these unresolved questions more than the new phenomenon of *Shira Emunit*—religious poetry or faith poetry—that has emerged in Israel over the last two decades. Poets of faith, among them Admiel Kosman, Yonadav Kaplun, and Miron Issakson, identify themselves or are identified by others as religious. This wave of religious poetry sought to create a poetic expression based on religiosity and an intense dialogue with traditional Jewish texts, which some critics labeled as "Midrashic poetry."[44]

Two different but interrelated developments have enabled the rise and prominence of religious poetry in Israeli literature during the last two decades. One is the crisis in poetry in Israel since the late 1970s, during which there was a notable decline in the status of poetry, partly due to an absence of a leading poet (or group of poets) such as Alterman, Shlonsky, Zach, and, Amichai. The other element is the fragmentation of the cultural and social environment. These two elements seem to parallel each other, and the result is that Israeli literature is now divided into many distinct and minor poetic voices without a major and defined center.

Likewise, there seem to be two contrasting views of what can be read as *Shira Emunit*. On one hand, there is a tendency to ignore the model of identity politics of religious and secular and to include much of Hebrew and Israeli literature under the rubric of more abstract religiosity (or its opposite, abstract secularism). In such a view, Admiel Kosman, Miron Issakson, and their colleagues carry on the tradition of Bialik, Berdichevsky, Amichai, Appelfeld, Oz, Zach, Rabikovitz, and others. On the other hand, there is the opposite tendency to classify the poetry as religious and secular based on the discourse and politics of identity and difference. According to this view, once the hegemony of secular-national Israeli culture was challenged, the seculars became only one of many groups, and the elite secular culture cannot be seen as defining an Israeli culture common to all Israelis or even Israeli Jews.[45]

Finally, *Shira Emunit* seems to be defined by its critics and observers in two potentially different ways, which also allow for different notions of secularity. The first notion of religiosity is the engagement of an all-purpose spiritualist sensibility, which is not localized in any specific cultural milieu. The yearning for the divine, for faith, wonder, an encounter with the mystery of life, the sense of something greater than oneself, a sense of humbleness that can be associated with the religious experience (or at least with some aspects of it) are all values and sensibilities that are usually not associated with a secular worldview. A secular ethos is one that emphasizes self-deficiency, rationalism, and so on. However, this kind of religiosity can be regarded as lacking any specifically Jewish content, despite its use of Hebrew language and references to Jewish texts.

The other notion of religiosity in Hebrew literature is based on a specific engagement with (or disengagement from) traditional Jewish life as defined mainly by a relation to traditional Jewish texts and symbols.[46] Such an encounter, in the case of *Shira Emunit*, is presumably faith-based—that is, invested with recognizably Jewish approaches to the metaphysical. However, this assumption is not automatic or self-explanatory, since there are many literary texts that are based on intense dialogue with traditional Jewish texts and symbols, and yet they are not always understood as religious by the writers, readers, and others who participate in what can be called "the Hebrew literary community," or the "Hebrew literary republic."[47] This is one of the main conceptual difficulties as well as the reason for countless recent debates about the issue of the religiosity and secularity of Hebrew literature.

In historical perspective, few people will question the fact that the emergence of modern Hebrew literature presupposed a rejection of many normative Jewish beliefs. The cultural moment that lies at the heart of modern Hebrew literature is a complex experience in which negation and positive creativity are closely interwined. In many crucial moments in its history, modern Hebrew literature drew its creative force from the tradition against which it was revolting.[48] Paradoxically, if there are any characteristics that are prototypical of Hebrew (and perhaps also of Jewish) secularism, it is the existence of self-doubt about its own validity and achievements. The debates over the secularity and religiousness of Hebrew literature can be seen as a continual sign of its decline and weakness, as well as a healthy sign of a dialectic renewal and regeneration. After all, this is a culture whose icons are conflicted writers and intellectuals such as Bialik, Berdichevsky, Brenner, and Agnon. In this sense, current Isreali writers, both those who define themselves or who are defined as faith-based or religious, as well as some of those who are defined as secular, are true heirs of the complex and ever-changing cultural phenomena of modern Hebrew literature.

NOTES

1. Hanna Wirth Nesher, ed., *What Is Jewish Literature?* (Philadelphia: Jewish Publication Society, 1994); Ruth Wisse, *The Modern Jewish Canon* (New York: Free Press, 2000).

2. This is especially true in anthologies of "Modern Jewish Literature" in which Hebrew literature is represented. See, for example, Howard Schwartz, *Gates to the New City: A Treasury of Modern Jewish Tales* (New York: Avon, 1983). On the other hand, see the example of Anton Shammas, Sayed Kashua, Salman Matzlaha, and other Israeli Arab and Druze writers who write in Hebrew but are not Jewish, and who may or may not write about Jewish themes.

3. See Gershon Shaked, *Modern Hebrew Fiction* (Bloomington: Indiana University Press, 2000).

4. Gershom Scholem, "On Our Language," in *On the Possibility of Jewish Mysticism in Our Times* (Philadelphia: Jewish Publication Society, 2001).

5. Ch. N. Bialik, "Al-Ha'agadah," in *Dvarim She-Be'al Peh* (Tel-Aviv: Dvir, 1935), 71.

6. See Max Weinreich's description of traditional Jewish life in Ashkenaz as *Derech HaShas* (*The Way of the Talmud*). Max Weinreich, *The History of the Yiddish Language* (Chicago: University of Chicago Press, 1973).

7. Benjamin Harshav, *Language in Time of Revolution* (Berkeley: University of California Press, 1993), 17.

8. Fierberg, "Letter to Berdichevsky," in *Kol Kitve Fierberg* (Tel-Aviv: Dvir, 1940), 156–161.

9. Dan Miron, *Bodedim Be-Moadam* (Tel-Aviv: Am-Oved, 1987), 75–76.

10. Bialik, "Hasefer Haivri," in *Bialik, Divrei Sifrut* (Tel-Aviv: Dvir, 1965), 29. This is a direct reference to Nietzsche's dictum: "In order to build a temple one must destroy another one." See Azan Yadin, "A Web of Chaos: Bialik and Nietzsche on Language, Truth, and the Death of God," *Prooftexts* 21 (Spring 2001): 179–203.

11. See Israel Bartal, "The Ingathering of Traditions: Zionism's Anthology Projects," *Prooftexts* 17 (January 1997): 77–93.

12. Bialik, "Hasefer Haivri." See Paul Mendes-Flohr, "Cultural Zionism's Image of the Educated Jew: Reflections on Creating a Secular Jewish Culture," *Modern Judaism* 18 (October 1998): 227–239; Eliezer Schweid, *Hayahadut ve-hatarbut hahilonit* (Tel-Aviv: Hakibutz Hameuachad, 1981).

13. Ch. N. Bialik, "Hakdama," in *Sefer Ha'agada* (Tel-Aviv: Dvir, 1966); Ch. N. Bialik, "Lekinusa shel ha'agadda," in *Kol Kitvei Bialik* (Tel-Aviv: Dvir, 1953), 220–222.

14. Ch. N. Bialik, "The study of the Agadah," in *Dvarim sheBea-al Peh*.

15. Yosef Heineman, "Al darko shek Bialik be'agdat hazal," *Molad* 17 (1959): 266–274; E. E. Urbach, "Bialik ve-agadat hazal," *Molad* 31 (1974): 82–83; David Stern, introduction to *The Book of Legends* (New York: Schocken, 1992); Mark Kiel, "*Sefer ha'agadda:* Creating a Classic Anthology for the People and by the People," *Prooftexts* 17 (May 1997): 177–197.

16. Bialik, "Lekinusa shel ha'agadda," 221.

17. Bialik, "Al-Ha'agadah," 42.

18. Ibid.

19. Bialik, "Lekinusa shel ha'agada," 222.

20. Dan Ben Amos, introduction to *Mimkor Israel* (Bloomington: Indiana University Press, 1976); Zipora Kagan, "Homo Anthologicus: Micha Joseph Berdyczewski and the Anthological Genre," *Prooftexts* 19 (January 1999): 41–51.

21. M. Y. Berdichevsky, *Tsfunot va'agadot* (Tel-Aviv: Am-Oved, 1965), 11.

22. Mendes-Flohr, "Cultural Zionism's Image of the Educated Jew," 234.

23. Ch. N. Bialik, "Yotzer hanusah," in *Kol Kitvei Bialik*, 245–246.

24. Bialik, "Mendele veshloshet hakrahim," in *Kol Kitvei Bialik*, 242–245.

25. See Shachar Pinsker, "Old Wine in New Flasks: Rabbinic Intertexts and the Making of Modernist Hebrew Fiction" (Ph.D. diss., University of California, Berkeley, 2001).

26. Bialik, "Lekinusa shel ha'agada," 221.

27. Similar ambivalence can be found in Berdichevsky's writing. As oppose to his defiant call for "transvaluation of values" and his belief in the act of making religious Jewish texts into a folkloric literature, one can find in his stories and novels deep doubts and ambiguities. See, for example, "In Two Camps," "Beyond the River," and "The Red Heifer." For a comprehensive discussion of Berdichevsky's fiction and ideology, see Avner Holzman, *Hakarat panim: Masot al Micha Yosef Berdichevsky* (Tel-Aviv: Reshafim, 1993).

28. Here and elsewhere in his poetry, Bialik plays with the different meanings of the Hebrew word *Or* (light). On one hand, light is traditionally associated with the Torah and the activity of studying Torah. On the other hand, at least from the end of the eighteenth century—light is associated with the European (and Jewish) Enlightenment.

29. Dan Miron, ed., *Chaim Nahman Bialik: Shirim*, vol. 1 (Tel-Aviv: Dvir and the Katz Institute, 1983).

30. Ibid., 139.

31. Ibid., 137. English translation by Atar Hadari, *Songs from Bialik* (Syracuse, NY: Syracuse University Press, 2000), 15–16.

32. Bialik, *Songs from Bialik*, 137.

33. Ibid., 253.

34. Ibid., 255.

35. Ibid., 283.

36. Ibid., 283–284 (English translation in Hadari, *Songs from Bialik*, 27–28).

37. Dan Miron, *Boa Layla* (Tel-Aviv: Dvir, 1987), 183–185. For a similar perspective, see Alan Mintz, "*Sefer Ha'Agadah*: Triumph or Tragedy?" in *History and Literature: New Readings of Jewish Texts in Honor of Arnold J. Band*, ed. William Cutter and David C. Jacobson (Providence: Brown Judaic Studies, 2002), 17–26. A different perspective on Bialik's ambivalence toward the Agadah and other Jewish religious-traditional texts examines the mixture of the romantic and decadent tendencies in his poetry. This perspective was best articulated in Hamutal Bar-Yosef, *Maga'im shel Decadence: Bialik, Berdichevsky, Brenner* (Be'er-Sheva: Ben-Gurion University Press, 1997), 106–129.

38. An extensive version of the discussion in this section can be found in Shachar Pinsker, "And Suddenly We Reached God"? The Construction of 'Secular' and 'Religious' in Israeli Literature," *Journal of Modern Jewish Studies* 5, no. 1 (2006): 21–40.

39. Yonatan Ratosh, *Sifrut Yehudit balashon haivrit* (Tel-Aviv: Hadar, 1982), 37–50.

40. Baruch Kurzweil, "On the possibility of Israeli Fiction," in *The Search for Israeli Literature*, ed. Zvi Luz and Yedidya Itzhaki (Ramat-Gan: Bar-Ilan University Press, 1982); Baruch Kurzweil, *Sifrutenu Hahadash: Hemshech o mahpecha* (Jerusalem and Tel-Aviv: Shocken, 1960), 11–146.

41. Dov Sadan, *Ben din leheshbon* (Tel-Aviv: Dvir, 1963).

42. Dan Miron, *Im lo tihye Yerushalayim* (Tel-Aviv: Hakkibutz Hameuhad, 1987), 139.

43. Baruch Kimmerling, *The Invention and Decline of Israeliness* (Berkeley: University of California Press, 2001); Charles Liebman and Elihu Katz, *The Jewishness of Israelis* (Albany: SUNY Press, 1997); Eliezer Schweid, *Likrat Tarbut Yehudit Modernit* (Tel-Aviv: Am-Oved, 1995), 293–314.

44. Hannan Hever, *Sifrut She-Nichtevet Mi-Kan* (Tel-Aviv: Yediot Aharonot, 1999), 134.

45. A recent Israeli political and secular phenomenon like the *Shinui* party, which defines itself as secular rather than mainstream Israeli, means that the secular has become one sector or subculture in Israeli society. For a discussion of this development, see Baruch Kimmerling, *Mehagrim, Mityashvim, Yelidim* (Tel-Aviv: Am-Oved, 2004), 353–360.

46. Leaving of religion is also religious in its quality and should be considered as such. Grappling with the loss of faith is indeed a religious wrestling, and the literature produced by Jewish writers who lost their faith should be considered religious literature, in spite of its secular context. See Kurzweil, *Sifrutenu Hahadash*; Alan Mintz, "*Banished from their Father's Table": Loss of Faith and Hebrew Autobiography* (Bloomington: Indiana University Press, 1989); Pinsker, "Old Wine in New Flasks."

47. The notion of the "Hebrew literary republic" is developed in Miron, *Boa Layla*, 9–19.

48. See Alan Mintz, "Hebrew Literature as a Source of Modern Thought," in *Translating Israel* (Syracuse: Syracuse University Press, 2001), 227–242.

PART IV

SECULAR JEWISHNESS IN THE DIASPORA TODAY

Probably the most secular Jewry in the world is in the Slavic areas of the former Soviet Union. Prevented by the authorities from learning about Judaism or practicing it easily for about seventy years, Soviet Jews developed a surprisingly strong sense of Jewish identity, abetted by the state's official identification of them as such. But it was an identity without cultural content. Using the largest surveys ever taken of Russian and Ukrainian Jewry, Zvi Gitelman explores what being Jewish means to Jews who do not practice Judaism. Now that official identification by nationality has been abolished in Russia and Ukraine, and none of the successor states to the USSR pursue anti-Semitic policies, will Jewish identity survive? What will be its content and how will its boundaries be drawn?

Turning to American Jewry, Calvin Goldscheider's provocative chapter challenges three widely held beliefs: American Jews' religious commitment is declining, their sense of ethnic identity is weakening, and their secular culture is disappearing. Goldscheider argues that what sustains the ethnic and religious continuity of American Jews are communal institutions and social and family networks. Institutions are able to construct new forms of Jewish cultural uniqueness that redefine the collective identity of Jews. Jewish values are the sources of continuity and are anchored in the structural underpinnings of communities. The family may be the most important of those institutions.

The most radical separation of Judaism from Jewishness is found in secular Judaism. There are several types of secular Judaism. Adam Chalom uses textual and sociological analysis to discuss secular humanist Judaism. Secular Judaism uses celebration and study, not prayer, to articulate a cultural-ethnic Jewishness. Chalom describes the types of people who are drawn to secular humanist Judaism and the ideological debates that take place in the movement.

13   *Jewish Identity and Secularism in Post-Soviet Russia and Ukraine*

ZVI GITELMAN

Being Jewish has meant different things at different times to different people. Reiterating the observation of Melville Herskovits, "no word, one may almost conclude, means more things to more people than does the word 'Jew'. . . . Of all human groupings, there is none wherein the problem of definition has proved to be more difficult than for the Jews."[1] Not only are the Jews difficult to define, using conventional terms for different types of groups, but, like many other groups they redefine themselves with some degree of regularity. Jews confound conventional social science wisdom in two ways: (1) they were probably a nation before print capitalism, pace Benedict Anderson, and before print;[2] (2) They don't fit the usual categories neatly: race, nation, ethnic group, religion. Both these exceptions are due to the antiquity of the Jews, with relatively modern categories not able to capture them easily. Academics especially need to be reminded that these categories are invented—or, to put it more fashionably, constructed. They do not exist in nature but are designed by humans to make sense of and bring order to social phenomena. Therefore, if a collectivity does not fit neatly into one or another category—if it cannot easily be put into the pigeonholes marked "race,"[3] "ethnic group," "nation" or "religion"—it is not the group that is problematic and lacking but the categories and the larger conceptual system of which they are a part.[4] Perhaps the difficulty in classifying Jews helps explain diminishing interest in them in academic research, where a holy trinity of race, gender, and ethnicity has become so popular. Probably a more important reason is the fact that in Western societies most Jews have moved into the mainstream, even the "establishment," and that, for some reason, makes them less interesting to sociologists, psychologists, historians, and those engaged in "cultural studies."

Nevertheless, there remains an urge to classify in order to understand.[5] That urge is no less strong among members of the group itself than among those who would analyze it. As Michael Meyer has noted, "Long before the word became fashionable among psychoanalysts and sociologists, Jews in the modern world were obsessed with the subject of *identity*. They were confronted by the problem that Jewishness seemed to fit none of the usual categories."[6] Perhaps this is because Jews emerged in the ancient Near East, where religion and ethnicity were not differentiated. When Jews were emancipated in eighteenth-century Western Europe, the distinction between these two categories began to be made and, for the first time, Jews could choose not to be Jewish or to be Jewish *and* something else. Jews have struggled ever since to define themselves and establish whether they are a race, religion, ethnic group, nation, or a cultural group. Are they a chosen people or humanity's misfortune? This has not been just an academic exercise, since identity has attitudinal and behavioral consequences. Perhaps that is why "few subjects arouse so much passion and misunderstanding as the identity and status of the Jewish people."[7]

Discussions about the nature of the Jews are directly relevant to the question of secular Jewishness, because if being Jewish means only practicing the religion known as Judaism, there can be no secular expression of Jewishness. On the other hand, if being Jewish means belonging to an ethnic group, "nationality," or "nation," religion may be irrelevant. But does being Jewish ethnically admit of being Christian, Muslim, or Hindu, etc., religiously? If not, and if Jewishness is a fused ethnoreligious concept, in which one must not be a practitioner of Judaism but cannot practice any other faith, can one element of the fusion exist without the other, not so much in an abstract logical sense but in a practical way? Can self-described Jews be part of a religious community only, as Reform Judaism asserted in the nineteenth century, or part of an ethnic or cultural community that has no religious component and yet is distinctly and recognizably Jewish?

One way to answer such questions is to engage in logical, abstract argumentation about categories and their contents. Another is an empirical path wherein one examines historically how Jews have defined themselves and acted as Jews. In this chapter, we follow the latter. For most of world history, Jewishness was expressed in religious modes and categories. In modern times, several modes of Jewishness were devised. The content of Jewishness was shifted from religion (Judaism) to language by Yiddishists and Hebraists, to territory by Zionists and some others, and to culture by still others. This was the outcome of secularization, a term debated almost as much as "Jewish." We take it to mean the separation of ideas, activities, or things and institutions from their religious meanings.[8] Secularization need not mean the abandonment of faith, though it can include it, but a process wherein religion no longer is the primary driving force of thinking and acting. Religion is not omnipresent in daily life but is either abandoned or compartmentalized to a greater or lesser extent. Judaism becomes relegated to specific places (synagogues, temples) and times (holidays) with clearly religious rituals rather than being a constant guide to life. Therefore, secular expressions of Jewishness can be conceived as attempts to rescue the feeling of being Jewish and the contents of Jewish cultures from its separation from Judaism, the religion. Secular, but not necessarily antireligious, alternatives to expressing Jewishness were proposed that did not depend on theistic beliefs. For example, the Yiddishist ideologue Chaim Zhitlovsky claimed that a "complete revolution . . . the secularization of Jewish national and cultural life," had occurred and had been made possible by the substitution of Yiddish language and culture for religion. "The great significance of this Yiddish culture sphere is that it has succeeded in building a 'spiritual-national home,' purely secular, which can embrace Jews throughout the world." (Whether Zhitlovsky seriously thought that Sephardic Jews would adopt Yiddish, or whether he simply ignored their existence, is not clear, but telling.) For Zhitlovsky, Yiddish had become the content of Jewishness: "The Yiddish language form becomes for us a content of great weight, a fundamental."[9] Thus, for the first time, language was identified as the "distinctive characteristic" or "epitome of peoplehood" of the Jews. As it turned out, Yiddish was overwhelmed by socially more powerful languages in the Americas, Western Europe, and South Africa, and was being challenged by local languages in Eastern Europe, but then it was literally dealt a death blow during the Shoah.

During those years of mass murder, most of the adherents of secularist expressions of Jewishness were killed, and their ideologies mostly went with them. In Western Europe and North America, though not in Latin America, Jewish ethnicity was expressed mostly in religious forms, and it is not always easy to distinguish form from content. However, in the eastern part of Europe one may still find the largest concentration of self-conscious Jews, outside of Israel, who are not consistent and committed practitioners of Judaism but who have surprisingly strong Jewish feelings or awareness of being Jewish. Jews in Russia and Ukraine today constitute an unusual Jewish collectivity. If ethnicity consists of content and boundaries,[10] then the ethnicity of Soviet Jews was defined since the 1930s much more by boundaries than by content. Neither language, nor religion, nor dress, nor foods, nor territory (despite the creation of the Jewish Autonomous Oblast' in Birobidzhan) marked them off from other Soviet citizens. Rather, it was state-imposed identity and social perceptions. Despite the long-standing denial by Vladimir Lenin and Joseph Stalin that Jews are a nation, in 1918 for reasons that are still unclear, the Soviet government classified Jews as a *natsional'nost'* or ethnic group, one of well over a hundred such groups. After 1932 all urban residents had to carry an internal passport in which one's official "nationality" was recorded on the fifth line, which became notorious as the *piataya grafa*, because it could serve to make distinctions, often invidious, among individuals and peoples. Anyone who had two Jewish parents was classified as a Jew, irrespective of his or her subjective feelings of belonging, language, residence, religion, or desires. The very strong urge not only to acculturate (that is, to drop Jewish culture and acquire Russian or other cultures), but also to assimilate (that is, to change one's very identity from Jewish to Russian) was blocked by the state-imposed category of "Jewish"—this by a state committed to Marx's vision of a world without nations, to Lenin's notion of *sliianie*, or fusion of nationalities, and to the abolition of ethnicity as a bourgeois construct used to divide the working class. One of the many ironies of Soviet Jewish history is that the Soviet state preserved the Jewish identity of millions. This was complemented by popular perceptions and anti-Semitism, so that even thoroughly acculturated Jews could not assimilate.

At the same time as the *boundary* between Jews and others was maintained, and even strengthened, the *content* of Jewishness was being emptied. Official attacks on Judaism, Hebrew, Zionism, and the traditional *shtetl* way of life of the

1920s eradicated much of the traditional small-town Jewish way of life. Beginning in the mid-1920s, but ending about a decade later, some made efforts to create a secular, socialist, Soviet culture based on a de-Hebraized Yiddish language, which was also purged, as much as possible, of religious ideas and even terminology. The Soviet Union became the only state in history to fully fund a network of over a thousand Yiddish elementary schools—to what extent they were also Jewish is arguable—along with newspapers, magazines, theaters, and scholarly research institutions that conveyed a secular, antireligious Yiddish culture. However, many Jews rejected this secular substitute for the Jewish culture they and their ancestors had known on two grounds: (1) for those still clinging to tradition, this was an ersatz and even inimical culture; (2) for those aspiring to upward vocational, political, and—as they saw it—cultural mobility, Yiddish was the culture of the outmoded, backward prescientific *shtetl*, whereas Russian culture was a world culture that in its Soviet form stood for science, technology, rationality, and progress.

Purposive programs of cultural and societal transformation were complemented by the consequences of rapid industrialization and urbanization and the mass migration of hundreds of thousands of Jews to places beyond the old Pale of Settlement. The social and cultural effects of this migration were not much different from those resulting from the transoceanic voyages of the relatives and friends of the Jews of the Russian Empire. Language, clothes, foods, mores, vocations were changed, and the traditional barrier against marriage with non-Jews was increasingly breached. By 1936, 42 percent of Jewish men and 37 percent of Jewish women in the Russian republic who married that year married non-Jews. In the old Pale areas of Ukraine and Belorussia, the percentages were much lower (15 percent in Ukraine for men and women; in Belorussia, 13 percent for men and 11 percent for women).[11] Paradoxically, the rise of intermarriage rates occurred at the same time as grassroots anti-Semitism became more visible.

Following World War II, state-sponsored anti-Semitism reached its peak, and the remnants of Soviet Yiddish culture were destroyed. A sense of Jewishness was now maintained almost exclusively by boundaries, not cultural content, though there were still subtle cultural markers that set Jews off from others, such as urbanity, aspirations for higher education, close families, more amicable relations between spouses, and perhaps lower levels of alcoholism.

After the Soviet Union

Though Nikita Khrushchev and his successors ameliorated the position of the Jews somewhat, by the time Mikhail Gorbachev initiated his policy of perestroika in the late 1980s, there was still not a single Jewish school of any kind in the country. The only Jewish newspaper had few pages, was published in Siberia (Birobidzhan), had a small circulation, and could not be read by most Soviet Jews since it was in Yiddish. The literary journal *Sovetish haimland* that had begun publishing in 1961 initially had a circulation of 50,000 but ended with 7,000, a substantial portion of which were sent abroad. About ninety synagogues existed for a population of about 2.5 million Jews. Teaching Hebrew was generally treated as a subversive activity, and after 1967 there was hardly any contact with Israel, although the Jewish state was regularly excoriated in the mass media. Thus, when the USSR broke up in 1991, there was little "thick" Jewish culture available to the Jews of the successor states. Yet, as then the second largest Diaspora Jewish population, and probably now the third or fourth,[12] post-Soviet Jewry is a significant part of world Jewry.

Post-Soviet Jews have opportunities to fill the boundaries demarcating their Jewishness with content. Ethnic and religious "entrepreneurs" are offering a variety of forms of Jewish living and expression. What conceptions of Jewishness prevail among Russian and Ukrainian Jews? How do they mesh with those held in most other parts of the Jewish world, including Israel, and what do the similarities and differences portend for post-Soviet Jewry and for its relationship with world Jewry? In sum, what do the Jewish identities of these people mean to them and what are the practical consequences of these identities?

Identities

Identity is widely discussed in recent years in both social sciences and the humanities.[13] Identity is "a person's sense of self in relation to others, or . . . the sense of oneself as simultaneously an individual and a member of a social group."[14] Who you think you are or how others define you often determines how you behave and even how you think. This is crucial for individuals and for groups. Yugoslavia's fate illustrates how much it matters whether people who inhabit a state think of themselves as members of that state. The Yugoslav case also affirms that identity is not fixed but shaped by culture and events, by situations, ideology, and geography. When Serbs, Croats, and Bosnians identified less as Yugoslavs and reverted to earlier identities, which were ethnic and not civic, the Yugoslav state collapsed and its peoples could no longer live together. The failure to convince people that they were first and foremost Yugoslavs, and only then Serbs, Croats, Slovenes, et al., precipitated the fall of Yugoslavia.

Another example of the importance of identities is the fate of the USSR. Despite claims in the 1970s,[15] the Soviet regime failed to create enough "new Soviet men" or a new type of ethnos, the *Sovetskii narod* (people)—a meta-ethnic, civic identity—so that when the center collapsed in 1991, what was left were fifteen states at least nominally ethnically defined. The system broke down because of economic and political failure. The centrifugal forces in the Baltic, west Ukraine, and perhaps the Caucasus were not strong enough to tear the system apart by themselves. Indeed, Belarus and the Central Asian states, and perhaps Russia, were forced into independence because the center collapsed, but once it did, the shards of the USSR were shaped by the answer to the question "who and what are we?" As we observe the Middle East and other parts of the world, we see that it can make an important difference for a state's policies whether it sees itself as Islamic, Christian, Jewish, democratic, part of the developing world, etc.

Identity means two things: (1) *who* you think you are, how you label yourself; (2) *what* you think you are, what the label means. I will focus more on the second than the first, more on *what* is a Jew than on *who* is a Jew, on what one thinks it means to be Jewish rather than whether one is or is not. In the former Soviet Union, the state no longer determines and assigns nationality; people are free to define themselves and choose their identities. The emigration of large numbers of Russians, Germans, and Jews compels Russia, Germany, and Israel to deal with the status and identities of the emigrants and decide what responsibilities the states, and their people, have toward them. The question of what and who is a Jew is therefore not an academic one but a matter of practical policy, with profound personal and collective consequences.

To understand the Jewish identities of post-Soviet Jews and find out what they mean to them, I and two colleagues in Moscow—Vladimir Shapiro and Valeriy Chervyakov—conducted a survey of 3,300 Jews in three Russian and five Ukrainian cities in 1992/93, followed by a survey of the same number (but not the same people) in 1997/98 in the same cities—Moscow, St. Petersburg, and Ekaterinburg (formerly Sverdlovsk) in Russia; Kiev, Kharkiv, Lviv, Chernivtsi, and Odessa in Ukraine. Of course, the very fact that we were able to survey ethnic attitudes and that Russian and American researchers could cooperate in studying sensitive issues showed how much had changed since the Soviet period, when any empirical research on ethnic issues was deemed sensitive and possibly subversive. Cooperation in such research with bourgeois scholars was unthinkable. Any study of Jews and Jewish issues was also highly suspect. So this was a highly unusual opportunity to study the outlooks and conceptions of Jews in Russia and Ukraine, and it resulted in the largest such study ever undertaken. The geographical-cultural diversity of these cities and the fact that they include more than half the Jewish population give us confidence that the survey represents the broad cultural and geographical spectrum of Russian and Ukrainian Jewry. Face-to-face interviews were conducted in respondents' homes by interviewers of Jewish origin trained specifically for this project. Interviews generally lasted between one and one-and-a-half hours and were conducted in Russian. Respondents had to be at least sixteen years old, but there was no upper age limit. In 1992/93, our sample replicated very closely the gender and age distribution of the Jewish population over sixteen years of age in each city. Because of the lack of updated information, in the second wave we structured the local samples according to the 1989 age-gender distributions. The only important change from 1989 is the dramatic aging of the Jewish population owing to the very unfavorable birth-to-death ratio and the emigration of younger people, as can be seen in tables 13.1 and 13.2.

In the absence of a list of Jewish residents of each city, we created a "snowball" sample. First, in each city we created a group, or panel, of several dozen Jewish men and women of different ages and socioeconomic status. We did not interview them but asked them to name several of their relatives, friends, and acquaintances whom they considered to be Jewish and who would tentatively agree to be interviewed. Then we asked these friends and relatives for their agreement to be interviewed and asked them to identify, in turn, *their* friends and relatives who might be interviewed. Only one member of each family could be interviewed. The panels informed us of the gender, age, type of employment, and professional background

Table 13.1   Distribution of Russian Jewish urban population

Age	1989 census		Microcensus	Survey sample in Moscow, St. Petersburg, Ekaterinburg	
	Russia (%)	Selected cities (Moscow, St. Petersburg, Ekaterinburg) (%)	1994 Russia (%)	1992–93 (%)	1997–98 (%)
Men					
16–19	3.0	3.0	2.9	2.9	2.6
20–29	9.9	9.3	7.9	9.3	9.2
30–39	14.7	13.1	11.8	14.0	13.4
40–49	16.6	16.7	17.7	16.2	16.7
50–59	21.7	22.2	20.6	22.3	22.5
60 and older	34.1	35.7	39.1	35.3	35.6
Women					
16–19	2.6	2.5	2.6	2.6	2.5
20–29	7.9	7.3	6.5	7.0	7.1
30–39	11.9	10.5	9.5	10.9	10.5
40–49	13.6	13.5	14.6	13.2	13.2
50–59	18.1	17.7	17.3	18.7	18.0
60 and older	45.9	48.5	49.5	47.6	48.7

of potential respondents. This allowed us to adjust the sample structure constantly to conform to the parameters of the overall Jewish population over sixteen in each city.

Some might question the reliability of the responses we obtained on the grounds that former Soviet citizens are more likely than most to tell interviewers what they believe are the politically correct answers and those the interviewers would like to hear. We have several reasons to believe the responses were spontaneous and authentic. First, our response rate was very high. Remarkably few people declined to be interviewed, suggesting that there was no fear of participating. Second, interviewees were told that the sponsors of the survey were the Institute of Sociology, Russian Academy of Sciences, and the University of Michigan, not a state organ or Jewish organization. Third, respondents were promised anonymity (though several protested and said they wanted people to know what they thought). Finally, the issues that we probed were not political or related

Table 13.2   Distribution of Ukrainian Jewish urban population

Age	1989 census		Survey sample in Kiev, Odessa, Kharkiv, Lviv, Chernivtsi	
	UKRAINE (%)	SELECTED CITIES (KIEV, ODESSA, KHARKIV, LVIV, CHERNIVTSI) (%)	1992–93 (%)	1997–98 (%)
Men				
16–19	3.6	3.6	3.7	3.3
20–29	10.5	10.7	10.5	10.9
30–39	15.9	15.7	16.0	16.2
40–49	15.5	16.0	16.0	16.1
50–59	21.3	21.1	20.5	20.4
60 and older	33.2	32.9	33.3	33.1
Women				
16–19	2.9	3.0	3.0	3.3
20–29	8.4	8.7	8.8	8.3
30–39	12.4	11.9	12.5	12.5
40–49	13.0	13.2	13.2	12.9
50–59	18.5	18.1	17.7	17.6
60 and older	44.8	45.1	44.8	45.4

to income but those on which the interviewees, for the most part, had never had a chance to express an opinion. We also do not see any item on which there is a large proportion of people giving what could be construed as "correct" or "desirable" answers.

The Meanings of Jewishness in Russia and Ukraine

The dominant conception of Jewishness held by people in Russia and Ukraine who consider themselves Jews or who were registered as such by the Soviet authorities is that it is, in Soviet terms, a nationality (ethnic group). It is a category that is secular and ethnic, having little to do with Judaism, and is based on biological descent and an ineffable feeling of belonging. Jewishness is not based on language, territory, customs, or behaviors. For most Russian and Ukrainian Jews, sentiment and biology have largely replaced faith, Jewish law and lore, and Jewish customs as the foundations of their Jewish self-conceptions. Table 13.3 shows the components of Jewishness as understood in Russia and Ukraine.

Table 13.3 Components of Jewishness as understood in Russia and Ukraine

		Russia (%)		Ukraine (%)	
		1992	1997	1992	1997
1. Pride	Be proud of one's nationality	33.3	22.9	29.4	31.4
	Defend Jewish honor and dignity	27.1	17.3	21.4	19.7
	Not hide one's Jewishness	0.5	20.8	0.7	13.6
2. Judaism	Believe in God	2.7	4.2	3.9	5.4
	Know the basics of	1.0	0.7	0.2	0.3
	Judaism	0.2	0.1	0.2	0.1
	Circumcise one's son	0.0	0.0	0.0	0.1
	Observe *kashrut*	0.0	0.3	0.3	0.4
	Observe the Sabbath	0.0	0.1	0.2	0.1
	Attend synagogue				
3. Jewish knowledge	Remember the Holocaust	7.3	15.1	15.5	21.5
	Know Jewish history	5.0	2.8	3.0	2.1
	Know a Jewish language	2.2	1.2	1.6	0.4
	Give children Jewish education	1.2	0.8	2.0	1.3
4. Social closeness to Jews	Marry a Jew	1.8	1.1	1.1	0.8
	Help other Jews	7.1	4.3	6.6	6.4
	Feel a tie to Israel	4.2	4.3	5.7	2.8
5. Other	Share Zionist ideals	0.2	0.2	0.3	0.2

Judaism has little to do with Jewishness, which is secular and ethnic, though people are uncertain as to whether one can practice another religion and still be a Jew. Judaism as organized religion plays no role as a "facade for ethnicity" among Russian and Ukrainian Jews. This does not mean that they are without faith. They are without religion. Contrary to official Soviet hopes and expectations, belief in God was not eliminated, but religion as systematic theology, doctrines, and practices was largely repressed and hence is unknown. Substantial proportions of our

Table 13.4   Belief in God

	Russia		Ukraine	
	1992 (%)	1997 (%)	1992 (%)	1997 (%)
Yes, I believe in God	18.3	22.8	24.2	31.0
I am inclined to such belief	23.9	25.3	29.7	24.4
I am not inclined to such belief	19.1	17.2	18.3	17.1
I do not believe in God	31.1	28.3	23.2	22.1
Don't know/no answer	6.4	7.6	4.8	5.5

respondents believe in God, but even those who believe do not draw a connection to behavior or even beliefs prescribed by Judaism. A young Ukrainian Jew explains: "Believing is something spiritual, something completely not understandable . . . It doesn't obligate you to anything . . . but religiosity is simply a religious person . . . who is obligated to carry out certain things."[16] On the other hand, nonbelief does not point to militant activity against religion as the secular religion of Communism would prescribe.

Table 13.4 shows the answers to our straightforward question: do you believe in God?

Both among the general population of Russia (and some areas of Ukraine), as well as among Jews, it is the oldest and youngest who are most inclined to theistic belief. Among our respondents, those under thirty and, to a lesser extent, those over seventy, are the most inclined to belief. A Russian study maintains that Russian religiosity has two sources: traditional religious upbringing, which is what explains the beliefs of people over sixty, and what they call "avant-gardism," the desire by young people to be associated with Western civilization, which they perceive as standing for "democracy, human rights, the market, multiparty systems" and religion.[17] We cannot tell whether this is true of the Jewish respondents or whether their greater inclination to belief is due to their being targeted by "religious entrepreneurs" or "missionaries"—or some other reason.

But mark well that belief in God does not necessarily imply practice of Judaism. We asked which religion people preferred, and the results are summarized in table 13.5.

Even among religious believers—those who believe in God and also prefer Judaism to other faiths—Judaism is not the major mode of expressing their Jewishness. Having faith does not imply that one follows God-dictated commandments (*mitzvot*), nor that one sees God as intervening in human history, two major premises of Judaism. In the year preceding the survey in Russia in 1992, only about half the *religious* people fasted on Yom Kippur or participated in a Passover seder, rituals generally observed by Reform as well as Orthodox Jews. Significantly, in 1997

Table 13.5   Attractiveness of religions in Russia and Ukraine

	Russia		Ukraine	
	1992 (%)	1997 (%)	1992 (%)	1997 (%)
None	36.3	44.1	38.5	36.6
Judaism	33.2	26.7	37.6	32.4
Christianity	13.2	13.7	10.7	15.5
Islam	0	0	0.1	0.1
Other	4.4	5.4	0.0	2.9
Don't know/No answer	13.0	10.2	9.6	12.6

in Russia the proportion of religious people fasting on Yom Kippur increased only slightly, but nearly three-quarters participated in a *seder*, probably because these gained in popularity as communal events. In Ukraine, larger proportions (two-thirds to three-quarters) of religious Jews fasted on Yom Kippur, but only about 60 percent participated in a seder.[18] Only slightly more than a third of those we call "religious" observe the Sabbath in either country; less than a quarter say they observe the dietary laws. In Russia in 1992 only 14 percent said they observed Shabbat and 10 percent said they observed *kashrut*.[19] In all, only half of those affirming Judaism observe the religious laws about which we inquired, and a quarter do not observe them at all. Clearly, the term "religious Jews" does not necessarily describe people who adhere to traditional behavioral norms.

Jewishness is an ethnic matter. Russian and Ukrainian Jews accept without question the Soviet conception of Jews as a nationality. However, they are uncertain about the Zionist conception of Jews as a nation. Thus, they have a parochial or localized conception of Jewish nationality. The old slogan of the American United Jewish Appeal, "We are one," would be viewed skeptically by post-Soviet Jews. They feel much closer to Russian non-Jews in their own city than to Georgian or Mountain Jews. They are uncertain whether even Belorussian and Ukrainian Jews, from whence most Russian Jews derive, are part of the same group (not category—the Soviets made sure they were in the same category). In contrast to Russian Jews, more Ukrainian Jews feel affinity for Russian Jews than they do for local Russians, and they feel greater affinity for local Russians than for Ukrainians. Like Russian Jews, they are distant from the non-Ashkenazic Jews, though less so than Russian Jews. Other measures also indicate that Jews in Ukraine have a more powerful sense of Jewish kinship and affinity than Jews in Russia.

Jewishness is seen as biological. It is an inherited trait, and for most it is sufficient to inherit it from one parent; it does not matter which one (cf. *halacha*). Conversion to Judaism is not necessarily entry into the Jewish collectivity, contrary to Jewish norms where conversion confers membership both in the religion and the people (*"amaich ami ve-elohayich elohay"*—your people are my people and your God my God, says the biblical Ruth). From the viewpoint of the post-Soviet Jew, this separation of religion and ethnicity makes sense, since if Judaism is not an essential ingredient of Jewishness, why should acquisition of the former confer the latter? One respondent defines ethnicity so independently of religion that for her practicing Judaism does not make one a Jew (contrary to Jewish tradition, which admits any practitioner of Judaism to the Jewish people).[20] "I can be a French person and practice Judaism," she maintains, "but that does not make me a Jew."

Jewishness is based on feeling and is much more primordial than instrumental. A woman in Kiev, in her eighties, says she is not particularly proud to be Jewish and years ago might have preferred to be registered in her passport as something else, observes no Jewish holidays, and is not at all active in Jewish public activities. But she says, "There must be something hidden deep inside which is very hard to characterize. For example, when I hear Jewish songs, they touch something deep inside of me, even though I grew up in a Russian environment. We didn't observe any special traditions or anything. And even so something touches me." Two-thirds of 1992 Russian respondents say that "to feel oneself a part of the Jewish people" is what being Jewish is all about, and nearly as many say that "to be proud of the Jewish people" is the essence. The most frequent way of expressing these sentiments among our Ukrainian respondents in 1997 is "to feel yourself part of the Jewish people [*narod*]" or "to feel an inner kinship with Jews, to feel we're one family." Some find it difficult to express: "this is an internal feeling. It's difficult to transmit [*peredat'*] it." One respondent expresses his being a Jew in a classic primordialist manner: "I feel that way and I don't need any additional reasons for it," or, "I feel like one and that's that" [*ia oshchushchaiu takovym, i vsyo!*] Even starker is the statement by an elderly lady in Ukraine: *"Kto Evrei, to znaet chto on Evrei, i vsyo"* [Whoever is a Jew knows that he/she is a Jew, and that's that]. Finally, a resident of Kharkiv, where we found the lowest levels of Jewish commitment, describes a Jewish seminar he attended. "A euphoria enveloped me because nowhere and never before, in no group and not in my student days did people understand me so well and I understand them. Well, I . . . This is—mine! I felt it! Explain it? Explain it exactly? I don't know, I can't. . . . Maybe it's a mentality. . . . People find it simpler to find a point of contact with each other." This bears out the idea that in the Former Soviet Union one does not have to *do* anything Jewish, one simply *is* Jewish.

This parallels what Fran Markowitz found among Soviet Jewish immigrants in Brooklyn, New York. "[For them] being a Jew is an immutable biological and social fact, ascribed at birth like sex and eye color. It may or may not include belief in the Jewish religion, but being a Jewish atheist is not considered a contradiction in terms. Being a Jew is self-evident. . . . [whereas] In American society where one's Jewishness is not self-evident, it is necessary to demonstrate, both to the gentile world and the Jewish community, that one is a Jew by doing specifically Jewish things."[21]

Biology and sentiment may seem to be very different bases for ethnic attachment.[22] After all, "blood" is physical, concrete and determined, whereas sentiment is abstract and not preordained but developed through experience. The post-Soviet Jew might argue that "blood" is a prerequisite to feeling; if one—such as a convert—does not have the genetic background, he or she will not have the sentiment. This is not necessarily true, but what may be implied is that without a family background one does not have memories of Jewish events, foods, music, and rituals. One has not usually associated more with Jews than with others and has therefore not picked up on the "glances of recognition" by which members of a group acknowledge their ties to one another. In any case, in the former Soviet Union, where converts to Judaism are far more rare than in the United States, it is far more likely that one who "feels" Jewish has some Jewish ancestry, and vice versa.

Perhaps the feeling or knowledge that one is Jewish is externally generated, mostly the product of anti-Semitism. About 55 percent of the Russian respondents in 1997 cite anti-Semitism as the major factor contributing to their consciousness of being Jewish, though nearly as many cite reading books as the major factor. In Ukraine the figures are 40 and 44 percent, respectively. In both countries, fewer than 10 percent mention religion.

Even if encounters with anti-Semitism—or other forms of racial, religious, or ethnic discrimination and insult—are rare or occasional, and even if they have not been recent, they may leave a deep psychological mark. Slights experienced in childhood may have long-term effects. Alla Rusinek recalls her school experience in Soviet times. She describes her dread each year when on the first day of school each child had to announce his or her name, nationality, and father's occupation. "She asks my nationality and then it begins. The whole class suddenly becomes very quiet. Some look at me steadily. Others avoid my eyes. I have to say this word . . . which sounds so unpleasant. Why? There is really nothing wrong with its sound, *Yev-rei-ka* [Jewish girl]. But I never heard the word except when people are cursing somebody. . . . Every time I try to overcome my feelings, but each year the word comes out in a whisper: *Yev-rei-ka*."[23]

Especially when being Jewish does not usually involve extensive knowledge of Jewish culture, practice of the Jewish faith, or observing Jewish customs, labels largely devoid of content take on greater importance to the one labeled—and libeled. In the absence of positive cultural content or even sentiment, association of Jewishness with anti-Semitic feelings and expressions can produce a Jewish consciousness that is largely negative, a feeling that being Jewish is a curse that should somehow be removed (some, referring to the fifth line of the passport, call themselves "invalids of the fifth category"). Social scientists have long observed the phenomenon of *selbsthass*, self-hatred, especially frequent among minorities of one sort or another, and its occurrence among Jews is well known. It leads to alterations of one's comportment, language, culture, name, and even physiognomy in attempts to change one's outward appearance and hence perceived identity.[24] In Soviet times, people adopted various strategies to change their names, fairly easily done, and their passport registration, a much more challenging process and one often accomplished by bribery.

Strikingly, most people we interviewed associated their realization that they were Jewish with negative feelings. We asked an open question: "What were the circumstances in which you became aware of your Jewishness?" We coded the responses as having positive, negative, or neutral valences. In Russia in 1992, 45 percent associated negative emotions with their awareness of being Jewish, and 54 percent did so in 1997. In Ukraine, the figures were 60 percent and 52 percent. Only a quarter to a third of our respondents identified the circumstances in which they learned their nationality as positive (the rest were coded as "neutral," either without any emotional connotation or with a mix of positive and negative emotions). Some typical responses were the following: "I was the only Jewish girl in the class; the teacher and pupils acted toward me not with hostility but as toward someone strange; this influenced me a great deal." "I glanced for the first time at the class register under the rubric 'nationality' and discovered that all the others had the proud 'R' [Russian] next to their name, while only I had the slimy 'E' [*Evrei*, Jew]."

In almost all age groups the formation of Jewish identity is associated with negative rather than positive circumstances, but those under thirty and over seventy reported the most positive feelings about the discovery of their Jewishness. The oldest cohort was exposed to more positive expressions of Jewishness while growing up in the 1920s, when many Jewish traditions were still being observed and nontraditional Soviet Jews were attending Yiddish schools or reading Yiddish newspapers and books and felt themselves equal to other Soviet peoples. At the other end of the spectrum, the youngest people came to social and ethnic awareness largely in the post-Soviet period. This may tell us that Jewishness has lost much of its stigma since the collapse of the Soviet Union.

For some, Jewishness means possessing certain traits—though they are not essential components of Jewishness. Urbanity, education, a penchant for intellectuality, "decency," and tight-knit families are among these. An oft-repeated theme is that Jews have been socialized to study and work harder so that they can overcome the barriers placed in their paths. Another is that Jewish families are tighter knit, more caring, and that women are better treated in them. A Kievan feels that "Jewish mothers are more caring. They care more about their children, they watch over them more carefully. . . . Some people say that Jewish husbands are more devoted, more caring, more sympathetic, but I think that's all in the past. Nowadays everyone is the same—that's been my experience."

How Being Jewish in Russia and Ukraine Differs

In Soviet times, Jewishness was a largely private matter. Whereas in many Western societies Jewishness is demonstrated and affirmed in public—in synagogues, at meetings, rallies, dinners, and celebrations—in the Soviet Union it was manifested almost exclusively within the family, at home: in conversations among friends and families, in reading, in holiday celebrations of some sort. While in the United States organizational affiliation, Jewish philanthropy, and public observance of Jewish rites and holidays are the ways in which many express their Jewishness, these were impossible in Soviet circumstances. There was not a single Jewish organization to belong to, nor, aside from a few synagogues, was there an opportunity to give money to Jewish institutions or causes.

This is changing. As a result of communal reconstruction and the activity of ethnic entrepreneurs, many of them foreign, Jewishness is now being "performed in the public space," in the jargon of the "cultural studies" academics. Jews get together for communal *sedarim*, for Hanukkah and Purim parties, for fund-raising dinners and meetings, and they do so in places that have become defined as Jewish venues—synagogues and former synagogues, Jewish clubs, and the like.

Perhaps a more important and less changeable way that post-Soviet notions of Jewishness differ from Jewishness elsewhere is willingness on the part of a substantial portion of our respondents to cross two major boundary lines long essential to the definition of Jewishness and which still hold true for Israeli and Diaspora Jews: practicing a faith other than Judaism and marrying non-Jews. When Judaism was the defining hallmark of Jewishness, conversion was the definitive step out of the Jewish fold. At least from medieval times, converts were regarded as "traitors, as a weak and dispensable element, or simply as lost souls whose choice to leave the fold excised them conclusively from Jewish history," and certainly the Jewish community.[25] After religion and ethnicity were made distinct, the theoretical possibility of Jews practicing another religion was raised. The Brother Daniel case in Israel in the 1960s demonstrated the impossibility of Jewish ethnicity coexisting with active non-Jewish faith, when the Supreme Court of Israel, a secular body, ruled that a person could not be a practicing Catholic (the Carmelite monk Brother Daniel) and claim Jewish identity by virtue of ethnicity (he was born Oswald Rufeisen, a Jew, in Poland). A recent study among "moderately affiliated [American] Jews" found that the taboo on practicing a faith other than Judaism still holds, even while the stricture on intermarriage is weakening. In the United States, Jewishness is often defined by the fact that it is not Christianity: "The only way to lose this Jewish birthright is to choose a different religion for oneself."[26]

Today there is considerable uncertainty among Jews in the Former Soviet Union about that. Some are quite unequivocal that practicing Christianity removes one from the Jewish fold. As one Ukrainian Jew put it, "As far as I know, a Jew is a Jew because he professes Judaism. As soon as he ceases to do so, he ceases to be a Jew!" Or as someone from Odessa put it, quoting his *landsman* Isaac Babel, "a Jew who rides horses has become a Russian, not a Jew. . . . A Jew is a person who feels Jewish. If he crosses over to another religion that means he no longer feels Jewish and doesn't want to be one." Zhanna P., born in Moscow in 1956 and now in Israel, says: "A Jew who is an atheist—this is normal. But to convert to another religion—this is betrayal of your people."

But with just as much certainty, a Muscovite who says she is unsure how to define a Jew asserts, "There is a difference between a Jew-by-nationality [*Evrei*] and a Jew-by-religion [*Iudei*]. So a Jew can take on a different religion." This is quite logical: if Jewishness is ethnicity only, then one should be able to practice whatever religion one wishes without affecting one's ethnicity. In Russia and Ukraine, in both years of the survey, only 30–39 percent are prepared to condemn Jews who "convert to Christianity." While only 4 percent condone this, 60 percent say they would neither condone nor condemn Jews who become Christians. As one St. Petersburg member of Betar put it, "A Jew who practices a religion other than Judaism is not a bad Jew—it's his choice . . . If you want to believe in Jesus Christ, believe, please, who forbids you to do so?" Between 39 percent (Russia, 1997) and 48 percent (Ukraine) would neither condone nor condemn "Jews for Jesus," though fewer than 10 percent would support them.

Conceptions of Jewishness among post-Soviet Jews are bound to be inconsistent and uncertain because the Soviet state defined Jewishness as an ethnic form without content. Jews had no access to teachers, texts, and the Jewish cultures in the rest of the world. What remained were beliefs and practices of grandparents and great-grandparents, but these were often challenged by the state (e.g., attitudes toward religious observance or intermarriage) and by the society (attitudes toward Christianity and to Jews themselves). Therefore, Jews in the Former Soviet Union can be unaware of strictures against practicing other religions or marrying non-Jews. They attach no particular value to Jewish languages or texts. What seems to stir more people than anything else are music and foods, probably because they arouse pleasant associations with a dimly remembered past and a vaguely imagined culture and way of life. Moreover, Philip Converse long ago pointed out how attitudes are illogically and inconsistently held.[27] The messages brought by religio-ethnic entrepreneurs may confuse post-Soviet Jews even more, since, like most people, they gain only partial, fragmented—and sometimes inconsistent and self-contradictory—information. They may be told different things by Jewish Agency and Jewish Joint Distribution Committee (JDC) representatives, or by Orthodox and Reform.

A third possible explanation for the range of understandings of Jewishness is individuation. There has been no religious authority or authoritative ethnic leadership for decades, and each person is free to compound his or her own Jewishness. There were no books of formulae available, and those available now recommend different compounds. No person or institution can impose rules and norms, though Orthodox groups do this indirectly when they turn non-halachic Jews away from educational institutions or religious ceremonies. Especially in the post-Soviet atmosphere, where there is strong animus against doctrine and dogma, a single Truth and its presumptive guardians and interpreters, people are more inclined to pick and choose that which attracts them rather than submit to a discipline. This is, of course, true among Jews elsewhere. A classic example is Conservative Judaism. The 1990 National Jewish Population Survey (NJPS) shows that only 29 percent of Conservative Jews buy kosher meat only and 28 percent had two sets of dishes, practices unambiguously supported by Conservative teaching.[28] We can expect even less adherence to principle, dogma, and tradition among those who have not been taught the basics of Jewish faith and culture.

Intermarriage

The traditional ban on marriage to non-Jews, which goes back centuries, is, perhaps along with the dietary laws, the most explicit expression of the Jewish sense of apartness.[29] "A Jew converted to another faith ceased to be regarded as a Jew by all, except for some non-Jewish religious fanatics or racists from the Spanish Inquisition to the Nazis."[30]

In the Soviet Union at the same time, "the media and arts presented interethnic marriages as a sign of progress and of the younger generation's liberation from outdated views."[31] A well-known work on the "revolutionizing" of the *shtetl* includes a story of love and marriage between a Jewish woman and a non-Jewish man (in Russian).[32] A Yiddish poem about a Jewish girl who went to fight in the civil war and comes home with a Russian boy celebrates the passing of the matchmaker (*shadkhn*) and rabbi, and the triumph of interethnic love.

> Mame, frey zikh haynt in tsveyen
> Nokh a kind kh'hob dikh gebrakht,
> Zest dem bokher mit der peye
> Mit oygn, shvartse vi di nakht
> -vu zhe hostu im genumen
> un vos iz er far a mench?
> O,nit keyn shadkhn, nit keyn mume
> un keyn rov hot undz gebensht!
> [Mama, today you have a double joy
> Because I've brought you another boy
> See this fellow with the wave in his hair
> With eyes as dark as the night.
> 'Where did you get him
> And what kind of person is he?'
> Without a matchmaker, without an "auntie"
> And no rabbi blessed us!][33]

Today the taboo of intermarriage is weakening in most diaspora countries. In Sweden, where a third of those affiliated with Jewish communities are married to non-Jews, half the Jews surveyed in 1999–2001 agreed that a Jew should marry a Jew, 30 percent disagreed, and 20 percent were neutral.[34] In the United States the 1990 NJPS found that 52 percent of Jews who had married since 1985 had married non-Jews. In September 2000, a national study by the American Jewish Committee found that 56 percent said they would *not* be pained if their children married a gentile (16 percent "see such marriages as a 'positive good'"); about three-quarters said that rabbis should officiate at Jewish-gentile marriages; and only a quarter agreed that the gentile partner should be encouraged to convert to Judaism.[35] While nearly everyone in a sample of United Synagogue (Orthodox) members in London agreed with the proposition that "a Jew should marry someone who is Jewish,"[36] among our respondents in the Former Soviet Union only 37–43 percent agreed in 1997 that a Jew should choose a spouse of the same nationality, a decline from 1992.[37] Robert Brym's and Rozalia Ryvkina's 1993 survey of a thousand Jews in Moscow, Kiev, and Minsk found that "only 26 percent said that it was important for Jews to marry other Jews."[38]

Table 13.6   Preferences for Jews as spouses, Russia 1997

Age	Jews	No difference	Others	Don't know
16-29	35.3	58.3	2.2	4.3
30-39	37.2	55.8	0.0	7.1
40-49	41.6	52.8	0.5	5.1
50-59	41.3	52.3	1.1	5.3
60+	48.8	48.5	0.2	2.5

Table 13.7   Reaction to child marrying a non-Jew, Russia 1997

Age	Positive (%)	Indifferent (%)	Negative (%)	Other (%)	Don't know (%)
16-29	20.0	40.0	0.0	2.0	20.0
30-39	6.2	60.0	13.8	3.1	16.9
40-49	5.3	57.4	22.3	7.4	7.4
50-59	12.2	58.5	14.6	7.3	7.3
60+	0.0	73.3	20.0	0.0	6.7

In the Former Soviet Union, intermarriage, high mortality, and low fertility are undermining the biological base of Jewishness. In 1988, 48 percent of Soviet Jewish women and 58 percent of Jewish men who married, married non-Jews.[39] In 1993 in Russia, only 363 children were born to two Jewish parents. In 1996 in Russia, Jewish mothers gave birth to 930 children, only 289 of whom had Jewish fathers.[40] By 1996, the frequency of mixed marriages among all marriages in Latvia involving Jews was 85.9 percent for males and 82.8 percent for females, and in Ukraine this indicator was 81.6 and 73.7 percent, respectively—levels much higher than those of the Russia's Jews in 1988.

Among our respondents, even among those advocating marriage only to Jews, a third claim they would *not* be upset were their children to marry non-Jews. Thus, the historic boundary setting Jews off from others is rapidly blurring. This can be seen vividly in responses to our questions regarding attitudes toward intermarriage, illustrated in tables 13.6 and 13.7.

In no age group—not even the most elderly, among whom intermarriage rates are low—is there anything approaching a majority opposed to intermarriage, and among no cohort is there a majority willing to endorse the more benign proposition that Jews should marry Jews.

Attitudes toward ethnically mixed marriages vary clearly (and predictably) by age. The younger one is the more inclined to say that it is *not* necessary for Jews to choose a Jewish spouse. But even in the oldest cohort, those over sixty, only 57–58 percent in 1992 and 42–49 percent in 1997 believe that Jews should marry other Jews.[41] This is in line with the general trend between 1992 and 1997 toward greater acceptance of interethnic marriage. Indeed, as we have seen, these attitudes are in line with the actual tendency of Jews to marry non-Jews. One does not know, of course, whether the change in attitudes toward intermarriage preceded its actual rise and facilitated it, or whether increased intermarriage is due less to attitudinal change and more to the shrinkage of the Jewish marriage market and the ongoing weakening of tradition. I suspect that, faced with the reality of intermarriage, people's attitudes have changed accordingly, as they have apparently in the United States and other countries.

Rare is the person who says, as a twenty-three-year-old from Chernivtsi did, that Jews should marry other Jews in order to preserve Jewish culture through the generations. A woman of exactly his age and from the same city disagrees. Love, she says, "is a great feeling and it doesn't check one's passport before it comes." Besides, she argues, mixed marriages produce genetically stronger children. An older woman observes, "If you love someone you cannot start thinking about the fate of the Jewish people." Many are aware of the tension between personal interests and those of the Jewish collective. An elderly man whose wife is Russian and whose children do not consider themselves Jewish—"I failed to preserve their Jewishness"—says he is concerned about intermarriage because it reduces the diversity of humankind and "that's abnormal." "On the other hand we are dealing with the fate of two concrete people who fell in love with one another—one Jewish, the other Russian. How can we force them not to marry each other? Here we have the conflict between the fate of a person and the historical fate of one's people." Finally, a young woman who is very active in Jewish affairs bemoans the loss to "the Jewish tribe" that intermarriage causes but argues that "the main thing is happiness. If I meet a person with whom I will be happy for the rest of my life, it's not that important what 'nationality' he is. . . . After all, we are not living with the sole purpose of the revival of the Jewish nation. We are regular people and we want to be happy. And if the only person who can make us happy is of another 'nationality,' then why not?" Some struggle between what they see as their responsibility to the collective Jewish entity and their personal desires. In the United States fewer and fewer people seem to pay any attention to the former as the "me generation" engages in the pursuit of individual happiness. It may be that similar tendencies are appearing in the postcollectivist societies of the Former Soviet Union.

In the Former Soviet Union, there are some who *advocate* intermarriage. A poet in St. Petersburg insists that "I don't suffer from xenophobia" and "children born in mixed marriages are smarter and more alert. And that's a fact! And that's good! And it doesn't matter to me [that they become less Jewish]." A man whose parents were die-hard Communists and named their children after Lenin and other revolutionaries thinks the more intermarriage the better, since it will reduce ethnic conflict and hatred between nations.

People married to Jews are the one group firmly committed to the idea that Jews should marry other Jews. Of those married to Jews, no matter what their own origins, 70–80 percent believe it necessary for Jews to marry other Jews. And those who are fully Jewish and are married to Jews are twelve times as likely to oppose their children intermarrying as those who are married to non-Jews. It seems that once an intermarriage occurs, opposition to it naturally weakens, and it will be more likely to occur in succeeding generations, perhaps not so much because there will be less explicit opposition to it than because if one's parents have intermarried there would seem to be little reason not to do so.

Conclusion

The Jewish identities of Russian and Ukrainian Jews are stronger than many would suppose but are problematic in several ways. First, they may be uniquely the product of a Soviet environment that no longer exists. Ethnic identities are often reformulated and "Jewish identities in general are to be understood as constructs in response to the circumstances."[42] But Soviet circumstances were unique, not replicated even in allied socialist countries where nationality was not registered in one's identity document. In some of those socialist countries, Jewishness was defined as a religious, rather than ethnic, category. In the USSR, state-imposed identity and governmental anti-Semitism combined with grassroots anti-Semitism to maintain boundaries between Jews and others long after Jewish content had largely disappeared from Jewish ethnicity. Russia and Ukraine no longer impose official ethnic identity, and none of the successor states to the USSR pursues an anti-Semitic policy. Popular anti-Semitism, which may wax and wane, may be the last barrier to assimilation. So some of the ingredients of Soviet Jewish identity have been changed, though of course descent and feelings of kinship remain.

Second, the conceptions of being Jewish held by the great majority of Russian and Ukrainian Jews are so different from those prevailing in most of the rest of the Diaspora and in Israel that sensitive questions of mutual recognition inevitably arise. The criteria for admission to the Jewish club that are set in the Jewish world, though by no means uniform, are not shared by a significant portion of post-Soviet Jewry. Thus, the gatekeepers of the Jewish club, whoever they may be—this, of course, is one of the most contentious issues in world Jewry today—have three choices when Former Soviet Union Jews present themselves for admission. The gatekeepers can abandon the rules altogether and adopt the suggestion of some of our respondents that "whoever thinks he or she is a Jew, is a Jew." Thus, they would have to abandon any external criteria and include as Jews "Jews for Jesus" or anyone else declaring himself or herself a Jew, thus perhaps pleasing postmodernists for whom "essentialism" is a cardinal sin but emptying the category "Jew" of any meaning at all.[43] In addition, the gatekeepers can modify the rules for admission, but if they do so extensively the rules can become so loose as to be inoperative or meaningless. Or, they can stick to the rules they have evolved and turn away many who seek admission. The rejected may form their own, competing "Jewish club," or they may turn away from the gates altogether and seek membership elsewhere.[44]

Third, and most generally, the challenge of developing a viable Jewish identity in Russia and Ukraine is formidable because it involves constructing a secular

Jewish identity. Amyot and Sigelman find that "Religious devotion . . . is the main pillar of Jewish identity in America, although close interpersonal relations with other Jews also play an important role." To the extent that American Jews reject "ethnoreligion," they also renounce their ethnic heritage.[45] This is not the issue in Russia and Ukraine. One must assume that for the foreseeable future most Jewish identities in the European Former Soviet Union will be secular and that interpersonal relations with other Jews will decline along with the sheer number of Jews—unless Jewish communities develop.

Secular Jews have long struggled with the problem of maintaining ethnicity divorced from religion and its symbols. This is clearly brought out in Shachar Pinsker's chapter. A secular Yiddish educator observed that when the "secular ship" floats on the "Jewish sea," one permeated by religion, "it turns out that one floats empty, with no ballast. And a terrible similarity appears between secularism and simple assimilation."[46] Some secular Jews substituted ethics for religion, others the Yiddish language and culture, and still others a modern Jewish state. All found themselves reverting to symbolism emanating from religious sources, though they tried to infuse the symbols with new emphases. As one of the ideologists of secular Yiddishism put it, "if the Jewish Passover is kept because a people liberated itself from slavery and went out to seek a land in which to live its own life freely—though the whole story of the Exodus from Egypt is perhaps only a legend—the festival is of . . . great human significance. . . . On the understanding, of course, that there must be no supernatural elements introduced into the observance, nothing of confessional faith."[47] A Hungarian Jew explains the dilemma this way: "We want to belong without taking on the belief. We do not want to practice religion itself but we want to belong. . . . It is incredibly difficult, we are Negroes without the color."[48]

Almost from the establishment of the State of Israel "*toda'a Yehudit*" (Jewish consciousness) and the Jewish identity of the nonreligious population have been the subjects of discussion. Israeli educators continue to wrestle with the problem of how to convey Jewish history, literatures, values, and traditions to nonreligious students. In America, where Yiddish, the basis of East European secularism, yielded to English, Jews have maintained Judaism as a facade for ethnicity. One sociologist asserts that "Jewish self-definition is that of a religious group but few Jews are believers in any significant way. As a Reform rabbi stated the problem, 'Prayer is still the pretext, but the justification of the act, the real purpose, is now achievement of community, the sense of belonging.'"[49] In Britain, too, according to a sociologist, "a feeling of belonging, rather than belief in God, is the driving force behind synagogue attendance."[50] In the Soviet Union, because religious forms were unacceptable, they did not serve the same purpose as they do in America or Britain. Secular, socialist, Soviet forms devised by the Jewish Sections of the Communist Party were seen as ersatz and never replaced Judaism-based symbols and rituals. Nevertheless, secular Jewish identity in the Soviet Union was powerful because it was maintained by a combination of official designation, anti-Semitism—whether state-generated or grassroots—and a feeling of apartness, especially after the 1930s.

Today, as we have seen, some of these elements of identity are gone. Is popular anti-Semitism, which waxes and wanes, the last basis of Jewish identity? Aside from its being a completely negative cause of such identity, is it sufficient to maintain it, or can one now escape since the boundaries of ethnicity have become permeable and blurred as a result of intermarriage?

One possibility is that rituals and customs that are religious in origin may be maintained and elaborated as ethnic ones. For example, as in the case of Passover cited earlier, holidays and observances based on historic events can be observed without imputing religious meaning to them. Even holidays that do not claim to commemorate historical events, such as the High Holidays, have been used by secularists as occasions for reflection, rededication, or celebration of milestones. Whether these have the emotional power and personal significance that traditional holidays do is questionable. Moreover, there is a big difference between feeling a sense of obligation, being commanded to do something, and exercising an option to participate or not in an available activity.

In the USSR individuals marked Jewish holidays in their own way. Matzah, difficult to obtain, would be eaten along with ham. On Rosh Hashana, toasts would be made with vodka to the Jewish people and the new year. Traditional foods, one of the last ethnic markers to disappear, would be served on holidays, though few people knew the origins of the traditions. Thus, individualized, highly unorthodox ethnic—not religious—rituals took place. In the future, such rituals and observances, now observed more in public, may become the ethnic culture of post-Soviet Jews.

The interesting question becomes what new understandings will emerge. Is thin culture or symbolic ethnicity transferable across generations? How far can something that is already thin be stretched across generations before it breaks entirely? In other words, can Jewishness survive without Judaism? As Henry Feingold has written, "The survival dilemma posed by secular modernity is whether the corporate communal character at the heart of Judaism can accommodate the individuation that is the quintessence of modern secular life. It is whether Jewishness can become again a living culture without its primary religious ingredient, Judaism, from which it has become separated."[51] Secular Jewishness as it emerged just a century ago was based on a common language (Yiddish), territorial concentration of Jews (the Pale, ethnic neighborhoods), a high degree of concentration in certain professions (needle trades, artisanal trades, commerce and trade), and a strong sense of being part of a distinct Jewish entity. Jews were kept distinct both by anti-Semitism or—for immigrants—by their cultural apartness, and by their sense of cultural superiority in many countries (Lithuania, Russia, Romania), though in others they strove to the "higher culture" as they perceived it (France, England, Germany, the United States). Today in the United States, Yiddish and Hebrew are no longer used or even posited as ideals, Jewish neighborhoods no longer concentrate as high a proportion of the population or do not exist altogether, and the Jewish working class has disappeared, and with it Jewish dominance of certain trades. Thus, the bases of secular Jewishness have eroded or disappeared.

In such conditions, can there be a viable, transferable secular Jewish life? Today "classical Jewish identity has . . . broken up (if not also broken down) into multiple Jewish identities, some of which . . . trace connections with the more distant past, while others [as in the Former Soviet Union] define themselves more directly and explicitly through highly contemporary issues." Thus, if the classical definition of Jewish identity is discarded, as Jonathan Webber has noted, "there would appear to be no simple, self-evident, and adequate formula to replace it with."[52]

Perhaps the search for a single definition of Jewish identity is fruitless in an age of individuation, the erosion of communal authority, and the decline of humility. Empirically, one might expect post-Soviet Jewry to be populated by the same types of Jews and their commitments that one observes in diasporas generally. It seems to me that there are four ways in which Western Jews relate to their Jewishness, and they may appear in the Former Soviet Union, though in different proportions. There are those who are indifferent or even hostile to their ethnicity; there are the occasional participants in ethnic or religious public and private events; a third group is involved in Jewish life, but it is a part-time avocation and not their dominant identity; finally, there are people who are driven by Jewishness and for whom it is their primary identity (some are "professional Jews" and others are laypeople intensively involved and who see many issues through the prism of their Jewishness).

Whatever will emerge on the communal and individual levels, after a hiatus of more than seventy years, it is at last solely up to the Jews of the Former Soviet Union themselves to choose whether and how to be Jewish.

NOTES

1. Melville Herskovits, "Who Are the Jews?" in *The Jews*, ed. Louis Finkelstein (Philadelphia: Jewish Publication Society, 1949), 4:1168, 1153.

2. Benedict Anderson, *Imagined Communities* (London: Verso, 1983).

3. For an overview of discussions of Jews as a race, and a rejection of the category of race altogether, see Steven Kaplan, "If There Are No Races, How Can Jews Be a Race?" *Journal of Modern Jewish Studies* 2, no. 1 (2003): 79–96.

4. A handy Russian-language compendium of such terms and their meanings is V. I. Kozlov, ed., *Etnicheskiei i etno-sotsial'nye kategorii* (Moscow: Statistika, 1995).

5. It is instructive that a book that was for many years one of the most popular general histories of the Jews among Jews themselves, Nathan Ausubel's *Pictorial History of the Jews* (New York: Crown, 1953) begins with a discussion of whether Jews are a race, nation, religion, people, etc.

6. Michael Meyer, *Jewish Identity in the Modern World* (Seattle: University of Washington Press, 1990), 3.

7. Anthony D. Smith, "The Question of Jewish Identity," in *Studies in Contemporary Jewry* (New York: Oxford University Press, 1992), 7:219.

8. C. John Somerville, "Stark's Age of Faith Argument and the Secularization of *Things*: A Commentary," *Sociology of Religion* 63 (Fall 2002): 361–372.

9. Chaim Jitlovsky, "What Is Jewish Secular Culture?" in *The Way We Think*, ed. Joseph Leftwich (South Brunswick, NJ: Thomas Yoseloff, 1969), 1:92, 93, 95.

10. Stephen Cornell, "The Variable Ties That Bind: Content and Circumstance in Ethnic Processes," *Ethnic and Racial Studies* 19 (April 1996): 265–289.

11. Mordechai Altshuler, *Soviet Jewry on the Eve of the Holocaust* (Jerusalem: Centre for Research of East European Jewry, Hebrew University, 1998), 74.

12. There are probably about 400,000–450,000 self-defined Jews in the former Soviet Union; 260,000 in the Russian Federation; 103,600 in Ukraine; and about 25,000 in Belarus, with smaller populations in the other former Soviet republics. The "enlarged Jewish population" in Russia, which includes all non-Jewish members in the household is estimated to be 520,000. The difference between "core" and "enlarged" Jewish populations is testimony to very high rates of intermarriage. See Sergio Della Pergola, *Jewish Demography: Facts, Outlook, Challenges*, Alert Paper No. 2 (Jerusalem: Jewish People Policy Planning Institute, June 2003), 3.

13. A recent critique of the category argues that since those who use it "routinely categorize . . . it as multiple, fragmented, and fluid [it] should not be conceptualized as 'identity' at all. Identity as a category of analysis and as a category of practice is often blurred," and, in general, " 'identity' tends to mean either too much or too little." "Self-understanding" or "self-conception" are proposed as more useful terms. Rogers Brubaker and Frederick Cooper, "Beyond 'Identity,' " *Theory and Society* 29 (2000): 1–47. I do not accept the general thrust of their critique, though I agree that "self-understanding" or "self-conception" are just as useful as "identity," and perhaps more so. Another critique of "identity" comes from Mervyn Bendle, who claims, inter alia, that it is "a cultural and historical artifact peculiar to Western modernity and reflecting underlying processes of social change." "The Crisis of 'Identity' in High Modernity," *British Journal of Sociology* 53 (March 2002): 1–18.

14. Perry London and Allissa Hirschfeld, "The Psychology of Identity Formation," in *Jewish Identity in America*, ed. David Gordis and Yoav Ben-Horin (Los Angeles: Wilstein Institute of Jewish Policy Studies, 1991), 33.

15. E. Bagramov, "The Soviet Nationalities Policy and Bourgeois Falsifications," *International Affairs* (Moscow) (June 1978): 76–85. See also M. I. Kulichenko, "Socialism and the Ethnic Features of Nations: The Example of the Peoples of the Union of Soviet Socialist Republics," in *Perspectives on Ethnicity*, ed. Regina Holloman and Serghei Arutiunov (The Hague: Mouton, 1978), 426–427.

16. Rebecca Golbert, "Constructing Self: Ukrainian Jewish Youth in the Making," (Ph.D. diss., St. Cross College, Oxford University, 2001), 217.

17. Ibid., 14. The "traditionalist" believers have no such attachment to Western values. In fact, they display more authoritarian outlooks than others. They prefer strong government and have positive views of Lenin, the Bolshevik Revolution, and the Communist Party (14–20).

18. It is not clear why this should be so. Perhaps in the 1990s the communal seder was not as popular or widely available in Ukraine as in Russia.

19. It is difficult to explain the substantial increase in observance of these two rituals in Russia over the five years. It may be that "observing Shabbat and kashrut" may mean to respondents that occasionally they might engage in a ritual such as lighting Sabbath candles or eating kosher food, the kind of behavior that may well take place in communal settings and at the kinds of events that increased substantially in the 1990s.

20. See Zvi Zohar and Avraham Sagi, *Giyur vezehut Yehudit* (Jerusalem: Mosad Bialik and Machon Hartman, 1994).

21. Fran Markowitz, "Jewish in the USSR, Russian in the USA: Social Context and Ethnic Identity," in *Persistence and Flexibility: Anthropological Perspectives on the American Jewish Experience*, ed. Walter Zenner (Albany: SUNY Press, 1988), 81, 83.

22. Prof. Ben Nathans of the University of Pennsylvania first brought this point to my attention.

23. Alla Rusinek, *Like a Song, Like a Dream* (New York: Charles Scribner's Sons, 1973), 20.

24. Sander Gilman, *Jewish Self-Hatred: Anti-Semitism and the Hidden Language of the Jews* (Baltimore: Johns Hopkins University Press, 1986).

25. Elisheva Carlebach, *Divided Souls: Converts from Judaism in Germany, 1500–1700* (New Haven: Yale University Press, 2001), 2.

26. Steven M. Cohen and Arnold M. Eisen, *The Jew Within: Self, Family, and Community in America* (Bloomington: Indiana University Press, 2000), 23. In *Messianic Judaism* (Boston: Beacon Press, 1999), Carol Harris-Shapiro seems to suggest that American Jews should consider including "messianic Jews" in their fold (see 184–189).

27. Phillip Converse, "The Nature of Belief Systems in Mass Publics," in *Ideology and Discontent,* ed. David Apter (New York: Free Press, 1964).

28. Jack Wertheimer, *Jews in the Center* (New Brunswick, NJ: Rutgers University Press, 2000), 25, table 1.2.

29. See Genesis 24 and 27, Numbers 25, the prohibitions on marrying Moabites and Ammonites (Deuteronomy 23), and the condemnation of King Solomon for having taken non-Jewish wives. Of course, the Bible recounts many instances of marriage between Jews and non-Jews. Todd Endelman suggests that prohibitions on intermarriage in antiquity probably reflect greater contact between Jews and their neighbors and that when Jews were ghettoized it was less necessary to make such prohibitions explicit. Intermarriage became a serious issue again when Jews were emancipated and could mix with non-Jews.

30. Baron, "Problems of Jewish Identity," 33.

31. Mordechai Altshuler, *Soviet Jewry on the Eve of the Holocaust: A Social and Demographic Profile* (Jerusalem: Hebrew University and Yad Vashem, 1998), 70.

32. V. Tan Bogoraz, *Evreiskoe mestechko v revoliutsii* (Moscow: Gosizdat, 1926), 84. I am indebted to Dr. Anna Shternshis for this reference.

33. "Gitele fun Komsomol," *Yungvald* 2 (1925): 10–11 (my translation). This material was also kindly supplied by Anna Shternshis, who points out that "there are definitely more intermarriage stories in Russian than in Yiddish. It is in fact hard to find one: most Yiddish stories are about friendship between children (Jews and gentiles), joint work, but not going out or marrying. The same is true about Yiddish songs of the period—they like to get married without the rabbi, but to a Jew. However, working together with a non-Jew is fine." Shternshish, personal communication, May 29, 2002.

34. Dencik, "Jewishness in Post-Modernity."

35. American Jewish Committee, 2000 Annual Survey of American Jewish Opinion, New York, 2000, 3.

36. Stephen Miller, "Religious Practice and Jewish Identity in a Sample of London Jews," in *Jewish Identities in a New Europe,* ed. Jonathan Webber (Oxford: Littman Library, 1994), 199.

37. In 1992, 53–55 percent agreed that one should marry a Jew. The decline over five years reflects the increase in intermarriage and the greater proportion of endogamous marriages among émigrés.

38. Robert Brym and Rozalina Ryvkina, *The Jews of Moscow, Minsk and Kiev* (New York: New York University Press, 1994), 26. Only 69 percent of the sample said they were registered as Jews in their passports (see 22–23). One can reasonably assume that if a higher proportion of registered Jews had been interviewed, the proportion opposed to intermarriage would have been higher.

39. Mark Tolts, "Jewish Marriages in the USSR: A Demographic Analysis," *East European Jewish Affairs* 22, no. 2 (1992): 8.

40. Mark Tolts, "Recent Jewish Emigration and Population Decline in Russia," *Jews in Eastern Europe* 35 (Spring 1998): 21.

41. The question was worded in Russian as "Kak vy schitaete, evreiam sleduet vybrat' sebe suprugu(a) svoei natsional'nosti, drugoi natsional'nosti, ili eto ne imeet znacheniia?"

42. Jonathan Webber, "Modern Jewish Identities," in *Jewish Identities in the New Europe,* ed. Jonathan Webber (London: Littman Library, 1991), 82.

43. Rebecca Golbert criticizes scholars for "their applications of certain fixed external criteria to measure the self-identification of Jews" and for "ignor[ing] the local frameworks for self-definition and cultural continuity and the multi-linear processes of social and political change which have affected them." She performs an important service in pointing out that there are

subtle ways in which Jewish identity was expressed and transmitted in the Soviet Union, but in her zeal to establish a new paradigm she ignores the questions of multigenerational viability and external validation or recognition of the peculiarly Soviet—or, Russia, Ukrainian, etc.— identity that evolved. Rebecca Golbert, "In Search of a Meaningful Framework for the Study of Post-Soviet Jewish Identities, with Special Emphasis on the Case of Ukraine," *East European Jewish Affairs* 28 (Summer 1998): 15.

44. Ronald Suny argues that two different ideas of nation-making should be distinguished. "In the first, the nation exists even when people argue about what it is; in time they will get it right. In the second, the nation is precisely that cultural and political space where people create and recreate their sense of who they are. Like culture, it is an arena of contestation, an argument about membership and boundaries, of authenticity. It is in the debate that the nation exists and is created and recreated." Comment at conference on "A Century of Modern Jewish Politics: The Bund and Zionism in Poland and Eastern Europe," Frankel Center for Judaic Studies, University of Michigan, February 15–16, 1998. The second notion is compelling, but it is hard to see how people can be admitted or barred from a "cultural and political space." The nation is surely an "arena of contestation," but the contestants must agree on some boundaries for the arena itself.

45. Robert Amyot and Lee Sigelman, "Jews without Judaism? Assimilation and Jewish Identity in the United States," *Social Science Quarterly* 77 (March 1996): 187–188.

46. Yudl Mark, "Yidishkayt un veltlikhkayt in un arum undzere shuln," in *Shul-Pinkes*, ed. Shloime Bercovich, M. Bronshtain, Yudl Mark, and Y. Ch. Pomerantz (Chicago: Sholem Aleichem Folk Institute, 1948), 14.

47. Chaim Jitlovsky, "What Is Jewish Secular Culture?" in *The Way We Think*, ed. Joseph Leftwich (South Brunswick, NJ: Thomas Yoseloff, 1969), 1:95.

48. Andras Kovacs, "Antisemitism and Jewish Identity in Postcommunist Hungary," in *Anti-Semitism and the Treatment of the Holocaust in Postcommunist Eastern Europe*, ed. Randolph Braham (New York: Rosenthal Institute for Holocaust Studies, City University of New York and Columbia University Press, 1994), 138.

49. Paul Ritterband, "Modern Times" (unpublished paper, March 1991), 22–23.

50. Miller, "Religious Practice and Jewish Identity," 200.

51. Henry Feingold, *Lest Memory Cease* (Syracuse, NY: Syracuse University Press, 1996), 8.

52. Webber, "Modern Jewish Identities," 8.

14

Judaism, Community, and Jewish Culture in American Life

CONTINUITIES AND TRANSFORMATIONS

CALVIN GOLDSCHEIDER

Observers and analysts of the American Jewish community have constructed three flawed but compelling arguments about the Jewish past and present. These arguments have been based, in part, on social science theories, and they have gained legitimacy in Jewish communities in the United States and around the world as a basis for policy formation, research agendas, and strategic planning. They are also consistent with a set of ideological orientations that have been current in the Jewish community for more than a century. Although somewhat oversimplified, these arguments can be summarized as follows.

According to the first argument, over the last century Jewish communities have moved away from a foundation in religion and religious activity toward secularism. In modern, open voluntary societies, Jews, like others, have become more secular, less attached to religious activities, religious institutions, and a religious way of life. Whatever religious orientations their grandparents and great-grandparents had, contemporary Jews have fewer. Religion is simply less central in their lives today, so it is argued. Judaism itself, with its associated religious institutions, has become more secular. Therefore even those who are religiously committed are more secular than their forebears. This so-called secularization theme has been applied to all communities of Jews in and outside of Israel.

The second argument, which focuses on the ethnic or "peoplehood" dimension of Jewish identity, states that Jews in the past had a distinct sense of being a people apart from the Christian and Muslim societies where they lived—that is, Jews were a social minority, not only a religious minority. Their minority status reduced access to social and economic opportunities and involved political constraints and discrimination in everyday life, at times to extreme levels. However, with the increasing openness of society, the expansion of political rights, citizenship, economic opportunities, and the acceptance of Jews into society, the ethnic component of Jewishness has diminished. Like other white social minorities subject to decreasing discrimination, over the generations Jews have assimilated ethnically into Western societies. Jews have accepted their new situation and have been accepted by others. As generational distance from immigrant origins has increased—fewer and fewer American Jews have grandparents who began their lives outside of the United States—the ethnic distinctiveness of American Jews has faded. Jews have become thoroughly and indistinguishably American.

A third argument flows directly from and combines the secularization and minority assimilation arguments. It assumes that as religious identity weakens and ethnic identity fades, the cohesiveness of the American Jewish community weakens. External stimuli are needed to ignite the dying embers of Jewishness. These sparks might come from a cultural attachment and pride in a new nation-state (Israel) or some recognition of Jewish vulnerability to external forces that threaten group survival. In their anti-Semitic and pro-Israel guises, these external factors tend to be unpredictable and to remain marginal to the daily lives of most Jews outside of Israel. Thus, as secularization diminishes Judaism and assimilation decreases Jewish ethnicity, few internally generated Jewish values or features of Jewish culture remain to sustain continuity of the community or continuity of identity. The Jewish community in America is therefore characterized only by symbolic religion and symbolic ethnicity. As Judaism and Jewishness fade, according to this argument, nothing beyond externals can undergird the viability of American Jewish communities.

Hence, some perspectives from social science and history postulate that the American Jew is vanishing and that the American Jewish community is eroding.[1] According to these views, the decline of Jewish communities outside of Israel is in sight—if not in the present generation, then soon. These three arguments about secularization, assimilation, and cultural distinctiveness have in one form or another informed discussions and analyses of the American Jewish community over the last decades.

However, a systematic body of evidence challenges the main implications of these arguments, which do not describe accurately the paths Jewish communities have taken in modern, open pluralistic societies. Although Jews have clearly assimilated, their communities have not always proportionately weakened, and many have been strengthened anew. Furthermore, the fundamental dichotomy between religious and ethnic identity is not as useful among Jews as it may be among other groups. Because of their ethnic identity and culture, Jews are not simply a religious group like Protestants, Catholics, Mormons, and Muslims. But because of their religious culture, Jewish Americans are also not an ethnic group like Italian Americans or Hispanic Americans.

Furthermore, because Judaism readily incorporates the secular, the distinctions between religious and secular identities are also not clear. Empirically, there are multiple links between religious and ethnic secular indicators of Jewishness, although Judaism and ethnic Jewishness are not identical. The distinctions between religious and secular or between ethnic and religious do not neatly distinguish among institutions of the community. Synagogues and temples have diversified their activities to incorporate strong ethnic components, and secular Jewish institutions have often stressed sacred themes.[2] So the survival paradigms—the dichotomies of ethnicity versus religion, minority versus majority—are not very useful as guidelines for studying contemporary American Jewish communities (if they ever were in the past, and regardless of their usefulness for studying other groups).

How can we make sense of the historical changes in American Jewish communities? How can we go beyond current arguments about decay, which cloud our analyses to new understandings? How do we go beyond the clichés of social science, the nuances of assimilation versus transformation, and the rhetoric of optimists versus pessimists that trivialize the basic issues? Indeed we should move away from the selective truths of Jewish ideology and Jewish organizational propaganda to delve more systematically into the fundamentals of Jewish continuity and change in the past and in the future. I aim to move beyond oversimplified demographic arguments to assess the major forms of "Jewish quality." As I have argued elsewhere, the issues of the American Jewish community are mainly associated with the quality of Jewish life, and that quality needs to be operationalized, measured, and analyzed.[3]

American Jewish Distinctiveness

Instead of asking whether the grandchildren and great-grandchildren of Eastern European Jewish immigrants to America are assimilating, or whether they are surviving as a community (they are doing both), some social scientists have reformulated the central analytic questions about Jews and other ethnic and religious minorities in the United States: (1) What factors sustain the ethnic and religious continuity of American Jews in the absence of overt discrimination and disadvantage? (2) What structural and cultural forces sustain continuity in the face of pressures toward the disintegration of the uniqueness and distinctiveness of their communities? The short answer to these questions is that communal institutions and social and family networks are the core elements sustaining communal continuity. Communal institutions are able to construct new forms of Jewish cultural uniqueness that redefine the collective identity of Jews. Jewish values are the source of continuity and are anchored in the structural underpinnings of communities.

Three features of social life form the basis for my assessment of the transformation of American Jews. First, I focus on the structural, not only the cultural, features of Jewish communities. Second, I emphasize the contexts (networks and institutions), not only the values, that distinguish Jews from others. Third, I target communities and families rather than individuals as themes of interpretation and analysis. To assess the formation and development of the community over time, I argue that we need to examine the quality of Jewish communal life in its broadest meaning. With the emergence of the fourth and later generations, distance from immigrant origins has faded as the major axis of change in the community. Although individuals exit and enter the community, the institutions and the collectively shaped culture sustain ethnic continuity and commitments.

Social class and family patterns of American Jewish communities are the core of generational continuity, and institutions are the sources of the communities' distinctiveness. Jews have been transformed from an immigrant group defined by a combination of religious and ethnic distinctiveness to an American ethnic community defined by a distinctive cultural construction of Judaism and Jewishness with central, particularly American features. This transformation makes historical comparisons by generation particularly problematic and cross-national comparisons using similar indicators of continuity distorting. I argue for the importance of context and structure in shaping comparisons over time. Changes over the life course as families are re-formed and expand are the bases for exploring group distinctiveness in a wide variety of social spheres.

Several analytic themes shape my orientation: First, changes over time in the characteristics of Jews and their communities do not necessarily imply the decline of the community or total assimilation. There is no simple inference that can be extrapolated from change to communal continuity. Hence, the identification of changes over time may imply the transforming of community but not its disintegration. Second, my focus is on the cohesion of communities, based on the extent and contexts of intra- and intergroup interaction, along with a shared constructed (and often changing) culture. Sharing and interaction may occur in specific institutional or religious contexts but are also likely to occur in the daily round of activity associated with multiple spheres of social activities—work, school, neighborhood, leisure, and family. Nevertheless, an examination of interaction in any one sphere may not have implications for interaction in other spheres. Third, time can be viewed both in terms of generations, historical context, and the life course. I expect that ethnic and religious identity, at both the individual and communal levels, varies over time as context changes. The life course is one perspective at the micro level for studying a variety of unfolding and emerging changes in the context of ethnic communities.

Wide varieties of structural and institutional features link Jews to one another in complex networks and mark Jews off as a community from those who are not Jewish. These features include family and social connections, organizational, political, and residential patterns, and religious and ethnic activities that can reinforce the values and shape the attitudes of American Jews. I will review some of these core features to identify their role in the integration of Jews into American society. At the outset, I reiterate that institutions play a powerful role in ethnic communities as they continually construct the cultural basis of community and represent conspicuous communal public symbols of community. Family and social networks reinforce shared cultural constructions of Judaism and Jewishness. Declines or increases in any one sphere do not necessarily imply similar changes in all spheres. For example, evidence of generational decline in organizational participation or synagogue attendance does not mean the decline in other forms of communal activities. Similarly, low levels at some stages of the life course do not necessarily imply low levels at other stages. Thus we need to examine a variety of social processes over time to assess future directions in the transformation of the Jewish community.

Some Historical Perspective

Examining cross-sectional survey data to understand the transformation of the American Jewish community without attention to some historical perspective provides limited results. Therefore, we will briefly consider the historical context of

American Jewish communities. The immigrant generation at the turn of the twentieth century could not shed its Jewishness, but it could change it. The foreignness of the immigrant population, which fit structural and cultural characteristics, prevented or constrained their full assimilation, as did the discrimination they encountered. Residential, educational, and occupational networks combined with family and organizational networks to reinforce a cohesive ethnic community. These bases of cohesion would inevitably change over time as the children of immigrants moved to new neighborhoods, attended different schools for longer periods of time, obtained better jobs, and faced the economic depression of the 1930s and war in the 1940s. Yet the children of immigrants were raised in families which were cohesive and supportive, where an ethnic language was distinctive, where cultural closeness to origins was undeniable, and where networks and institutions were ethnically based. Together, these powerful elements made the second generation Jewish by both religion and ethnicity. But their ethnicity (in the sense of national origin) was fading and their Jewishness was becoming Americanized. Although sharply different from the Jewishness of their parents' generation, their children's Jewishness was clear and distinctive by American standards. The issue of change and continuity among Jewish Americans, critical for both scholars and the community, focuses initially on generations in the sense of closeness to foreign origins and to length of time in American society. The continuation of integration into the third and fourth generations, distant from their cultural origins, directly raises the question about the changing culture (i.e., quality) of American Jewish life.

At work, in neighborhoods, in schools, as well as in religious, political, and social activities, immigrant Jews and their children interacted with other Jews. Yiddish and socialist schools competed with public and religious schools for enrollment, and Yiddish newspapers competed with English ones. Credit associations, *landsmanshaftn*, and local fraternal and communal institutions were formed and expanded. Although they were learning English, Yiddish remained the language of business and social life among Jewish immigrants. Even when their children rejected Yiddish, it still formed the cultural environment of their upbringing. In the pre–World War II period, most Jews in America interacted with other Jews in their community. Jewish families and communities rejected those who, through intermarriage or by their behavior, rejected their community. For most Jews, the number of bases of communal cohesion was large indeed. The overlap of occupation, residence, and ethnicity was as high in America as anywhere in urban Europe. Jews left the Old World behind—but not all of it—to become American. Their Jewishness was conspicuous by their background, culture, and social structure.

What happened to the community and to ethnic and religious identity among the descendants of immigrants? Clearly the third and later generations faced a very different social and economic context. The role of the educational and occupational opportunity structure was to shape generational social and residential mobility. In turn, stratification—the concentration of Jews in particular social classes—became one of the conspicuous forms of communal cohesion in the United States. I will briefly examine the education and occupation of Jews using evidence from 1910, 1970, 1990, and 2000 national data sources (U.S. censuses and sample surveys) on Jewish men and women in comparison to other white, non-Hispanic populations.

Education

The story of the changing educational profile of the American Jewish community from the turn of the twentieth century to its end is for the most part clear and well known. Jews in the United States have become the most educated group of all American ethnic and religious groups, of all Jewish communities around the world, and of all Jewish communities in recorded Jewish history. This is quite a feat, considering the low level of education of the American Jewish community three to four generations ago. This accomplishment reflects both the value that Jews place on education and the educational opportunities available in the United States. Over 90 percent of contemporary American Jewish young men and women go to college, and their parents' generation also attended college, forming two generations of college-educated men and women. Moreover, many have grandparents with exposure to at least some college education. Increases in the educational level of the American Jewish population have been documented in every study carried out over the last several decades, and the level attained is a distinguishing feature of American Jewish communities. Therefore, it may be considered a core value of contemporary American Jewish culture.

National data sources allow us to analyze this dramatic change in detail. Elsewhere I have used the 1970, 1990, and 2000 National Jewish Population Surveys along with comparable data on the non-Hispanic white population from U.S. census and Current Population Survey data to construct the educational attainment levels of American Jews born in the pre-1905 period to the 1960s and 1970s. These cohorts show how school enrollment ranged throughout the twentieth century, and the reconstructed data highlight several important features of the educational transformation of American Jews.[4]

First, cohorts of Jewish men and women born before 1905 had relatively low levels of education, which increased first for men and then for women. Viewing these cohorts as the experience of a generation, Jewish men and women born in the first decade of the twentieth century aggregated at low educational levels. Even those who completed high school were exceptional within the Jewish community as well as among their non-Jewish age-peers. In contrast, those who were raised at the end of the twentieth century are college graduates; those who do not finish college have become clear exceptions among Jews. In contrast, those born in the 1920s and 1930s were much more educationally heterogeneous than cohorts born before or after them. These middle cohorts lived through a period of transition in the schooling of American Jews, where the rate of educational change and the choices about whether to continue schooling at various stages were at a maximum. These contrasts clearly reflect the transformation from a generation characterized by low levels of education to a generation where two generations of Jews are characterized by college levels of education. The transitional generation (born in the

1920s–1930s) also exhibited the greatest tension between foreignness and American integration. Furthermore, generational conflict as revealed by levels of educational attainments was greatest during this middle period.

These educational data refer to individuals, retrospectively constructed, with generation and compositional changes inferred. At the turn of the twentieth century, census data on those whose mother tongue was Yiddish (or who lived in a household where Yiddish was spoken) had distinctively lower school enrollment and literacy levels than comparable white Americans. By the end of the twentieth century, Jews had become a community with distinctively high levels of education, higher than other groups in the United States. The overall increase in the educational levels over the last several decades has only marginally reduced the gap between Jews and others. On the whole, the Jewish community has become concentrated at the upper end of educational distribution, reducing the educational heterogeneity among Jews, and thereby creating a new structural basis of community and commonality between generations.

Occupation

Consistent with the literature and with educational patterns, the 1910 census data show that a majority of American Jews were either skilled or semiskilled workers.[5] Few were professionals or managers. When Jews worked in white-collar jobs, they gravitated toward "sales" work. In 1910 Jewish women were heavily concentrated in these same categories of blue-collar work, and few held professional and managerial jobs. At the beginning of the twentieth century, both Jewish men and women were therefore distinctive in their occupational concentration in sales and factory work.

In the two generations until 1970, the Jewish occupational pyramid was upended: it shifted from having 55 percent of males in worker or service positions in 1910 to having 69 percent in professional and managerial positions in 1970; from 73 percent of Jewish women with jobs classified as worker or service categories in 1910 to 46 percent in professional and managerial jobs and 37 percent in clerical jobs in 1970. Between 1970 and 2000, even this category was formed by an increase in professional occupations among Jewish men and women, along with a rather sharp decline (over 50 percent) in managerial positions among Jewish men.

These radical shifts over time in the occupational structure and in type of jobs have resulted in new forms of Jewish occupational distinctiveness in the United States in comparison to white, non-Hispanics in metropolitan areas. Particularly conspicuous is the greater concentration of Jews not only in professional jobs, but in specific occupations. Without going into detail, these data show an enormous transformation in occupational concentration with new forms of distinctiveness. Considering the decline in self-employment of American Jews from around 40 percent to 15 percent (1910–2000) and the convergence between Jews and other males, the Jewish level continues to be distinctive. Clearly the meaning of self-employment has also radically changed. Self-employed professionals and self-employed tailors not only require different levels of education, but also are likely to have different implications for generational occupational transfers and for ethnic networks. Both occupational diversity and new types of occupational concentration emerged among Jews by the 1970s, patterns that continued through the end of the twentieth century.

Implications of Stratification for Jewishness

There are two views on the implications of these changes in education and occupation for the continuity of the American Jewish community. On the one hand, increases in educational attainment and the diversification of occupational types result in greater interaction with "others" who are not Jewish. These new contexts of interaction between Jews and non-Jews challenge the earlier segregation of Jews and, in turn, the cohesion of the Jewish community. The institutional contexts of schooling and the workplace may also expose Jewish Americans to new networks and alternative values not ethnically or religiously Jewish. The combination of interaction and exposure may result in a diminishing of the distinctiveness of the community over time through family changes and generational discontinuity. Therefore stratification is often associated with new intergroup interaction patterns that in turn result in diminished community cohesion.

On the other hand, there is a different interpretation of stratification. The emerging commonality of social class among Jews and the distinctiveness of Jews relative to others are themselves important sources of cohesion within the Jewish community. Jews are both marked off from others and linked with other Jews by their resources, networks, and lifestyles. These are the obvious implications of their occupational-educational distinctiveness and their high levels of attainment. To the extent that community is based on both shared interaction among members and a common set of values and lifestyles, the occupational and educational transformations among American Jews suggest significantly stronger bases of communal cohesion than at midcentury, when there was more educational and occupational heterogeneity. The mobility of Jews away from the occupations characteristic of the immigrant generation has been a dominant theme in research. However, missing from analyses has been an emphasis on the new forms of educational and occupational concentration that have emerged.

These two alternative outcomes of the educational and occupational transformations that Jews have experienced in twentieth-century America are often presented in oversimplified and extreme forms. Clearly American Jews cannot be characterized as either a totally assimilated community (in the sense of the loss of communal cohesion) or as an isolated, totally cohesive community. There should be more direct ways other than by inference to assess the impact of stratification changes on the quality of Jewish life. However, researchers have achieved no consensus about how or even what to measure to reveal the quality of Jewish life in the United States. Nor is there sufficient evidence about the nature and implications of the educational and occupational networks Jews have developed over the life course and generationally. Thus the emerging balance of Jewish communal life and its link to educational and occupational changes experienced by Jews cannot be assessed fully.

Nonetheless, there are national data on selected aspects of Jewish life that can be linked to the educational and occupational patterns I have outlined. A review of some analytic explorations along these lines is suggestive. Measures of Jewishness that tapped the multidimensional ethnic and religious expressions of Jews in 1990—including seasonal ritual observances (Passover and Hanukkah), traditional rituals (*kashrut* and Shabbat observances), organizational participation (Jewish educational and organizational activities), associational ties (Jewish friends and neighbors), philanthropy (contributions to Jewish charities), and intermarriage attitudes—were related statistically to the occupational and educational characteristics of households. Not surprisingly, the results are complex and revealing. First, many of the measures of education and occupation are not related directly to contemporary indicators of Jewishness. Jewishness reflects the family life course (e.g., age, family structure, and presence and ages of children) rather than educational or occupational attainment. Occupational measures were only weakly related to most of the Jewishness factors that were examined. It appears that the commonality of jobs and self-employment are not directly linked with religious and most ethnic ties.

The data are consistent with the argument that occupational concentration and related measures have altered over the generations and, hence, the implications of these factors for Jewish continuity may also have changed. In the past, occupational mobility and educational attainment were linked to disaffection from the ethnic community. This is no longer the case. The absence of a relationship between occupation and measures of Jewishness may also imply that having these occupational ties is an important basis for Jewish interaction and Jewish networks. If occupational networks substitute for Jewish communal and religious networks, then we should expect that the relationship between occupational concentration and measures of Jewishness would be weak. There are no measures of ethnic economic resources, ethnic networks, and ethnic business connections to test out these arguments directly.

The situation is clearer for education. The evidence using several indicators of education shows that higher levels of education reinforce and strengthen Jewish expressions, particularly those that are tied to participation in Jewish communal activities. College education seems to promote Jewish-related activities for the age group below forty-five, although this is less the case among older cohorts. In this sense, the relationship between attending college and Jewishness negatively related to Jewishness in the past changed significantly by the 1990s. Again, this is consistent with the view that Jewish alienation presumed to be associated with higher levels of educational attainment occurs when higher education is an exceptional group feature, characteristic of the few. When exposure to college and university education is an almost universal experience for American Jews, its impact on Jewishness becomes minimal or is reversed.[6]

Finally, there is no systematic evidence that the changed stratification profile of the American Jewish community results in the abandonment of the Jewish community in terms of the wide range of Jewish expressions. There is no systematic relationship between becoming a professional, working for others, or being in a job where there are few Jews, on the one hand, and most, if not all, of the measures of Judaic expression as individual measures or as part of a general Jewishness index, on the other.

Contexts of Assimilation

The evidence points to the conclusion that neither high levels of educational attainment nor being in managerial and professional jobs weaken the intensity of Jewishness in all of its multifaceted expressions. Yet the commonality of social class among American Jews and their high levels of educational and occupational reconcentration are not likely to be sufficient to generate the intensive in-group interaction that characterized the segregated Jewish communities in some areas of Eastern Europe and the United States a century ago. The benefits of these stratification transformations in terms of networks and resources have not re-created the cultural and social communities of Jews of a different era. Nevertheless—and this is the critical point—the evidence indicates that the emerging social class patterns are not a threat to Jewish continuity in the transformed pluralism of American society.

The educational and occupational transformations of twentieth-century America clearly mark Jews off from others as well as connect Jews to one another. The connections among persons who share history and experience and their separation from others are what social scientists refer to as community. The distinctiveness of the American Jewish community in stratification patterns has become sharper.

When these stratification profiles are added to the residential concentration of American Jews, the community features become even clearer. Many have observed the migration away from areas of immigrant residential concentration, the residential dispersal of American Jews, and the reshaping of new forms of residential concentration for the second and later generations of American Jews. But new forms of residential concentration have emerged. The development of Jewish neighborhoods in large urban areas, middle- and upper-class suburban areas with large Jewish populations, and smaller concentrations in the South and West also encourage interaction among Jews. Jewish networks have formed around schools, country clubs, and religious institutions that reinforce ethnic and religious culture. So the national data on residential concentration combined with educational and occupational concentration reveal new forms of community interaction. The occupational concentration of Jews, attendance at selective schools and colleges away from home, and work in select metropolitan areas have resulted in new powerful forms of networks and institutions. For a voluntary ethnic white group several generations removed from foreignness and not facing the discrimination of other American minorities, the geographic concentration of American Jews is astonishing.

The value placed by Jews on educational attainment as a mechanism for becoming American (and obtaining good jobs and making higher incomes) is clearly manifest in the context of the opportunities open to Jews in the United States. Their higher level of education and their concentration in professional and managerial jobs has not led to the "erosion" or total assimilation of the Jewish community. While these stratification changes may result in the disaffection of some individual Jews from the community, it may also result in the greater incorporation within the Jewish community of some who were not born Jewish, increasing the general attractiveness of the community to Jews and others.

Educational, residential, and occupational concentration implies not only cohesion and similarity of lifestyle among Jews, but also exposure to options for integration and assimilation. Education implies exposure to conditions and cultures that are more universalistic and less ethnically based, even when most Jews are sharing this experience together and are heavily concentrated in a select number of colleges and universities. If high levels of educational attainment and occupational achievement enhance the choices Jews make about their Jewishness, then Jewish identification and the intensity of Jewish expression are becoming increasingly voluntary in twenty-first-century America. In that sense, the new forms of American Jewish stratification have beneficial implications for the quality of Jewish life. A balance exists between the forces that pull Jews toward each other, sharing what we have called "community"—families, experiences, history, concerns, values, communal institutions, religious commitments and rituals, and lifestyles—and those that pull Jews away from each other, often referred to as "assimilation." The available evidence suggests that the pulls and pushes of the changing stratification profile toward and away from the Jewish community are profound. They are positive in strengthening the Jewish community and represent a challenge for institutions to find ways to reinforce their communal and cultural benefits.

The Value of Education

Education has become one of the core values of contemporary American Jewish culture. In the past, it was a powerful path toward social mobility. Education led to better jobs, higher incomes, and escape from the poverty of the unskilled and skilled labor characteristic of one's parents, and from the neighborhoods and networks that consisted of the foreign-born. Education was a means of escape from the association of foreignness with a foreign language, a foreign culture, and foreign parents. Likewise for many, education was an escape from Jewishness and Judaism. In short, education was the path to becoming American, but it required leaving the community.

Education has almost always been celebrated among Jews with pride in the group's accomplishments. When children and grandchildren became doctors and lawyers, skilled businesspeople and teachers, it was thought that this was the "Jewish" thing to do. But in those early years there was a cost: for Judaism and Jewishness, and more important, for generational relationships. Although parents encouraged their children to obtain a high level of education, the lifestyle associated with higher education often meant disruption and conflict between parents and children who had different educational levels, and between siblings and peers who had different access to educational opportunities.

Looking beyond the costs, over the last two generations Jews have now appreciated the value of education. The value of education has not lessened, but opportunities have increased and spread. Education has not disrupted Jewishness but has increased generational similarities and removed one source of the generation gap. So the meaning of two generations of college-educated Jews becomes not simply a note of group congratulations and pride, and not only a changed relationship to Jewishness as a basis of intergenerational commonality; educational attainment has also become a feature of families that is not disruptive to them and that points to increasingly shared common experiences.

An analysis of educational attainment points to the increased power of families, the generational increase in resources and the common lifestyles that far from divide families but bind parents and children together into a network of relationships. Emphases on education and achievement and on family cohesion and values have become group traits that make the Jewish group attractive to others. Unlike in the past, when interaction and marriage between Jews and non-Jews was also a mechanism of escape from Jewishness and foreignness, the Jewish group has now become attractive because of their family and communal traits—particularly, but not only—education. Hence, like education, intermarriage cannot have the same meaning in the modern context of generations as it did in the former context of rejection and escape. By binding the generations, education has become a family value.

The Content of Jewishness: Religion and Religiosity

But what about the content of this generational commonality? What are families sharing Jewishly? Are they sharing Jewish culture and Judaism? Let us do a brief mental exercise. Think about the meaning of Judaism two hundred years ago in Eastern Europe, where the majority of Jews in the world lived and where most ancestors of American Jews originated. Let us consider a social scientist who decided to take a survey of these communities. Under financial constraints of the Jewish organizational sponsor and under pressure from local rabbis, the researcher included on the survey a question about synagogue membership, the frequency of attending religious services, and the extent of Jewish education as indicators of religiosity. In carrying out the statistical analysis of this survey, the social scientist is surprised by the following findings: Almost no women attend synagogue services (except in a few large cities) and then only a few times a year. Few young boys past the age of Bar Mitzvah, and even fewer young girls of any age, have any Jewish education. Neither have their parents. Many men do not attend services regularly because they do not have a quorum of ten adult men (living in communities where there were few Jews), except for a few times a year when they are able to come to a larger town with a greater Jewish population. Questions on studying religious texts or knowledge about religious ritual were excluded because no one expected the frequencies to be high.

Although almost all the synagogues were filled with worshipers, not all people were able to attend daily or weekly services because they lived too far from the synagogues or lived in towns or locations where there was no *minyan*, a quorum of adult male Jews. Many Jews lived in places where there were few synagogues, few Jews, and no Jewish institutions. Most Jews were busy with the difficult task of making a living and surviving economically, which occupied most of their time and energy. Most neither had a formal Jewish education nor provided any for their children.

Our social scientist also was able to make some further observations. The bitter cold of late fall in the rural areas of Eastern Europe and the absence of access meant that other Jewish rituals in the annual Jewish calendar were neglected—such as building a *sukkah*, purchasing their own *Lulav* or *Etrog* for Succot, or other family ritual activities. These were simply out of reach for most of the poor Jews in these communities. The poverty even limited giving charity—too many of the Jews were themselves poor. Together, climate, geographic access, money, and leisure time availability were constraining features in the expression of Judaism a century or two ago.

The picture was not much different when we consider formal Jewish education. Few persons were educated in Jewish institutions two hundred years ago; there were few Jewish schools, no adequate Jewish curriculum, and the tutors or teachers were themselves poorly educated. If judged by partial and anecdotal evidence, these teachers were more often a discouragement to education than a stimulus to knowledge. (Much of the Jewish education of a generation or two ago in the United States was a major turn-off to thousands of American youngsters for much the same reason.) Most Jewish men and women in the beginning of the nineteenth century were not literate in any language. Even if Jews could afford Jewish books, there were few to be purchased, and few could read them. Jews were living in a Jewish cultural wasteland. At least in terms of synagogue attendance, the depths of Jewish literacy, and Jewish education, and even the observance of some public and family religious rituals, Jews in America by the end of the twentieth century fared much better. However, despite this and extensive other information collected in our hypothetical survey, only an incompetent social scientist would have concluded that Jews two centuries ago were not religious, that they did not "value" Jewish education, or that their communities were eroding.

Correctly, you would admonish me for presenting such superficial historical comparisons: The comparisons are distorting because formal Jewish education, synagogue attendance, and ritual observances were limited by available resources and by the absence of choice. In the home and within families, Jews were committed to their Judaism as much as circumstances permitted. They were Jewish by necessity if not always by choice, being responsive to the peer pressure of their Jewish friends and the discrimination of their non-Jewish neighbors.

Those are powerful arguments, because they highlight the centrality of family and community in the development of Judaism and the quality of Jewish life in the home. Identical points can be made about contemporary American Judaism and Jewish education. American Jewish communities are not confronted with the same constraints of the past, but new constraints and newly emerging pressures operate in similar ways, limiting exposure to Jewish education and the performance of some religious rituals. At the same time, new forms of communication and technologies bring Judaism to remote areas of the country and from distant places to the homes of American Jews. New Jewish rituals—Jewish craft fairs; annual Jewish

Federation meetings, which pull together Jewish organizations representing over eight hundred localities and millions of Jews in the United States; celebrations for Israel's Independence Day; Holocaust Memorial Day; scholar-in-residence weekends; and certain special lectures on Jewish themes in universities—dot the American Jewish calendar as never before. Perhaps these replace some public religious rituals of the past. A glance at local annual calendars of Jewish communities throughout the United States reveals the enormous range of impressive activities characterizing today's Jewish communities.

Being Jewish in the past was part of everyday life; it was the focal point of family and community. The major distinguishing feature of Judaism was its connection to the totality of Jewish life, which meant association ties and family-economic networks, the omnipresence of community and the positive impact of being distinctive, and shared lifestyle and values. The totality of Jewish life was intensive and cohesive, reinforcing the values and shared experiences of individuals.

Yet I argue that religious ritual observances, formal Jewish education, and attending religious services are no more and no less valid indicators of contemporary American Judaism than of Judaism two hundred years ago. Then, the work Jews performed, the jobs they had, the institutions and their cultural forms they created—i.e., the shared totality—reinforced a sense of distinctiveness and Jewish community. Moreover, non-Jews reminded them that they were a minority. Likewise in America today, the numbers show that most Jews at the beginning of the twenty-first century share Jewish holidays and ritual occasions with other Jews (Passover, Hanukkah, and the High Holidays being the most popular), share commitments to the State of Israel, and give charity to Jewish causes. Most see other Jews as their closest friends, work with other Jews, attend Jewish institutions, and want to provide some Jewish education to their children to transmit Jewish culture to the next generation. In general, Jews consider being Jewish important in their lives, even when being Jewish is as abstract as "tradition" and "family values." Indeed, in the minds of American Jews, being Jewish in some form is one of the most expressed and deeply felt values. If poverty and lack of access to opportunities used to be the preoccupation of Jewish communities, contemporary American Jews are distracted by wealth and resources. The commonality of religious expression between the generations at the end of the twentieth century reinforces the bonds created in the home. Just as educational similarities between the generations are sources of family bonds and communal cohesion, the commonality of religious expression binds the generations. This is the case even when the religious base of both generations is weak.

Unlike generations ago when immigrants and their parents were raised in homes that were characterized by different levels of religious observance, and certainly unlike the immigrant generation and their children, the religious attitudes of the third and fourth generation in America have much in common culturally. To be sure, their Judaism is secularized and transformed, but it is not a source of generational conflict. Among the younger generation, Judaism is not a source of rejection and escape, as it was in the past.

Yet what is the content of contemporary Jewish institutions? What distinguishes them as Jewish? Institutions selectively construct Jewish history and cultural memory, providing one basis for cultural and religious continuity. This pattern is similar to families and generations of the past that constructed their own version of Jewish culture and religion, even as the content of their culture had changed. It is the community, the networks, the shared lifestyle, values, and concerns of American Jews that bind them together. The form and content are radically different today than in the past. I argue that the community itself and the institutions that shape the culture of the community are critical in terms of ethnic continuity. Institutions are the visible and conspicuous symbols of Jewish culture and the basis of Jewish communal activities.

In contemporary America, the evidence suggests that a critical part of Jewish continuity is connected to whether there are Jewish-based communal institutions. Jewish schools and Jewish libraries, Jewish homes for the aged, Jewish community centers, and many diverse temples and synagogues are important elements in the development of American communities. Jewish institutions compete with one another for loyalty and commitments. Playing golf with other Jews in a mostly Jewish country club, swimming and playing softball at the Jewish Community Center, or using day care facilities in a Jewish institutional setting do not seem to be very Jewish on the surface, but they are. They are part of the total round of activity that makes for a community of intertwined networks. These secular activities within Jewish institutions can enhance the values of Jewish life, intensify shared commitments, and increase the social, family, and economic networks that sustain the continuity of the Jewish community. They may also reinforce the value of Jewish religious rituals and religious institutional activities. Using Jewish institutions to create networks forms the potential to improve the quality of Jewish life and to ensure its continuity. All of these activities together—not only the formal educational and religious ritual ones—form what we mean by community. Indeed, our studies show that the secular activities of Jewish life reinforce the religious and vice versa, because so many Jews participate in them. The intensities often go together because they lead to the same place—the Jewish community. And it is community that shapes the lives and future of Jews in America, as it has in the past. The connection between the family and these communal institutions therefore becomes a central feature of Jewish continuity.

I have focused on the transformation of religion in America, the development of institutions, and the remarkable choices Jews have made about their Jewishness and Judaism. This is not to argue that there is no decline in some aspects of Jewish communal life, which clearly there are. But taking a broader perspective, I have suggested how Jewish communities in America have changed and how they have developed new and creative forms of Jewish culture. I do not define change as decline, nor the development of new forms of Jewish culture and religion as secularization. Rather, I have argued for a more dynamic view of change that implies the value of choice, diversity, and creativity in the emergence of new forms. Some social scientists have missed these new forms by solely measuring the older forms, and some have dismissed them as the last gasps of a dying community. I reject both points of view by arguing that Jewish cultural forms are emergent and developing and are likely to form the new basis of American Jewish communities in the coming generations.

Jews create institutions—federations, Hillels, synagogues and temples, schools, Jewish community centers, museums and Holocaust foundations, philanthropies, and other local organizations—in which they invest, on whose boards they serve, and which they expand. These kinds of institutions provide major benefits to the community as a whole. From an organizational goal point of view, these institutions define the nature of Jewish culture, Jewish creativity, and Jewish continuity. The old joke about the lone shipwrecked Jew who had built two synagogues, one that he attended and one that he did not, symbolizes the enormous capacity of Jews to build institutional Jewish life.

Concluding Thoughts

Let us revisit the themes that help us understand the contemporary American Jewish community. Defining who is included in Jewish communities is not simply a social science research question, but a profound theoretical and practical concern. In a voluntary community, people define themselves in and out of the community at various points in their lives. One consequence is that those who have taken snapshots of the community at one survey time period (and not dynamic moving pictures) obtain distorted pictures of ethnic identity and community. Life course transitions, such as when children are not living at home and have not yet started their families, are particularly vulnerable. People's ethnic and religious identity is often in flux, and their communal commitments throughout life are difficult to forecast.

Categorizing some Jews as "core" and others as "periphery" (as was done in the formal reports of the National Jewish Population Surveys in the United States) does more than establish an arbitrary classification system. The distinction becomes a social construction of the margins of the community, which culturally polarizes and justifies policy initiatives directed at the "core" and not at the "periphery." The categorization itself is based on a cross-sectional snapshot, formed by asking questions over the telephone about current Jewish identification.

While family values and cohesion are central to the understanding of contemporary Jewish communities, few studies have had a family focus. Social scientists have been primarily concerned about individual identity. When we focus on family we tend to measure only group processes of fertility and family structure. Yet we have argued theoretically for the power of networks as a basis for continuity among ethnic populations. Thus we need to refocus directly on these family networks. The American Jewish community's obsession with marriage and intermarriage has not led to studies of children and young adults when they are not living at home. We argue about generational continuities—the core of communal changes—but we do not study life course transitions.

How do we conceptualize the Jewish family? Too often we start (and end) with indicators of family deterioration. Rather, we can study how Jewish families strengthen our communities by beginning systematic studies of blended families, reconstituted families, intermarried families (not only couples), stepfamilies, and their children. When we study families, we should look beyond the nuclear family to identify the roles of extended relatives and kin. Incorporating an emphasis on gender in our research also requires us to examine the relationship between men and women and the intergenerational relationships between parents and children. For example, the gender switch in Jewish intermarriages from mostly Jewish males marrying out to a more equal pattern for men and women may be of particular importance in evaluating Jewish continuity. These in turn need to be related to institutional structures, such as synagogues and Jewish organizations, and what is happening within Jewish homes.

Furthermore, how do we take religious transformation into account? Sociologists have incorporated in surveys measures of the intensity of religious expression: for example, most, if not all, Jewish surveys since the 1960s have included questions on candle lighting on Friday night, or on Hanukah or Passover Seder celebrations. On the basis of these and other similar questions about ritual, we have made conclusions about changes and variation in religious activities of Jews. We have also made conclusions about religious decline and secularization. However, if we only had the survey questionnaires as a guide to what constitutes Judaism, we would have a distorted view. If the survey questionnaire were our Judaic text, we would conclude that some religious rituals are more important than others. For example, is lighting candles more important to measure than people doing good deeds or having a Friday night dinner with family members, or visiting the sick? The rabbis of the Talmud could not prioritize among the *mitzvot*, and therefore it seems arrogant for social scientists to do so. How distorting to assert that we understand contemporary Judaism by examining the results of our past national surveys. Have we biased our views of those "Jews on the periphery" by measuring whether they publicly attend the synagogue regularly or how often they fast on Yom Kippur? Do we dismiss their Seders on Passover and Hanukkah celebrations by noting that they are "only" occasions of family get-togethers and Hanukkah is "only" the Jewish counterpoint to Christmas in America? It is on the basis of these questions asked in a cross-sectional survey that sociologists have inferred about changes toward secularization.

Institutions, let alone networks, seem to be missing from research. Of course we have included in our surveys whether people are synagogue members or give charity (to the Federations), but we do not ask whether living in a community that has a Jewish community center or a Jewish day care center or home for the aged matters for the quality of Jewish life. Do we find out in our surveys whether Jewish day care strengthens Jewish networks and community? Does our emphasis on national Jewish studies mask the rich diversity among Jewish communities? To conclude that ethnic ties and networks decline on the basis of simple questions about formal organizational membership and the number of Jewish friends reduces the theoretical richness of the argument to empirical trivia (especially when life course changes are not considered).

Finally, we should evaluate Jewish education and not only study how many years and in what types of institutions people obtain their education. I have often argued that the quality of a university course can be measured by how much the instructor learns. I would similarly argue that the quality of Jewish education, especially at younger ages, is seen by how much the parents learn. As far as I know, systematic information on these aspects of education has not been obtained in our demographic/community surveys.

The key and most powerful finding of our research is the reinforcement of the importance of examining the quality of Jewish life. Clearly there is an interaction between the numbers and quality (indeed you need a *minyan* for some purposes), but who is counted toward that quorum is not a social science question where hard data can shed light.

Two critical points need to be stressed: the diversity of Jewish communities and the process of continual change. What works for one community may not work for others. If our premise that contexts (including social, political, cultural, and economic in addition to institutional and historical contexts) matter is correct, then it follows that when context changes, Judaism changes. When contexts vary, Jewishness and Judaism vary as well. Our expectation is that community variation is normal, not exceptional. Hence we should not be surprised that the measures of what characterizes the community in various places should vary. We are not likely to consider the extent of monthly *Mikvah* use in the twenty-first century as an indicator of Jewish identity, nor would examining the wearing of clothing made of wool and linen (*Sha'atnez*) be useful. (These categories may have been useful in analyzing nineteenth-century Morocco or Slobodka.) Similarly, we would also not use only the public celebrations of Hanukah and celebration of Rosh Hashanah as indicators of how communities in the 1950s expressed their Judaism.

We have entered a new century and a new millennium. Continuity with the past is limited when the communities we are studying have changed so drastically. Therefore, we should focus on community and families, instead of diverting our energies from grand questions about Judaism and the Jewishness of our homes to obsess about biology. Imagine if 90 percent of American Jews were ending up with marriage partners who happened to be born Jews but cared little about their Jewishness. There would likely be no perceived crisis, and we would not be concerned about Jewish continuity in America. There would be no perceived erosion, no perceived demographic decline, and we would probably be arguing among ourselves about the right ways to investigate the decline of Judaism.

Whatever the message the American Jewish community thinks it is sending to the next generation, most of them hear the following: "We Jews are great musicians. Your grandparents were musicians, as were their parents before them. For centuries our people have made the most extraordinary music. Therefore the number one priority of our community is that whomever you marry should have a mother who is a musician."[7] Young people are perplexed by this message. "We don't get it," they might say. "There was relatively little music in our homes when we were growing up. A couple of times a year we went to big concerts where we didn't know the score. We enjoy hearing the music from time to time even though we can barely read a note. If music is so important to our family and to our community, why is it that the only thing I hear them talking about is whether or not my potential mother-in-law is a musician?"

Jewish families and Jewish institutions, homes, and communities have been the music of Jewish lives. My personal hope is that Jews and their children and their partners, and their children's children and their partners, will learn to play this music and contribute to this great unfolding Jewish symphony.

NOTES

Some ideas for this paper were developed in C. Goldscheider, *Studying the Jewish Future* (Seattle: University of Washington Press, 2004).

1. See Alan Dershowitz, *The Vanishing American Jew: In Search of Jewish Identity for the Next Century* (Boston: Little, Brown, 1996); Bernard Wasserstein, *Vanishing Diaspora: The Jews in Europe since 1945* (Cambridge, MA: Harvard University Press, 1996). See also Sergio Della Pergola, *World Jewry Beyond 2000*: The Demographic Prospects (Oxford: Oxford Centre for Hebrew and Jewish Studies, 1999).

2. See Jonathan Woocher, *Sacred Survival: The Civil Religion of American Jews* (Bloomington: Indiana University Press, 1986).

3. See especially Calvin Goldscheider, *Studying the Jewish Future* (Seattle: University of Washington Press, 2004).

4. See the empirical details in Calvin Goldscheider, "Stratification and the Transformation of American Jews," in *Papers in Jewish Demography*, ed. Sergio Della Pergola and Judith Even (Jerusalem: Avraham Harman Institute of Contemporary Jewry, Hebrew University, 2001), 27:259–276; Calvin Goldscheider *Studying the Jewish Future*.

5. See, for example, Barry Chiswick, "Jewish Immigrant Skill and Occupational Attainment at the Turn of the Century," *Explorations in Economic History* 28 (January 1991): 64–86; Thomas Kessner, *The Golden Door: Italian and Jewish Immigrant Mobility in New York City, 1880–1915* (New York: Oxford University Press, 1977); Stanley Lieberson, *A Piece of the Pie: Blacks and White Immigrants since 1880* (Berkeley: University of California Press, 1980); Calvin Goldscheider, *Jewish Continuity and Change* (Bloomington: Indiana University Press, 1986).

6. Esther Wilder, "Socioeconomic Attainment and Expressions of Jewish Identification: 1970 and 1990," *Journal for the Scientific Study of Religion* 35 (June 1996): 109–127.

7. This is taken from an insightful essay by Michael Brooks in *Sh'ma* (October 1999).

15

Beyond Apikorsut

A JUDAISM FOR SECULAR JEWS

ADAM CHALOM

In rabbinic literature, the term *apikoros* (derived from the Greek philosopher Epicurus) refers to a Jewish heretic who is both familiar with and scornful of rabbinic wisdom and knowledge. The *Mishnah* declares that the apikoros has no share in the world to come, along with "he who says resurrection of the dead is not in the Torah" and one who asserts that "the Torah is not from Heaven."[1] The Talmud describes an apikoros as one who insults a scholar (*Sanhedrin* 99b), and elsewhere in *Sanhedrin*, the wise are warned: "R. Eliezer said: Be diligent to learn the Torah and know how to answer an Epikoros. R. Johanan commented: They taught this only with respect to a Gentile Epikoros; with a Jewish Epikoros, it would only make his heresy more pronounced." This Jewish heretic is particularly difficult for traditional Judaism, for unlike the *am ha'aretz* (ignorant), the apikoros knows the rules he is breaking and continues to break them anyway. As the medieval Talmudic commentator Rashi noted in reference to the passage above, "With him, therefore, discussion is not advised since he is deliberate in his negation and not therefore easily dissuaded."[2]

Versions of secular Judaism have certainly similarly defined themselves by their rejections of Jewish law, rabbinic authority, and the constraints and theology of traditional Judaism. Jewish anarchists "celebrated" the Jewish New Year with explicitly antirabbinic observances:

> The ticket of admission to this affair in 1890 read in part: "Grand Yom Kippur Ball, with theater. Arranged with the consent of all new rabbis of liberty . . . The *Kol Nidre* will be offered by John Most. Music, dancing, buffet, Marseillaise, and other hymns against Satan." . . . Anarchists determined to scandalize Orthodox Jews, particularly on Yom Kippur. One year they advertised on the eve of the Day of Atonement that a certain restaurant . . . in New York's Lower East Side would remain open on the following day to feed all freethinkers. Many outraged Jews came to protest and the ensuing battle between traditional Jews and the atheists brought out the police reserves.[3]

These were people and organizations that were called, and to some extent, called themselves, *"apikorsim."* But secular organizations that are primarily negative have limited staying power; after all, the second generation does not understand why those other Jews fast on the night of the Kol Nidre ball. They know the punch line but cannot get the joke.

The issue at hand is the risk that secular Jews and scholars of secularism generally treat organized secular Judaisms as only or primarily *apikorsut*, or heresy. For Jews raised in the Sholem Aleichem *shule* system, Arbeter Ring (Workmen's Circle) communities, or secular Jewish camps like Kinderland and its noncommunist socialist rival Kindering,[4] their secular celebrations of socialist- and Yiddish-oriented Passover or Hanukkah were experienced as a Jewish fusion of modern ideas and historical Jewish culture. American Reform Rabbis claimed in the 1885 Pittsburgh Platform both that "[they] accept as binding only the moral laws and maintain only such ceremonies as elevate and sanctify [their] lives, but reject all such as are not adapted to the views and habits of modern civilization" and that "[they] are convinced of the utmost necessity of preserving the historical identity with [their] great past."[5] Just as Reform Judaism is generally presented and certainly self-understood as a Jewish response to the modern world and as an alternative to total assimilation, secular Judaisms should be considered likewise.

Classifying Jews can be exceedingly difficult. If one were studying "Conservative Judaism," Conservative Jews could be defined by the official *halachic* (religious Jewish legal) pronouncements of the Rabbinical Assembly. Or they could be studied through the formal public liturgy and ritual behavior of Conservative Jews in synagogue. Or they could be classified by the private behavior of ordinary Conservative Jews. Each of these lenses would yield different understandings of what "Conservative Judaism" means. For instance, official pronouncements might highlight strong *kashrut* (dietary law) observance, while private behavior may be a hodgepodge of traditional kashrut, kosher in the home but not in restaurants, "kosher-style," or not kosher at all. An official spokesperson might say that the latter examples are not "truly" Conservative Jews but are members of Conservative synagogues and would self-identify on surveys and in public as Conservative Jews. The truth is that different *aspects* of the phenomenon of Conservative Judaism can be understood simultaneously through each lens, if one is willing to explore these aspects as a sociologist rather than as a theologian.

This mirrors the approach we will take to explore secular Jewishness in America. We will first examine a formal approach to Jewish identity that appeals to secular and secularized Jews called Secular Humanistic Judaism. We will then determine how the official philosophy of Judaism translates into one model of Jewish community life, through texts as well as my own experiences raised in, trained as a rabbi for, and working within this movement with congregations of the Society for Humanistic Judaism. Finally, we shall get an idea of the kinds of people drawn to such Jewish ideology and community based on my experience as well as recent statistics from the founding congregation of Humanistic Judaism, the Birmingham Temple in suburban Detroit.

If it is difficult to classify Conservative Jews, it is even more challenging to define American secular Jews who do not agree on a label and who may never join anything. The term *secular* could mean anything from "opposed to religious institutions and authority" to "this-worldly/anti-supernatural." The Yiddish term for "secular," *veltlekh,* can be understood as either "worldly" (i.e., cosmopolitan) or "this-worldly" (as opposed to "supernatural").[6] Thus the paradox presented by the *American Jewish Identity Survey* of 2001, discussed by Zvi Gitelman in his conclusion to this volume, in which almost half of the Jews who called their outlook on life "secular" still believed in a God that performs miracles and answers prayers.[7] On the other hand, if one accepts self-chosen labels as definitive, this group of Jews that has much in common is split into many subgroups—fifty "cultural" Jews, forty-five "secular" Jews, thirty-five "atheist" Jews, and so on. One could similarly separate "ultra" Orthodox, Modern Orthodox, and Hasidic Jews, even though they have much in common conceptually and in liturgy and practice.

Some of the other labels that certain American Jews might choose for themselves that we can subsume under the general heading of "secular" include the following:

- Secular (capital *S*): a self-aware member of a Secular Jewish community, such as those in the Congress of Secular Jewish Organizations;[8]
- cosmopolitan: a "citizen of the world" who happens to come from a Jewish background;
- secularized (lowercase *s*): someone influenced by the general secularization of Western European and American culture;
- anti-institutional: the proverbial "spiritual but not religious" individual who may have supernatural beliefs but is personally or emotionally opposed to organized religion and religious institutions;
- unaffiliated: not a member of a Jewish congregation, a category that at any one time includes around 50 percent of the American Jewish population;[9]
- cultural: an increasingly popular label in multicultural America;[10]
- just Jewish: consistently a popular survey choice when offered;
- of Jewish origin: someone with at least one Jewish parent, but sometimes with two.[11]

None of these include *personally* secular Jews who are members of religious Jewish congregations for any number of reasons: their spouse is active; they live in a small Jewish community and want to publicly identify; or for emotional or historical reasons.[12] Each of these possible labels defines a piece of the whole, and many labels may apply to the same person or group of people at once.

Even within a somewhat organized movement like Secular Humanistic Judaism, there are disagreements regarding terminology. Some members of that movement prefer the term *Humanistic* and object to the label *secular,* because they consider *Humanistic* a more positive term, and, after all, they *are* organized in religious forms (many as congregations, some of which employ rabbis), and they meet religious needs.[13] Others in that movement prefer *Secular* (capital *S*) and reject the description "religious" because, for them, Jewish *religious* organizations center on God, Jewish tradition, and commandments, and this movement does not. A prominent affiliate of the Congress of Secular Jewish Organizations describes its vision of Jewish identity as "Secular Jewishness"[14]—capital-*S* Secular, preferring "Jewishness" over the term "Juda*ism*" (i.e., a belief system) to translate *"yidishkayt."* Despite this semantic difference, secular and secularized Jews attracted to Secular Humanistic Judaism have much more in common. The problem stems from the paradox that "Secular Humanistic Judaism is an expression of a non-contradictory, bona fide secular religion."[15] Or, in other words, it supports a congregational model that can appeal to secular Jews.

A Judaism for Secular Jews

Secular Humanistic Judaism embraces a human-centered philosophy that affirms the power and responsibility of individuals to shape their own lives independent of supernatural authority. . . . Secular Humanistic Jews value their Jewish identity and the aspects of Jewish culture that offer a meaningful connection to the past and a genuine expression of their contemporary way of life. Secular Humanistic Jewish communities celebrate . . . inspirational ceremonies that draw upon, but are not limited to, traditional literature.[16]

Secular Humanistic Judaism is a blend between a humanistic philosophy and a cultural and ethnic Jewish identity. It does not use prayer and worship but rather celebration and study to articulate Jewishness. It understands Jewish and human history through scientific and academic study rather than through traditional wisdom, and it sees ethics as a function of personal and social consequences rather than the keeping of commandments (*mitzvot*). Secular Humanistic Judaism is a balance between connecting with Jewish tradition and articulating contemporary values and beliefs.

There is an irony in articulating a Judaism aimed at secular Jews, because they are often individuals who are opposed to and alienated by organized religion. To some extent, Secular Humanistic Judaism sees itself as descriptive rather than prescriptive. "Most humanistic Jews do not know that they are what they are. . . . They have never bothered to articulate the real beliefs that lie behind their lifestyle— because, to do so, would force them to deal with the discrepancy between what they say they believe and what they actually do believe."[17] Those raised in Humanistic congregations, of course, are taught to understand Jewish identity through this perspective. But the majority of its members were raised in other Jewish settings, and find that this approach articulates what they already believe rather than teaching them what they *should* believe. One member has reflected: "It was the first time in a Jewish congregation that I didn't feel a need to escape, the first time that I experienced no cognitive dissonance."[18]

In its connections with Jewish culture, Secular Humanistic Judaism considers Judaism as the total culture or civilization of the Jewish people:

Bible is Judaism, Talmud is Judaism, everyday life is Judaism, Jewish history is Judaism, Jewish poetry is Judaism, Jewish customs are Judaism, Jewish food is Judaism, Jewish jokes are Judaism; just as religion is Judaism. But you cannot argue that Judaism equals the religious beliefs of Jews; first, because these beliefs were and are different, even mutually contradictory; and second, because religion was and is just one aspect of Jewish existence; today, for many Jews, it is not even that. Judaism, then, is everything that the Jewish people in their very long history have produced. Judaism is Jewish civilization, Judaism is Jewish culture.[19]

In this approach, there are important similarities with Reconstructionist Judaism, though it is significant that Secular Humanistic Judaism does not see Judaism as primarily a *religious* civilization, but rather as a culture that subsumes religion. One can see in this passage the importance of historical study and consciousness, as well as the removed or secularized anthropological stance that religion is "just one aspect" of Jewish identity.

From this general orientation toward Jewish culture, Secular Humanistic Judaism derives three conclusions. First, if Judaism is a culture, one may connect to his or her Jewish identity in many ways, such as lighting Shabbat candles or reading Jewish history. Food is as Jewish as fasting. Second, if Judaism is a culture, then it was created by the Jewish people, evolved through the Jewish historical experience, and can even be changed today. In the words of an early Jewish secularist, Chaim Zhitlovsky, "We created the Jewish religion: Judaism exists by virtue of the existence of the Jews. We elevated religion to a national duty of every Jew because our people needed it and because religion had the power to maintain us as a nation. In these times, however, religion is being transformed into a private matter of individuals alone, for it is now deemed that every individual has the right to believe as he wishes."[20] According to this perspective, even the Torah and Talmud were created by people and thus should be treated with the reverence of ancestral but *not* supernatural wisdom. Third, if Judaism is an ethno-cultural identity rather than primarily a religious identity, as defined by rabbinic Judaism, then Jewish family and communal celebrations, such as holidays and life cycle events, can signify more than rabbinic observance. For example, *Pesah* (Passover) may be explored as a harvest holiday, a spring celebration of universal significance, and a family observance that evolved differently through 1,500 years of rabbinic Judaism and the Diaspora. New connections with modern life can be made through creative *hagadot*, stories of migration and liberation, recalling the Warsaw Ghetto Rebellion (which began *erev* Pesah, 1943), and even by placing an orange on the Seder plate to assert gender equality. As we shall see, this open approach to Jewish culture/civilization as *the* vehicle to articulate Jewish identity will lead to significant changes in Jewish ceremonial life.

On the philosophical side, the "secular humanistic" perspective of Secular Humanistic Judaism derives from both the Jewish and the human experience. Rather than Secular Humanists who happen to be of Jewish background, "from the beginning we have been Humanistic Jews, rooted in the history and culture of the Jewish people. Our humanism has always been enhanced by our Jewish connection, because the message of Jewish experience is that we cannot rely on the kindness of the fates. . . . The rabbinic establishment may have told us that we are the Chosen People. But our memories tell us that we are the victims of a cruel destiny. If the Jewish people survived, it is only because of human self-reliance, courage, and cooperation."[21] In other words, humanism is a philosophical conclusion drawn from one's personal understanding of the Jewish experience. Furthermore, there are many examples of historical Jewish emphasis on the importance of human actions: the tradition on Yom Kippur that one must be forgiven by the person one has wronged before asking for divine forgiveness; commandments in the Torah and rabbinic literature to personally attend to the widow and orphan; and even in the skepticism of Jewish folk stories and humor.

> Judaism is made up of two categories of expectations. The first is *mitsvot bein adam lamakom*, commandments between man and God. For us, these are not really commandments—there being no commander—but teachings. Interestingly, the word *mitsva* has come, colloquially, to mean "good deed"; and that is because the second category is known as *mitsvot bein adam lekhaveiro*, teachings governing interpersonal behavior, guided by values and ethics, including social action to benefit members of the community and strangers in need.[22]

In the Yiddish saying *"a foyln iz gut tsu shikn nokhn malech-ha-moves"* (it's good to send a lazy person for the angel of death), one can hear some doubt regarding angelic efficiency.

To be sure, these sources of Jewish literature and folklore often phrased their emphasis on human action in religious language. But in looking for evolutionary ancestors, contemporary setting may be less important than emphasis:

> There are many stories that clearly express essential humanistic values. They teach us to question authority, resist injustice and respect human dignity within a Jewish cultural/religious context.
>
> In Jewish folklore, one can find Mother Rachel teaching God compassion, rabbis challenging God's injustice, freethinkers questioning traditional pieties and ordinary Jews defying unjust laws. Exploiters of the poor are castigated, religious fanaticism is denounced and the virtues of *mentshlekhkayt* are elevated over ritual observances. There is plenty of humor too. This is a rich source of Jewish humanism that we ought to tap.[23]

In response to the objection that these stories are being taken out of their original religious context and serving "secular" aims, it should be recalled that citing texts and phrases out of their original context to highlight new insights is nothing new to those familiar with rabbinic literature. More important, because Secular Humanistic Judaism understands Jewish culture and literature as human creations rather than revelation, it sees its Jewish connection based on ethnicity and history more than on theology: "The Jewish personality that emerged out of the Jewish experience was heavily laced with skepticism. Jewish ambition and self-reliance did not come from piety. They arose out of the deeply-felt conviction that the fates were not as dependable as the rabbis made them out to be."[24] The culture created by that "Jewish personality" is the source of Jewish connectedness.

The second derivation of the "secular humanism" of Secular Humanistic Judaism is from the human experience in general—for example, characteristics of human life such as the suffering of the just, natural disasters, or the power of scientific knowledge—that has led both Jews and non-Jews to humanistic conclusions. Secular Humanistic Jews "share a humanist agenda with other humanists. Humanist philosophy, ethical education, and the defense of the secular state are some of the [shared] items."[25] In addition to affirmations of Jewish cultural and historical connection, we also find the following in the "Core Principles" of the Society for Humanistic Judaism: "We affirm the value of study and discussion of Jewish and universal human issues. We rely on such sources as reason, observation, experimentation, creativity, and artistic expression to address questions about the world and in seeking to understand our experiences. We seek solutions to human conflicts that respect the freedom, dignity, and self-esteem of every human being. We make ethical decisions based on our assessment of the consequences of our actions."[26] These general philosophical conclusions such as rationality and consequential ethics are not uniquely Jewish in either derivation or application and are supported intellectually by philosophers such as John Stuart Mill, A. J. Ayer, and Jean Paul Sartre (even though not Jewish). The scientific attitude stems from a human-centered approach to knowledge, focusing on "what we can know" about the world as well as what we cannot know. As one Secular Humanistic Shabbat celebration of science affirms, "'I do not know' is a brave and dignified answer, especially when it is true."[27] Consequential ethics also emerge from a human focus on behavior and its consequences. If Leviticus 19:18 states "you shall love your neighbor as yourself; I am the Lord," commanding mutual respect through divine fiat or because each is in the divine image, Secular Humanistic Judaism accepts the formulation with another rationale: love your neighbors as yourself because they are in the image of you.

To summarize, the official ideology of Secular Humanistic Judaism is both philosophic and cultural, both ethnic and universally human. It is not unique in Jewish history to have drawn on non-Jewish philosophy (e.g., Maimonides and medieval neo-Aristotelian philosophy). What is distinct is that Secular Humanistic Judaism uses philosophical tools to draw conclusions on major issues explicitly different from those drawn by traditional Jewish sources, rather than create new philosophical defenses or apologetics for old beliefs and practices. "Humanistic Judaism is a nontheistic religion that combines a humanistic philosophy of life with the holidays, symbols and ceremonies of Jewish culture. Its principles affirm the value of reason, individuality, and freedom. It interprets Jewish history as the product of human decisions and actions rather than the unfolding of a divine plan."[28] Both sides of this identity—"secular humanism" and "Judaism as Jewish culture/civilization"—are clearly evident in the above description and the one cited at the beginning of this section. The way this ideological approach will translate into communities remains to be seen.

Congregations for Secular Jews

Congregations and rabbis were useful inventions. Secular Jews need full-service communities, and they need trained leaders who can respond not only to their

Jewish cultural needs but especially to their human needs for coping with the human condition. . . . In many ways Humanistic congregations function in the lives of their members in the same way as Reform, Conservative and Reconstructionist synagogues do. They provide the same services, ask the same questions—even though they provide different answers.[29]

Again we find an irony in speaking of congregations for secular Jews, many of whom define themselves as individualists and are against organized religion. Historically, American secular Jewish organizations were more often schools or mutual-aid societies, but because of their political orientation to the left, they tended to be opposed to formal leadership, and certainly clergy-like leadership. These organizations included "the Sholem Aleichem *folkshuln*, which were ostensibly Yiddishist and nonpolitical, and the Arbeiter Ring (Workmen's Circle) schools, which were secular, socialist-oriented institutions reminiscent of the Bundist academies of Poland."[30] Through these leftist Jewish organizations, early American secular Jews felt a Jewish connection: "The Jewish labor movement and its institutions became the secular substitute for the old community. In many ways, the Jewish immigrant workers looked upon the institutions of the Jewish labor movement . . . as their contribution to Jewish continuity."[31] The students themselves and their parents, as well as thousands of "unaffiliated" Jewish families, lived in densely Jewish neighborhoods where being Jewish was a function of language and residence as much as belief and ritual practice. Thus they felt little need to join a congregation to self-identify as Jews.

Yet how can we explain current attempts of Humanistic Judaism to attract secular Jews to a congregational model? Two trends have provided the impetus. First, American Jews have been socially and economically successful. As many sociologists have noted, in the last fifty years Jews have moved in great numbers from predominantly ethnic neighborhoods to dispersed suburban subdivisions. No longer in Jewish neighborhoods or densely Jewish professions, Jews have experienced a greater need for community identification, which out of necessity takes the form of a chosen association, such as the synagogue model, a common form for the last two generations. As this move to dispersal progressed, American Jews also became more professional, and by 1971 "nearly 90 percent of American Jews in the labor force were white-collar workers."[32] As a result, it should not be surprising that as aspirations to radical social change became less attractive as they became more successful, "most second generation Jews chose a middle-class secular ethnicity, unencumbered with a radical ideology."[33] The accompanying demographic and organizational decline in secular socialist Jewish institutions created an intellectual or institutional space for something new.

The second trend is more personal and is formed by Jews raised in religious congregations who are dissatisfied with their experience. The narrative of one Humanistic rabbi's journey from his conventional Jewish upbringing to Humanistic Judaism is typical of this trend:

As a child, I learned the *Sh'ma* and the *Borchu*, *"Hiney Ma Tov"* and *"Ayn Keloheynu."* But I never paid attention to the words. . . . Only later did I wonder who was this God to whom I was praying, only later did I question the core beliefs of traditional Judaism that I had simply accepted on the authority of inherited doctrine.

It was while conducting funeral services as a rabbi that I first began to find inconsistencies between my own beliefs and the prayers. . . . In the face of death and tragedy, and certainly after the Holocaust and nuclear devastation, I could not accept God as a shepherd whose rod and staff were supposed to comfort me.[34]

Some of these individuals remain in the mainstream religious Jewish world if only temporarily—for example, while their children are in Bar or Bat Mitzvah training, or because of familial or emotional ties. But as evidenced by affiliation statistics, many others do not stay. Some in this latter group are willing to try something different—such as in a *havurah* or Humanistic Judaism—that articulates their beliefs and ritual connections more satisfyingly. At the same time, unlike the vituperative break from traditional Judaism shown by early American secular Jews, these more recently secularized Jews are open to communities that to some extent retain the congregational model with which they are familiar.

This forms the general background for the origins of Humanistic Judaism. A new Reform congregation in suburban Detroit, founded in the fall of 1963 and led by Reform-trained Rabbi Sherwin Wine, quickly evolved beyond Reform Judaism by removing the term *God* from its liturgy in favor of increased attention to the human condition. This created much local and even national controversy at the time, but it also generated interest from likeminded Jews. By 1969, the Society for Humanistic Judaism was formed with three congregations, and today it claims over thirty congregations of varying sizes, with significant congregations (around one hundred family member units) in New York; Chicago (two); Washington, DC; San Francisco; Sarasota; Boston; Orange County, California; and suburban Detroit, where the founding congregation boasts around four hundred memberships.[35] In 1982, the Leadership Conference of Secular and Humanistic Jews was organized in cooperation with lay leaders of the Congress of Secular Jewish Organizations. This ultimately led to the creation of the International Institute for Secular Humanistic Judaism (IISHJ), a leadership training institution, in 1985. The IISHJ began its North American rabbinic training program in 1992, and as of the fall of 2007, the IISHJ Israeli rabbinic program has graduated seven rabbis. Other Humanistic rabbis have been ordained by different rabbinic training institutions. Finally, the International Federation of Secular Humanistic Jews, established in 1986, provides support to likeminded organizations outside of North America and shares space and staff with the Center for Cultural Judaism in New York City.[36]

While congregations of the Society for Humanistic Judaism neither pray devoutly nor observe *halacha* (Jewish religious law), from my personal experience, they are indeed congregations, providing Shabbat and holiday celebrations, schools, life cycle celebrations, and community support. Many have trained leader-ship, either rabbis trained within the movement or in other seminaries, or

"Leaders" trained by the IISHJ. Some are organized primarily around schools or discussion groups and may prefer the term *community* to *congregation*, but a neutral observer might call them congregations nevertheless: "Imagine a recently arrived Martian taking a tour of religious institutions as their devotees are engaged in their distinctive practices. Assume also that our extraterrestrial friend has not yet gained a clear understanding of the content distinguishing the respective religions from one another. By observing behavior, the Martian would find no appreciable difference on the basis of which to deny that Secular Humanistic Judaism is a religion."[37] Moreover, congregational life in Humanistic Jewish congregations has all of the benefits and challenges common to all congregations, such as politics, gossip, and interpersonal conflict.

Yet the most important overarching difference between Humanistic Jewish congregations and Reform or Conservative synagogues (aside from official theology) is the attitude toward "tradition." If one personally or philosophically differs from one's inherited liturgical or ritual tradition, but nevertheless desires a positive connection, one finds a balance between integrity and continuity: "Humanistic Judaism seeks equilibrium between continuity with Jewish civilization and creative expressions of a new Jewish identity."[38] Giving primacy to integrity means saying words and performing actions that clearly reflect what one believes, which requires creativity when those beliefs differ from historical Judaism. Giving primacy to continuity means forging direct connections with the past by using words and rituals created and celebrated by one's ancestors, even if the content is philosophically problematic. Most liberal Jewish congregations tend to follow the latter course, making minor changes to a few texts and using English "translations" that are more acceptable than literal ones. For example, a current Reform prayer book translates the end of the song *Oseh Shalom* as "among us, all Israel, and all the world" while the Hebrew *"aleynu v'al kol yisra'el"* refers only to "upon us and all Israel."[39] This same prayer book, like its predecessor two decades prior, uses gender-neutral references to human beings, and in this version "the gender-neutral approach is extended to English-language references to God, and, *in some degree*, to the Hebrew [my emphasis]."[40] The desire to use the traditional Hebrew text is thus more important than the modern commitment to gender neutrality at all times.

Another strategy, common to Reconstructionist Judaism, is to maintain traditional liturgy but to supplement or reinterpret: "The readings play an important role by providing a counterbalance to the Hebrew. Changing huge sections of the Hebrew liturgy would sever our roots in traditional prayers. So missing themes must find their place elsewhere. . . . For example, the voices of women emerge in the readings."[41] We can clearly see the importance of "roots in traditional prayer," even if the original Hebrew text is in need of a "counterbalance." As for interpretation, what one is encouraged to think about while reciting the traditional *Shema* and the first following paragraph (Dt 6:4–9), including loving God with all one's heart and soul, etc., is very different from traditional theology (even though the Hebrew and translation follow the original): *"ve-ahavta,"* and you must love. You shall love your God intellectually, emotionally, and with all your deeds. Whatever you love most in these ways is your god. For the Jewish people, the deepest love should be for freedom, justice and peace."[42] A God that is the abstract human concepts of "freedom, justice and peace" could hardly perform the actions credited to him/it in traditional liturgy, but it may be more palatable to a modernized audience than the literal content of the Hebrew texts.

Implicit in both of the described approaches of Reform and Reconstructionism—minimal editing with creative translation or interpretation—is a third Jewish "strategy" that affirms continuity over integrity. This strategy is rarely articulated explicitly, but it is one with which many are familiar: do not worry about what the prayers mean "because they're in Hebrew and no one understands it anyway." As one Humanistic rabbi observes about Jews with such an approach, "It is possible for them to recite blessings and prayers that bear no relationship to their lives or actual values and attitudes—indeed, that contradict their actual values and attitudes—with no sense of the discrepancy. The *words themselves have become ritualized* to the extent that their meaning is ignored as irrelevant."[43] Continuity with Jewish tradition trumps integrity because the difference between personal philosophy and prayer content is unknown or even ignored. The result of these affirmations of continuity over integrity is prayer services that are similar in structure and significant portions, even if the balance between Hebrew and English varies from one to the next.

If the balance tilts the other way and one emphasizes integrity over continuity, one is willing to change traditional texts, even in the Hebrew, that are objectionable to modern sensibilities, as Reform and Reconstructionist Judaism did with the *Avot* (ancestors) blessing but were unwilling to do in other cases.[44] One may also create new and original texts and rituals that more clearly articulate one's contemporary beliefs and values. Thus, Marcia Falk's feminist *The Book of Blessings* includes a new *Shema*: "*Sh'ma, yisra'eyl—la'elohut alfey panim, m'lo olam sh'khinatah, ribuy paneha ehad*" (Hear, O Israel—The divine abounds everywhere, and dwells in everything; the many are one.)[45] This *Shema* begins with *Shema Yisrael* and ends with *ekhad*, but the rest of the Hebrew is entirely different. The same is true for her standard blessing introduction: "*n'vareykh et eyn hahayim*" (let us bless the source of life).[46] This new formula is more impersonal than the traditional "*baruh atah Adonai*" (blessed are you [masculine] our Lord), which avoids gendered God language, is more ambiguous on theological beliefs, and is more supportive of imminent (God in humanity) as opposed to transcendent (God ruling humanity) theology. While other feminist Jews have tried substituting "*Shehina*" (divine presence) for "YHWH" (the name of God read as "*Adonai*" or Lord), in Falk's opinion, "the retention of the formulation 'Blessed are you' has its own limitations. This passive construction is ultimately disempowering in that it masks the presence of the speaking self . . . that is performing the act of blessing. Perhaps more important, the statement 'Blessed are you' leaves the traditional view of God as Other unchallenged—and this theology is clearly problematic for many Jews today."[47] Falk is aware of how controversial her work is: "How does one dare to rewrite such words? I have no answer to this question beyond the raison d'être of this book as a whole, which is, simply, that we ought to try to say what we mean when we pray."[48] If one no longer believes the content of traditional prayers, then one must change the text one reads and sings to accomplish this goal.

Similarly, the liturgy and celebrations of Humanistic Judaism differ markedly from the traditional Jewish prayer service in both structure and content. Where traditionally Jews asked God to make peace (*oseh shalom*) for them and Israel, Humanistic Jews sing modified words to the same melody:

Na'ase shalom ba'olam	Let us make peace in the world.
Na'ase shalom aleinu	Let us make peace for us,
V'al kol ha-olam	And for the entire world.
V'imru shalom	And let us say: peace.[49]

Continuity is provided by the traditional melody, similar-sounding Hebrew, and a similar overall theme of hope; integrity is provided by the emphasis on human action and universal scope. Traditional songs and rituals consistent with Secular Humanistic Jewish perspectives, like *Hinay Ma Tov* or the Passover Four Questions, are sung or read in the original texts, but modern Israeli music and poetry are also used to provide Hebrew content for Jewish celebration.[50] The large majority of liturgical text and almost all prose and responsive reading is in English, with many (though by no means all) songs in Hebrew. Blessings tend to either begin "*Baruh haor ba'olam*" (Blessed is light in the world) and end with traditional formulae like "*hamotzi lehem min ha'aretz*" (brings forth bread from the earth), or they focus on the people performing the action being blessed: "*b'ruhim ha-motzi'im lehem*" (blessed are those who bring forth bread, etc.). Entirely original Hebrew songs are also used; for example, a song written by Sherwin Wine early in the movement's history is one of the most commonly used:

Ayfo Oree? Oree Bee.	Where is my light? My light is in me.
Ayfo Tikvatee? Tikvatee Bee.	Where is my hope? My hope is in me.
Ayfo Kohee? Kohee Bee.	Where is my strength? My strength is in me.
V'gam Bah.	And in you.[51]

For those raised in this movement, these texts, songs, and blessings are much more familiar and have more familial and emotional resonance than the traditional *Shema*, *Kaddish*, and other classical texts of historical Jewish prayer.

From my experience, for secular Jews in Humanistic Jewish congregations there are two general standards for Jewish practice: personal meaning and philosophical consistency. Some may choose to fast on Yom Kippur, and others may not. Some may choose to observe Passover rules regarding grain, even if they do not observe kashrut in general—like the Israeli who eats a Tel Aviv McDonald's cheeseburger on a matzah-meal bun during Pesakh. They may read the Bible, or Saul Bellow, or even scholarly studies of Jewish life to experience a personally meaningful Jewish connection. In the standard of personal meaning, Humanistic Jews are no different than most Conservative or Reform Jews who pick and choose which practices they will follow based on personal preference: kashrut at home but not at restaurants, wearing *talit* or *tefilin* in synagogue but driving home afterward. As sociologist Steven Cohen and theologian Arnold Eisen have suggested, "The principal authority for contemporary American Jews, in the absence of compelling religious norms and communal loyalties, has become the sovereign self."[52]

Philosophical consistency, the second standard for Humanistic Jews, would apply in certain cases: wearing tefilin is both clearly fulfilling a commandment and a practice commonly understood to be this, and for those unsure of any "commander" and striving to say what they mean and mean what they say, such a practice would not be clearly consistent. The result of the application of these two standards—personal meaning and philosophic consistency—is that practice varies within a range from congregation to congregation and from individual to individual. For example, some may consider fasting on Yom Kippur philosophically inconsistent because, historically, it was a way to fulfill the commandment to "afflict your souls,"[53] while others may give fasting a secular significance, such as solidarity with the hungry, a test of will, identification with past Jewish generations, or a personal purification for the new year. Despite this diversity, throughout the congregation as a whole there is generally broad agreement on both the philosophical basis for the organization and on the practical expression of that identity. However, it should be noted that Humanistic congregations are susceptible to ritual and liturgical debates as much as congregations of any other denomination.

Who Are Secular Humanistic Jews?

The final lens we will use to explore this vision of Judaism aimed at American secular Jews is the demographic composition of families involved in a Humanistic Jewish congregation, provided by statistics from a self-conducted survey of the Birmingham Temple (about four hundred member families) in 2003–2004, as well as my personal impression of other communities in the national movement.[54] It should be noted that these may not be the relative proportions of American secular Jews as a whole; rather, this represents a self-selected group of secularized Jews who (1) are attracted to this model; (2) were interested enough to have joined the congregation and filled out the survey; (3) live in a community with a Humanistic Jewish congregation; and (4) have heard of the movement in the first place. Other Humanistic congregations may have different proportions of each group. So who are the individuals to whom a Humanistic Jewish congregation may appeal?

- The Native: like myself, someone who was raised in a secular, cultural, or Humanistic Jewish identity. They may have grown up in a socialist or Yiddishist school, in a Workman's Circle, or even in a Humanistic Jewish congregation. They comprise 10 percent of the Birmingham Temple membership.
- Evolved: the most typical member of a Humanistic Jewish congregation, as much as half of any congregation. They were raised in a conventional liberal Jewish religious identity, but that identity does not match who they have become as adults. Between personal philosophical questions and the

difference between what they experience in synagogue and how they live their private lives, they find in Humanistic Judaism a Jewish connection that fits their beliefs and behavior. In the Birmingham Temple survey, 20 percent of the respondents were raised as Reform and 30 percent as Conservative Jews.

- Rebelled: people who were raised very traditionally (often Orthodox or even ultra-Orthodox) and broke away. They are looking for a Jewish cultural and ethnic identity but reject strict ritual requirements and traditional theology. They are also attracted to Humanistic Judaism's willingness to say "I don't know" and to ask questions rather than provide dogmatic answers. Of the Birmingham Temple, 7.5 percent fit this category.

- Ethnic or Cultural: individuals who are "unaffiliated Jews" or "just Jewish." They often *know* they are Jewish, even though they have had little formal Jewish education outside of home holidays. Jews from the former Soviet Union could also fit into this category. They want a stronger Jewish connection for themselves or for their children (in part because of the declining ethnic experience described above), but they do not accept traditional theology and do not connect with a traditional lifestyle. This group represents 15 percent of the Birmingham Temple.

- Secular Israeli: Here there is no question of a Jewish ethnic or national connection, and many Israelis have strong affinities for Jewish language, history, and literature as the major components of a modern Jewish cultural identity. Sometimes Humanistic Judaism is a natural fit for this group. However, like some Russian Jews, many Israelis are dubious about the "right" to change traditional texts and practices ("the synagogue I don't go to is Orthodox"). Israelis also tend to desire more Hebrew language in their celebrations and schools than most Humanistic Jewish congregations provide. This group represents only 1 percent of the Birmingham Temple survey responses.

- Blended: Many families with one non-Jewish partner find homes in Humanistic Judaism because both partners are welcome as equal members, and families are allowed to explore the cultures of both parents on their own without hiding that fact. The Humanistic Jewish congregation can support the Jewish side of a mixed cultural identity. At the Birmingham Temple, 17 seventeen percent of respondents were not raised Jewish, statistically suggesting that at least one-third of the membership is involved in an intercultural marriage. In other congregations, the percentages are higher.

Understandably, congregations with members from such diverse backgrounds have a challenging time creating celebrations that speak to all of these personal experiences.

At the same time, Secular Humanistic Judaism does appeal emotionally and intellectually to individual members. It is not the only version of a secular Jewish identity that exists today or that could exist, and many more individuals (consciously or not) agree with the general philosophical approach of Secular

Humanistic Judaism than are currently members of Humanistic Jewish congregations. This can be seen by surveys such as the American Jewish Identity Survey (AJIS) or National Jewish Population Survey (NJPS), as well as in behavior: many Jews affiliate only temporarily to celebrate a Bar or Bat Mitzvah because the religious congregation does not relate to their lifestyles; many others drop in or only buy tickets for High Holidays because their Jewish and human selves are not closely connected; Jewish community programs like cultural festivals, Israel walks, and music performances draw crowds that otherwise might come to nothing; and charitable donations from unaffiliated Jews to Israel and Jewish Federations demonstrate ethnic solidarity in the absence of synagogue membership.

So why do not more of these individuals join a Secular Humanistic Jewish congregation? Some simply have not heard of it, and others live in smaller Jewish communities and join what is already available there. Some are repelled either by congregational structure or the associated financial burdens, and some have so strongly rejected their Jewish background that they are opposed to any "institutions," "organized religion," or "religious authority." Some do not agree with making changes to traditional Jewish language and practices, and many American Jews care much less about ideas and philosophy than about conventionality and community. And like every Jewish movement, some join Humanistic Jewish congregations to educate their children and then drop out when they are done, since being Jewish in general is simply not as important to them as adults.

But for those who *do* find it meaningful, Secular Humanistic Judaism provides Jewish communities that justify and celebrate their secular lifestyle while creating connections to an ethnic Jewish identity they value. A Jewish identity addressed to secular Jews that does not demand conformity to traditional models is not a way out of Jewish identification, but rather a way in. Secular Humanistic Judaism is not simply an Apikoros heretical rejection of Jewish tradition in favor of secular freedoms, but rather the free adoption and adaptation of Judaism by secularized Jews to the secular lifestyle they already enjoy. They could have chosen to be nothing; they have chosen to identify as part of a Jewish community instead.

NOTES

1. *Mishnah Sanhedrin* 10:1. Philip Blackman, ed., *Mishnayot (Order Nezikin)* (New York: Judaic Press, 1963–64), 285.

2. Sanhedrin 38b; Israel Epstein, ed., *Babylonian Talmud* (London: Soncino Press, 1952), cited from Jewish Classics Library.

3. Philip Goodman, comp., *The Yom Kippur Anthology* (Philadelphia: Jewish Publication Society, 1971), 331.

4. See "A Brief History of Camp Kinderland," at http://www.kinderland.org/campkinderland/history/history.htm.

5. "The Pittsburgh Platform (1885)," in *The Jew in the Modern World*, ed. Paul Mendes-Flohr and Jehuda Reinharz (New York: Oxford University Press, 1980), 371–372.

6. Uriel Weinreich, *Modern English-Yiddish Yiddish-English Dictionary* (New York: YIVO Institute for Jewish Research, 1968), 285.

7. Egon Mayer, Barry Kosmin, and Ariela Keysar, *American Jewish Identity Survey* 2001, Exhibit 13, http://www.gc.cuny.edu/studies/ajis.pdf.

8. See http://www.csjo.org. The constituent organizations of this body are the heirs of the secular *shule* movement of previous generations of American secular Jews. See the Sholem Community of Los Angeles at http://www.sholem.org.

9. This label may be temporary; many of this group will affiliate at some point in their lives, usually around the age of a child's Bar or Bat Mitzvah.

10. See, for example, the Center for Cultural Judaism at http://www.culturaljudaism.org.

11. For example, see Mayer et al., *American Jewish Identity Survey* 2001 for their discussion of their statistical category of "Jewish Parent: No Religion," http://www.gc.cuny.edu/studies/ajis.pdf.

12. See Michael B. Herzbrun, "The Silent Minority: Nonbelievers in the Reform Jewish Community," *Central Conference of American Rabbis Journal* (Summer 1998).

13. See articles by Sherwin Wine, David Oler, and Walter Hellman in *Humanistic Judaism: Is Humanistic Judaism a Religion?* 30 (Winter 2002).

14. The Sholem Community of Los Angeles, at http://www.sholem.org/secular.asp.

15. Joseph Chuman, "What Do the Courts Say?" *Humanistic Judaism* 20 (Winter 2002): 13.

16. "The International Institute for Secular Humanistic Judaism," in *A Life of Courage: Sherwin Wine and Humanistic Judaism*, ed. Dan Cohn-Sherbok, Harry T. Cook, and Marilyn Rowens (Farmington Hills, MI: International Institute for Secular Humanistic Judaism, 2003), 311.

17. Sherwin Wine, *Humanistic Judaism* (Buffalo, NY: Prometheus Books, 1978), 2.

18. Barbara Behrmann, "Reclaiming My Jewish Identity," *Humanistic Judaism* 29, (Spring/Summer 2001): 12.

19. Yehuda Bauer, introduction to *Judaism in a Secular Age: An Anthology of Secular Humanistic Jewish Thought*, ed. Renee Kogol and Zev Katz (Farmington Hills, MI: International Institute for Secular Humanistic Judaism, 1995), xiv.

20. Chaim Zhitlovsky, "Unzer tsukunft do in land" [1915], cited in Mendes-Flohr and Reinharz, *The Jew in the Modern World*, 388.

21. Sherwin Wine, "Reflections," in Cohn-Sherbok et al., *A Life of Courage*, 293.

22. David Oler, "Securing the Future of Humanistic Judaism," *Humanistic Judaism* 29 (Autumn 2001): 8.

23. Bennett Muraskin, *Humanist Readings in Jewish Folklore* (Farmington Hills, MI: International Institute for Secular Humanistic Judaism and Milan Press, 2001), 2–3.

24. "Jewish Humor," *Humanistic Judaism* 21 (Summer/Autumn 1993): 41.

25. Sherwin Wine, *Judaism Beyond God* (Jersey City, NJ: Ktav Publishing House, 1995), 217.

26. "Core Principles" (adopted October 8, 1999), http://www.shj.org/CorePrinciples.htm.

27. Sherwin Wine, *Celebration: A Ceremonial and Philosophic Guide for Humanists and Humanistic Jews* (Buffalo, NY: Prometheus Books, 1988), 157.

28. Daniel Friedman, *Jewish without Judaism: Conversations with an Unconventional Rabbi* (Amherst, NY: Prometheus Books, 2002), 92.

29. Wine, "Reflections," in Cohn-Sherbok et al., *A Life of Courage*, 291–292.

30. Henry L. Feingold, *A Time for Searching: Entering the Mainstream, 1920–1945* (Baltimore: Johns Hopkins University Press, 1992), 119.

31. Lucy Dawidowicz, "The Jewishness of the Jewish Labor Movement in the United States," in *The American Jewish Experience*, ed. Jonathan Sarna (NY: Holmes and Meier, 1986), 160.

32. "National Jewish Population Study, 1971," cited in Dawidowicz, "The Jewishness of the Jewish Labor Movement, 158.

33. Deborah Dash Moore, *At Home in America: Second Generation New York Jews* (NY: Columbia University Press, 1981), 55.

34. Peter H. Schweitzer, "A Rabbi's Journey to Humanistic Judaism," in *Humanistic Judaism* 29 (Spring/Summer 2001): 3.

35. Society for Humanistic Judaism Board of Governors meeting material, May 2005.

36. More information on each organization is available at their respective Web sites. For the society, see http://www.shj.org; the leadership conference, http://www.lcshj.org; the institute, http://www.iishj.org; the federation, http://www.ifshj.org; and the center, http://www.culturaljudaism.org.

37. Chuman, "Courts," 11.

38. Adam Chalom, "To Destroy and to Build: The Balance of Creativity and Continuity," in Cohn-Sherbok et al., *A Life of Courage*, 104.

39. Chaim Stern, ed., *Gates of Prayer for Shabbat and Weekdays: A Gender Sensitive Prayerbook* (NY: Central Conference of American Rabbis, 1994), 124.

40. Ibid., iv. A well-known example of such a Hebrew change, not only in Reform Judaism, is the addition of matriarchs Sarah, Rebecca, Rachel, and Leah to the *Avot* (ancestors) blessing in the *Amida* (standing prayer).

41. *Kol Haneshamah: Shabbat Vehagim* (Wyncote, PA: Reconstructionist Press, 1994), xxiii.

42. Ibid., 277.

43. Daniel Friedman, "Humanistic Judaism: For the Many or the Few," in Cohn-Sherbok et al., *A Life of Courage*, 169–170.

44. Stern, *Gates of Prayer for Shabbat and Weekdays*, 124.

45. Marcia Falk, *The Book of Blessings* (Boston: Beacon Press, 1996), 170–171.

46. For example, *"hamotzi'ah lekhem min ha'aretz"* (that brings forth bread from the earth). Falk, *The Book of Blessings*, 18–19.

47. Ibid., 419.

48. Ibid., 432.

49. Wine, *Celebration*, 423.

50. Peter H. Schweitzer, *The Liberated Haggadah: A Passover Celebration for Cultural, Secular and Humanistic Jews* (NY: Center for Cultural Judaism, 2003), 9, 36. A few Humanistic congregations choose to modify *"shevet ahim"* (brothers/siblings dwell) to *"shevet amim"* (nations dwell) because of gender sensibilities.

51. Wine, *Celebration*, 397.

52. Steven Cohen and Arnold Eisen, *The Jew Within: Self, Family, and Community in America* (Bloomington: Indiana University Press, 2000), 2.

53. Lv 23:27.

54. The study was facilitated by APB Associates of Southfield, Michigan, and statistical results were distributed to congregation leadership. There were 439 individual respondents to the survey. For this question, respondents were asked, "In what denomination were you raised?" and given the following choices: "Conservative," "Humanistic or secular," "Orthodox," "Reform," "'Just Jewish' (no denomination)," "Other Jewish (SPECIFY)," and "Non-Jewish."

Conclusion

THE NATURE AND VIABILITY OF JEWISH
RELIGIOUS AND SECULAR IDENTITIES

ZVI GITELMAN

As has been made clear in this volume, Jews are difficult to define and have redefined themselves periodically, most often as a religious or ethnic group.[1] Writing in the 1960s, C. Bezalel Sherman suggested that Jews "would seem to be all of these and more": a religious group, a "historical continuum," a "cultural group with peculiar racial traits," a "people." However, he noted, "Collectively, American Jews regard themselves as first of all a religious community."[2] At the same time, other sociologists noted that most Jews in New York City had no synagogue or temple affiliation and that what really linked them was a "sense of common fate." "But we know from experience that when asked, 'what is your religion?' even [nonreligious and antireligious Jews] answer, 'Jewish.'" Glazer and Moynihan concluded that "the common fate is defined ultimately by connection to a single religion, to which everyone is still attached by birth and tradition, if not by action and belief."[3] Bernard Levin averred in *The Times* (London) that he was a nonbeliever, but "when I am filling in a form on which there is a space labeled 'Religion,' I don't hesitate, but put Jew. . . . Am I a Jew? If I do not pray with the Jews, and sing with the Jews, and refuse to eat pork with the Jews, and read books backwards with the Jews, how can I be a Jew? Well, don't forget the form that I filled in."[4]

A decade after Moynihan and Glazer, Charles Liebman and Steven Cohen argued that for Jews, "ties to tradition and minority experience are far more important than common belief, making it more an ethnic than a religious collectivity in many respects."[5] They called "familism" the "key element of the Jewish collective consciousness." Jews see themselves as part of an extended family, "a group into which a person is born and of which the person remains a part regardless of what he or she does."[6] Thus, American and other Jews conceive of, describe, and present themselves differently at different times and in different places. The debate about the nature of the Jewish entity continues within and outside it, and not in the United States alone.

At the turn of the twentieth century, there were available in the marketplace of Jewish identities perhaps five conceptions of who and what Jews are. These were the traditional ethno-religious fusion; Reform Judaism's restriction of Jewishness to religion and denial of Jewish nationhood; Zionism's claim that Jews are a modern as well as ancient nation and hence deserve a state; a secular Diaspora nationalism that justified the existence of a people but saw no need for a state; and assimilationism, the idea that whatever Jews might have been in the past, their future was to merge into the peoples among whom they lived.

The oldest conception is that Judaism is a tribal religion. Whoever adheres to Judaism is considered a member of the tribe or people, unlike the "universal" religions, Christianity and Islam, whose adherents are of different peoples or nationalities.

In this respect, the Jewish people resemble the Greeks, where to be Greek one must be Greek Orthodox.[7] There is a wide spectrum of the relationship between religion and ethnicity. It ranges from the congruence of religion and ethnicity, as in the Jewish, Saudi Arabian, Tibetan, Greek, and perhaps Amish cases, to a close association of the two—as in the Polish/Catholic and Italian/Catholic cases—to countries of immigration, such as the United States, Canada, and South Africa, where the association between religion and ethnicity is tenuous or nonexistent. Then there are largely secular societies such as the Scandinavian, where the association between ethnicity and religion is largely historic. Nevertheless, Denmark, one of the most secular states in the world if judged by the church attendance of its nominally largely Christian population, has a constitution that still makes the Evangelical Lutheran Church the established church of Denmark, and, as such, it is supported by the state.

For the present purpose, I differentiate between Judaism and Jewishness. By Judaism I mean a religion with a distinct set of beliefs and practices.[8] Jewish*ness*, on the other hand, is a sense of being Jewish, in whatever way one—or, importantly, *others*—chooses to define it. It may be defined, of course, primarily through religion, Judaism. At a minimum, Jewishness may be defined as what people are *not*—not Christians or Muslims, not Arabs or Poles.

Secularization

Secularization is a process whereby that which had been explained and understood in religious terms comes to be understood without reference to the divine and metaphysical. On the behavioral plane, the behaviors emanating from those understandings change or dispense with the rationale for those behaviors. Behaviors may continue, but they are no longer motivated or undergirded by the same rationales. The process of secularization occurs on two planes, which may not always be as connected as might be expected. Secularization is an intellectual process, often but not exclusively occurring among people who ponder issues of cause and effect, belief and evidence, teaching and experience. But it is also a behavioral process, not necessarily informed by philosophical consideration. On the first level, secularization is due to what is perceived as new knowledge, especially in science and history, and conclusions drawn from the consequent argument.[9] As a mass behavioral or social process, secularization has often been the concomitant of mass migration, new technology, or urbanization, rather than of a conscious mass rethinking of previous ideas. The process of secularization is "neither one-dimensional nor inevitable and varies in pace, incidence and impact from place to place, depending on such factors as the socio-cultural situation, the conflicting groups involved, and the impact of functional rationality on society and its different spheres."[10] These generalizations apply to European societies, including those in which Jews have lived, and they may also be relevant to Jews in Israel and North America, if not necessarily to Arabs in Israel and non-Jews in North America.

As several authors in this volume point out, Jewishness was expressed in religious terms until modern times. If we examine secularization as an intellectual process, Baruch Spinoza is often identified as the first modern Jew to question systematically and publicly, by virtue of his writings, some of the sacred doctrines of Judaism, especially in his skepticism regarding the scientific reliability of biblical accounts. Despite inferences made by some contemporary advocates of secular Jewishness, Spinoza did not launch a movement and did not sketch out an ideology that would preserve a secular Jewishness while rejecting the main tenets of Judaism. It was not the ideas of one man or even a group that stimulated mass-level secularization. Rather, it would seem that for most Jews the process of secularization was on the second level, where behaviors were changed by mass movements and radically changed social situations.

It is not clear when Spinoza began to be read by Jews. His *Tractacus Theologico-Politicus*—it is doubtful that many Jews read it in the Latin original—was first translated into French in 1679 and into English a decade later.[11] In the mid-nineteenth century the *maskil* ("Enlightened Jew") Solomon Rubin translated into Yiddish a play about Uriel da Costa, another "heretic," and in so doing "transformed da Costa into a radical, skeptical, anticlericalist maskil fighting to defend his views."[12] Rubin translated some of Spinoza's writings into Hebrew in 1857 and advocated that Jews abandon the study of Maimonides for Spinoza's writings. But "moderate maskilim could not bear the idea of Spinoza as a major historical hero,"[13] and some opposed any attempt to portray Spinoza as a faithful Jew. Nevertheless, Meir Letteris published in 1845 "The History of the Wise Scholar Baruch Spinoza, may his Memory be Blessed" in *Bikurei ha'itim hahadashim*, and, according to Shmuel Feiner, "the maskilim were already familiar with Spinoza and his philosophy."[14] They identified him as a persecuted maskil and were more interested in his biography than in his philosophy.

Only at the turn of the twentieth century did works by and about Spinoza appear in Yiddish.[15] The first Yiddish booklet (sixty-four pages) about Spinoza appeared in 1905.[16] About 1926, a self-described group of "Spinozists" in New York launched "active work on the Jewish street" aimed at attracting "Jewish workers and *folks-inteligentn*" to a class on the *Ethics* and to symposia on Spinoza's thought.[17] Needless to say, this was not a mass movement. In 1932, an academic appraisal of Spinoza appeared in a Warsaw Yiddish literary journal.[18] Apparently, the first Russian edition of Spinoza's works did not appear until 1935. Despite the intentions of the New York Yiddishist Spinozists, his works never became popular reading among the Jewish proletarian or religious masses.

Some believe that Jewish secularism as an intellectual movement began with the *Haskalah* ("Enlightenment"). Among those Orthodox Jews whose knowledge of the classic texts and of Jewish history is gained from the Art Scroll editions and similar contemporary tendentious publications, it is often assumed that the *Haskalah* was an antireligious movement. The truth is more complicated. The founding

father of the *Haskalah*, Moses Mendelssohn, remained an observant Jew throughout his life, though his children converted to Christianity.[19] One scholar of the
Haskalah in Galicia-Poland describes it as a "moderate, reasonable, and religiously-
informed movement."[20] As Nancy Sinkoff observes, "Enlightened Jews on both
sides of the Oder River on Prussia's eastern border sought to balance the relationship between traditional religious obligation and modernity's commitment to indi-
vidualism and moral autonomy."[21] The maskil Mendel Lefin (1749–1826) in Podolia
(now in Ukraine) and Galicia was faithful to rabbinic culture and "believed in individual intellectual autonomy because it was a gift from God."[22] Lefin and other
maskilim "did not reject the rabbinic culture of Ashkenaz in its entirety."[23] Perhaps
the virulence of the critique of Hasidism by many maskilim makes it easy to con-
strue the *Haskalah* as an antireligious movement, especially by those whose ideological agenda is well served by rejection of science and general or "secular"
culture, a rejection that was not the universal position of East European rabbis in
the seventeenth and eighteenth centuries.[24] The *Misnagdim*'s critique of Hasidism
was no less sharp and biting, but such luminaries as the Vilna Gaon can hardly be
accused of secularism, so the wrath of the putative defenders of Orthodoxy was
directed more at the maskilim.[25]

As Mordechai Zalkin notes, the relationship between *Haskalah* and religion varied from place to place. It could be assumed that the maskilim of Odessa, a newly
established port city, of which it was said that "seven miles around it, the fires of
gehenom [hell] burn," would be nonreligious. But in Vilna (present-day Vilnius)
most maskilim had studied in yeshivas. They did not look to cut the tie with religion and tradition. Isaac Baer Levinson's *Teudah beYisrael*, "which was to the East
European maskilim what Mendelsohn's writings were to the West European maskilim," argued that "if there is no Torah there is no [general] wisdom, and if there is
no [general] wisdom there is no Torah."[26] The Vilna maskilim of the first half of
the nineteenth century had opened themselves to new ideas, but they lived their
lives according to traditional norms.

However, a "radical *Haskalah*" developed later in the nineteenth century and
"became increasingly pessimistic and disillusioned with the Enlightenment and all
its fine ideas that were never realized."[27] Some turned to science "in the hope that it
would provide . . . a secular, precise, true and certain explanation and would foretell
the inevitable events of the future."[28] The more radical maskilim advocated religious change and attacked the rabbinic leadership, provoking a counterattack by the
latter. Before the 1860s, maskilim had explicitly rejected the kind of reform that was
going on in Germany, but later some called for a revision of *Halacha* and the
Shulhan aruch, the most important code of Jewish law. The *kulturkampf* in Europe at
the time, in which the Catholic church fought the loss of control over education and
Pope Pius IX declared the doctrine of papal infallibility, influenced some maskilim
who became vocally anticlerical. Thus, by the late nineteenth century the *Haskalah*
movement encompassed a spectrum of attitudes toward Judaism, but most maskilim, even the anticlerical among them, did not espouse explicitly antireligious positions, though many advocated "modernization" and reform of Judaism.

Shmuel Feiner sums up the relationship between secularity and the Haskalah thus:

> The enlightenment revolution in eighteenth-century Jewish society was a secular one [but] most of the maskilim did not declare a cultural war on religion itself. They did not wish to sever their followers' ties to the religious sources, the sacred tongue or the observance of the commandments or the holidays . . . as some enemies of enlightenment claimed. . . . They tried to shape a Jewish tradition that was compatible with the Enlightenment and emphasized moral values and reason. It was, however, a secular revolution, because it weakened the public standing of religion and of the clergy and established, alongside them or in their place, a secular culture and institutions. . . . One broad and diverse development took place, in the course of which the sacred and the profane were separated. In this way, two blocs of knowledge, institutions, and patterns of behavior were created, and each of them gained autonomy. They drew upon different sources of authority—one of them from the sanctity of divine authority, the other from the reason, experience, and human will himself [*sic*].[29]

The question of authority has been further complicated in recent decades in many societies, including those in which most Jews reside. In addition to religious and secular institutions of authority, to which individuals had previously paid allegiance, the authority of the individual has been reasserted, not so much in terms of rights, as was the case in the eighteenth and nineteenth centuries, but as the entity most qualified to decide what is best and correct for that individual. The decline of deference in speech and public and private behavior is a manifestation of "individuation," the idea that individual assessments and beliefs take precedence over systematic and generalized ideologies. In the religious realm, individuation involves a "stress on inner authenticity and autonomy . . . a personal quest for meaning."[30] Thus, while "organized religion" may decline, new forms may arise. The popularity of "spirituality"—intensely personal and rarely institutionalized—and of kabala, which makes few institutional or behavioral demands, at least in its current popular interpretations, attest to changing fashions in religious expression. Such trends may have greater implications for a collectively oriented, ethnicized, and communally based religion as Judaism than for other religions, which are more toward the universal side of the tribal-universal spectrum.

Secularism and Its Jewish Expression

The common ground of several definitions of "secular" is removing spheres of life from the sacred (*kodesh*) and treating them without reference to a divine being or to another world (*hol*). Foods (no dietary laws), clothing (nothing prescribed or proscribed), governance, and economics are relatively easy to desacralize. As Americans have become increasingly aware, sexual relations, education and beginning-of-life and end-of-life issues are much harder.

In Karl Dobbelaere's view,[31] secularization means three things: (1) functional differentiation in society, so that religion becomes one subsystem among others and loses its overarching claim; (2) organizational secularization involves the change in values, beliefs, morals, and rituals of a religious group (Reform Judaism and Unitarianism might be examples); (3) individual secularization means the diminishing congruence between the norms of religious groups in beliefs, rituals and morals and the attitudes and conduct of their members. American Catholics who ignore Vatican teachings on birth control and abortion; American Conservative Jews who do not follow their movement's rulings on dietary laws, driving to synagogue, etc.; Orthodox Jews who violate state laws—all exemplify individual secularization.

The secular/religious dichotomy is not as sharp as it may seem. When a Szatmar *hasid* who abjures secular education, has no television or computer in his house, and reads only religiously sanctioned literature steps into an elevator and pushes the button—not on *shabbes*, of course—has he entered the secular world of technology and science? Or does he do so only when he rejects a belief in the existence of God or, short of that, the divinity of the scriptures? When a teacher in a secular institution attends a class (*shiur*) on *Halacha*, is he performing the religious act of Torah study, as his counterpart in the yeshiva is doing, or is he engaging in the same kind of textual analysis and intellectual exercise as his university colleague? Of course, we may answer the question by examining intent, but the activity itself, whether observed by an outsider or reflected on by the person performing the act, is probably neither wholly religious nor wholly a-religious. Were the university teacher to read the text to discover its inconsistencies and logical flaws in order to desacralize it, perhaps he might be more clearly engaged in a secular—and secularizing—act.

Uncertainties, ironies, and subtleties in the religious/secular dichotomy were reflected in the quip of the late philosopher Sidney Morgenbesser a few weeks before his death when he was in great pain. "Why is God making me suffer so much? Just because I don't believe in him?"[32] Morgenbesser, who had once contemplated the rabbinate as a career but became a nonbeliever, often demonstrated his Jewishness publicly at Columbia University at a time when it was not customary to do so. Perhaps Judaism, because of its ethnic component, blurs the lines between the secular and the religious more than most religions.

An early example of blurring of the religious and secular, Judaism and Jewishness, religion and ethnicity, is the Book of Esther, incorporated into the biblical canon by the rabbis of the Talmud after some discussion.[33] Some suggest that this book was the first seemingly purely secular and purely ethnic expression of Jewish ethnicity. "The lack of religious piety in the Hebrew version of Esther is notorious. God is not mentioned by name at all.[34] Neither Esther nor Mordecai display any concern for any of the laws of Judaism . . . Esther becomes the sexual partner and then the wife of a Gentile; she lives in his palace and eats his food with no recognition of the laws of kashrut. . . . There are no prayers, sacrifices or other acts of conventional religious piety . . . Jewish identity in Esther is ethnic, and Jews can successfully hide that identity."[35] Others argue that there may be at least a hint of Divine intervention in the phrase *"revah vehatzalah ya'amod mimakom aher"* (salvation and delivery will come from another place) with *Makom* (place) one of the attributes or names of God.[36]

In any case, modern experiments in a-religious Judaism or Jewishness began in nineteenth-century Europe. Among them were what might be called familism, Yiddishism, territorialism, autonomism, Jewish socialism, Zionism, and the Soviet experiment in secular socialist Yiddish culture. By "familism" I mean—to expand on Liebman and Cohen—nothing more than social association, the strong proclivity for endogamous marriage, and the feeling of belonging together. This was exemplified in the founding of B'nai Brith, until some years ago the largest Jewish organization in the world, followed by "social orders" such as B'nai Abraham, B'nai Zion, Knights of Pythias, and their equivalents in several countries, and by "Jewish" fraternities and sororities in European and American universities.[37] A common language, food and dress cultures, vocational niches, territory, and lack of full acceptance by non-Jewish society, or merely compact settlement, were sufficient bases for Jewish solidarity. In other words, Jews were seen as a social group, identified as such by themselves as well as by non-Jews.

In the Russian Empire a variant of Jewishness developed that was largely unknown in Western Europe, secular Jewish nationalism based on language and autonomy within the Diaspora. An ideology of Yiddish*ism* developed.[38] An architect of this ideology, Chaim Zhitlovsky, claimed that the substitution of Yiddish language and culture for religion "succeeded in building a 'spiritual-national home,' purely secular, which can embrace Jews throughout the world."[39] For Zhitlovsky, Yiddish had become the content of Jewishness. "The Yiddish language form becomes for us . . . a fundamental."[40] For the first time, language was identified as the "distinctive characteristic" or essence of the peoplehood of the Jews.[41] In the early decades of the twentieth century the idea of a Jewish people based on a culture, rather than religion, was popular across a wide political spectrum, from Zionists to Diasporists—that is, those who believed Jews could form a viable national entity without their own state. "In postreligious society, culture was to become the main ingredient of secular attachment to Jewish peoplehood, filling the enormous niche hitherto occupied by religion. Yiddish literature was seen as the most important component of secular, modern culture."[42] Though probably few of the advocates are aware of it, those who today are promoting Jewish culture in English and other non-Jewish languages are heirs to this ideology, with the crucial difference that not only is Judaism no longer the nexus of Jewishness, but neither are Jewish languages.

In the Yiddishist movement language replaced religion, but as David Fishman, a contributor to this volume, points out, the movement was not uniformly antireligious or even a-religious. The movement failed for several reasons. Most Yiddish speakers were murdered by the Nazis and their collaborators. But even beyond the grasp of the Nazis, Yiddish did not survive transplantation from its native soil to the new worlds of the Americas. It could not compete in the marketplace of languages and cultures, ceding preeminence to English, Spanish, and French.

At the beginning of the twentieth century, historian Simon Dubnov argued that "a proper understanding of Jewish history in the Diaspora, to be achieved through historical research, would be the foundation of a new secular Jewish national identification based in the Diaspora."[43] He complemented this naive view of the nature of national identity with the promotion of a modernized, democratized *kehilla* as the organ of national autonomy within Diaspora states. More than a century before Will Kymlicka and others now arguing the cause of collective group rights and representation, Dubnov vehemently rejected the idea, first proposed by the Comte de Clermont-Tonnere to the French in the late eighteenth century, that Jews could have equality with others as long as they abjured all claims to national, collective rights. Dubnov opposed the notion that only as individuals did Jews need and deserve rights. Each nation—which Dubnov but not Clermont-Tonnere considered Jews to be—should have some form of collective rights. The *kehilla* would be democratic, secular, and nationally conscious—if not nationalist—and it would administer Jewish affairs. The weakness of this scheme is that it depended on two dubious assumptions, that states would permit this autonomy and that in such states Jews would prefer communal autonomy to direct integration, even assimilation, into the larger body politic, bypassing the Jewish communal substate.

It is instructive to compare this idea of a Diaspora nation sustained by its culture, history, and autonomous self-governance with the Polish experience. Like Jews and many others, the Poles lost their state, once one of the largest and most powerful in Europe, in the late eighteenth century. Polish intellectuals nevertheless kept the national political aspirations of their people alive through language and culture. Eventually, Poles regained their sovereignty and reestablished Poland as a state in 1918. Could Polish peoplehood have been sustained over many generations without a state? The Polish and Jewish cases are not analogous because Jewish statelessness lasted 1,878 years and Polish statelessness only 123. Moreover, while there was a significant Polish political and later economic emigration, most Polish people continued to inhabit their native territories, which Jews did not. But as with the Jews, religion played a major role in sustaining the national consciousness of Poles. They counterposed their Catholicism to Prussian Protestantism and Russian Orthodoxy, not as purely theological but as cultural and hence national difference.[44] The Russian authorities tried to suppress Polish religion, language, and culture, but that only made mobilization around these more plausible and effective for nationalist Poles. Thus, though Poles and Jews lived side by side in a common state of statelessness for over a century, Polish success in using culture and language as the means of national survival does not offer a useful analogy to the Jewish situation.

Jewish Diaspora territorialism and autonomism were beaten out by Zionism, which emerged from the wreckage of World War II as the prominent solution to Jewish powerlessness and vulnerability. Jewish socialism, most prominently Bundism, was dealt mortal blows by the murder of most of its adherents, the rise of Jews out of the working class in all Diaspora countries, and the association of socialism with Stalinism and Soviet communism, however unfair and simplistic that might be. The Soviet experiment with Yiddish-based secular, socialist Soviet Jewish culture failed, not only because the state withdrew its support, but also because Soviet Jews developed the same outlooks as their cousins abroad who regarded Yiddish as the archaic, somewhat ludicrous language of the "old country" or of the *shtetl*, one which would not serve well either in the new countries or in the cities of the industrializing USSR. In 1931 there were 1,100 Yiddish schools in the USSR enrolling 150,000 students, but by 1948 there were no schools and no students. True, the government refused to allow them to reopen after the war, but already in the 1930s many Soviet Jews had rejected state-manufactured Jewishness as inauthentic, an ersatz creation of the very people who had robbed them of their real traditions and ways of life. Systematically stripped of its religious and traditional references, Soviet Yiddish seemed to some a desiccated caricature of the language. Others rejected Yiddish education and institutions as impractical and useless for educational, vocational, and social mobility.

An American visitor to a pre–World War II Yiddish school in Kiev observed that pupils preferred Russian textbooks and concluded that "Russian is the language of a culture stronger than the secular non-Hebrew culture conveyed by the Yiddish language in the Soviet Union; Russian is also the language spoken . . . generally in the USSR; and all those pupils, and parents too, who ever expect to move freely about the Union must have complete mastery of the Russian language."[45] A porter at a meeting of transport workers in 1924 put it directly when he argued against having his trade union operate in Yiddish. "The matter is quite simple . . . For many years I have carried hundreds of *poods* on my back day in and day out. Now I want to learn some Russian and become a *kontorshchik* [office worker]."[46] Since Yiddish had been made into practically the only legitimate content of Jewishness, the failure of Sovietized Yiddish to win the allegiance of the masses had important consequences for the future of Jewish identity in the USSR.

In general, language does not appear to have been a very powerful nexus for Jewish ethnicity. It has not been the "distinctive characteristic" or "epitome of peoplehood" for Jews.[47] As Professor Roman Szporluk once remarked to me, "Jews are linguistically promiscuous." Though Hebrew is a language unique to one people—unlike Arabic, Spanish, English, or French, but like Japanese and Hindi—and Jews elevated it to the status of the holy tongue, *"lashon hakodesh,"* Jews have not been completely loyal to it. They have picked up and dropped languages with impressive frequency, though abandoned languages have left their traces on successive Jewish vernaculars. Even some very traditional and highly conscious Jews have adopted non-Jewish languages: Georgian has long been the dominant vernacular of even the very traditional, religious Georgian Jews, as Italian was the common language of all kinds of Jews in Italy, and Arabic or French the languages of North African and Middle Eastern Jews. Culturally isolated and religiously fervent Szatmar Hasidim and other Hungarian groups seem to have no hesitation in using Magyar. More recently, English has gained wide acceptance even among Hasidim in communities such as Borough Park in New York and Stamford Hill in London. At the same time, Yiddish and Hebrew literature are neither written nor very much read today in any Diaspora community. Ironically, after the establishment of the State of Israel, whose main language is Hebrew, it may be that fewer non-Israeli Jews in the Diaspora speak the language or, certainly, write prose, poetry and dramas in it than before Israel's emergence.[48]

If a Jewish language is not a plausible foundation for a Diasporic Jewish culture, are there other forms of a-religious Jewish culture that pass the test of viability?

One way to define viability is that a culture should be transmissible across at least three generations. It should be more than symbolic and be able to constrain and direct behavior. And it should engage a substantial proportion of the population associated with it.

Do *religious* forms of Jewishness meet that standard? Orthodox Judaism does, though it was not long ago that many doubted it was either transmissible or transplantable, as it seemed to fade very rapidly with immigration to the Americas and, to a lesser extent, Western Europe. Conservative Judaism seems to be in crisis, as its membership declines and ages, and its ideology seems uncertain.[49] Reform Judaism seems transmissible, but it is also a default position of Jewishness, the last stop on the way out of Jewishness, because its rules of admission are so flaccid as to accommodate half-Jews, inattentive Jews, non-practicing Jews. Perhaps we dare generalize about most Reform, most Conservative, and most "cultural" Jews: theirs is "symbolic ethnicity," in Herbert Gans's term, less a determinant of everyday behavior and more a symbolic manifestation of origin, some positive sentiment, and filial piety. Of course, those active in "civic Jewishness," participating in nonreligious Jewish organizations, social and cultural activities, and working for Jewish causes and institutions have an active ethnicity, one that is important to them and takes much of their time and other resources. Many observers of American and other Jewish societies believe the proportion of such people is shrinking in Jewish populations.

For one thing, a-religious Jewishness is difficult to maintain in a heavily churched society such as the United States, where 95 percent of the population claims to believe in God and 40 percent claim they attend church regularly (the proportions are considerably lower among Jews). But it is perfectly acceptable and is even the norm in Russia, Ukraine, Hungary, Denmark, and other countries.[50] In the United Kingdom, where religion is weak and weakening, there seems to be a decline in attachments to Judaism.

In most Western Jewish populations, as religious commitment seemed to decline for several decades after World War II, support for Israel and identification with the Holocaust were the main pillars of Jewish identity. They assumed a prominent role in Jewish literature, public commemorations, art, music, civic activity, fund-raising, museum building, education, and travel abroad. Recently, mass pro-Israel sentiment and active support has declined, especially among younger people in the United States and United Kingdom.[51] This may reflect disagreement with Israeli policies, increased salience of other issues, or disenchantment with what was once seen as a noble social experiment whose failures have become increasingly apparent. Or, this may simply reflect a distancing from Israel as a *Jewish* state. But, according to one report, "Strikingly, there was no parallel decline in other measures of Jewish identification, including religious observance and communal affiliation."[52] Only 57 percent agreed that "caring about Israel is a very important part of my being Jewish," compared with 73 percent in a similar survey conducted in 1989.

The only experiment in secular, cultural Jewishness that succeeded in achieving its goals and being transmitted from one generation to the next is Zionism, the most successful a-religious movement in Jewish history. It has achieved three of four of its major aims: the establishment of a Jewish state that would be a safe haven for persecuted Jews; the "ingathering of the exiles" (in a few decades Israel will have more Jews than any other country in the world); *mizug galuyot*, the fusion of people of many different cultures and from widely scattered lands into an Israeli nation. The fourth aim, that of establishing a model state (*or laGoyim netaticha*) has not been attained. But perhaps precisely because of these attainments, most Zionist youth movements and adult organizations are moribund, the World Zionist Organization is a retirement home for failed politicians, and there is much talk among Israeli intellectuals on the left of post-Zionism.

As the Shoah passes from living, personal memory, and as it is routinized or institutionalized in curricula, a proliferation of museums and an ever-increasing volume of publications, people begin to get used to it. Though politically incorrect to say so, it is likely that a person who has seen the iconic photos of the *Shoah* may times—the little boy with his hands up in the Warsaw Ghetto, the shooting of a man in a ravine near Vinnitsa, the survivors of Auschwitz behind the wire photographed by the Red Army movie cameraman, the piles of emaciated corpses at Buchenwald or Bergen-Belsen—is less and less moved by them. As the *Shoah* passes from *personal* memory to *collective* memory, from experience into history, it will take its place with the destruction of the Temples in Jerusalem—formally mourned, commemorated on a special day, and occupying a prominent place in history books—but not very personally meaningful to most. This may not happen for decades, but it probably will happen, especially as human beings continue to ignore the "lessons of history" and slaughter each other in Cambodia, Rwanda, Sudan, or the Balkans.

Nevertheless, Israel and the *Shoah* are examples of how alternatives to synagogue-based Jewishness can become very meaningful and command action, but for relatively short periods. *Bechol dor vador*—in every generation—in modern times, nonreligious expressions of Jewishness have emerged, become popular to one degree or another, and mostly waned. We have seen Yiddishism, Zionism, a Jewishness of civic action and social justice, "Federation" Jewishness, and cultural Jewishness. A century and more ago both the Reform movement and the socialists emphasized social justice as the core of Judaism and attempted to make it "relevant" or appealing to contemporary Jews. The Reform movement continues to stress social action—it has a highly visible special committee dedicated to that element of Reform Judaism—but it never abandoned the synagogue or temple, and in recent years many in the Reform movement have moved toward traditional Jewish forms (increased use of Hebrew, Friday night and Saturday morning services, wearing *kippot*, and Zionism).

Jewishness as a civic religion inspired by the social justice ideals of the prophets still enjoys currency in the Jewish world, though the Orthodox seem increasingly focused on ritual and less concerned with prophetic ideals. *Tikun olam* (making the world a better place) has been the one Hebrew phrase that most Jewish civic leaders, otherwise blissfully ignorant of Hebrew and any other Jewish language, repeat as a mantra. But the disillusion with the left in Europe, with the African American movement in the United States, and with much of the third world, as well as the *embourgeoisement* of world Jewry has made this channel for the expression of Jewishness less popular than it was from the 1930s to the 1960s. At the same time, many Jews ask why social justice need be sought in a "parochial" Jewish context, just as some Jews see no further need for Jewish athletic or social clubs.

Following the Six Day War in 1967, for about thirty years a new form of Jewish activism and expression became popular. This was a civic Jewishness, expressed by being active in communal politics and projecting a Jewish political agenda onto local, state, and national arenas. Perhaps the nomination of Joseph Lieberman in 2000 by the Democratic Party to be vice president of the United States marks the *decline* of that mode of Jewish expression, since he showed that a highly visible, even traditionally religious, Jew could be in the mainstream of American politics. Jews need not be on the sidelines with special agendas but could be in the thick of things and yet maintain their own values. Similarly, the current decline of federations and their role in local and national Jewish life signals that the path to upward Jewish mobility does not lie exclusively through them. The heyday of federation Jewishness in the United States, and perhaps of civic engagement in British, French, German, Russian, and other Jewish communities, may be over. Riven by organizational disputes, diminished by rapid personnel turnover, damaged by the poor quality and Jewish ignorance of some of the Jewish "civil service," federations, still the largest fund-raising institution of American Jewry, attract fewer people to their conventions, have not increased their fund-raising even though Jewish wealth continues to grow, and may not be attracting the same caliber of activists as they did earlier. Now that Jews can serve on the boards of local symphonies, national museums, and the most exclusive organizations, federations are no longer the main channel for upward social mobility and high communal visibility.

In Europe, national Jewish bodies have been challenged by upstarts and have been at times stained by corruption. In the former Soviet Union, they have failed to inspire and organize the Jewish population, and in other post-Communist states (Czech Republic, Croatia, Lithuania, Ukraine) they have fractionated into publicly feuding groups. Similarly, the World Jewish Congress, badly damaged by internecine disputes and recriminations, may enjoy much more authority with non-Jewish bodies than with Jews themselves.

Could it be that this shift from one form of civic Jewishness to another is precisely the *strength* of an a-religious Jewishness? It reflects the ability to adjust to changing circumstances, shifting tastes, new fashions. But it can do so only as long as there is a critical mass of people committed to their Jewishness, its expression and perpetuation, whether by primordial sentiments, intellectual conviction, or even inertia. They must be willing to posit their Jewishness as an identity that, though its forms and even content may shift, will always command their loyalty. Judaism (religion) also changes, of course, though its fundamental beliefs seem to persist. It demands undivided loyalty, though lately some have argued for the possibility of a Jewish-Christian identity.

Finally, in recent years artistic and literary expressions of Jewish culture have been touted as important ways of being Jewish in Europe and the United States.[53]

The death of Saul Bellow signaled a transition to the new generation of Allegra Goodmans, Jonathan Foers and others who are regularly reviewed in both the *Forward* and the *New York Times*, awarded literary prizes, funded by the National Foundation for Jewish Culture and others, and make frequent appearances at Jewish Community Centers, the 92nd Street Y, and college campuses. Is literature, generally considered a pastime for nonwriters, sufficiently demanding and informative to shape people's lives, or is it at most reinforcement for what one already does and believes—perhaps provoking an occasional reevaluation—and at a minimum entertainment? Much celebrated in Jewish media as evidence of a "Jewish revival," expressions of Jewishness in the arts do not have the power to direct behavior that religion does. Reading literature is for most people an occasional activity. Even if regularly accompanied by visits to Jewish museums and concerts, can literature and the arts constitute or even support a way of life? Perhaps the consumer of Jewish arts does so because he or she has a basic underlying commitment to Jewishness—to *Jewish* literature and *Jewish* art—born of a primordial sense of belonging and identification with the tribe and its culture. For such a person, Jewishness may not be a *way* of life, but it is a *part* of life. The choice of reading books on Jewish themes is not accidental, but does it portend more than that? We shall return to this issue.

In the United States, Israel, and some other major centers of Jewish population—probably not in the Former Soviet Union—there has been a shift to emphasis on the individual ("individuation") and the satisfaction of his or her wants (or perceived needs) and away from the collective. As observed earlier, this is expressed in "spirituality," "Jewish renewal," the adaptation and distortion of kabala to a "new age" fad, a renewed emphasis on personal creativity and artistry, as exemplified in the Jewish cultural festivals, artistic endeavors, and the foundations that support them. In Israel, the demise of kibbutzim and youth movements are manifestations of the same de-emphasis on the collective. Whatever else they do, these new modes of Jewish expression affect the collective. Some believe they *weaken* the collective by encouraging centrifugal forces that impede the sense of collective belonging and commitment, creating a cacophony that prevents outsiders from hearing a single voice of the Jewish people. Others argue that by accommodating diverse expressions of Jewishness, more people are brought into a larger tent of Jewishness, enabling the harmonization of personal expression with collective belonging.

There the spectrum of attitudes toward Jewishness and concomitant behaviors range from militant, conscious secularism of the kind that once led the anarchists to have balls on Yom Kippur; to a de facto secularism, one born largely of indifference and inattention; then to a de facto religionism created by conformity to what are seen as communal norms in America and its Jewish population (and this obeisance to communal expectations exists no less in the Orthodox than in the other denominations); and finally to conscious, considered, committed religiosity. What makes contemporary Jewry in Europe and the Americas different from the Jewry of a century ago is that, to cite a popular cliché, Jews today are all "Jews by choice." Not only can belief not be coerced, which was never really possible, but even public behavior and expression of Jewishness cannot be commanded—which once was possible—but must be gained in fierce competition with other allegiances and even identities.[54]

We should remember that ethnic groups are defined not only by cultural content, but by boundaries—that is, the lines drawn by those inside the group and outside it which determine who is in and who is out. In multicultural, diverse America, the boundaries between Jews and others have been blurred by intermarriage and its acceptance, acculturation, social integration, and the erosion of a distinct culture. Though the boundaries between Jews and others have greatly eroded in the United States, they are still quite discernible in Eastern Europe and in parts of Western Europe. In Europe, the side of the wall constructed by the group inside the boundary (Jews) may have eroded, but the side constructed by those outside has generally not eroded as much. In any case, it could be rebuilt.

The near disappearance of militant secularism in America, Western Europe, and the post-Communist states (though one could conceive of it reviving in America in reaction to the Christianizing of the public square) and the indifference of secularism-by-default means that for most Jews on this end of the religiosity spectrum there is no longer a thick Jewish culture, one with strong, tangible, visible manifestations such as distinctive language, customs, foods, clothing, areas of residence, and occupations. Yiddish, Jewish neighborhoods, Jewish foods, and types of clothing, and the concentration of Jews in the needle trades are subjects of nostalgia and memory rather than components of contemporary Jewishness. Instead of these, we have a thin culture, a "common and distinct system of understandings and interpretations that constitute normative order and world view and provide strategic and stylistic guides to action."[55] The Orthodox, especially the ultra-Orthodox, retain a thick Jewish culture, but most a-religious Jewish cultures have been very much thinned. There are groups of nonreligious or non-Orthodox Jews involved in thick cultures—those who teach and take Judaic studies courses, activists in Jewish organizations, and Jewish civil servants and teachers. But the vast majority of Jews in the Diaspora give only occasional expression to their Jewishness. It is a pastime, not a vocation; a luxury, not a necessity; occasional rather than constant and all-embracing. How much stamina does thin culture have? Does it inevitably move from thin culture to symbolic ethnicity,[56] and then to assimilation and hence the disappearance of Jewishness ("straight line theory"), or does it have a long shelf-life, a self-sustaining capacity?

That question should be answered empirically, rather than speculatively or by wishful thinking. So we turn to empirical data on the question of contemporary secular and religious expressions of Jewishness. The American Jewish Identity Survey took a survey by phone of 1,668 people who were identified as Jewish. The interviews lasted only seven minutes on average and did not permit exploration or clarification of ambiguities (e.g., "What do you mean when you say. . . .?").[57] There are at least two other problems with this study. It was sponsored by advocates of secular or cultural Judaism rather than by a disinterested body. The results were interpreted by the survey's sponsors as showing that more than half of American Jewry considers itself secular. However, the survey did not define *secular* either to the respondents or in its report. Thus, there is no way to know what those who designed and responded to the survey understood by *secular*. Does it mean agnostic, atheist, believing in a deity but not in organized religion? Is it to be understood as not adhering to the prescriptions and proscriptions of a religion while retaining a nominal affiliation with it? Does it mean working and living in an a-religious environment? The confusion and lack of clarity this engendered can be seen in the following findings. On one hand, 42 percent of those who say they are Jewish "by *religion*" describe their outlook as "secular" or "somewhat secular." But of these 42 percent, only 14 percent deny (even "somewhat") the existence of God. Only 23 percent of Jews with "no religion" deny God's existence. Are they deists who believe that God exists but do not believe in religion? The biggest conundrum is in table 13: 53 percent of those who are "fully secular" believe God exists and 55 percent believe God hears prayers. In fact, 12 percent of the respondents define themselves as both "secular" and "Orthodox." So what on earth—or in Heaven's name—does *secular* mean?

Does it mean that they do not follow a religious lifestyle, whatever that may be? That they never participate in a religious ceremony? We are told that two-thirds of American Jews participate in a Passover *seder*.[58] Is that seen as a religious act or just food, family, and fun? Are these people analogous to the *masortim* described by Liebman and Yadgar in this book? Curiously, only 1 percent of the respondents identify themselves with the secular humanist branch of Judaism. From this survey we learn next to nothing about how secularism is understood, and so we are no better off in understanding what secularism means to American Jews than we were before the survey.[59]

The problematic 2001 National Jewish Population Survey also sheds no light on the question. While in 1990 the NJPS estimated that 16 percent of American Jews had been born Jewish but had no religion currently, and thus were classified as "secular,"[60] the results of the 2001 NJPS do not seem to include this category.[61] In Great Britain, 26 percent of Jews surveyed nationally in 1995 defined themselves as secular, and another 18 percent as "just Jewish." In Russia and Ukraine, while over a third of Jews surveyed in the early and late 1990s declared a belief in God or inclination to such belief, very few professed to follow the Jewish religion. Thus, there is no doubt that a-religious Jews form a substantial portion of several Jewish populations, though their proportion in the American Jewish population, still the largest in the world, is uncertain. But I believe it is misleading to assert, as some have, that the majority of Jews worldwide self-define as secular—that is, they live a nonreligious, non-halachic lifestyle—since this would include all Reform, Reconstructionist, and the great majority of Conservative Jews in America, the masortim in Israel (perhaps 40 percent of adults) and many people affiliated with the (Orthodox) United Synagogue in the United Kingdom. They may live "a non-religious, non-halachic lifestyle," but would they see themselves as secular? Except for the masortim, analyzed by Liebman and Yadgar, the others do not generally adhere to Halacha. Yet, I suspect most of them would deny that they are secular.

Jewishness and Judaism

We tend to periodize "ages of" something. We speak of "the age of reason" or an "age of secularization." These may be useful as heuristic devices. They help simplify and order events and tendencies, but they should not be taken literally. In each one of these "ages" there have been and probably always will be countertrends to the dominant one. Thus, in a "religious age," there might well be nonreligious voices and activities. If the present age is one of secularization—that seems to be true in Western Europe—we observe the concurrent strengthening of religious beliefs and behaviors in other parts of the world.

Church attendance and belief in God have plummeted in Western Europe, even in such formerly religious countries as Spain and Italy. In 2004, only 44 percent of Britons said they believed in God, in contrast to the 77 percent who asserted such belief in 1968, and a third of the young people surveyed described themselves as agnostics or atheists. Fully 81 percent said Britain was becoming more secular.[62] Ronald Inglehart's and Pippa Norris's study in many countries confirms this tendency—except in America, of course.[63] Here we have a religious resurgence, a form of American exceptionalism that no one has been able to explain satisfactorily. In the last ten to twenty years religion seems to have replaced class as the organizing principle of many people's political thinking and behavior. About 40 percent of Americans surveyed in 2002 considered themselves evangelicals or "born-again" Christians. The president, vice president, Speaker of the House, and the House majority leader, as well as the former attorney general at the time all defined themselves as members of this group.[64] Rodney Stark titles his article analyzing the decline of secularism as "Secularism, R.I.P."[65] Jeffrey Hadden writes of "Desacralizing Secularization Theory" and maintains that sociologists who discern secularization as the trend of the times are making a "silent prescriptive assertion that this is good," but "there is no substantive body of data confirming the secularization process. To the contrary, the data suggest that secularization is not happening [in the United States]."[66]

The data on Jews are too sparse to judge whether they are becoming more secular. Significant numbers of Jews may be attracted to Judaism, but other powerful forces pull even greater numbers away from it. Still, as long as America remains a "churched" society and social expectations are that one has at least a formal affiliation with a religion—no candidate for major political office has declared or would declare himself or herself an atheist—Jews will be pressured to have at least a nominal affiliation with Judaism. Adam Chalom's chapter illustrates how even a secular humanist variant of Judaism or Jewishness is cloaked in religious forms ("temple," "congregation," meetings on the Sabbath). But it seems that Jewishness will be a secondary, tertiary, or even more remote driving force of most Diaspora Jews' thinking and behavior. Those whose professions or leisure time commitments involve them heavily in Jewish affairs will be the minority, as they are now. This does not mean that Jewish culture will be irrelevant or inconsequential to the majority. Just as there are opera fans who attend several performances a year and pay heavily for the privilege, and just as some spend some time outside the opera reading and thinking about it, so too will Jewish culture, however expressed, continue to entertain, fascinate, attract, and engage. But, like opera, it will not be a guide to life.[67] It is not clear that forms of Jewishness that will engage large numbers of nominal Jews exist apart from religion today, except in the State of Israel. Stephen Whitfield postulates that "only religion can form the inspirational core of a viable and meaningful Jewish culture," at least in America,[68] and Yadgar and Liebman come to the same conclusion in their chapter on secular Jews in Israel. That was not true in Eastern Europe before the Second World War, and it may not be true in parts of Europe today, but it is difficult to find good reasons to dispute Whitfield regarding the largest Jewish Diaspora community. It may be equally difficult to ascertain what constitutes "sufficient" Jewish involvement and commitment to assure the survival and intergenerational transmission of nonreligious Jewishness. In some countries, anti-Semitism can still be counted on to force Jewish consciousness on those who otherwise would not have it. But, as in the case of Soviet Jewry, a negative Jewish consciousness can also increase the incentives to abandon Jewishness. In any case, most Jews believe that Jewish culture or Judaism have more to offer than being an object of scorn and persecution. On what precisely that is, there is no agreement. As long as significant numbers of people debate the issue, the survival of Jewishness is assured.

NOTES

1. For a survey and analysis of nineteenth- and twentieth-century social science studies of Jews, see Mitchell Hart, *Social Science and the Politics of Modern Jewish Identity* (Stanford: Stanford University Press, 2000).

2. C. Bezalel Sherman, *The Jew within American Society* (Detroit: Wayne State University Press, 1965), xi, 218.

3. Nathan Glazer and Daniel Patrick Moynihan, *Beyond the Melting Pot* (Cambridge, MA: MIT Press, 1963), 140–142.

4. "The Jews Who Choose," *London Times*, October 6, 1995. Strikingly, none of the five letters to the editor reacting to Levin's article even hinted that one could be a Jew without practicing Judaism (*London Times*, October 10, 1995, 19).

5. Wade Clark Roof and William McKinney, *American Mainline Religion: Its Changing Shape and Future* (New Brunswick, NJ: Rutgers University Press, 1987), 102. Similar conclusions are reached by Barry Kosmin and Seymour Lachman, *One Nation Under God* (New York: Harmony Books, 1993), 121.

6. Charles Liebman and Steven Cohen, *Two Worlds of Judaism* (New Haven: Yale University Press, 1990), 17.

7. The historical relationship between Christian Orthodoxy and nationality is traced in Victor Roudometof, *Nationalism, Globalization and Orthodoxy* (Westport, CT: Greenwood, 2001); on the Greek case, see Adamantia Polis, "The Greek Concept of National Identity," *ASEN Bulletin* 7 (Spring–Summer 1994), 11–14; on Romanian Orthodoxy and ethnic identity, see Gavril Flora, Georgina Szilyagi, and Victor Roudometof, "Religion and National Identity in Post-Communist Romania," *Journal of Southern Europe and the Balkans* 7 (April 2005): 35–55.

8. Karl Dobbelaere defines religion as "a unified system of beliefs and practices relative to a supra-empirical, transcendent reality that unites all who adhere to it into a single moral community." *Secularization: An Analysis at Three Levels* (Brussels: PIE—Peter Lang, 2002), 52.

9. Owen Chadwick, *The Secularization of the European Mind in the Nineteenth Century* (Cambridge: Cambridge University Press 1975), 250.

10. Dobbelaere, *Secularization*, 103.

11. Personal communication from Steven Nadler, April 1, 2005. The French title is *Reflexions curieuses d'un esprit des-interrese . . .*, and the title page indicates it was published in Cologne by Claude Emanuel. Apparently, the French translation was published surreptitiously, with three different title pages.

12. Shmuel Feiner, *Haskalah and History* (Oxford: Littman Library, 2002), 145.

13. Ibid., 147.

14. Ibid, 145.

15. Personal communication from Alan Nadler, April 3, 2005.

16. Philip Krantz, *Boruch Shpinoza, zayn lebn un zayn filosofie*, cited in Jacob Shatzky, *Spinoza buch* (New York: Spinoza Institute in America—Yidisher optayl, 1932), 176.

17. Ibid., 7.

18. K. Gutenboim, "Shpinoza motivn," *Globus* 4 (October 1932): 1–24. The editor stated that "in a forthcoming number," Aharon Zeitlin would publish "God, Man and Geometry," an article about the "'godless' god of the philosophers, the man-less [*mentsh-lozn*] god of Boruch Shpinoza, and the living man-god of Lev Tolstoi" (24). In an earlier issue of *Globus*, Leo Finkelshtain reported on a Spinoza conference in The Hague. "These are congresses of fervent fans. The Hasidim are going to the rebbe's grave. It's a Spinoza community which makes periodic pilgrimages [*oileh regel*] to The Hague."

19. See Alexander Altmann, *Moses Mendelssohn: A Biographical Study* (London: Littman Library, 1998), and Dominique Bourel, *Moses Mendelssohn: La Naissance du Judaisme moderne* (Paris: Gallimard, 2004).

20. Nancy Sinkoff, *Out of the Shtetl: Making Jews Modern in the Polish Borderlands* (Providence: Brown University Press, 2004), 272. A Soviet Marxist interpretation of Lefin and his followers can be found in Maks Erik, *Etiudn tsu der geshichte fun der haskole, 1789–1881* (Minsk: Meluche farlag, natsektor, 1934). For example, Erik writes, "The right wing of the Galician Haskalah under the leadership of Lefin, Perl, Rapaport, Krochmal represents a closed system of ideas—the ideology of a reactionary detachment of the bourgeoisie, still confined to feudal views and concepts, the ideology of a stratum which marches forward to capitalist development, but cautiously, fearfully, looking backwards" (191). The Soviet rhetoric should not put one off from a valuable study.

21. Ibid., 5.

22. Ibid., 9.

23. Ibid., 90.

24. Jacob Raisin cites many examples of secular knowledge and writings among East European rabbis and concludes that "it must not be supposed that supremacy in the Talmud was secured at the cost of secular knowledge. . . . Not a few of the prominent men united piety with philosophy, and thorough knowledge of the Talmud with mastery of one or more of the sciences of the time" (*The Haskalah Movement in Russia* [Philadelphia: Jewish Publication Society, 1913], 35). Nevertheless, because of some radical maskilim, *Haskalah* became "synonymous with apostasy or licentiousness. . . . To be called 'Berlinchick' or 'Deitschel' was tantamount to being called infidel and epicurean, anarchist and outlaw" (131, 133). "Thus began the bitter fight against Haskalah, in which Hasidim and Mitnaggedim, forgetting their differences, joined hands, and stood shoulder to shoulder" (134). On the conflict between Hasidim and Maskilim, see Raphael Mahler, *Hahasidut vehaHaskalah* (Merhaviya, Israel: Sifriat Poalim, 1961).

25. On the opposition to Hasidism, see Alan Nadler, *The Faith of the Mithnagdim: Rabbinic Responses to Hasidic Rapture* (Baltimore: Johns Hopkins University Press, 1997).

26. Quoted in Mordechai Zalkin, *Be-alot hashahar* (Jerusalem: Magnes Press, 2000), 263.

27. Shmuel Feiner, *The Jewish Enlightenment* (Philadelphia: University of Pennsylvania Press, 2002), 371.

28. Ibid.

29. Feiner, *The Jewish Enlightenment*, 371.

30. Dobbelaere, *Secularization*, 143.

31. Ibid.

32. Obituary, *New York Times*, August 4, 2004.

33. Talmud Bavli, Tractate Megilah, chap. 1, 7b.

34. Some have seen the reference to salvation coming from "*Makom aher*" (literally, another place; 4:14) as a reference to God since one of God's names is "*Makom*."

35. Sidnie White Crawford, "Esther and Judith: Contrasts in Character," in *The Book of Esther in Modern Research, ed.* Sidnie White Crawford and Leonard Greenspoon (London: T&T Clark, 2003), 68.

36. Whether the book is the first in the Jewish canon to separate ethnicity and religion, it certainly is the prototype of the classic Diaspora Jewish political strategy of *shtadlones*, or political intercession and begging for concession and protection, a strategy typical of weak minorities.

37. On "Jewish" fraternities, see Marianne Sanua, *Going Greek: Jewish College Fraternities in the United States, 1895–1945* (Detroit: Wayne State University Press, 2003).

38. See Emanuel Goldsmith, *Architects of Yiddishism at the Beginning of the Twentieth Century: A Study in Jewish Cultural History* (Rutherford, NJ: Farleigh Dickinson University Press, 1976), and David Weinberg, *Between Tradition and Modernity: Haim Zhitlowski, Simon Dubnow, Ahad Ha-Am and the Shaping of Modern Jewish Identity* (New York: Holmes and Meier, 1996).

39. Whether Zhitlovsky seriously thought that Sephardic Jews would adopt Yiddish, or whether he simply ignored their existence, is not clear.

40. Chaim Jitlovsky [Haim Zhitlowski], "What Is Jewish Secular Culture?" in *The Way We Think*, ed. Joseph Leftwich (South Brunswick, NJ: Thomas Yoseloff, 1969), 1:92, 93, 95.

41. Ibid., 13. Weinberg believes that ultimately the secularists of the "transitional generation could not shake their deep-seated belief that the core of Jewishness lay in spiritual and ethical ideas that were eternal and independent of outside influences."

42. Gennadi Estraikh, *In Harness: Yiddish Writers' Romance with Communism* (Syracuse: Syracuse University Press, 2005), 28.

43. Simon Rabinovitch, "The Dawn of a New Diaspora: Simon Dubnov's Autonomism, from St. Petersburg to Berlin" (unpublished manuscript).

44. In Hapsburg-ruled Galicia, there was no conflict between the religion of the rulers and ruled.

45. Harold Weinstein, "Language and Education in the Soviet Ukraine," *Slavonic and East European Review* 20 (1941): 138.

46. *Der emes*, April 6, 1924, quoted in Zvi Gitelman, *Jewish Nationality and Soviet Politics*, (Princeton: Princeton University Press, 1972), 369.

47. "We may define the 'ethnie' or ethnic community as a social group whose members share a sense of common origins, claim a common and distinctive history and destiny, possess one or more distinctive characteristics, and feel a sense of collective uniqueness or solidarity" (Anthony D. Smith, *The Ethnic Revival in the Modern World* [Cambridge, 1981], 66).

48. The last Hebrew magazine published in America, *Hadoar*, closed in 2005 after many years of declining readership.

49. According to the 2001 National Jewish Population Survey, a third of American Jews define themselves as Conservative, down from 38 percent in 1990; 39 percent call themselves Reform, down from 42 percent; and 21 per cent are Orthodox, up from 7 percent a decade earlier. Some of these changes may be due to sampling errors and other errors in method in both years of the survey. According to NJPS 2001, a high proportion of Reform Jews were raised in Conservative homes, indicating that Conservatism is weakening, just as Orthodoxy had early in the twentieth century when most Conservative Jews had been raised in Orthodox homes.

50. See chapters by Dencik on Denmark; Miller, Kosmin, and Goldenberg on the UK; Gitelman on Russia and Ukraine; and Kovacs on Hungary in Zvi Gitelman, Barry Kosmin, and Andras Kovacs, eds., *New Jewish Identities in Contemporary Europe* (Budapest: CEU Press, 2003).

51. Steven M. Cohen, "Poll: Attachment of U.S. Jews to Israel Falls in Past 2 Years," *Forward*, March 4, 2005, p. 1.

52. Ibid.

53. Jonathan Webber, "Notes Towards the Definition of 'Jewish Culture' in Contemporary Europe," in Gitelman et al. *New Jewish Identities*, 317–340.

54. "Secular identity formation also differs from the premodern in that it is not organically of one piece. The secular persona is necessarily split and divided to enable him and increasingly her, to function in the complex modern world. . . . Of all the roles he plays, it is the professional

or working role that is the integrative one. Ask modern man who he is and his likely to tell you what he does." Guidance of family and tribe are diminished. "The quest for self-actualization becomes the prime organizing principles [sic] of secular life, playing the role that tribe or church did for premoderns. . . . One cannot be commanded; one must be persuaded" (Henry Feingold, "From Commandment to Persuasion: Probing the 'Hard' Secularism of American Jewry," in *National Variations in Jewish Identity*, ed. Steven M. Cohen and Gabriel Horenczyk [Albany: SUNY Press, 1999], 165).

55. Ibid., 271.

56. Herbert Gans, "Symbolic Ethnicity," *Ethnic and Racial Studies* 2 (1979): 1–20.

57. Egon Mayer, Barry Kosmin, and Ariel Keysar, *American Jewish Identity Survey*, 2001 (New York: Center for Jewish Studies, Graduate Center of the City University of New York).

58. *National Jewish Population Survey*, 2001.

59. In a message to me on January 10, 2002, responding to my question about what *secular* means in the survey, the late Egon Mayer wrote: "Yes, it would have been and would be interesting to find out what people mean by any one of these terms. But . . . we simply set a different goal: how do people choose among the terms 'religious,' somewhat religious,' 'somewhat secular,' and 'secular' when they describe their outlook? Then we sought to describe that sorting by a host of demographic variables." But the meaning of *secular* to the surveyors and respondents is still undefined, and it would seem that all the survey tells us is which terms respondents chose, but not what the terms mean to them or anyone else.

60. "They reported 'none,' 'agnostic' or 'atheist' to a question on their current religion. They are commonly referred to as 'secular Jews'" (*Highlights of the CJF 1990 National Jewish Population Survey*, 3).

61. In a 1995 national Jewish survey in Great Britain (n = 2,180 surveyed by mail), 26 percent defined themselves as secular and 18 percent as "just Jewish" (Stephen Miller, Marlena Schmool and Antony Lerman, *Social and Political Attitudes of British Jews: Some Key Findings of the JPR Survey*, JPR Report no. 1, February 1996, 10).

62. (Johannesburg) *Star*, December 28, 2004.

63. *Sacred and Secular: Religion and Politics Worldwide* (Cambridge: Cambridge University Press, 2004).

64. Gallup poll, cited in Edward Rothstein, "Reason and Faith, Eternally Bound," *New York Times*, December 20, 2003.

65. Rodney Stark, "Secularization, R.I.P.," *Sociology of Religion* 60, no. 3 (1999): 249–273.

66. Jeffrey Hadden and Anson Shupe, *Secularization and Fundamentalism Reconsidered* (New York: Paragon, 1989), 22.

67. "A Jewishness based on identity rather than an assumed way of life complicates matters for Jewish survival, but, at the same time, seems to be the only way to achieve Jewish survival in our times. The question remains as to whether even that is enough. First, identity must be built or established and then ways must be developed to translate that identity into concrete and continuing manifestations. . . . Speaking social scientifically, it does not seem likely that it will be a successful project. It requires too much voluntary effort on the part of a population that essentially is becoming more ignorant of what being Jewish all about, generation by generation if not even more quickly. In addition, it must be achieved in the face of horrendous [sic] competition which, precisely because it seems so open and welcoming, is so dangerous to the success of the project, imposing its norms and ways on the Jewish people in the name of freedom, choice, and democracy, very real values in their own right. At the same time, however, Jews have confounded social scientists or their predecessors for many centuries. Hence, as long as the effort is made, no final verdict can be registered" (Daniel Elazar, "Jewish Religious, Ethnic, and National Identities: Convergences and Conflicts," in *National Variations in Jewish Identity*, ed. Steven M. Cohen and Gabriel Horenczyk [Albany: SUNY Press, 1999], 41).

68. Stephen Whitfield, *In Search of American Jewish Culture* (Hanover: Brandeis University Press, 1999), 224.

Contributors

GABRIELE BOCCACCINI is professor of Second Temple Judaism and Christian Origins at the University of Michigan. Author and editor of numerous publications in the field, he is the founding director of the Enoch Seminar and the editor-in-chief of the journal *Henoch*.

MIRIAM BODIAN is professor of Jewish history at the University of Texas, Austin. The author of *Dying in the Law of Moses: Crypto-Jewish Martyrdom in the Iberian World* (2007), she is now working on a book about an unusual trial of the Portuguese Inquisition.

ADAM CHALOM is the dean for North America of the International Institute for Secular Humanistic Judaism and the rabbi of Kol Hadash Humanistic Congregation in Highland Park, Illinois. A Ph.D. from the University of Michigan in Near Eastern Studies, his dissertation was entitled "'Modern Midrash': Jewish Identity and Literary Creativity."

YARON ELIAV is the Samuel Frankel Associate Professor for Rabbinic Literature at the University of Michigan. He studies the multifaceted cultural environment of Roman Palestine, with emphasis on the encounter between Jews and Graeco-Roman culture. His latest book is *God's Mountain: The Temple Mount in Time, Space, and Memory* (2005).

TODD M. ENDELMAN is the William Haber Professor of Modern Jewish History at the University of Michigan. A specialist in the social history of European Jewry and in Anglo-Jewish history, he is the author most recently of *The Jews of Britain, 1656–2000* (2002).

DAVID E. FISHMAN is professor of Jewish history at the Jewish Theological Seminary of America. He is the author of *The Rise of Modern Yiddish Culture* (2005).

ZVI GITELMAN is professor of political science and Preston Tisch Professor of Judaic Studies at the University of Michigan. He is the author or editor of fourteen books. The second edition of his *A Century of Ambivalence: The Jews of Russia and the Soviet Union, 1881 to the Present*, was recently published in Russian (2008).

CALVIN GOLDSCHEIDER is professor emeritus of sociology and Ungerleider Professor of Judaic Studies at Brown University. He is now Polinger Scholar in Residence at American University. Among his many books are *Israel's Changing Society* (2002); *Cultures in Conflict: The Arab-Israeli Conflict* (2002); and *Studying the Jewish Future* (2004).

JULIAN LEVINSON is the Samuel Shetzer Professor of American Jewish Studies and associate professor of English at the University of Michigan. His book, *Exiles on Main Street: Jewish American Writers and American Literary Culture*, was published in 2008.

CHARLES S. LIEBMAN (1934–2003) was professor of political science and sociology at Bar-Ilan University. He was an Israel Prize Laureate in Political Studies and published extensively on Israeli and American Jewish identities. Among his works related to this volume are *Choosing Survival: Strategies for a Jewish Future*, with Bernard Susser (1999) and *The Jewishness of Israelis: Responses to the Guttman Report*, with Elihu Katz (1997).

STEVEN NADLER is William H. Hay II Professor of Philosophy and Max and Frieda Weinstein/Bascom Professor of Jewish Studies at the University of Wisconsin–Madison. His books include *Spinoza's Heresy* (2002) and *Rembrandt's Jews* (2003). His latest book is *The Best of All Possible Worlds: A Story of Philosophers, God and Evil* (2008).

SHACHAR PINSKER is an assistant professor of Hebrew literature and culture at the University of Michigan. His research and publications focus on modern Hebrew and Yiddish writers. He recently coedited (with Sheila Jelen) *Hebrew, Gender, and Modernity: Critical Responses to Dvora Baron's Fiction* (2007). His forthcoming book is *The Making of Modernist Hebrew Fiction in Europe: 1900–1930*.

SCOTT SPECTOR teaches history and German Studies at the University of Michigan. He is the author of *Prague Territories: National Conflict and Cultural Innovation in Franz Kafka's Fin de Siècle* (2000). He is currently completing a book on sexual and criminal identities and cultural fantasies of violence in central Europe from 1860 to 1914.

MARK TESSLER is Samuel J. Eldersveld Collegiate Professor of Political Science at the University of Michigan, where he also serves as vice provost for International Affairs. His recent publications include an updated edition of *A History of the Israeli-Palestinian Conflict*. He is currently conducting political attitude surveys in seven Arab countries as part of the Arab Barometer project, which he directs in collaboration with scholars in the Middle East.

YAACOV YADGAR is a senior lecturer at Bar-Ilan University's department of political studies. His current research focuses on Jewish identity, ethnicity, and nationalism among Israeli Jews.

Index